PLEIN AIR
TECHNIQUES
FOR ARTISTS

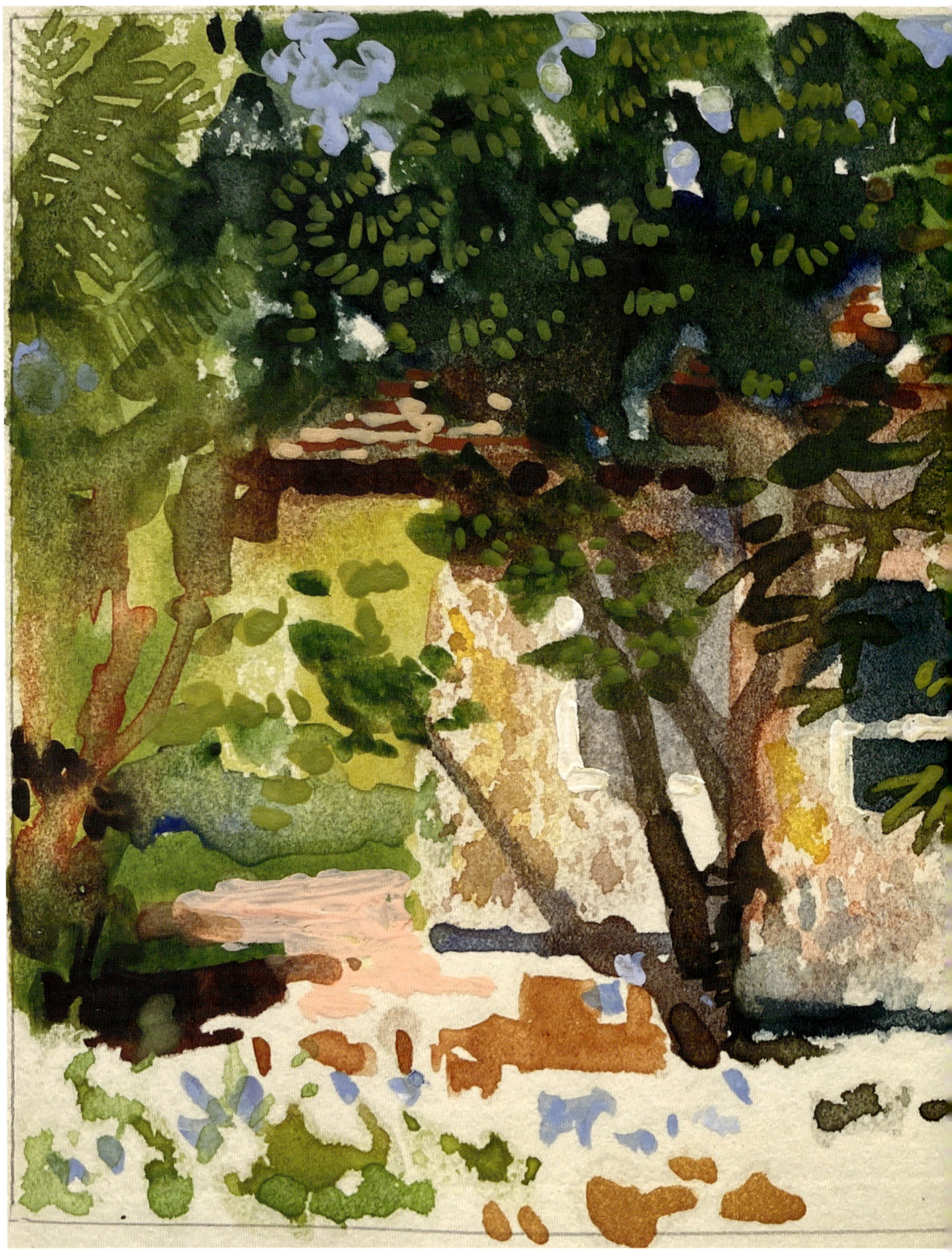

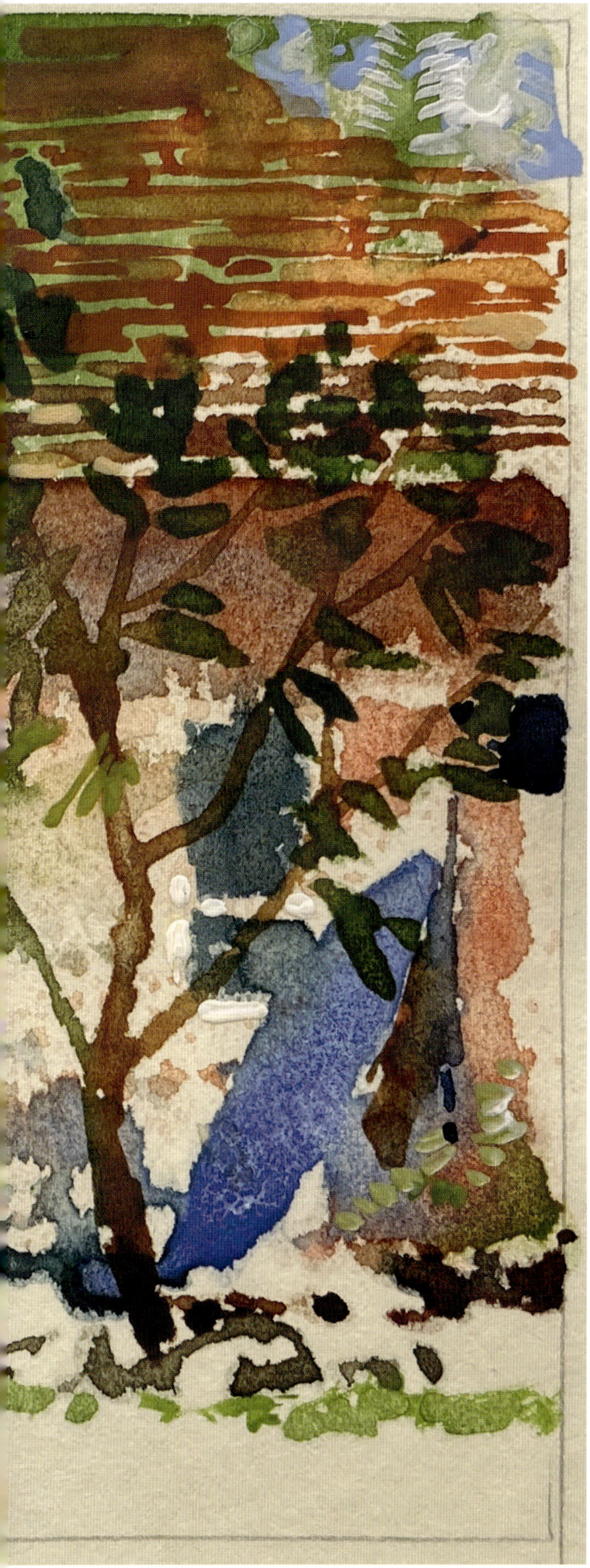

PLEIN AIR
TECHNIQUES
FOR ARTISTS

Principles and Methods
for Painting in Natural Light

AIMEE ERICKSON

CONTENTS

Introduction 6
Finding "The Zone" 8

1 | MATERIALS AND GEAR 11
What's Your Medium? 12
Brushes and Brushstrokes 14
Supports: Canvas, Panels, and Paper 17
Plein Air Painting Kit 19

2 | COMPOSITION AND VALUE 23
Making Interesting Compositions 24
Black and White 32
Sketchbook Exercise: Notan 33
Value 35
Exercise: Simplified Value Studies 39

3 | COLOR 41
Speaking of Color . . . 42
Color Exercises 45
Exercise: A Color Chart, Emphasizing Value 46
Exercise: Color Ladders 47
Limited Palettes 50
Color Development of Value Studies 54

4 | SUNLIGHT AND SHADOW 57
Seeing Skills: Shift Your Perception 58
Light, Shadow, and Color 59
Demonstration: Light and Shadow on Architecture 60
Where to Start 63
Exercise: The Color of Light 66
Raking Light 68
Technique: Stain It, Draw It, Paint It 69
Perspective 71
Foreground Solutions 73

5 | INDIRECT LIGHT 77
Dappled and Filtered Light 78
Technique: Starting with a Mid-Tone Canvas 79
Demonstration: Large Scale Work 80
Demonstration: Dappled Afternoon Light 82
Overcast Light 84
Demonstration: A Two-Session Painting 87
Technique: Cutting In 90
Painting Makeover: Light and Shadow Relationships 92
Technique: Using a Broad Brush 94
Shade and Reflected Light 95

6 | BACKLIGHT 99
Rim Light 100
Contre-Jour: Against the Light 102
Transmitted Light 104
Technique: A Loose Start 107
Painting Makeover: Perspective 110

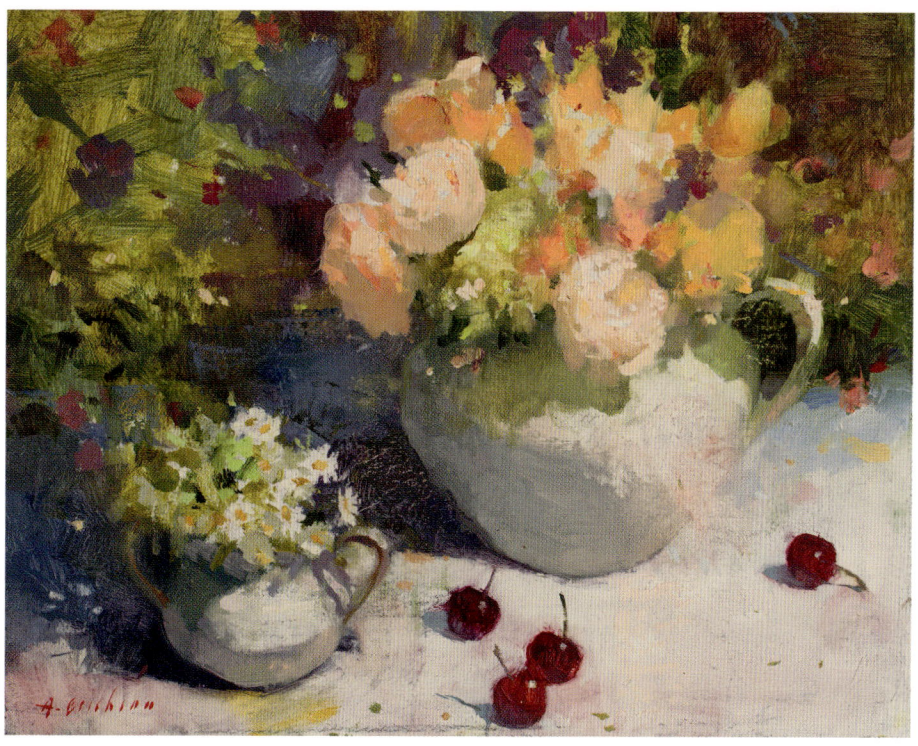

Aimee Erickson, *Still Life with Flowers and Cherries*, oil on muslin panel,
16" × 18" | 40.64 × 45.7 cm

7 | FRONT LIGHT   **113**
Front Light: A Dramatic Fully Lit Effect   114
Technique: Direct Impasto Brushwork   118
Painting Makeover: More Color   120

8 | NOCTURNES   **125**
Twilight   126
Nighttime   128
Demonstration: Nocturne   129

9 | SPECIAL EFFECTS   **133**
Glow   134
Demonstration: Multiple Light Sources   136
Glare   137
Reflections   139
Heavy Atmosphere   144
Demonstration: Fog   146

10 | DESIGN AND THE VISUAL IDEA   **151**
Beyond Representation   152
Technique: Paint Manipulation   153
Multiple Small Studies   156
Strategy: Serial Studies of a Subject   157
The Camera's Role   160
Improvisation   161

Glossary   162
Plein Air Quick Reference   164
    Field Painting Strategies   164
    What to Do If You Don't Have an Idea   165
    Summary of Perspective Principles   166
    If Your Composition Isn't Working   167
Contributing Artists   168
Acknowledgments   170
About the Author   171
Index   172

INTRODUCTION

A SERIOUS, PLEASANT PURSUIT

Plein air painting is a wonderful way to spend your time. It's an active meditation, a reason to travel, and a way to interact with friends and nature. Plus, it's not easy. There's always a challenge if you want to meet it.

In painting, color is used to describe light. Plein air painting is primarily about responding to the conditions of the day, about making some kind of visual record of what you see. But the landscape changes with the light, its appearance shifting almost as if it's trying on different outfits. How to cope? Do we freeze a moment with a photograph and paint that, or do we chase the sun across the landscape?

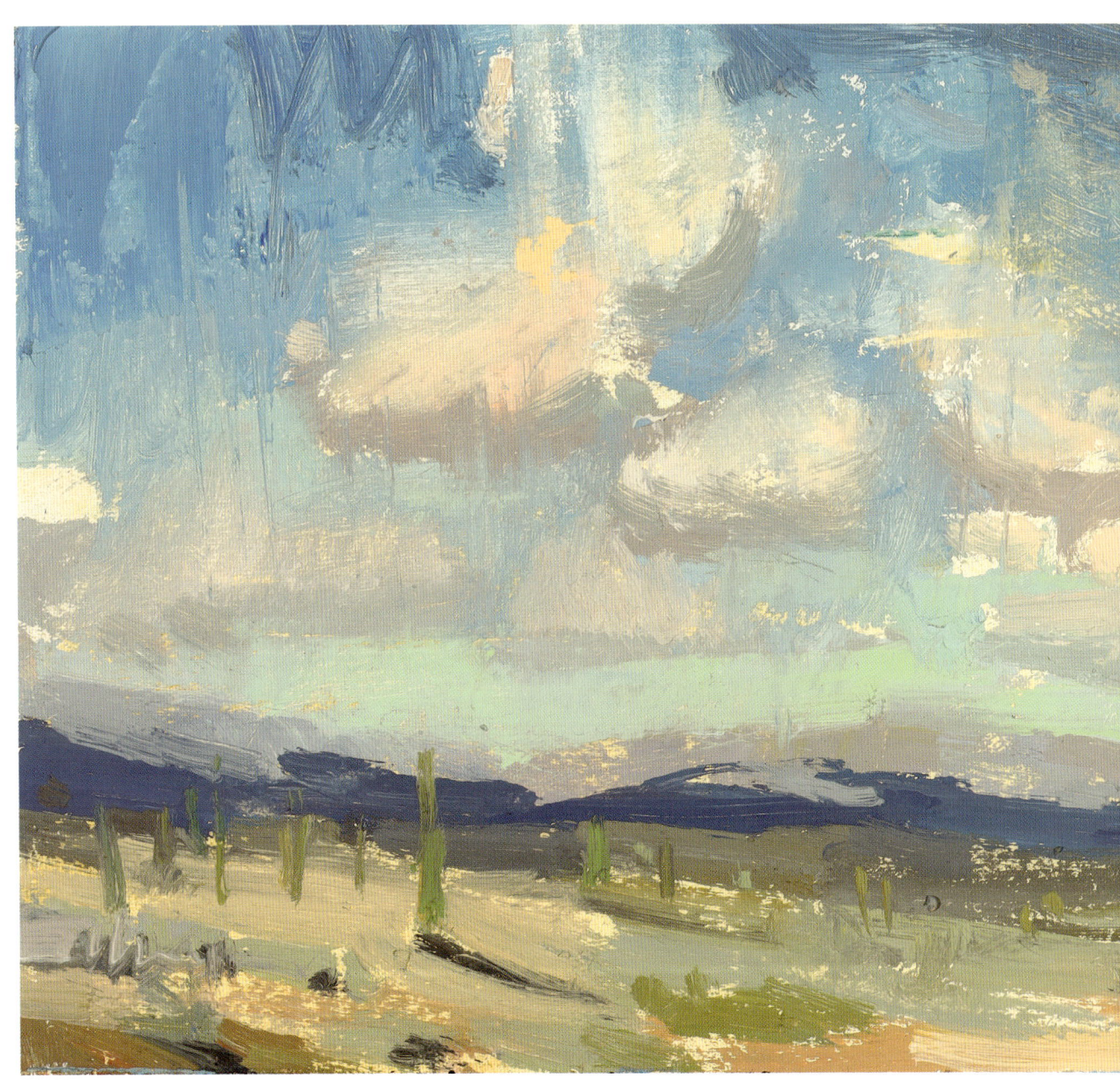

How about neither: If we learn to recognize and understand various lighting scenarios, our knowledge can be the filter we see through. We can identify a phenomenon and paint *that*. The painting becomes a record of the artist's understanding.

En plein air means "in open air" in French and carries the connotation of being in the great outdoors. For the purposes of this book, the term means painting from life. It means directly observing nature and painting outdoors—unless you're indoors or in the car. It means your subject is lit by natural light—unless you're doing a nocturne and all the light is artificial. It means painting quickly to capture the conditions of the day—unless you're working slowly or over multiple sessions or on a very large canvas. It means working directly, without a sketch or plan—unless you plan or sketch first. There's a difference between studio painting and plein air, but we can save that discussion for another day. Let's go paint.

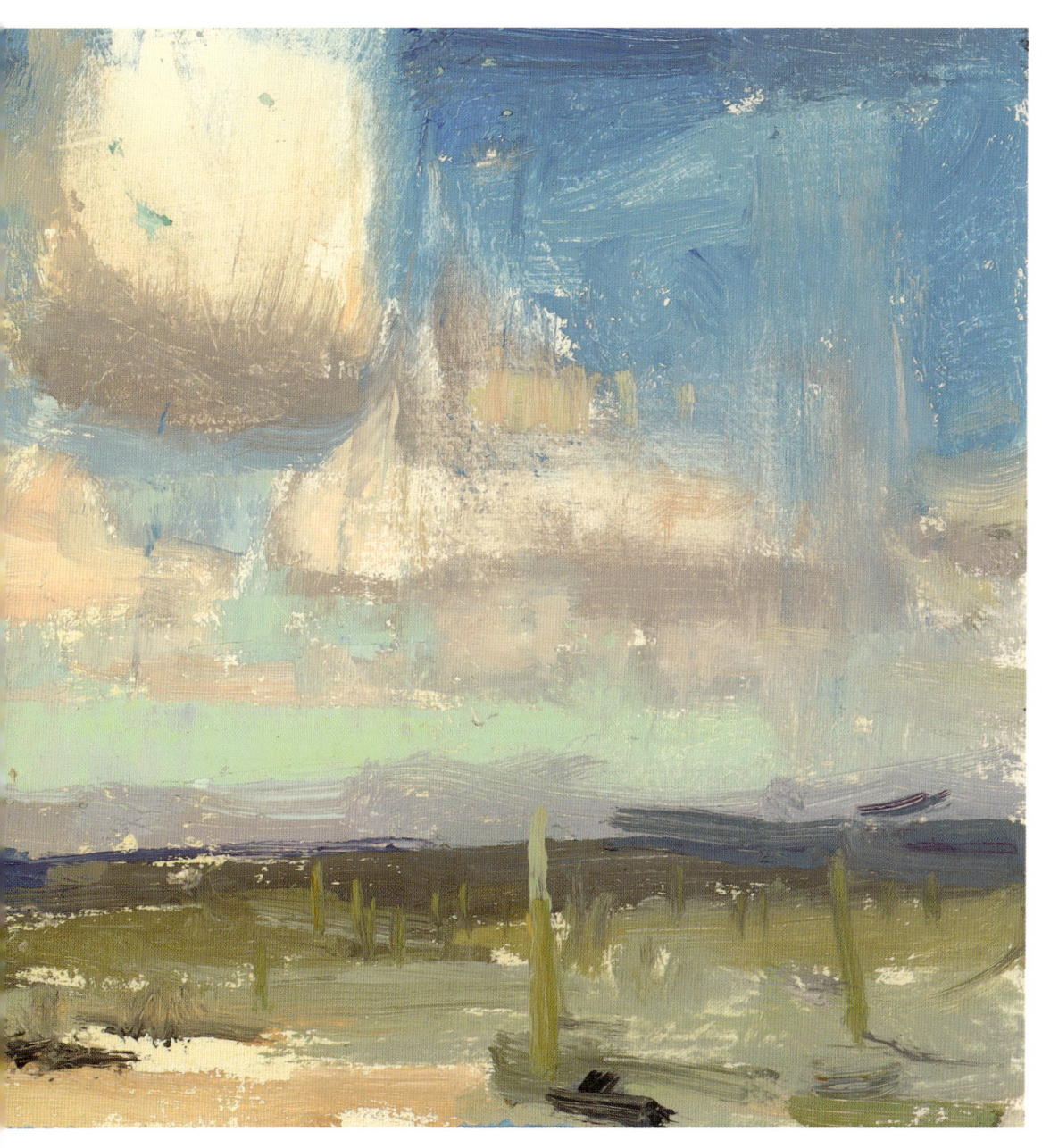

Aimee Erickson,
*Cloud study,
Bulldog Canyon*,
oil on muslin
panel, 6" × 12" |
15.2 cm × 30.5 cm

FINDING "THE ZONE"

AN AWARENESS OF YOUR EMOTIONAL STATE AS A GUIDE TO BEING AN EFFECTIVE LEARNER

Imagine yourself in a circle.

Inside the circle is everything you know: principles you have integrated and skills you have mastered. Outside the circle is everything you don't know. There's a lot out there, and there always will be.

In the realm of the unknown, some things are distant, and others are closer in. These are the things you're aware of, recognize, and may have even attempted. Some of these things are right on the edge, just outside your circle, ready for you to learn.

As a student, a learner, your goal is to expand your circle at a pace that feels right. Pay attention; give time and effort to your Next Thing.

Think of how you learned to write your name. You were introduced to letters and learned to recognize them. You practiced each stroke. Now, you can dash off a signature without effort. This is how the circle expands.

There are three things that can happen as you're working, and you can know exactly where you are by how you feel.

1. When you're operating inside your circle, there's nothing new. It's all familiar, and you can do it without thinking. There's no challenge. You'll know you're here if you lose interest.

2. If you're tackling a lot of things that are outside your circle, trying too many new things at once, you'll feel overextended or frustrated.

3. The third way, the middle way, is when you are solidly in your circle and giving your attention to one new thing. This is where you're engaged, you have ideas, and time is suspended. We call this "the zone." Your brain loves this state. This is where the best learning happens. Even imagining it feels good.

So, if you need more of a challenge, ask yourself, "What's one new thing I can try?"

If you're overwhelmed, pause and ask yourself, "How many new things am I attempting?" Then ask, "When was I last in my comfort zone?" Reset, wait if you need to, then find a starting place for one new thing.

You may sometimes be so overwhelmed that you can't think. The best strategy I know to overcome this is to slow down, take a breath, and then do something I'm good at— just one thing, something I can do easily and well—and do it until I regain stability.

▸ Aimee Erickson, *Lilacs on a Tiled Table*, oil on canvas, 27" × 24" | 68.6 × 61 cm

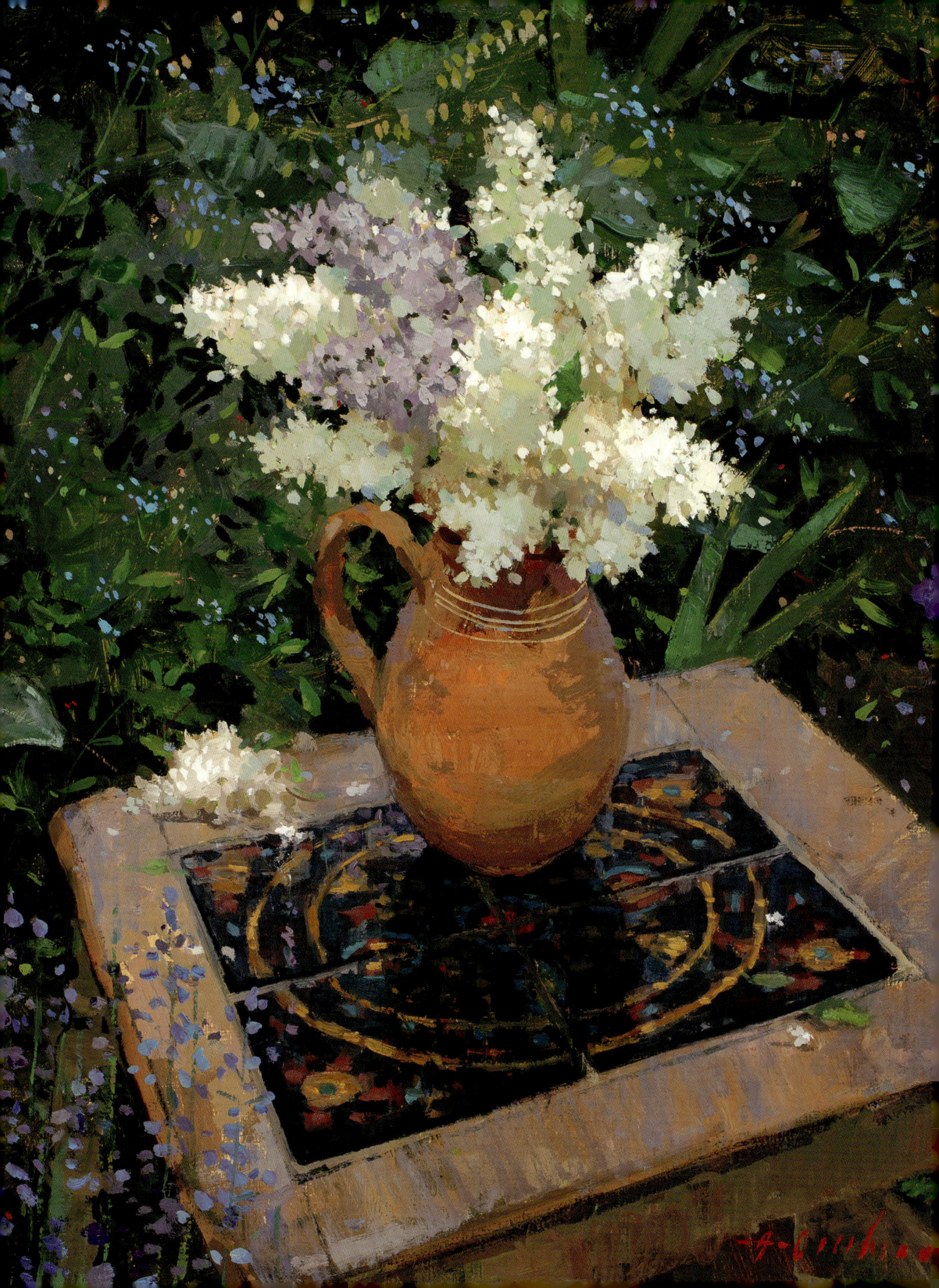

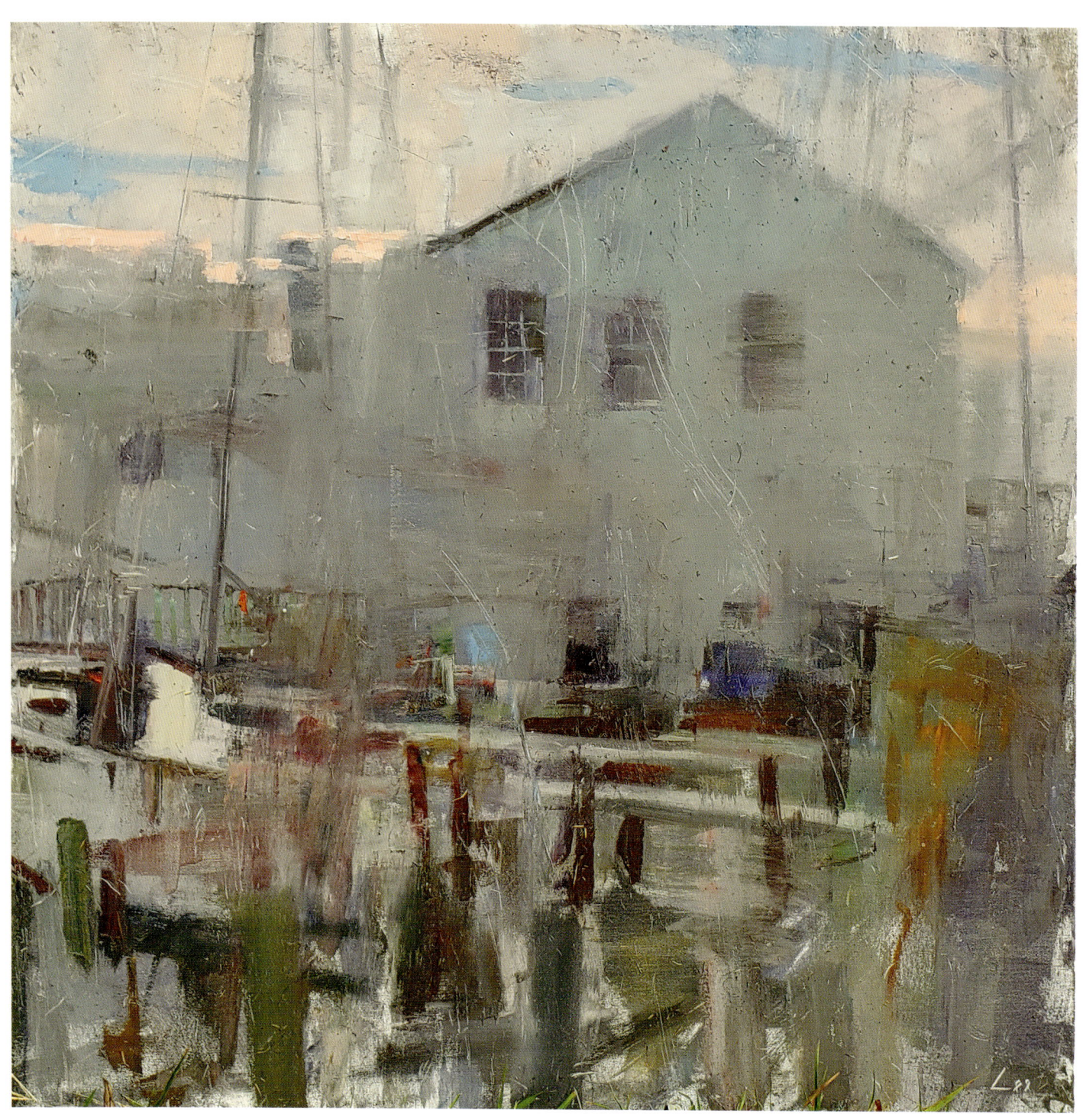

Patrick Lee, *Oyster House, Solomons, MD*, oil on canvas, 36" × 36" | 91.4 cm × 91.4 cm

1

MATERIALS AND GEAR

At a minimum, you'll need a pencil and a sketchpad.

There is no maximum. I tell you this from observation. The only limit is how much a person (or their vehicle, or attendants and mule team) can carry.

I myself have a clear inner switch that tells me when I have too much gear. It's funny. I sometimes have to choose between my camera and my umbrella. I think it's because I need my attention pointed toward decision-making during the painting instead of mucking around keeping track of stuff. I'm happiest when I have a handful of brushes and a couple of panels—as long as they're my preferred brushes and the panels I really like.

Aim for a happy medium. No fluff, just everything you need. If you're just starting out, here are my recommendations: Get a lightweight easel or box that sets up quickly; commit to a single panel size, not too big, and have fifty or a hundred of them prepared; start with three or four brushes; use a limited palette, even just black and white. And plan on being in the experimental stage for as long as it takes!

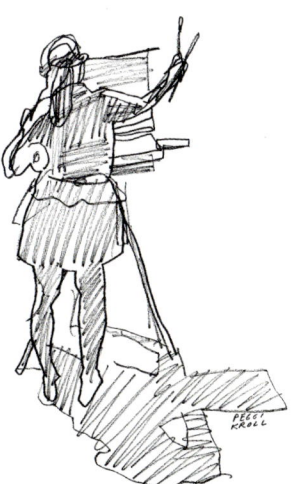

Peggi Kroll Roberts, *Artist Working*, marker on paper, 8½" × 9" | 21.6 cm × 22.9 cm

WHAT'S YOUR MEDIUM?

The word *medium* is used to identify different types of paint—oil, watercolor, and so on—as well as for additives that adjust flow or drying time. It comes directly from the Latin word, meaning *the middle*. In painting, it has one meaning, of "the liquid with which pigments are ground or mixed to give them desired fluidity," also called the *vehicle* or *binder*. The history of the word reminds us that it's only the binder that changes: The pigments are consistent, although naturally, the look and behavior of pigments is affected by what binds and carries them.

Every type of paint—every medium—has its own qualities and working properties. The vehicle for the paint is going to dictate the mark that you get, the layering possibilities, and the appearance of the colors.

OILS

In oil paint, the binder is traditionally linseed oil, a drying oil with a long open time, and its solvent is (nowadays an odorless version of) turpentine or mineral spirits. Oil paint dries by oxidation. Any surface can be used for oil paint if it's properly prepared with gesso (for canvas or wood) or shellac (for paper).

Water-miscible oils use a miracle of modern science to make oil paints water-soluble. Water-miscible oils are not compatible with traditional oils. Choose one or the other.

Painting itself is a medium for expression of emotion or perception.

Andy Evansen, *Cold Call*, watercolor on Saunders Waterford 140lb. rough, 14" × 21" | 35.6 cm × 53.3 cm

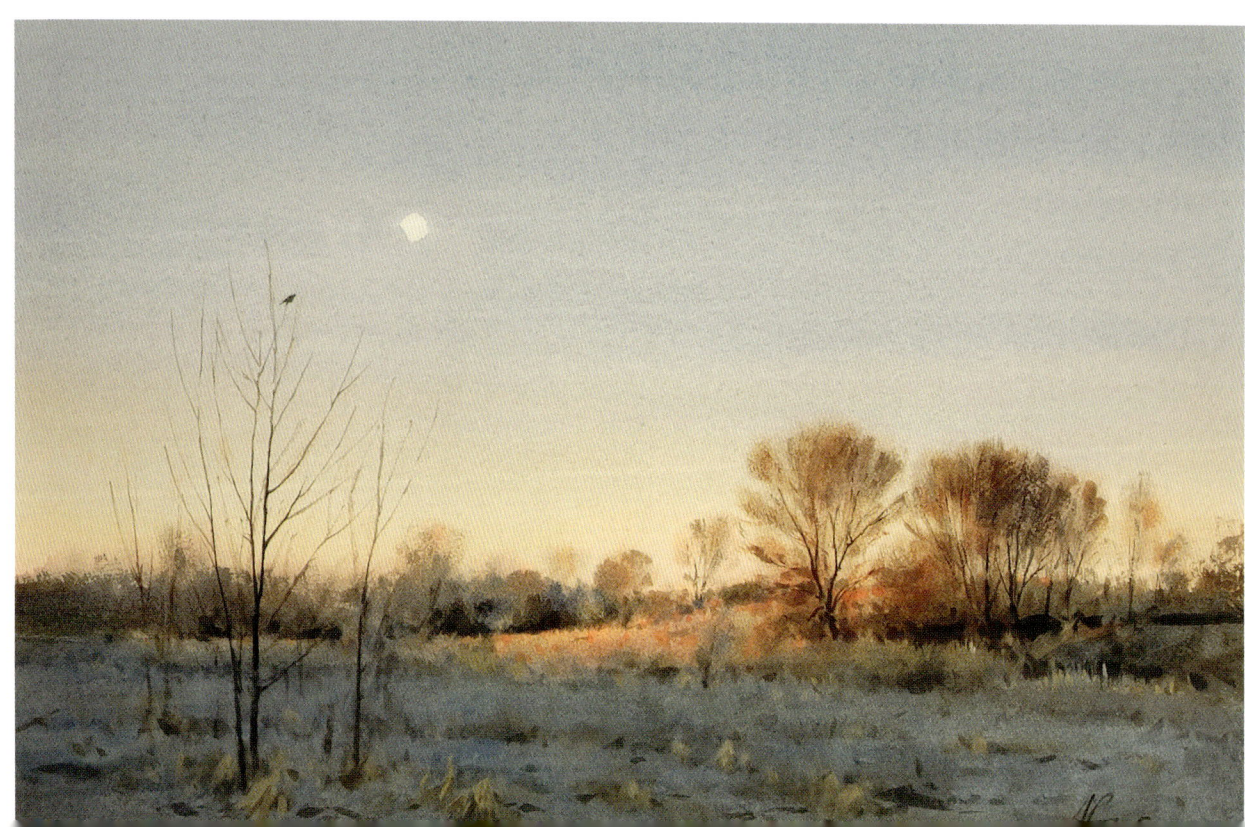

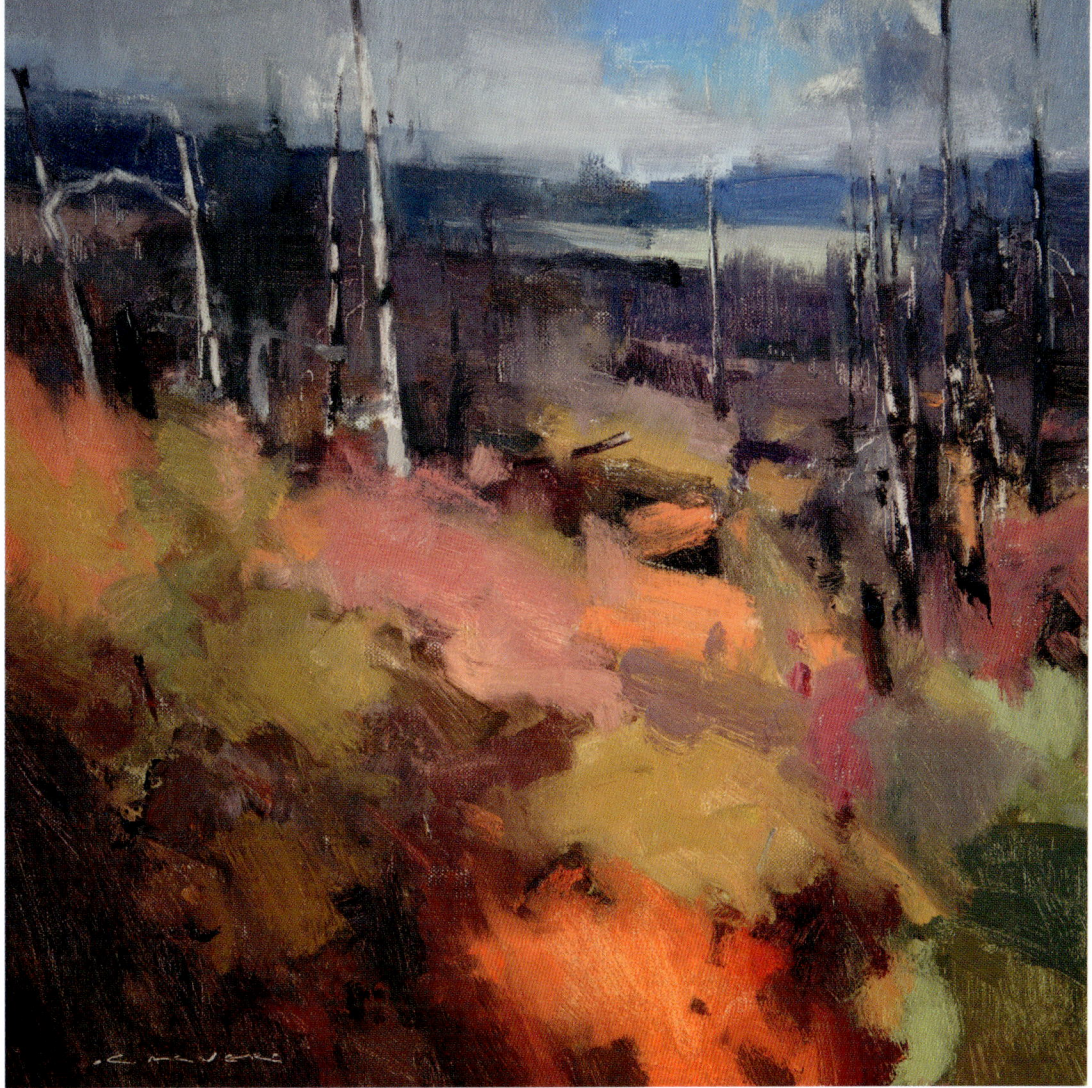

Jill Carver, *September Squall in Glacier*, oil, 14" × 14" | 35.6 cm × 35.6 cm

OPAQUE WATERMEDIA

In **acrylic paints**, the binder is an acrylic polymer, thinnable with water. Acrylics dry by evaporation and are waterproof when dry but can be dissolved with rubbing alcohol. **Acryla gouache** (acrylic gouache) is an acrylic formulated with larger solids, which sit on the surface of the paint film to create a matte appearance. Acrylics can be applied to any gessoed surface, usually canvas or hardboard.

Casein uses milk protein as a binder. It is soluble in water and dries by evaporation. It is essentially waterproof when dry (unlike watercolor or gouache). The common support for casein is paper.

Gouache (pronounced "gwash") is an opaque watercolor made of gum arabic treated with a higher pigment load and an inert white pigment that gives the colorant more opacity. Gouache can be applied to paper or a gessoed surface.

TRANSPARENT WATERCOLOR

In watercolor, the binder is gum arabic and the solvent is water. Watercolors dry by evaporation. The traditional support is watercolor paper and does not require a ground; non-absorbent surfaces like plate finish bristol board are also an option and allow pigments to be lifted or "erased."

BRUSHES AND BRUSHSTROKES

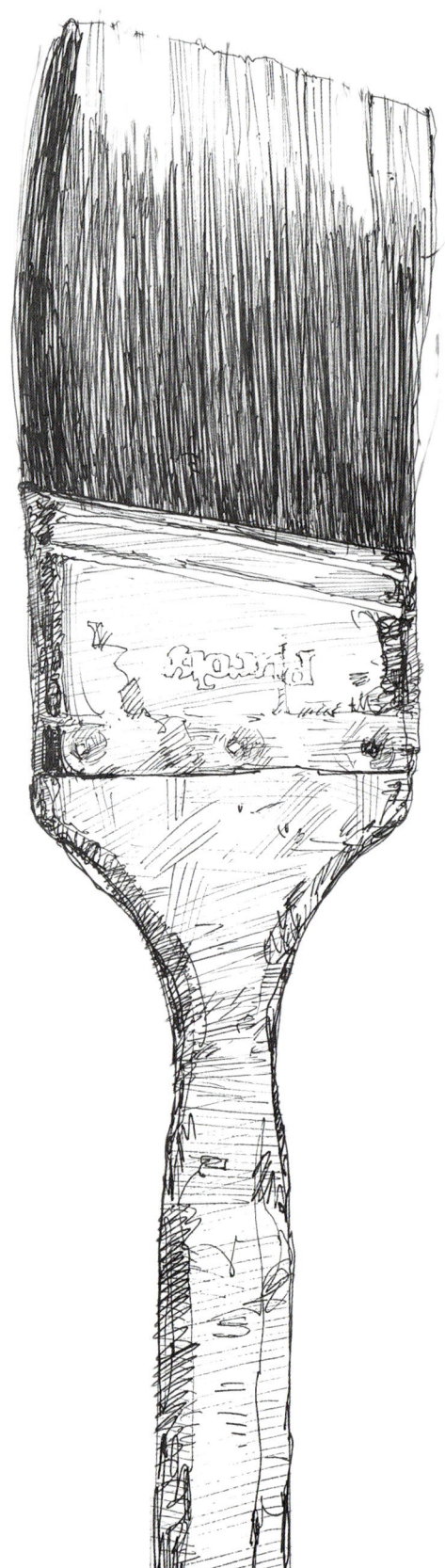

Several things contribute to a beautiful brushstroke. Decent brushes are one. Confidence is another. If you make a tentative brush stroke, and its color, shape, and placement are correct, what you've got is a correct, tentative (or worse, fearful) brushstroke. But gather yourself and your confidence and make a strong brushstroke with clear intention. The mark will be strong *even if it's not perfect in other ways.*

One more thing to be aware of: It's hard to overstate the degree to which the direction of a brushstroke can indicate form.

The parts of a brush:

- **Bristles.** Natural or synthetic.
- **Ferrule.** Bright metal tube that holds the bristles and is crimped to the handle.
- **Handle.** Made of wood, which grew, has grain and strength and flexibility, and is shaped to balance in your hand.

The bristles extend into the ferrule. If paint gets in there and dries, it pushes the bristles apart, splaying them as though they exploded. After use, get the wet paint out of the bristles with a vigorous rinse in solvent. Later, you can wash them with a mild soap (Murphy's Oil Soap is great for oil painters' brushes) and water, then press them dry with a towel and reshape the bristles.

(Left) Purdy 2½" (6.4 cm) angled sash brush, good for applying gesso. **(Right)** Rosemary & Co Series 99 Pointed Pure Sable size 0, good for powerlines and signing paintings.

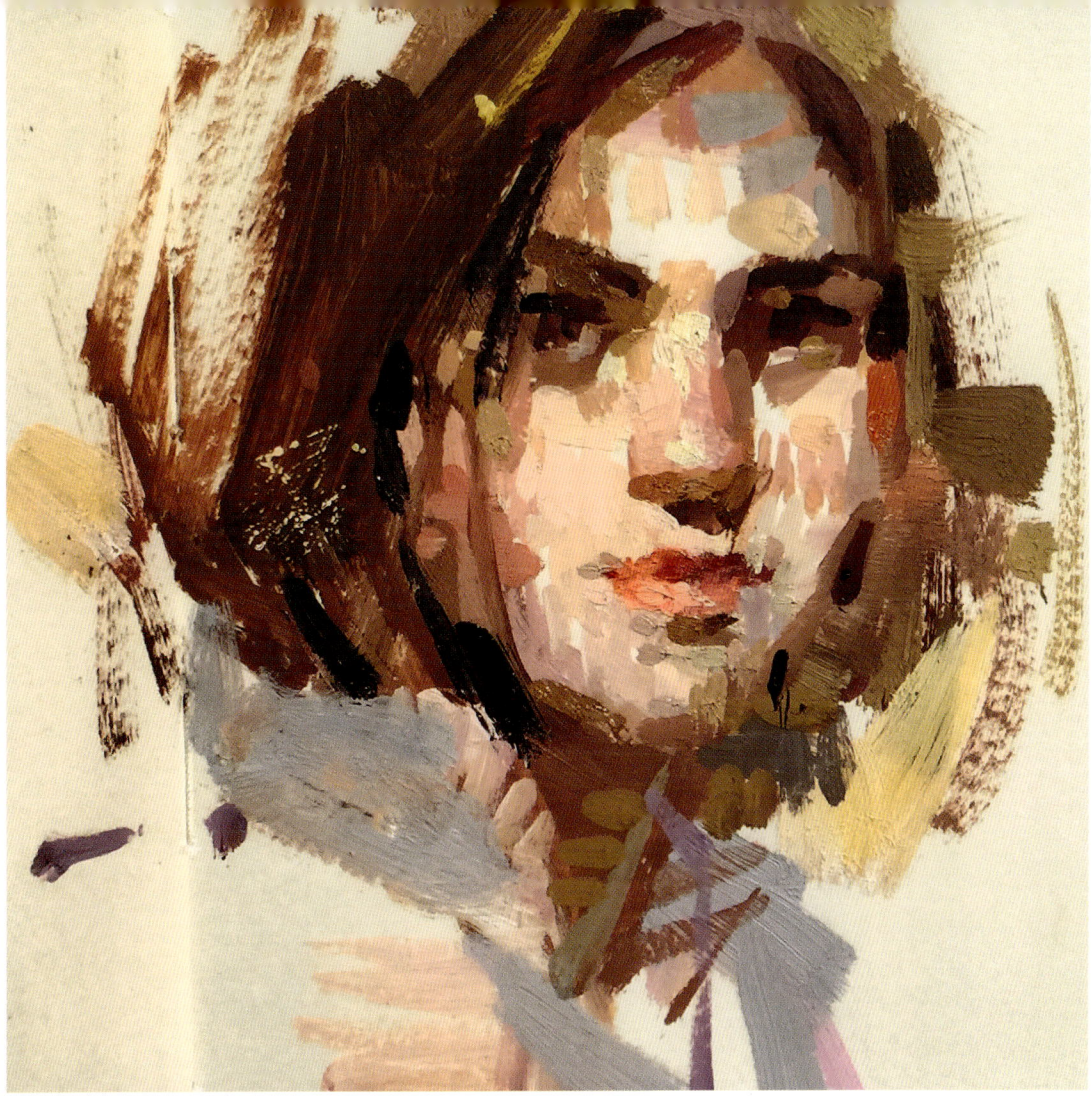

Aimee Erickson, *Portrait Study, Michael's Daughter*, oil on Moleskine heavy sketch paper, approximately 8¼" × 7" | 21 cm × 17.8 cm

THE WELL-INFORMED BRUSHSTROKE: WHAT MATTERS

PAINT

- Quantity of paint on the brush.
- Consistency—Is it drippy, or silky, or heavy like clay? This can be adjusted with a medium.
- Number of paint colors loaded up at once.

BRUSH

- Size and shape.
- Bristle quality.
- Angle of the brush relative to the surface.
- Springiness of the bristles.
- How much paint it holds.

SURFACE

- Surface texture, anywhere from smooth to very rough.
- Absorbency— Does the paint sit on the surface or get sucked in?
- Wet or dry and how much paint is on the canvas already.

THE PAINTER

- Knowledge and intention.
- Gesture, motion of the hand.
- Amount of force applied to the brush: Is there more pressure at the beginning of the stroke, the middle, or the end?

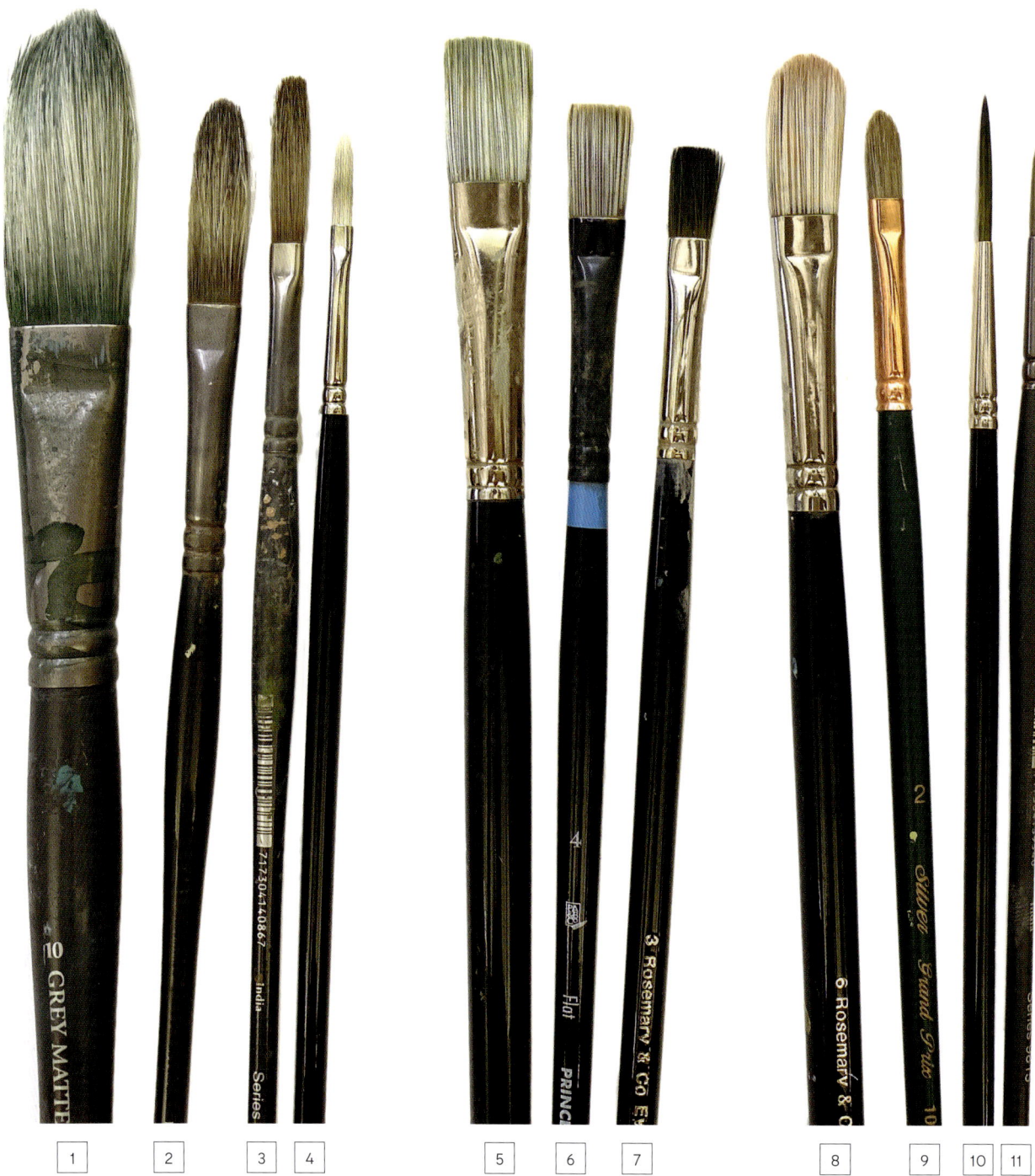

| 1 | 2 | 3 | 4 | | 5 | 6 | 7 | | 8 | 9 | 10 | 11 |

A few of my favorite oil-painting brushes:

1 Richeson Grey Matters Series 9845
   No. 10 Egbert

2 Rosemary & Co Series 2085 Chungking
   Egbert No. 4

3 Richeson Grey Matters Series 9845
   No. 2 Egbert

4 Rosemary & Co Ivory Long Filbert No. 0

5 Rosemary & Co Ivory Long Flat No. 7

6 Princeton Aspen 6500F Flat No. 4

7 Rosemary & Co Evergreen Long Flat No. 3

8 Rosemary & Co Ivory Long Filbert No. 6

9 Silver Grand Prix 1003 Filbert No. 2

10 Rosemary & Co Evergreen Rigger No. 4

11 Richeson Grey Matters Series 9815 No. 2

SUPPORTS: CANVAS, PANELS, AND PAPER

The *support* is the substrate, and is usually coated with a primer, or *ground*, most often acrylic gesso. There are plenty of commercially available supports for all types of media, in a range of quality and cost. If you're just starting out, find a suitable surface that's not too expensive—having affordable materials makes it easier to experiment.

I've found that inexpensive homemade panels are my favorite. You can make your own canvas panels by gluing muslin to Masonite, Gatorfoam Board, or Multimedia Artboard.

Treating paper with shellac seals the fibers and makes a lovely painting surface that maintains the tooth of the paper, is archival, and most delightfully, does not warp. Shellac is also a traditional way to prep wood panels for oil painting.

Try different surfaces to gain an appreciation of their differences. There's no single best choice because it comes down to personal preference.

An extra coat of gesso or two, and maybe a light pass with sandpaper, fills in the pinprick holes in the weave of commercial pre-primed canvas and improves the surface.

CANVAS TONE

A toned canvas is one that has a thin layer of paint applied over the gesso, to establish a color/value tone under the painting. It can be neutral or colorful, and it can be applied in advance and allowed to dry or be applied at the start and painted into.

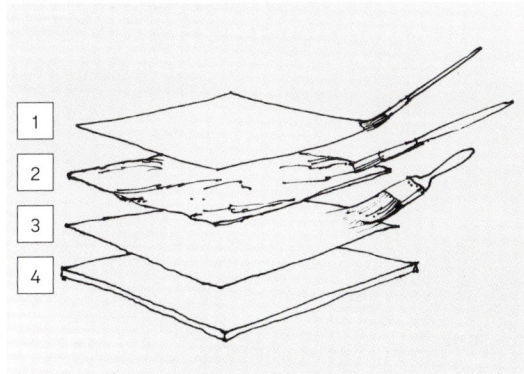

Layers of an oil painting

1 Varnish (optional).

2 Paint film.

3 Ground: The primer coat, usually acrylic gesso (pronounced "jesso").

4 *Support* is the broadest term for the substrate, which can be paper, cotton or linen canvas (stretched or adhered to a panel), or wood.

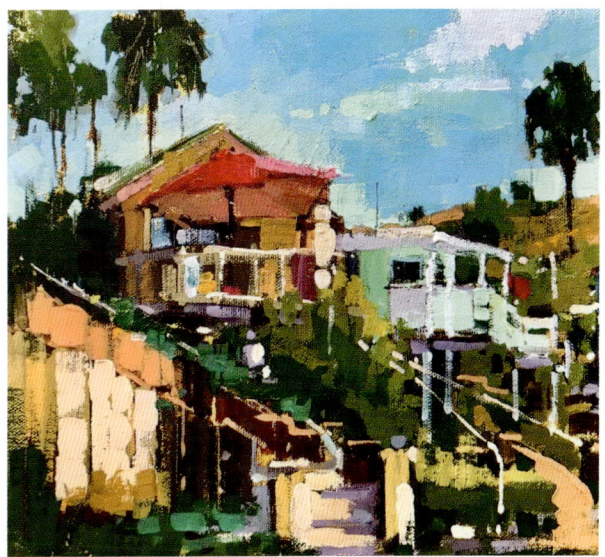

Michele Usibelli, *Beach Cottages* (detail), gouache on canvas panel, 9" × 12" | 22.9 cm × 30.5 cm

Usibelli often uses metallic gold paint as her canvas tone.

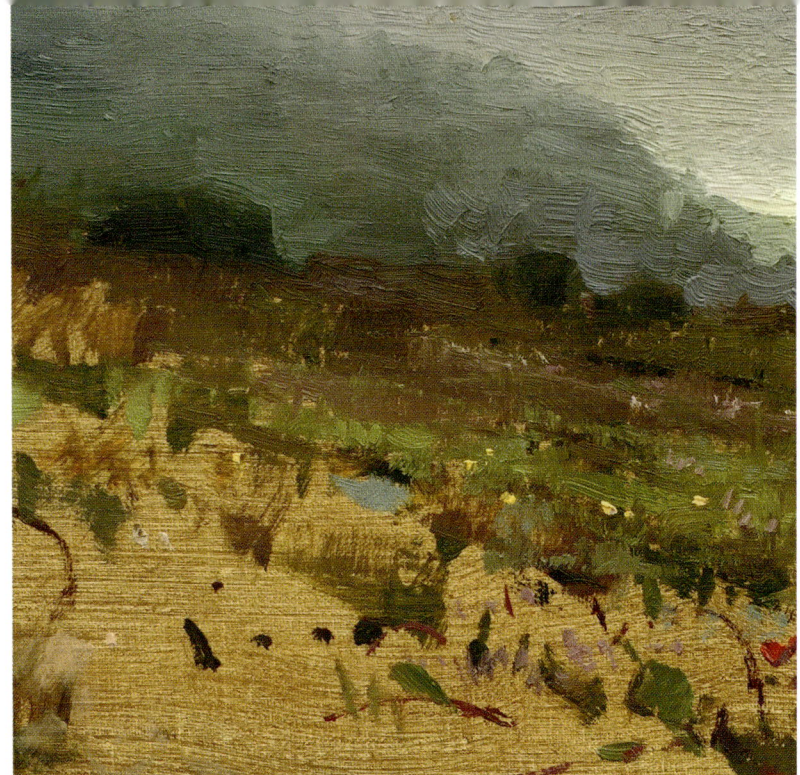

Aimee Erickson, *Brightening* (detail), oil on muslin panel, 7" × 12" | 17.8 cm × 30.5 cm

This panel was toned ahead of time with a mixture of Old Holland Raw Umber with a little white to make the tone a bit cooler and more opaque. In this case, it worked out to leave a good deal of tone visible in the foreground.

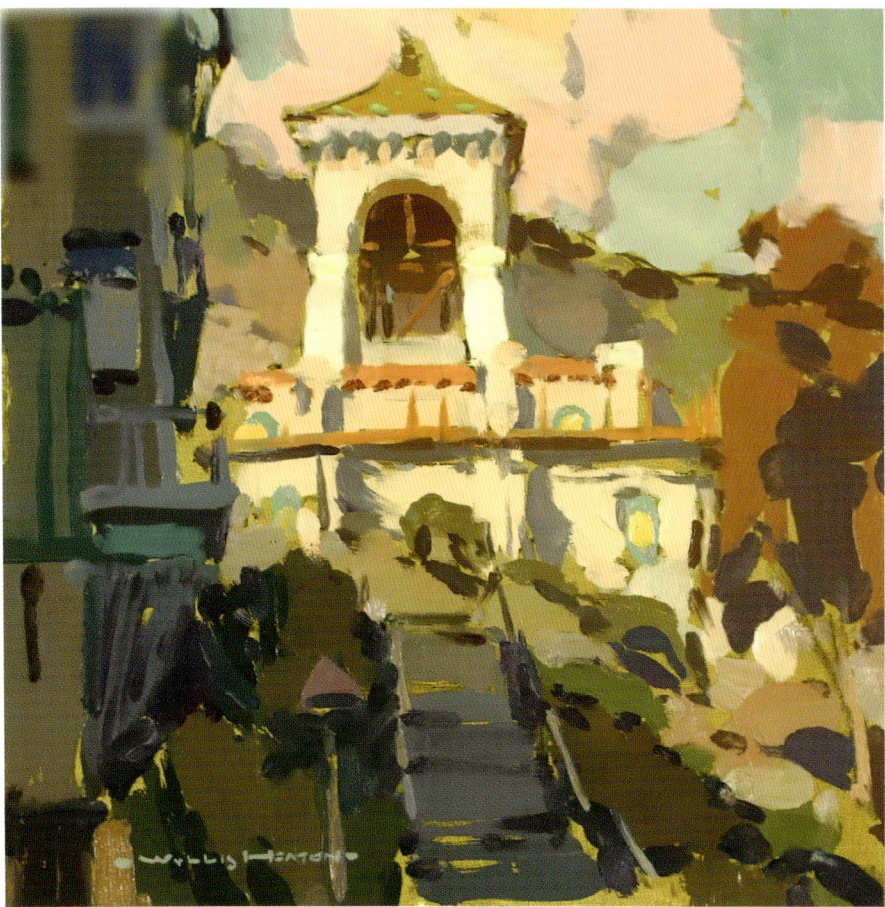

Wyllis Heaton, *Chimes Stairway*, oil on canvas panel, 12" × 12" | 30.5 cm × 30.5 cm

For sunny-day paintings—or for overcast days if he wants to build in a lit quality—Heaton starts with a mix of Indian Yellow, Raw Umber, and Alizarin Crimson to tone the canvas. It makes a nice olive gold color, visible between his direct, clean brushstrokes.

PLEIN AIR PAINTING KIT

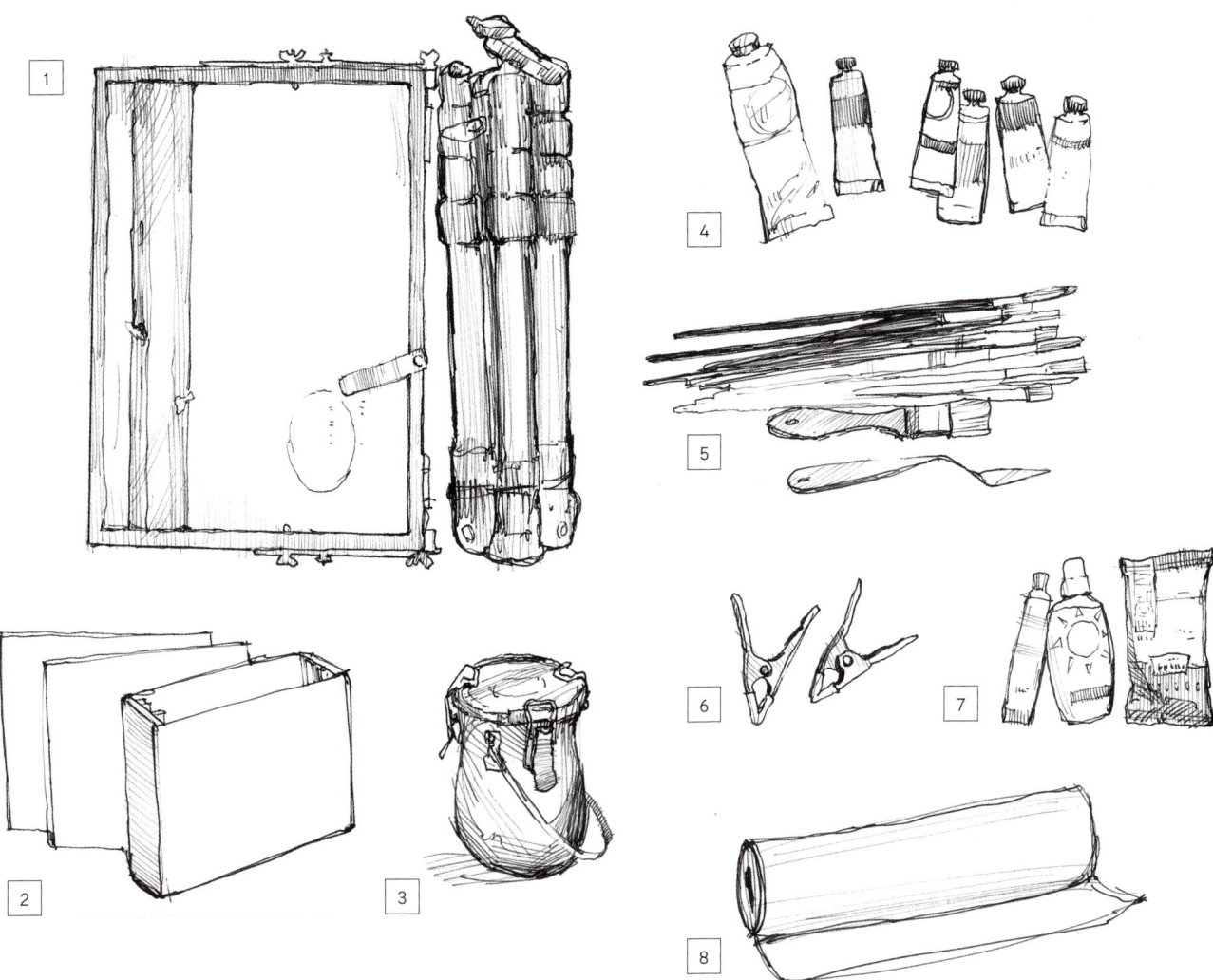

FOR OILS (OR OPAQUE WATERMEDIA)

1   A folding easel, or a pochade box and tripod. I use the 11" × 14" (28 cm × 35.6 cm) Open Box M, with a Benro tripod.

2   Panels and wet panel carrier.

3   Turps can with a gasket and clamp-on lid (or a container for water).

4   Paints and medium.

5   Brushes and palette knife.

6   Clamps. I use them to attach the turps can to the tripod leg and for smaller panels.

7   Insect repellent, sunscreen, and a snack.

8   Paper towels and trash bag.

Some useful extras: an umbrella, a sun hat, a viewfinder, and a battery-powered clamp light for nocturnes.

PLEIN AIR WATERCOLOR KIT

Watercolor is well-suited to outdoor work. It dries quickly, so the finished paintings are easy to pack and transport. Generally, watercolor paintings take less time than the other media. The white areas in watercolor are untouched paper, meaning there needs to be a plan—a pencil drawing—at the start that identifies those areas.

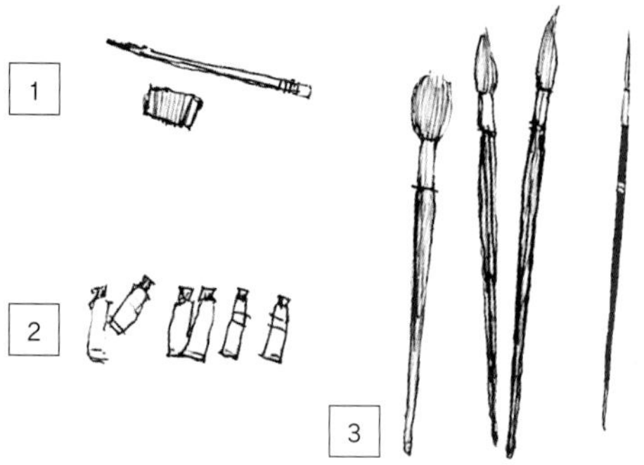

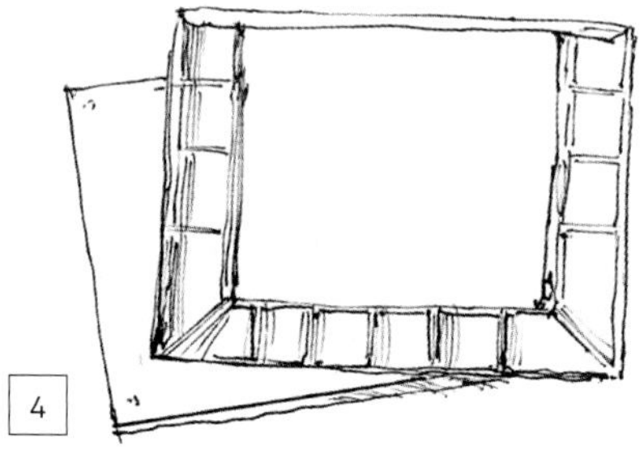

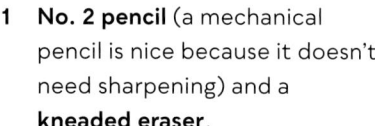

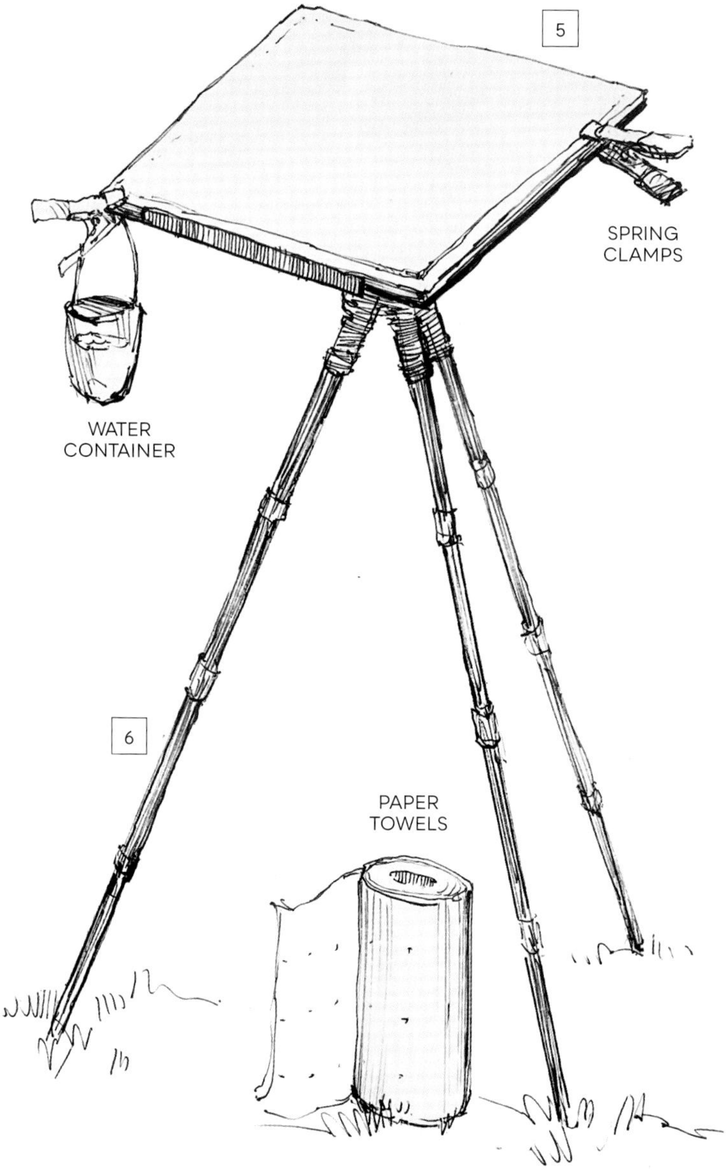

1. **No. 2 pencil** (a mechanical pencil is nice because it doesn't need sharpening) and a **kneaded eraser**.

2. **Paint.**

3. **Brushes.** Good brushes hold a lot of water and come to a nice point. You'll need one big mop brush, a couple of middle-sized brushes, and a rigger.

4. **Palette.** The palette should have deep wells and a big mixing area. The wells each hold a single tube of paint. Empty the entire tube into the well. No, it won't dry out—at the end of the session, clean the mixing areas and put the lid on the palette till the next time.

5. **Paper.** A watercolor pad of paper, sketchbook, or loose sheets; paper quality makes an enormous difference in the behavior of watercolors. (If you use loose sheets, you'll also need a board and a roll of artist's tape.)

6. A **tripod** with an adjustable tabletop/pad (so the painter can control gravity's effect on a wet wash).

SPRING CLAMPS

WATER CONTAINER

PAPER TOWELS

SKETCHBOOK WATERCOLORS

A sketchbook and a small set of watercolors with a collapsible brush make up the entirety of my painting kit when I want to travel light. At right is my sketchbook from a 2003 cross-continental bicycle tour. I kept it in my handlebar bag so I could sketch whenever I wanted.

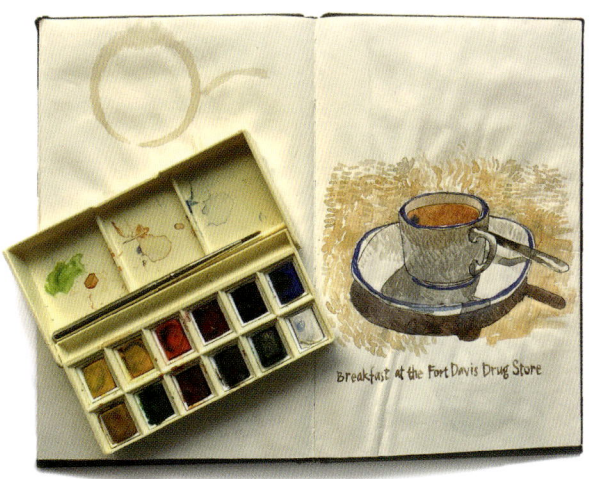

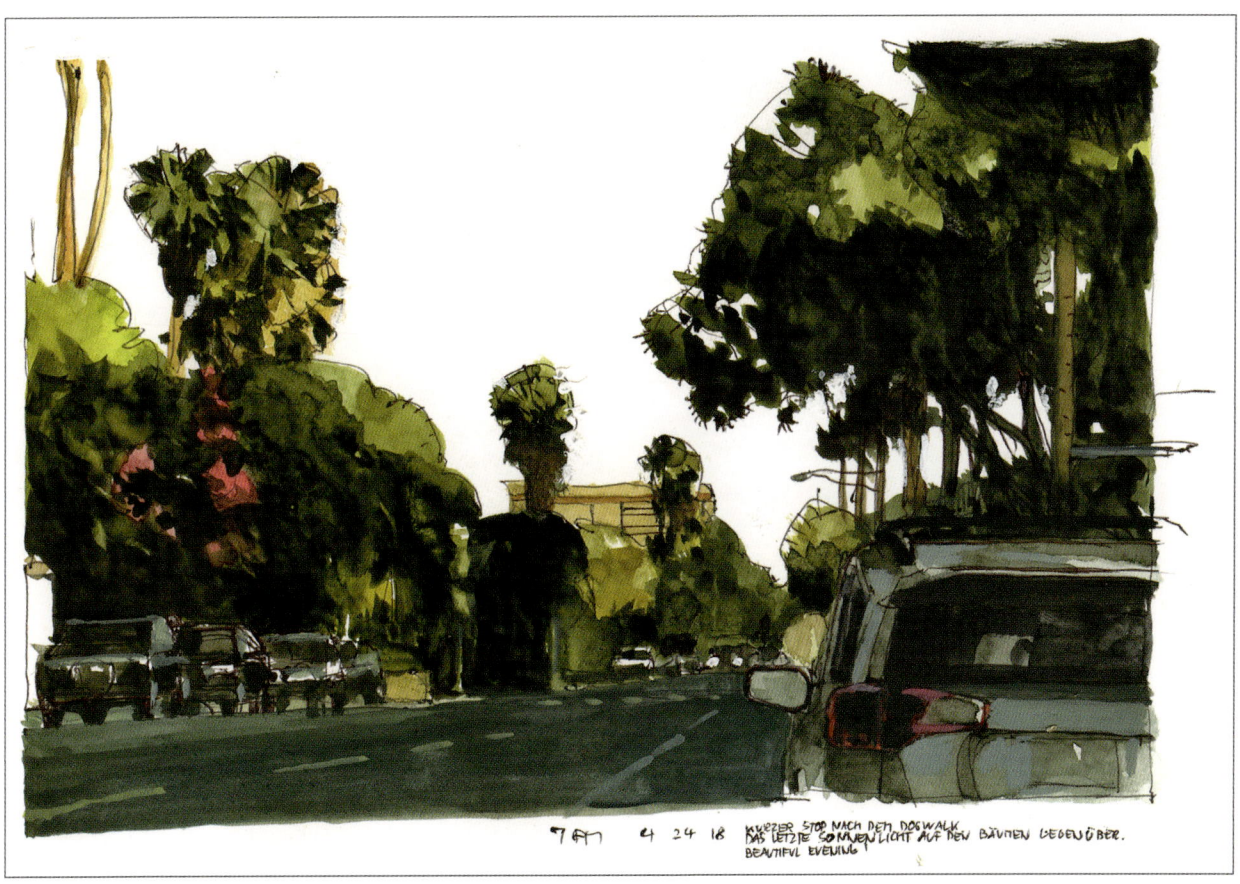

Christian Schellewald, *Talmadge Street*, LAMY Ballpoint Pen, Holbein Watercolor, and Holbein Gouache on paper, 7" × 5" | 17.8 cm × 12.7 cm

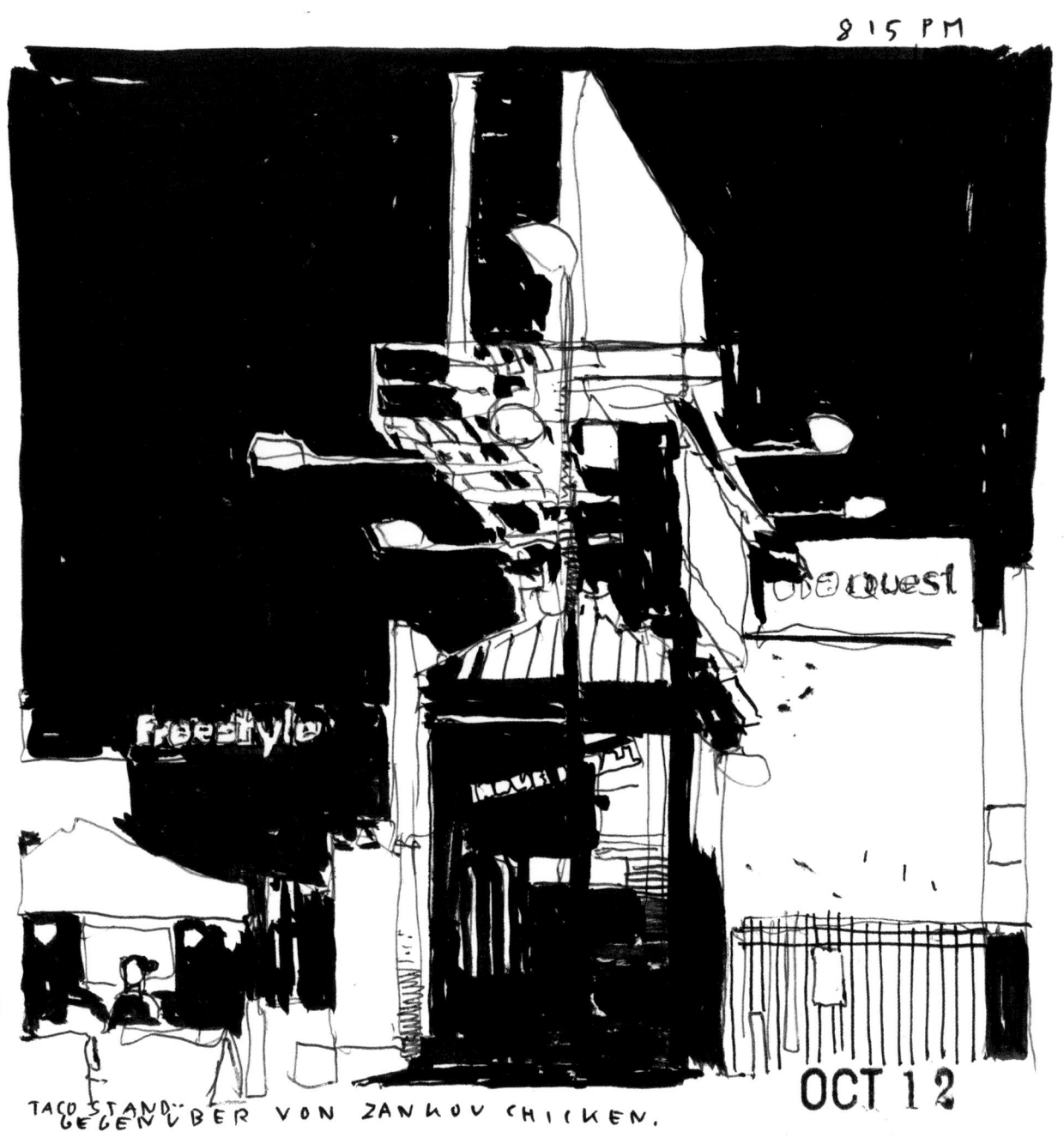

Christian Schellewald, *Sunset Boulevard*, ballpoint pen and brush pen on paper, 6" × 5" | 15.2 cm × 12.7 cm

Using shape and line in black and white.

2

COMPOSITION
AND VALUE

Composing a picture has a parallel in music: There are only so many notes, but the number of tunes is unlimited.

In painting, we begin with the format: the picture plane, defined by the four sides of the canvas. The first mark within that space has an energy relative to the frame. Every subsequent mark creates new relationships. The elements we have to work with—color, value, line, edges, shape, texture—can all be manipulated to achieve the artist's intention. (See image below.)

This artistic sense is what differentiates us from mechanical means of recording images. This sense, this ability, is what we want to develop: being attuned to the inherent *feel* of things.

Teaching composition is an interesting proposition. To introduce it to beginners, we have to break it down into some sort of a system: some number of steps, a formula for something that is by nature not formulaic, but bigger and less specific. When we actually paint, it isn't always an academic step by step. We might start with lines, or shapes, but sometimes we skip lines and shapes and go straight for the energy of it.

Here are three shapes, each one a common panel proportion: 5:4, 3:4, and 1:1. Each one has four sides, but, with differing proportions, each one has a different feel. Even without words, we can sense a different dynamic from each of them. We can even allow our body to respond with a gesture that embodies that dynamic—taller, more upright, more alert; wider, spreading, more relaxed; and square, compact, stable, balanced. We have a built-in visceral sense of the dynamic "feel" of shapes. Each mark made within the frame shifts that dynamic.

MAKING INTERESTING COMPOSITIONS

Compositions are ultimately successful or not, but "Make a successful composition" is not a helpful starting place. We need a paradigm that provides a way to manipulate the elements within a picture. Consider this: Composition occurs on a scale from static to dynamic, with very static being dull and very dynamic being chaotic. Adopting this paradigm and engaging our natural sense of the feel of things gives us a practical way to understand what makes a composition successful.

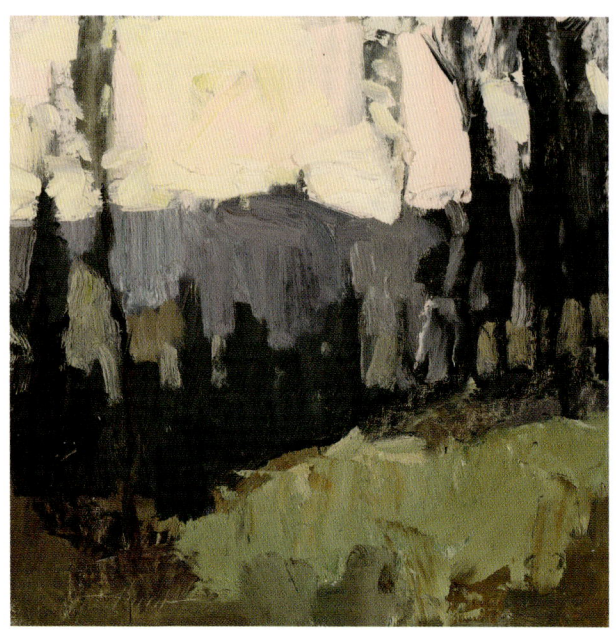

Jason Sacran, *Untitled*, oil on panel, 12" × 12" | 30.5 cm × 30.5 cm

COMPOSITION

STATIC · DYNAMIC

| BORING, DULL | CALM | INTERESTING AND ENGAGING | LIVELY | CHAOTIC |

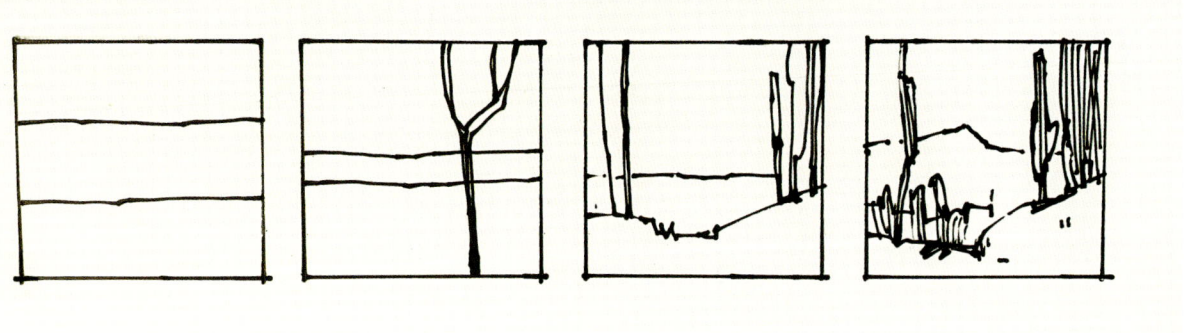

Four thumbnails, from static to dynamic.

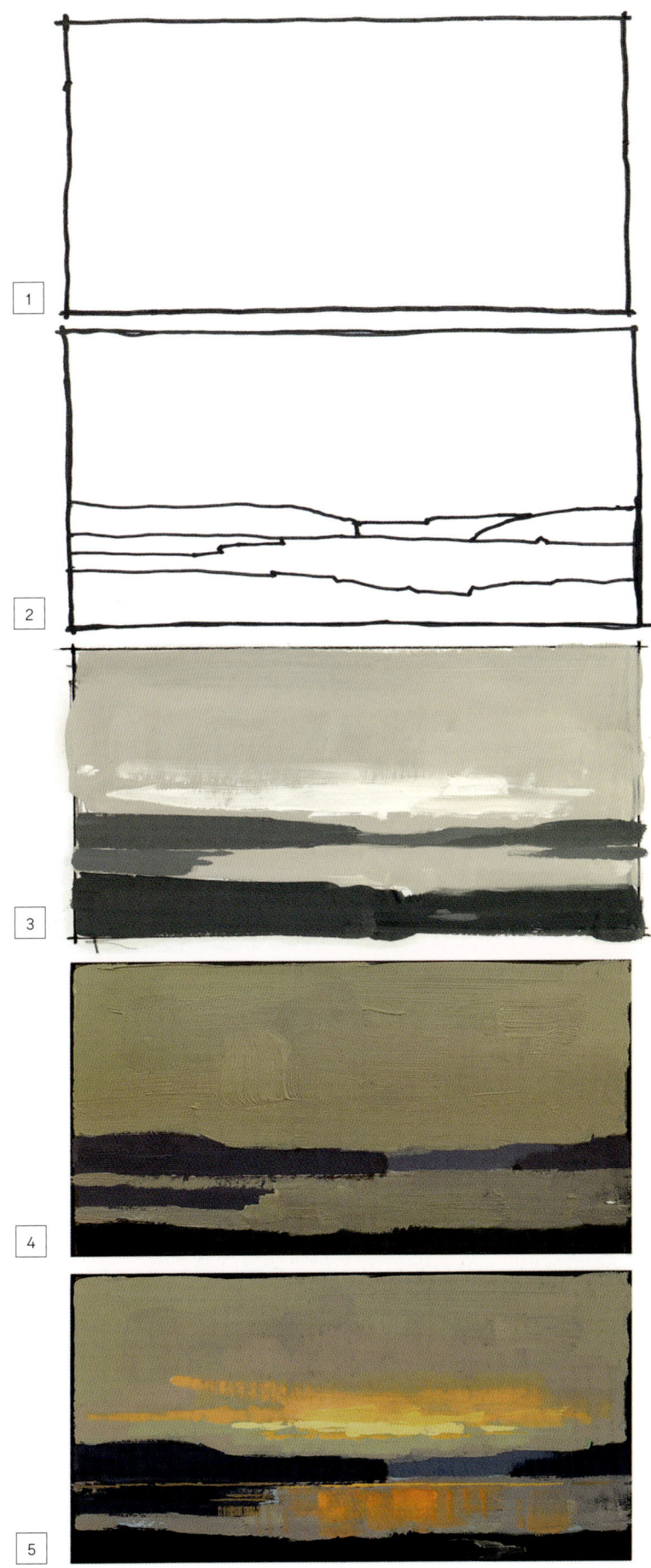

THE FUNDAMENTALS OF SHAPE-BASED PAINTING

In this familiar and useful approach for composing pictures, including plein air work, we think of composition as *the arrangement of shapes within a frame.*

1. First, you have a frame, or format: the four sides of your composition.

2. Second, that format is divided into shapes.

3. The shapes then have value assigned: black and white being the simplest. A more complex value structure uses shades of gray, usually not more than five.

4. Then, the values have color. There's more than one color solution for any value structure.

5. Last is detail and identity as "things." If a solid value structure is the cake, and beautiful color is the icing on the cake, this stage is the sprinkles, the final, small, yet not insignificant touches that are often the first thing the viewer will notice.

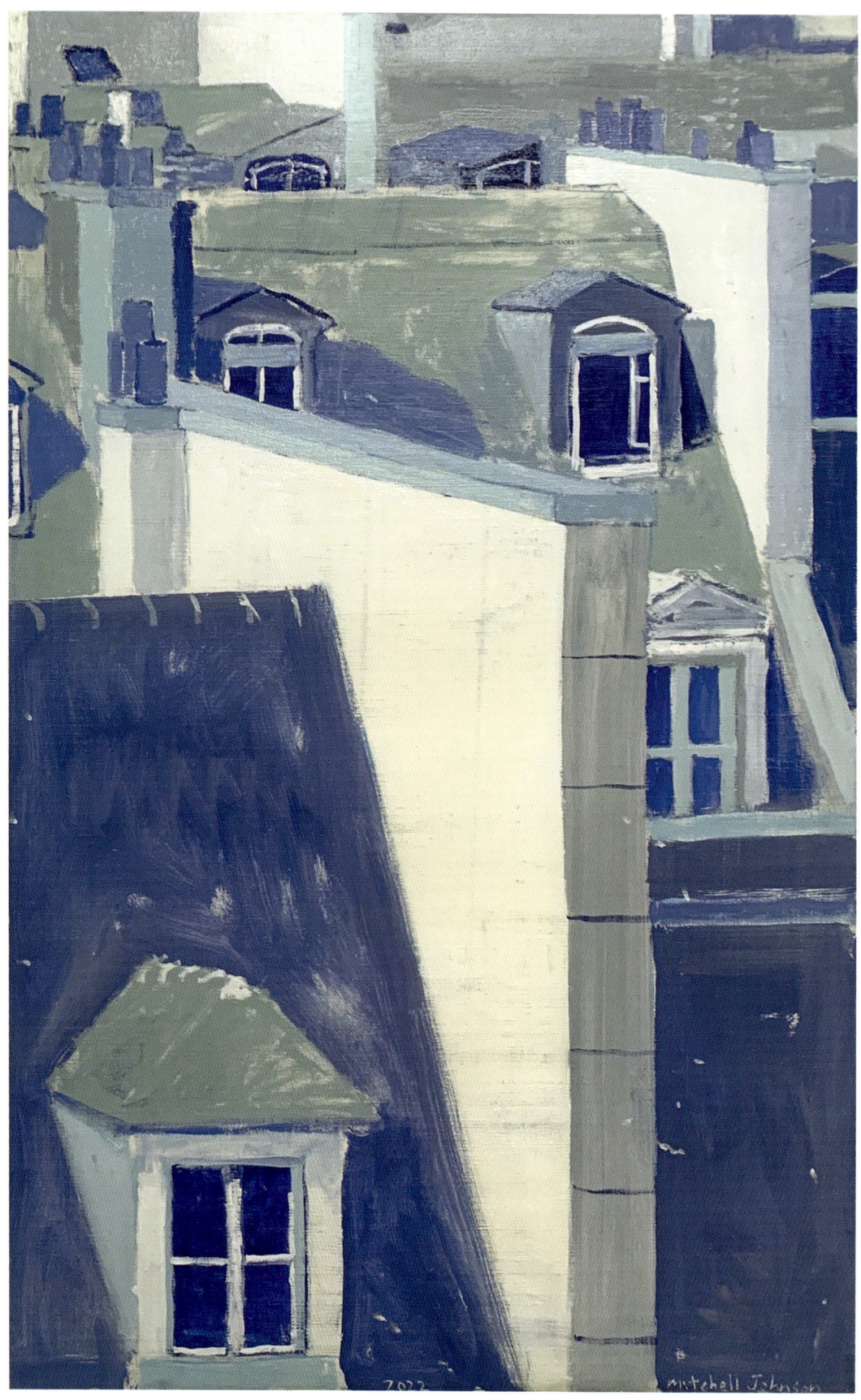

Mitchell Johnson, *Paris Blue*, oil on canvas, 31" × 20" | 78.7 cm × 50.8 cm

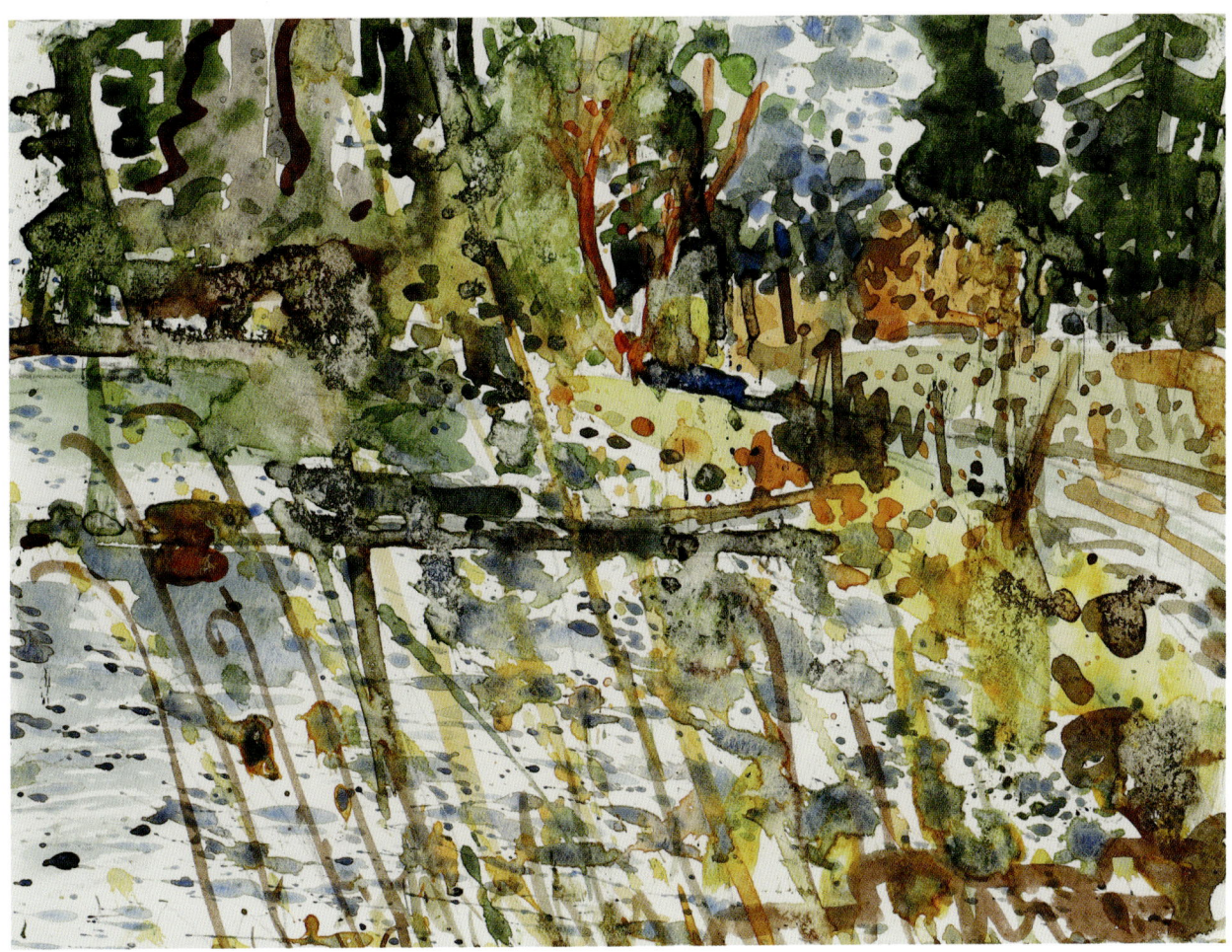

Peter McLaren, *Untitled*, watercolor on paper, 6" × 8" | 15.2 cm × 20.3 cm

MOTIF VS. THE FORMAL ASPECTS OF PAINTING

The *formal aspects* of painting are those terms in which any painting can be discussed: value, color, paint handling, edges and transitions, and paint quality. *Motif* is subject matter.

NON-SHAPE-BASED PAINTINGS

I can think of two ways a painting can move away from being shape-based, although both of them can be successfully merged with a shape-based approach. One is when form is developed or rendered to a degree that supersedes shape. The other is when color and brushstrokes are applied across the canvas in a confetti-like effect known as *equalization*, so called because the entire surface is treated equally. (A third way is just a lack of knowledge.) Between equalization and shape-based painting is a wide range where shapes and brushwork coexist, in dialogue within a painting.

MARK-MAKING

It seems to me that mark-making comes naturally to us, and border drawing–outlining and coloring within the lines–is learned. Both approaches are important. There's no substitute for drawing as training for the eye and hand. In the real world there are no boundary lines; there is just light revealing color that our brains interpret as form. This is how we see.

If you are holding a pencil and want to define, say, a roughly square shape, you draw a square. If you're painting, you can pick up a big, square brush and make a single mark. The tool you're holding allows your thinking–and your energy–to change.

As painters, we get to choose. We can start with a complete drawing, making lines to indicate the edges of things, or we can make a broken series of marks to note the edges we see as critical. We can make shapes from the inside out, pushing paint to where we want an edge, or we can make mark after mark until they add up to something.

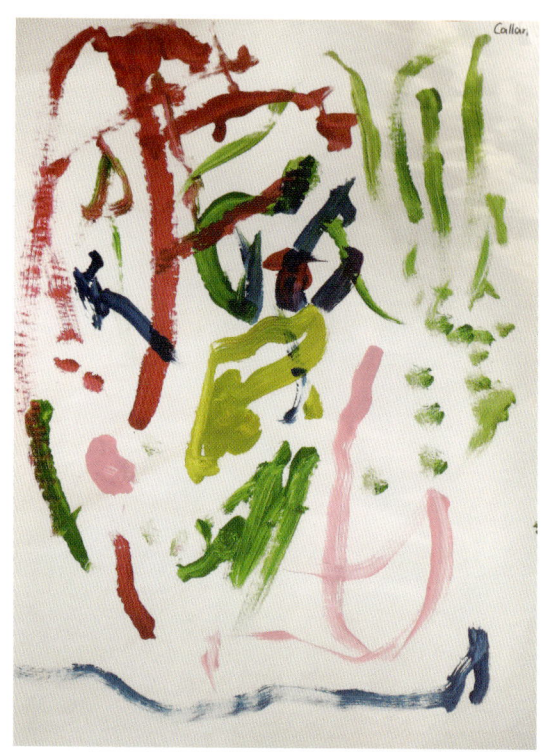

Callan McDonald, *Just Stop Talking*, tempera on paper, 25" × 17" | 64 cm × 43.5 cm

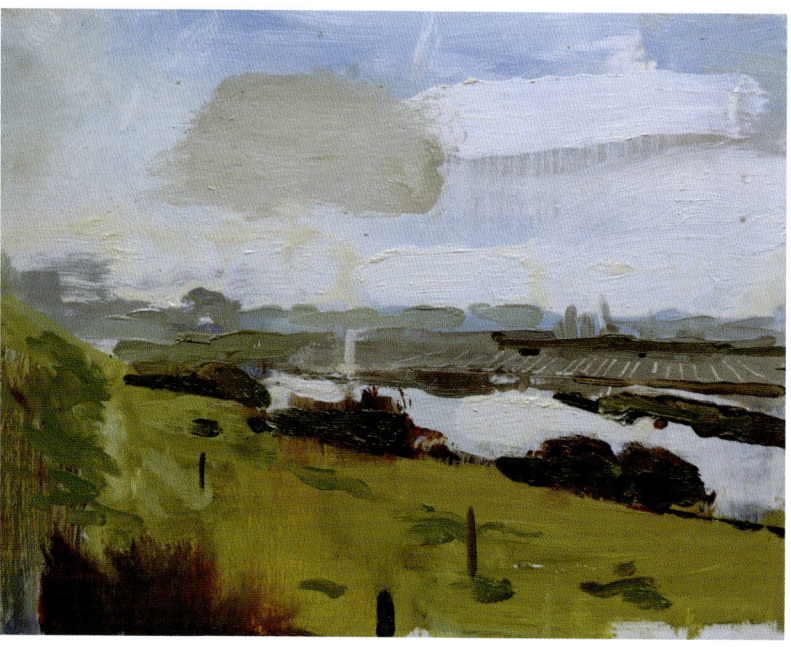

Stephen Hayes, *Sauvie Road Terminus*, oil on birch panel, 8" × 10" | 20.3 cm × 25.4 cm

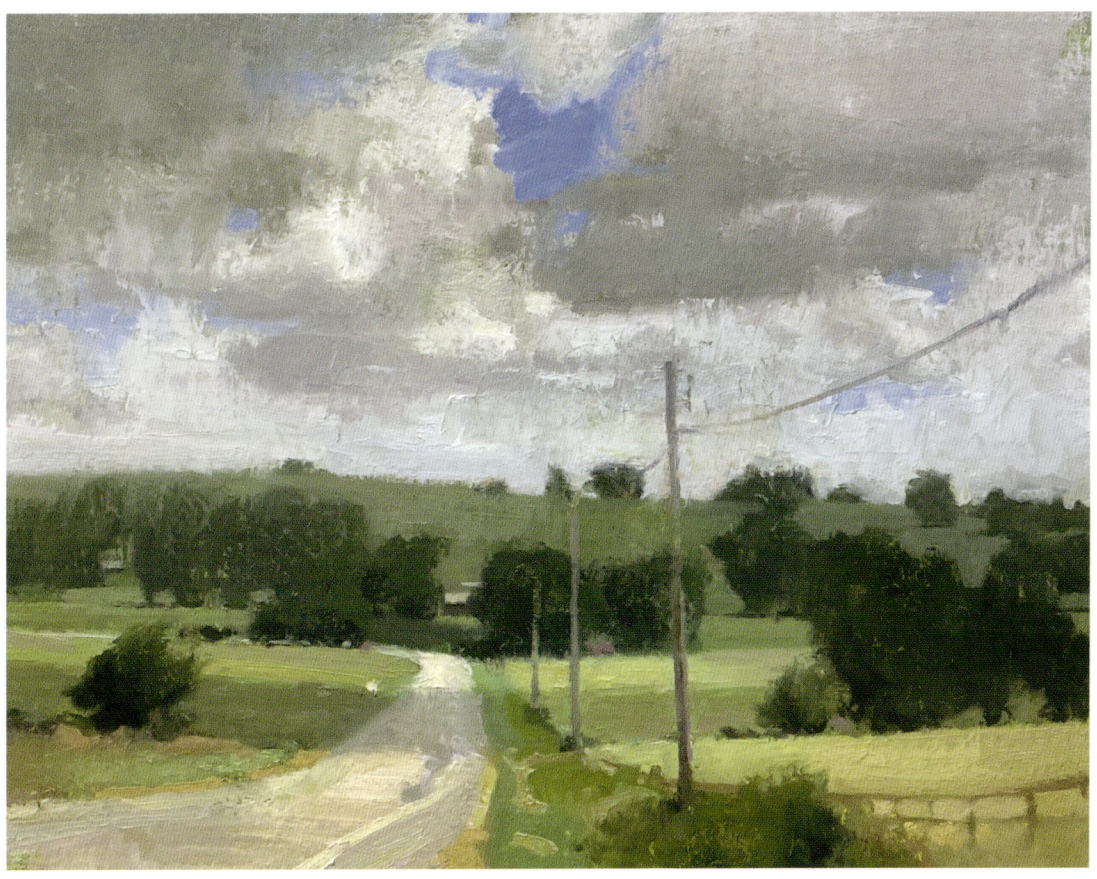

John P. Lasater IV, *Ozark Paysage*, oil on canvas, 14" × 18" | 35.6 cm × 45.7 cm

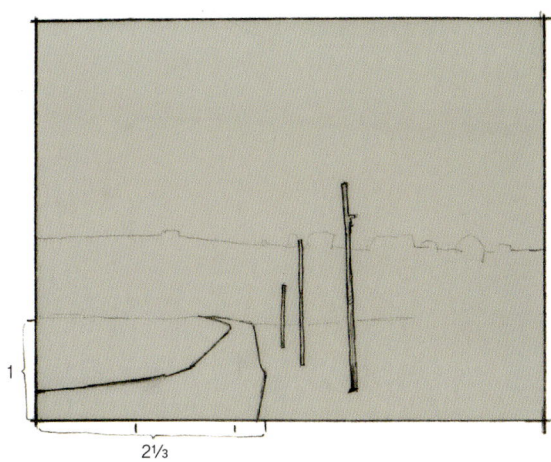

Here, I have outlined the road from John Lasater's painting, *Ozark Paysage*, to show the shape of the road and the size and spacing of the utility poles.

PERSPECTIVE: DIMINISHING SIZE

The drawing solutions to indicate distance include size, placement, and overlapping. In reality, distant objects have a smaller apparent size. In painting, we make distant things smaller to create a sense of distance. This applies easily to a series of similar objects, like people or utility poles. It also applies to the spaces between things.

More distant objects are placed closer to the horizon line; clouds at the top of the picture and shrubs at the bottom are (or seem) closer to us.

An apparent overlap is a clear way to indicate that one object is closer than the other.

DESIGNING WITH A VIEWFINDER

A viewfinder works like a window to define the subject, or help you choose, and blocks out everything around it. The marks make it easy to adjust it to match the format of the canvas.

Sometimes, what falls within the viewfinder makes a good composition. If not, we can rearrange elements to make a better design.

How to Measure Angles

This is what I call the *windshield wiper method*: Use a pencil or brush held at arm's length. Pretend it's held against a window or windshield, so it can't be pointed away from you, but can only move like the hands of a clock. Close one eye and rotate the pencil to match the angle of whatever you're measuring.

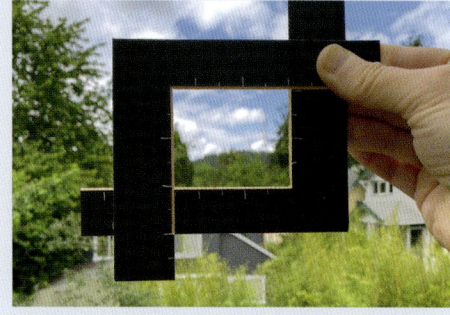

Using a homemade viewfinder.

THUMBNAILS AND SMALL SKETCHES

A thumbnail is a design sketch, about the size of a postage stamp, used to try out ideas quickly and explore divisions of space within the frame. Just as the shape of the frame itself has a feel, small changes within the frame make a difference in how the picture feels.

These thumbnail sketches are based on the photo at right.

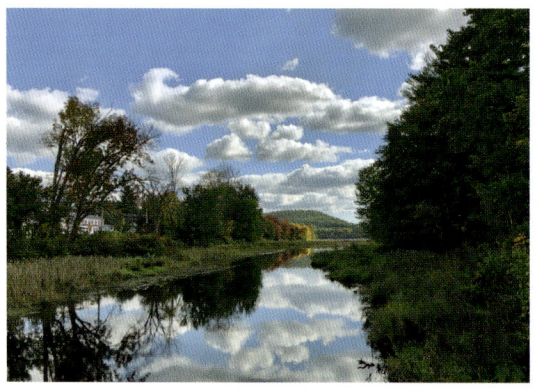

Photo by Patty Mynczywor.

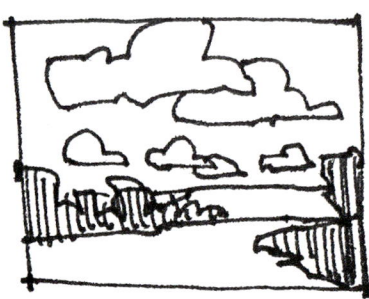

This thumbnail is designed to show the beauty of the clouds.

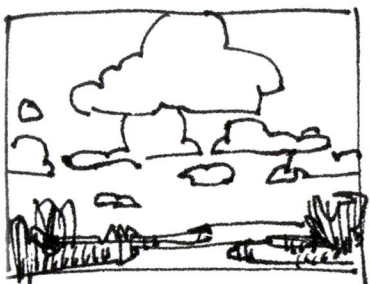

This one also shows off the clouds, and I like it better. The ground is compressed and the sky takes up even more space in the frame— it feels more spacious.

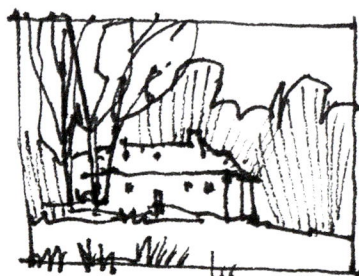

This one ignores the brook and shows the house nestled in the trees.

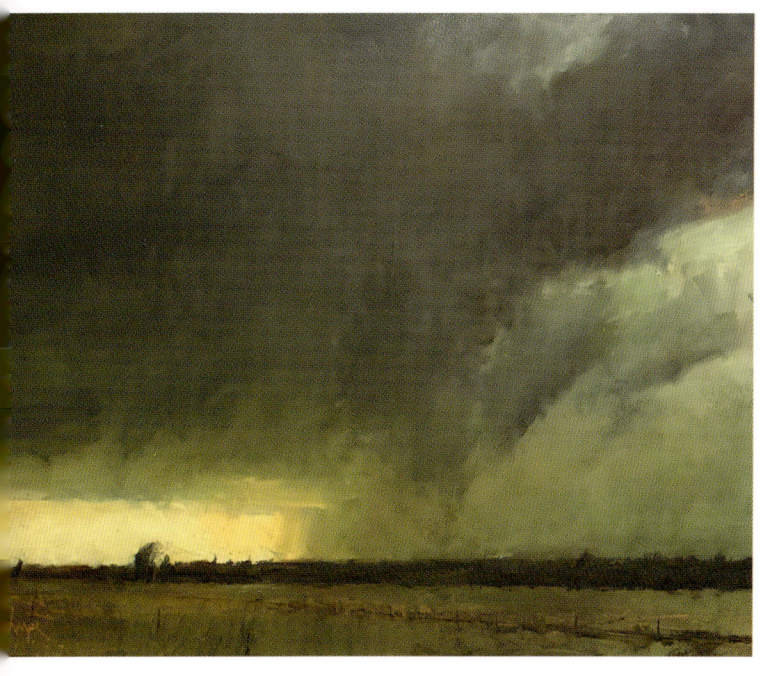

David Sharpe, *Clearing*, oil on wood panel, 12" × 12" | 30.5 cm × 30.5 cm

David Sharpe, *Lone Pine*, oil on wood panel, 9" × 12" | 22.9 cm × 30.5 cm

One of the primary compositional decisions we make is where to locate the horizon. There's a tendency to place it in the middle of the frame because that's how we perceive the world.

Learn, instead, to think of the placement of the horizon as a design decision.

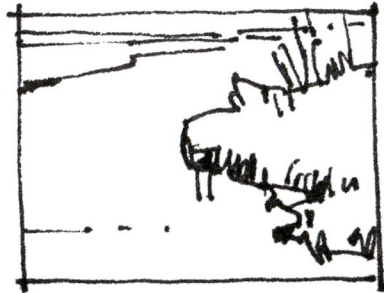

This one focuses on the riverbank.

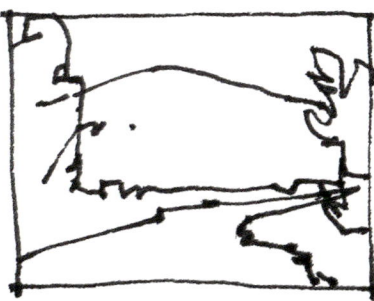

This one is designed to emphasize the mountain.

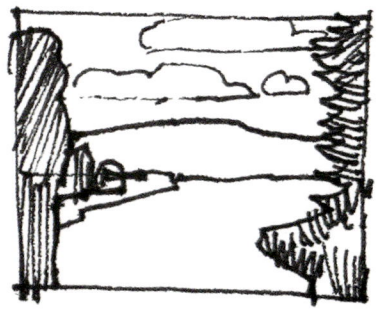

This one includes trees, water, mountain, and sky, without emphasizing any one thing. This is "as it comes," not designed.

BLACK AND WHITE

The simplest, strongest images are black and white: light and dark shapes, defined by each other. Composing with black and white forces us to be decisive, helps us learn to group things together, and hones our sensitivity to abstract shape relationships. This idea of the distribution of light and dark, strong and weak, within an image is the essence of the Japanese concept of *notan*. (In a less strict interpretation, notan can have three values.)

Decisions can be made based on light and shadow, on local value (the "home" value of an object), or on some combination of the two.

Edge vs. inside. Think about shape as having a perimeter–the outside edge–and an interior. When working in full value or color, we can do things inside of a shape, using value, hue, or chroma changes, but in notan, each shape is a single flat value.

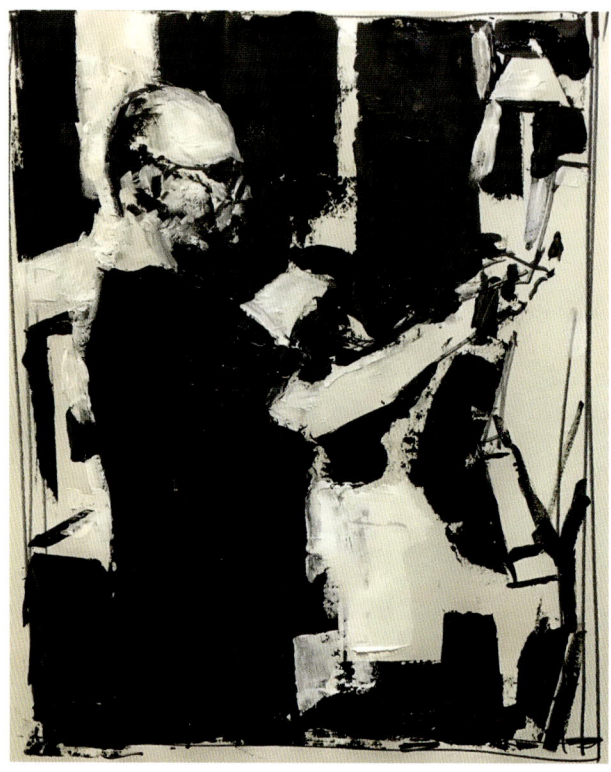

Patrick Lee, *The Artist*, Sharpie and acrylic on paper, 10" × 8" | 25.4 cm × 20.3 cm

A NOTE ABOUT THE EXERCISES

The best assignments are the ones you yourself invent to teach yourself something. (The best paintings are often those that arise from that same spirit of invention.) The exercises in this book are designed to allow you to learn some fundamental principles by doing, rather than simply having it explained. It's okay to adjust them to suit yourself.

SKETCHBOOK EXERCISE:
NOTAN

MATERIALS

- Pencil, markers, watercolor, or any opaque watermedia
- Sketchbook

Acrylic, gouache, and casein are great for making notans because they dry fast. You can refine shapes or make changes without blending. Markers or watercolor are also excellent. Sketch first with pencil so the whites stay clean. If you want to make corrections, you'll need to add another medium to get an opaque white. Work at a size that feels doable. You can let your brush determine the scale of your study or vice versa.

A Good Place to Begin. Start with making notan studies of paintings. Some paintings are more suited to this exercise than others. Look for works that have a strong light/dark structure. Your job is to decipher the existing composition into black and white. Information is always lost in this process. Consider it a game to see if you can make shapes that are simple and informative.

Process. Draw the four sides of the format and then lightly draw the subject in pencil. Find the shadow/dark areas and paint them black and then paint (or leave) the light areas white.

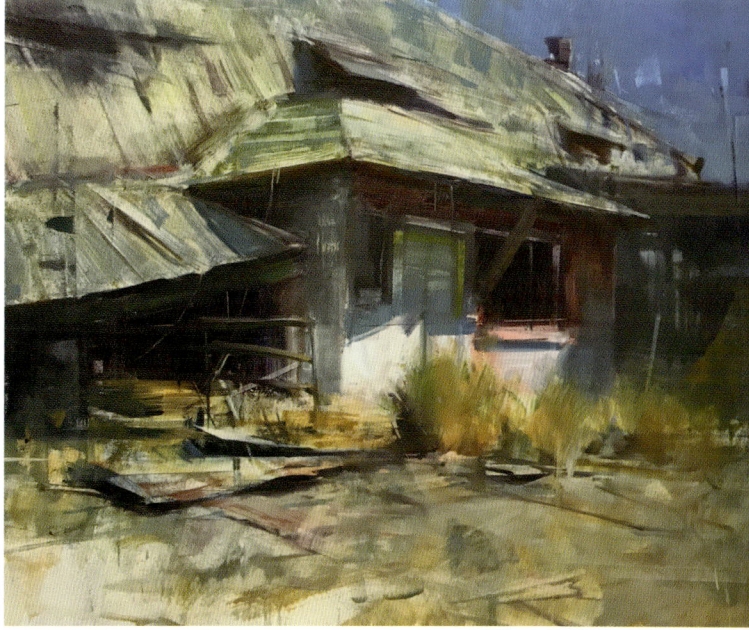

Bryan Mark Taylor, *Milk Farm*, oil on panel, 11" × 14" | 28 cm × 35.6 cm

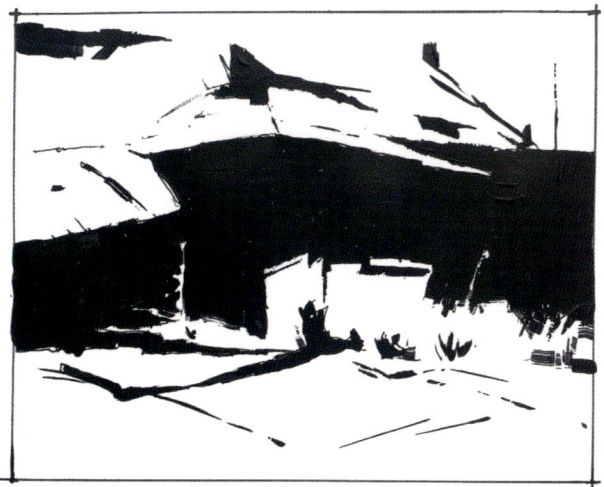

Notan in two values based on *Milk Farm* by Bryan Mark Taylor.

continued ▶

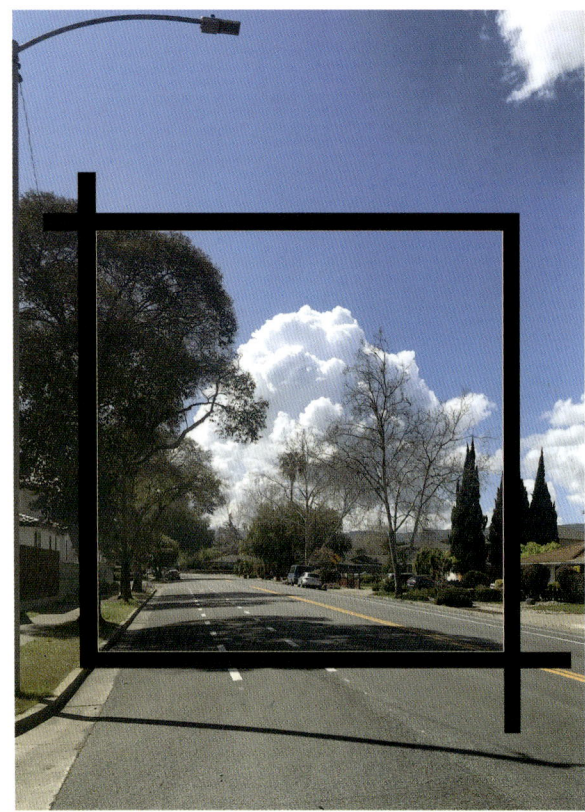

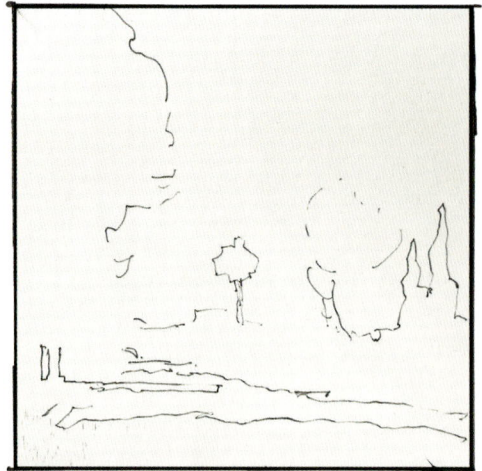

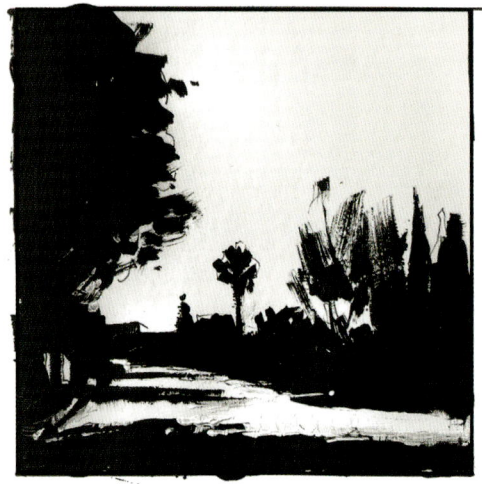

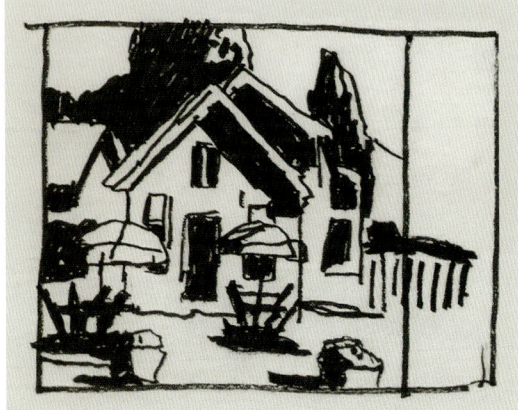

Peggi Kroll Roberts, *Notan*, permanent ink
on paper, 4" × 4" | 10.2 cm × 10.2 cm

The format and composition are inextricably
linked. Can I adjust my composition to fit inside
the format? Or do I need to change the format
to better fit my shapes?

More Advanced: Make Notans from Life.
The process is a combination of seeing
what's there and designing it to make a
strong composition. Use your viewfinder and
again lightly draw the shapes first. Again,
make your shapes simple *and* informative.
If what's there could be better designed, go
ahead and make it better. This is a process,
and it's okay to make several attempts as you
figure things out.

VALUE

Value means lightness or darkness. *Interval* is the difference between one value and another.

Composing with a range of grays is more complex than black and white and simpler than color. Black and white is an *either/or* proposition and a metaphor for no middle ground. In grayscale, it's *all about* the middle ground, and the question becomes, "Does this shape need to be lighter or darker, and how much?"

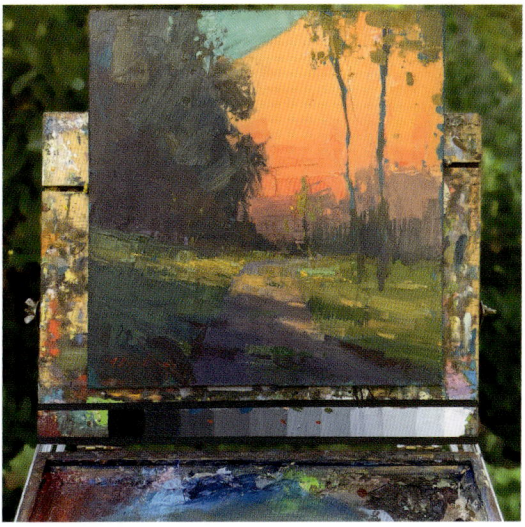

Having a value scale handy while painting is useful for checking your color values. Mine is painted onto my panel holder.

TINTING STRENGTH

Any time you mix two paint colors together, you have a moment of discovery: Which of the two is stronger? *Tinting strength* is a pigment's ability to influence other pigments.

Tip. If you're new to painting, start with a tube of black, a tube of white, and fifty panels. Take my advice! Color will be there when you're ready for it!

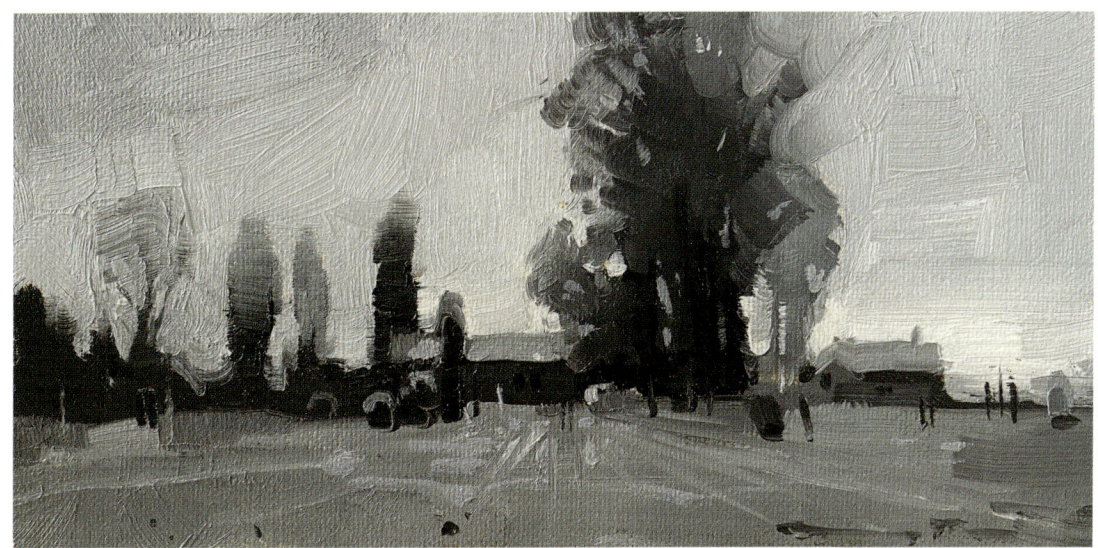

Aimee Erickson, *Grayscale study of Sonoma Farmland*, oil on canvas panel, 3½" × 7" | 8.9 cm × 17.8 cm

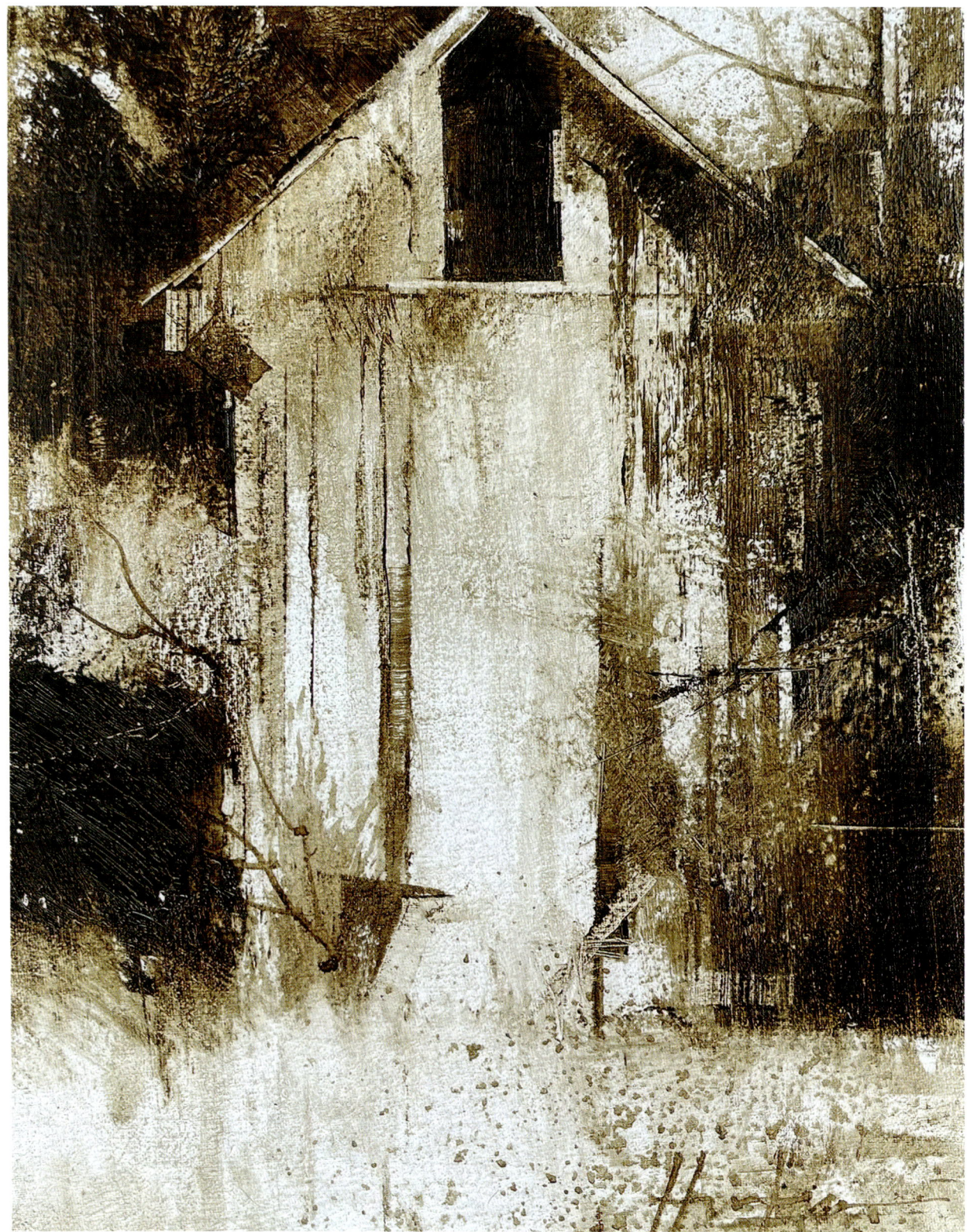

Charlie Hunter, *You Are Not Needed Now*, water-miscible oils on canvas panel, 8" × 6" | 20.3 cm × 15.2 cm

Charlie Hunter uses water-miscible oils and a one- or two-pigment palette to create images based on strong composition and value relationships. Since he's not using white, all the light values are the gessoed canvas showing through.

LIMITED VALUE STUDIES

A *limited value study* uses a few shades of gray, usually no more than five, to define the shapes within a composition. The goal is to simplify: Make fewer shapes with stronger presence. What can be left out? What can be merged into one shape? Are the shapes informative? There's no one best solution. Explore.

Tip. A strong value structure is the best foundation for color.

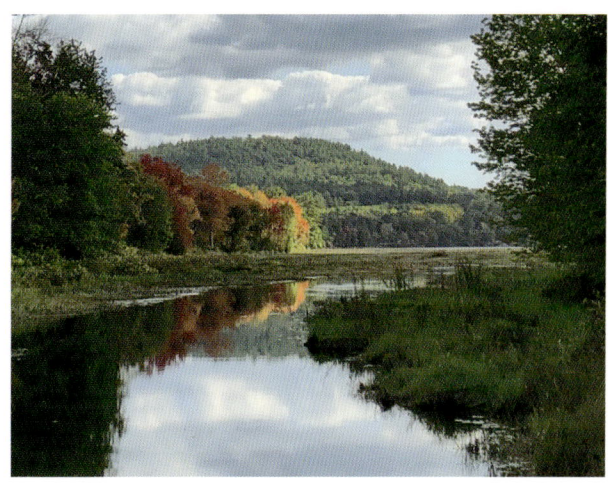

Photo by Patty Mynczywor (cropped).

Too complicated. There are three values used, but they aren't grouped into big shapes. This is not a simple solution and would be less effective as a value structure for color.

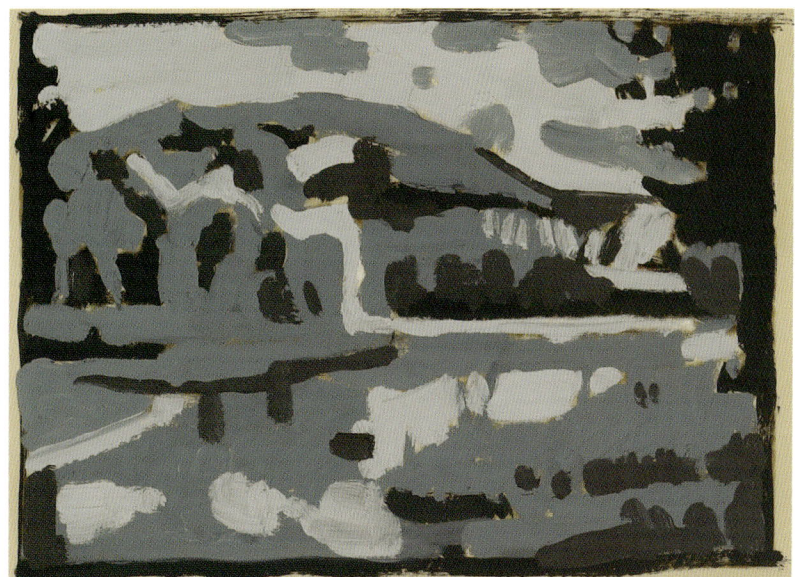

Better. Here, the primary value shapes have been made as simple and informative as possible. The foreground land- and tree-forms are darker than the water and mountain, and the mountain is darker than the sky. This is a solid foundation for later, when I use color to divide value from itself.

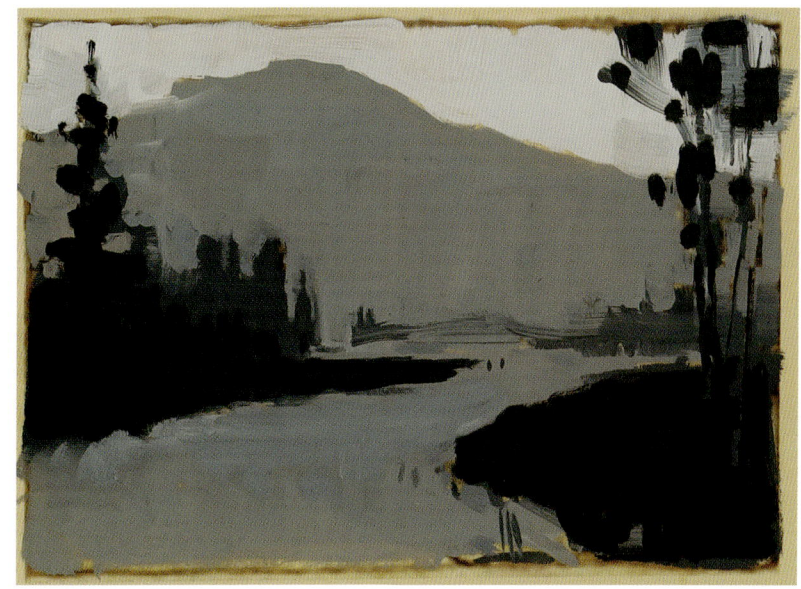

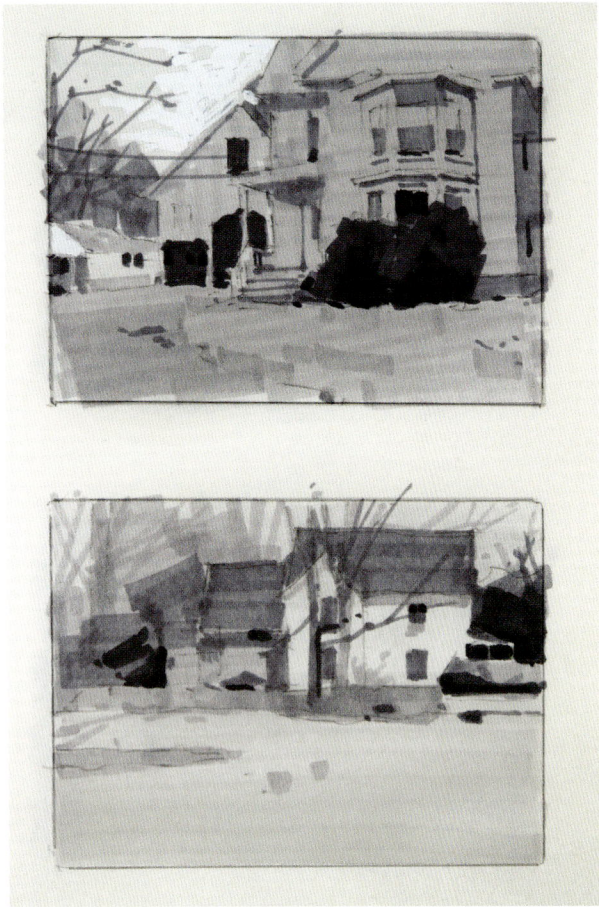

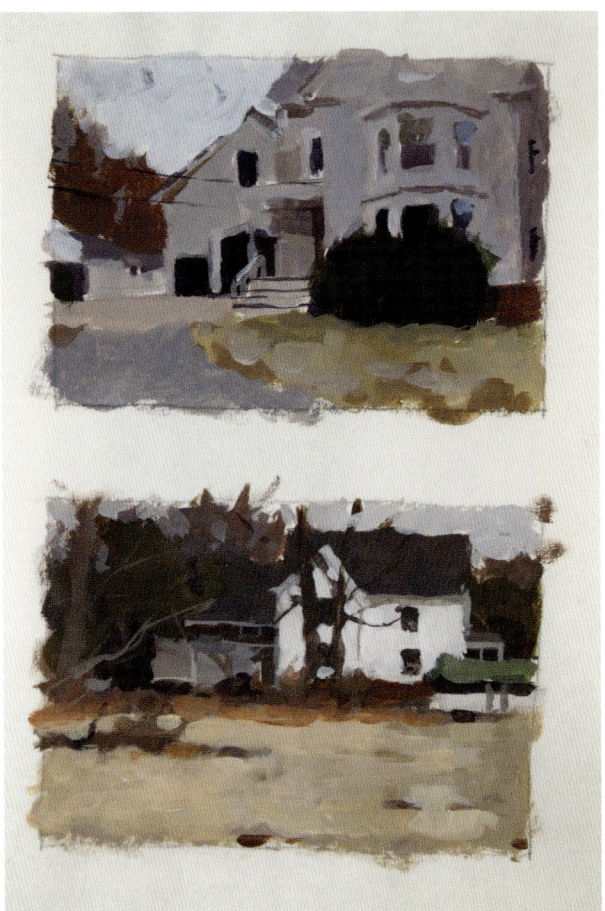

Gareth Jones, *value studies*, Copic markers on paper, subsequently developed in color.

Gareth Jones, *color studies*, gouache on paper.

Whether mixing your own or using tubed grays, be sensitive in your selection of *which* grays you use for your study—black, white, and a 50 percent middle gray might seem like an obvious choice, but there's no default palette here. When you're working only in value, the values matter and the intervals matter.

Another sketchbook option, more convenient than getting out your paints, is to use markers in a range of grays. Copic makes a set of six sketching grays.

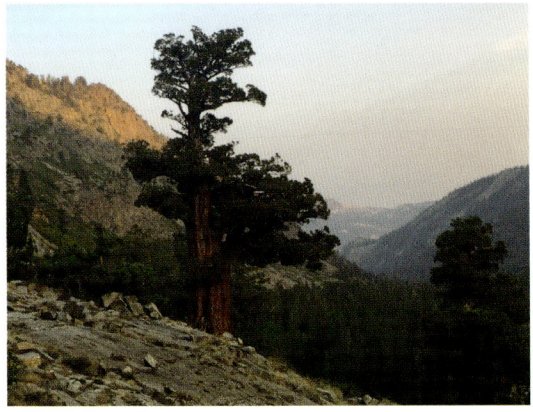

This is the reference photo for the value studies opposite.

EXERCISE:
SIMPLIFIED VALUE STUDIES

On location or working from a compositional sketch, find shape/value solutions using the simplest means possible, perhaps two or three or four values. See if you can reduce the overall number of shapes to just a few. Make them both simple and informative.

BRISTLECONE PINE VALUE STUDIES

Here are a series of explorations as an example of how many value patterns are possible from a single scene.

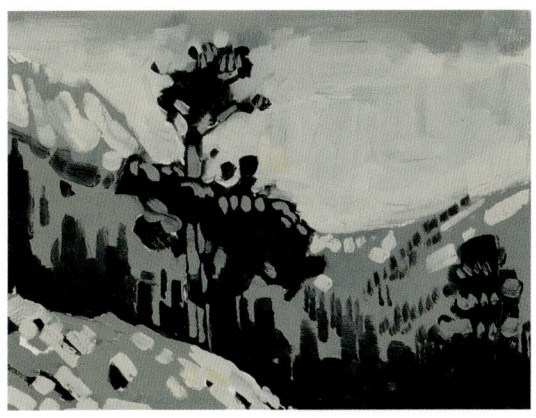

Three-value study, observing every value change I possibly can. My three values are alternating over the entire surface. It's interesting but busy and does not accomplish the goal of dividing the picture into large value shapes.

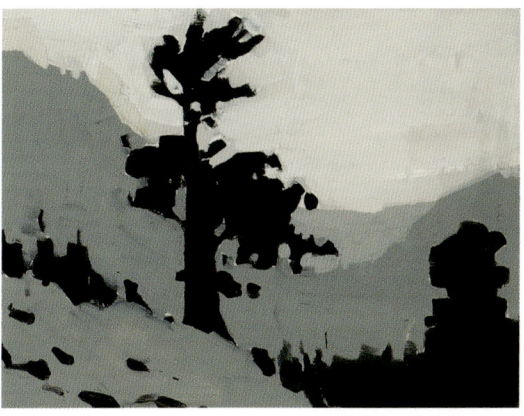

Three-value study, with the values organized into larger areas, and yes, I admit, a fourth value that's added on the distant horizon.

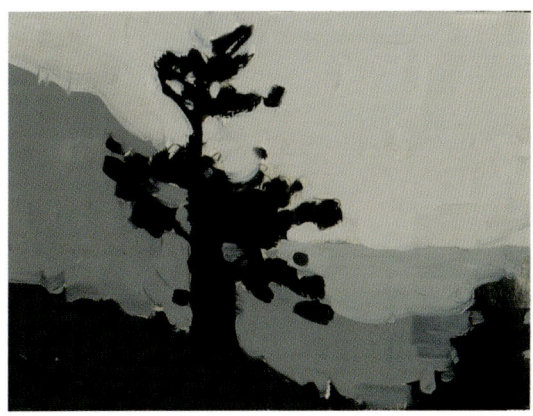

Here, I'm trying out an all-dark foreground.

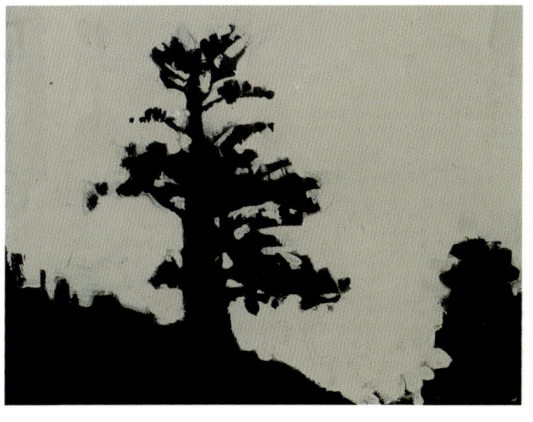

Two discrete values. I like the stark feel.

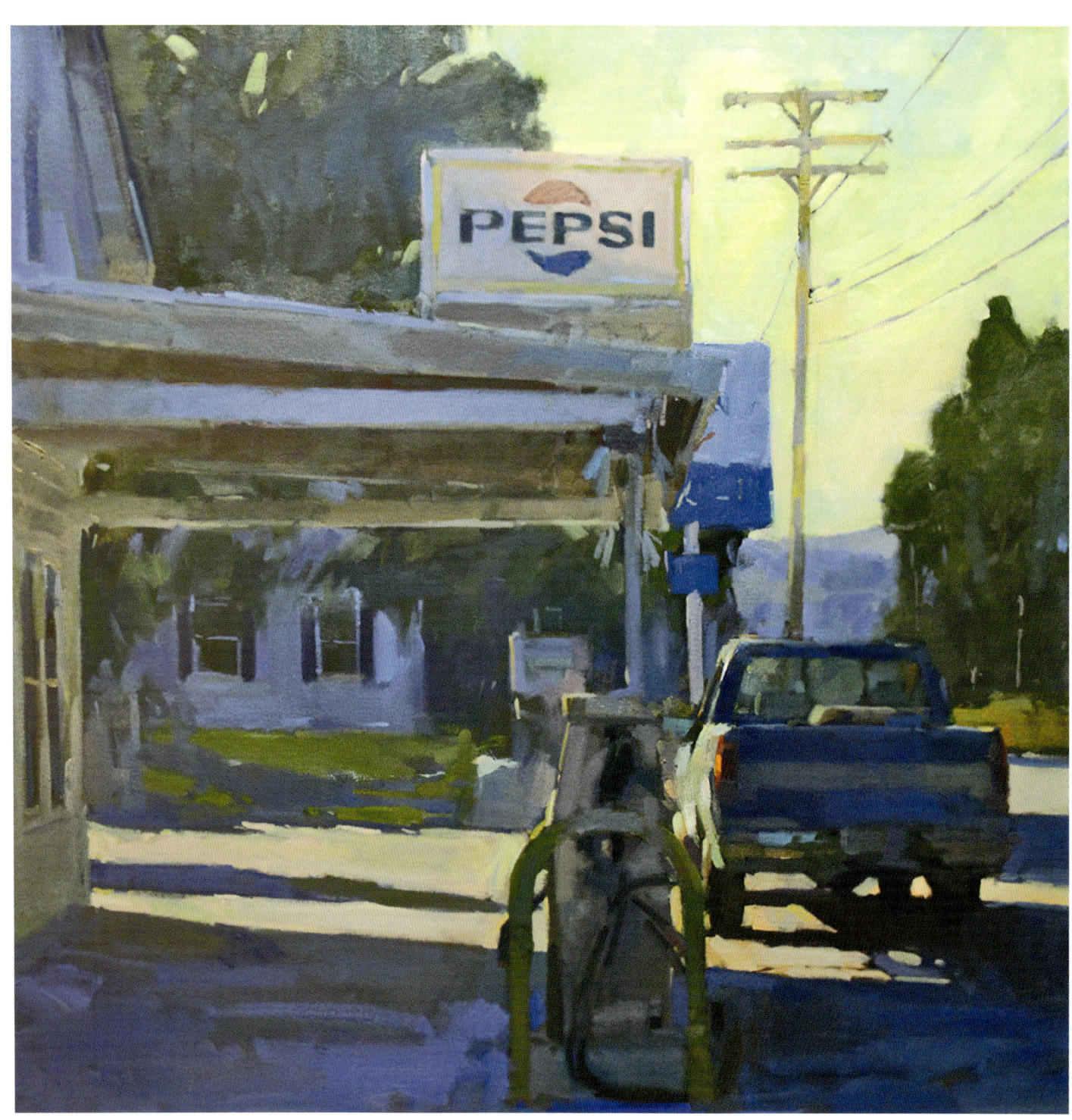

Colin Page, *Stop and Go*, oil on canvas, 32" × 32" | 81.3 cm × 81.3 cm

3

COLOR

When painting on location, color decisions result from three things:

- **Knowledge and intention.** This includes everything you know about color theory, color relationships, pigment interactions, and color schemes, plus what you like and *what you want* the colors in your painting to accomplish.

- **What's on your palette.** A single-pigment palette will result in a monochrome painting. Two pigments plus white produces a wider range of color, and a full palette allows for much more complex color relationships. (But more paint colors can't compensate for a lack of know-how.)

- **What you see.** This comprises not only what's there to be seen, but *how* you see it. From infancy, we learn survival-mode seeing: Is it a threat? Can I eat it? And once the thing has been identified, the brain moves on. But as artists, we slow down and look for the abstract visual information that makes up an object. Rather than "a blue chair," for example, we look for specific abstract shapes and a range of colors. We squint to simplify value relationships. We turn our head sideways to alter perception of color relationships. We learn the difference between looking long and sharply at something and a passing glance. And as we learn to see *more* and *differently*, our paintings can't help but evolve.

Knowledge and intention, palette, and what you see: All three of these come into play. They take turns being in charge of the color game, inventing rules, and finding solutions.

SPEAKING OF COLOR . . .

Does it matter what words we use to describe color? Of course it does. Vocabulary influences our perceptive ability because both words and perceptions are processed by the brain. Having a word for something brings it into our consciousness. There are two ways to describe color–the poetic and the scientific–and both are useful and necessary to us as artists.

POETIC COLOR VOCABULARY

In everyday language we speak of color in what I think of as *the poetic approach*. This language uses familiar objects or a string of descriptive color names to conjure up a color idea. It's evocative, connecting the color to an emotional dimension. House paint manufacturers use a poetic approach when giving colors names like Cairo, Slicker, or Coastal Fog. We have such a strong association between words and color that the description we use can affect our feelings for a color, for better or worse.

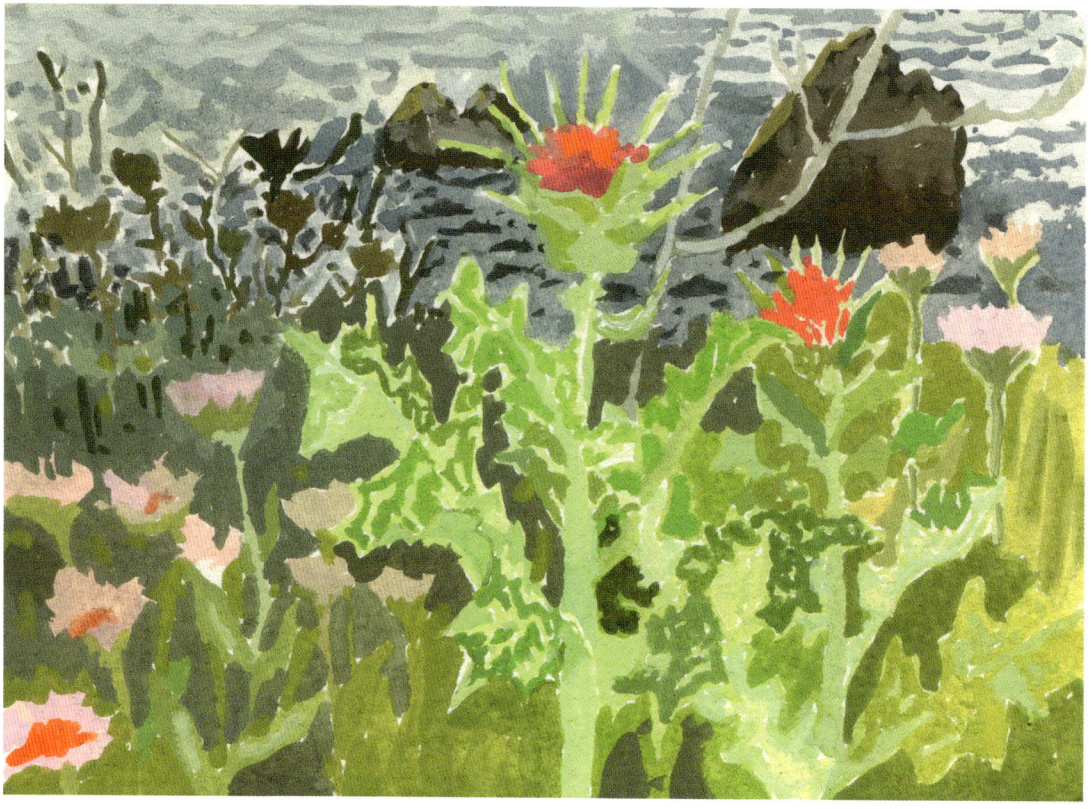

Michelle Morin, *Big Sur Bluff*, watercolor on paper, 9" × 12" | 22.9 cm × 30.5 cm

SCIENTIFIC COLOR VOCABULARY

As painters, we are not just on the receiving end of color, seeing it and feeling that emotion it conveys. *Au contraire*. We are on the back end, mixing the colors we want and juxtaposing one color with another to achieve a certain effect and convey a mood.

We need to be able to define color in a way that helps us engineer the effect we want. We need terms for our most common need: comparing one color to another. Borrowing from science, we can describe color in terms of its three defining characteristics: hue, value, and chroma.

Hue is the color family: red, orange, yellow, green, blue, or purple. Shown here is a gradual change in hue from blue to green, at a middle value.

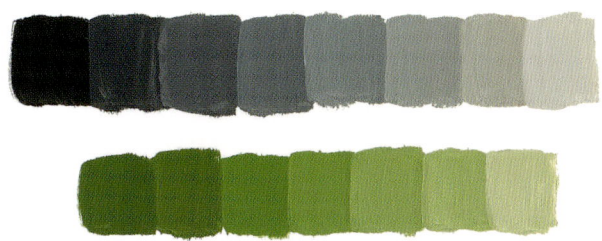

Value is the degree of lightness or darkness. Often when we discuss value we use grays to illustrate, since gray has value but no color. However, color also (and always) has value, as shown in this range of greens.

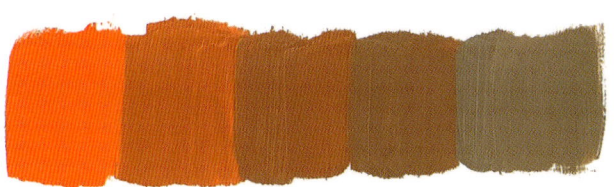

FIVE REDS, FROM STRONG (HIGH CHROMA)
TO WEAK (LOW CHROMA)

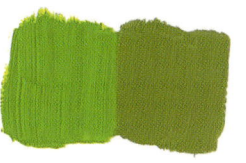

A BRIGHT (HIGH-CHROMA)
GREEN AND A LOWER-
CHROMA GRAY-GREEN

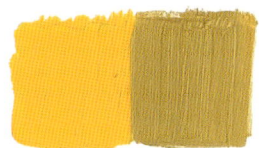

AN INTENSE (HIGH-CHROMA)
YELLOW AND A LOWER-
CHROMA YELLOW

Chroma refers to the intensity, or saturation, of a color. Fire-engine red is high chroma; brick red is low chroma. Shown here are five reds, from strong to weak, made by starting with pure cadmium red light and gradually adding gray to it. In poetic language, we might call those three intermediate colors *rust*, *terra cotta*, and *brown*, but in the scientific language of color theory, we identify them as red in hue, all of the same value and varying only in chroma.

COLOR TEMPERATURE

Color temperature is not a defining characteristic of color, but it is a very useful concept. Most importantly, color temperature is almost always relative. In terms of the color wheel, red, orange, and yellow are warm, and blue, green, and violet are cool, with orange being the warmest, and blue being the coolest. If, however, the comparison is between two reds, you may perceive that one is a warm red and the other is cool *relative to the first*.

Value is also a factor in color temperature: Darker is warmer and lighter is cooler. This is where color temperature becomes less straightforward.

If the concept of color temperature in a given context does not make sense to you, don't worry about it. Simply practice identifying color relationships in terms of hue, value, and chroma.

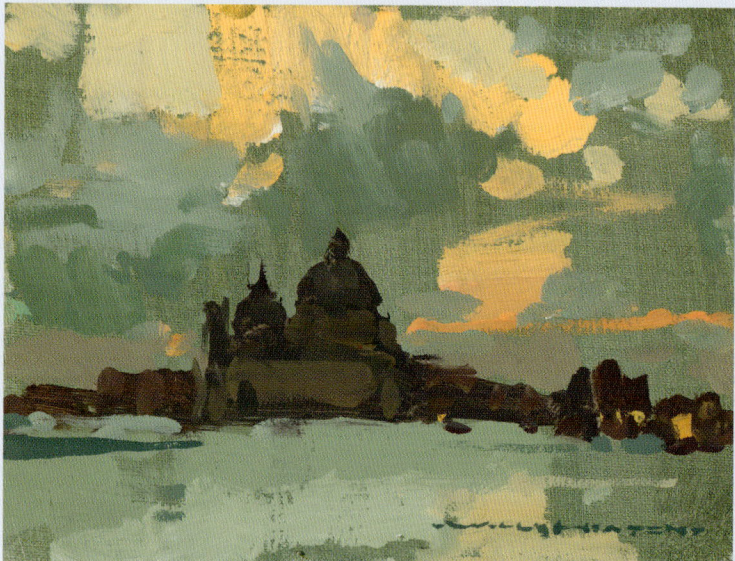

Wyllis Heaton, *Sunset over Venice*, oil on canvas, 9" × 12" | 22.9 cm × 30.5 cm

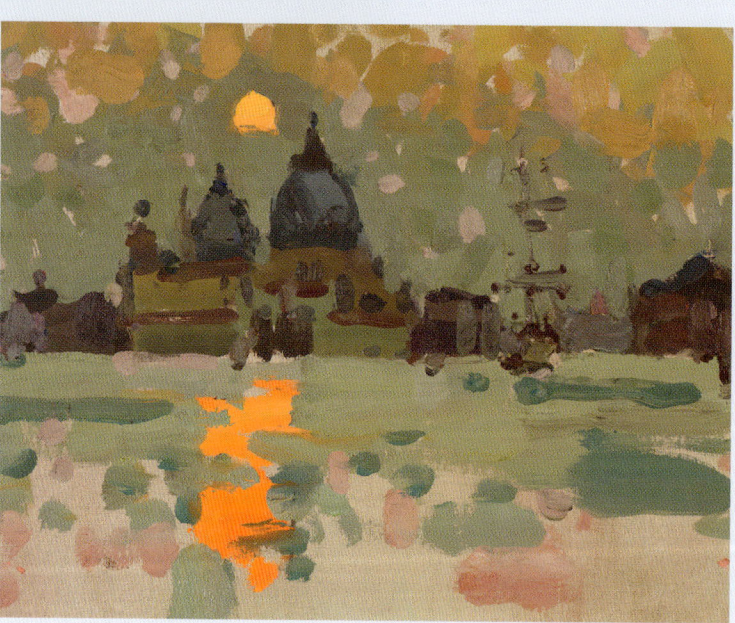

Wyllis Heaton, *Salute in Twilight*, oil on canvas, 6" × 8" | 15.2 cm × 20.3 cm

COLOR EXERCISES

These two exercises are a summary course in practical color mixing. They are designed to teach you what you need to know about hue, value, and chroma. An intellectual understanding isn't enough. Take your time—these are a wonderful way to spend studio time and will only benefit your work.

MATERIALS

- **Toned paper:** This is best as it makes judging values easier. I used a Strathmore 400 Series Toned Sketchbook (both the Warm Tan and Cool Gray are good).
- **Medium:** I did these examples in oil paint, on pages treated with shellac (surprisingly, wet oil paint hardly transfers to the opposite page at all when you close the book). Gouache and acrylic are also excellent choices and dry faster. They darken as they dry, so you have to learn to accommodate that.
- **Pigments:** This exercise can be done with any white, yellow, red, and blue. Black is optional. Make note of your pigments for reference. I used Scheveningen Yellow Light, Scheveningen Red Medium, and Ultramarine Blue.
- **Brush:** My brush is a Rosemary & Co Ivory Long Flat, No. 4.
- **Palette knife:** for mixing.

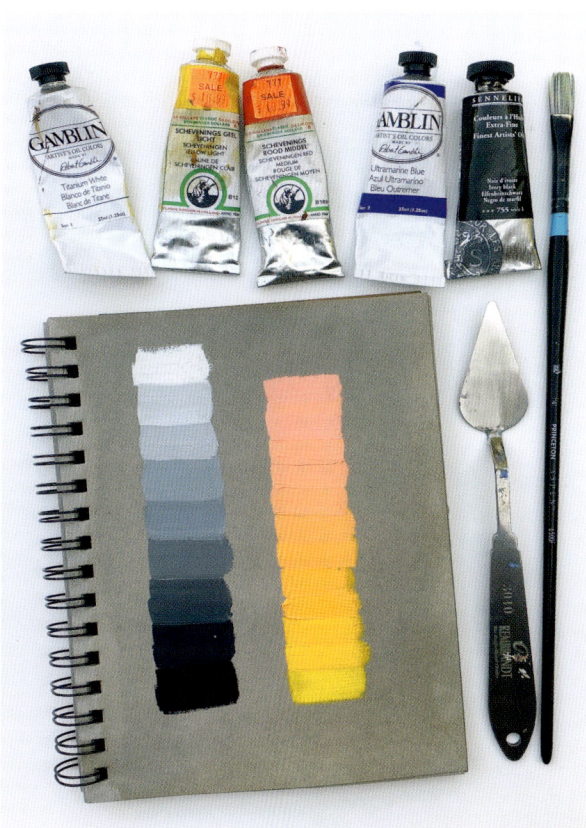

EXERCISE:
A COLOR CHART, EMPHASIZING VALUE

The purpose of this exercise is to mix colors *at specific values.* If you're an organized person who likes grids, you can draw a grid first. Freeform is also fine. The important thing in this exercise is to give yourself time and space to see the value of colors.

1. First, on the left side, make a four-value scale from dark to light. Black and white are outliers but are nice to have on the page as reference. (If you're going without black, make a dark neutral by mixing red + blue + a little yellow and use that as your "black.")

2. In a given row, you can put any hue, at any chroma, as long as it is *the same value as the gray* in that row. When you have trouble seeing value—if you can't tell whether your values match or not—find a way to give your eye different or more information: Dab some color onto the gray as I've done here, stand back from your work, look at it sideways, make a bigger swatch to compare, or make some variations in the value of the color you're mixing. Play with it. You're learning a new skill, and your brain is accustomed to identifying hue over value.

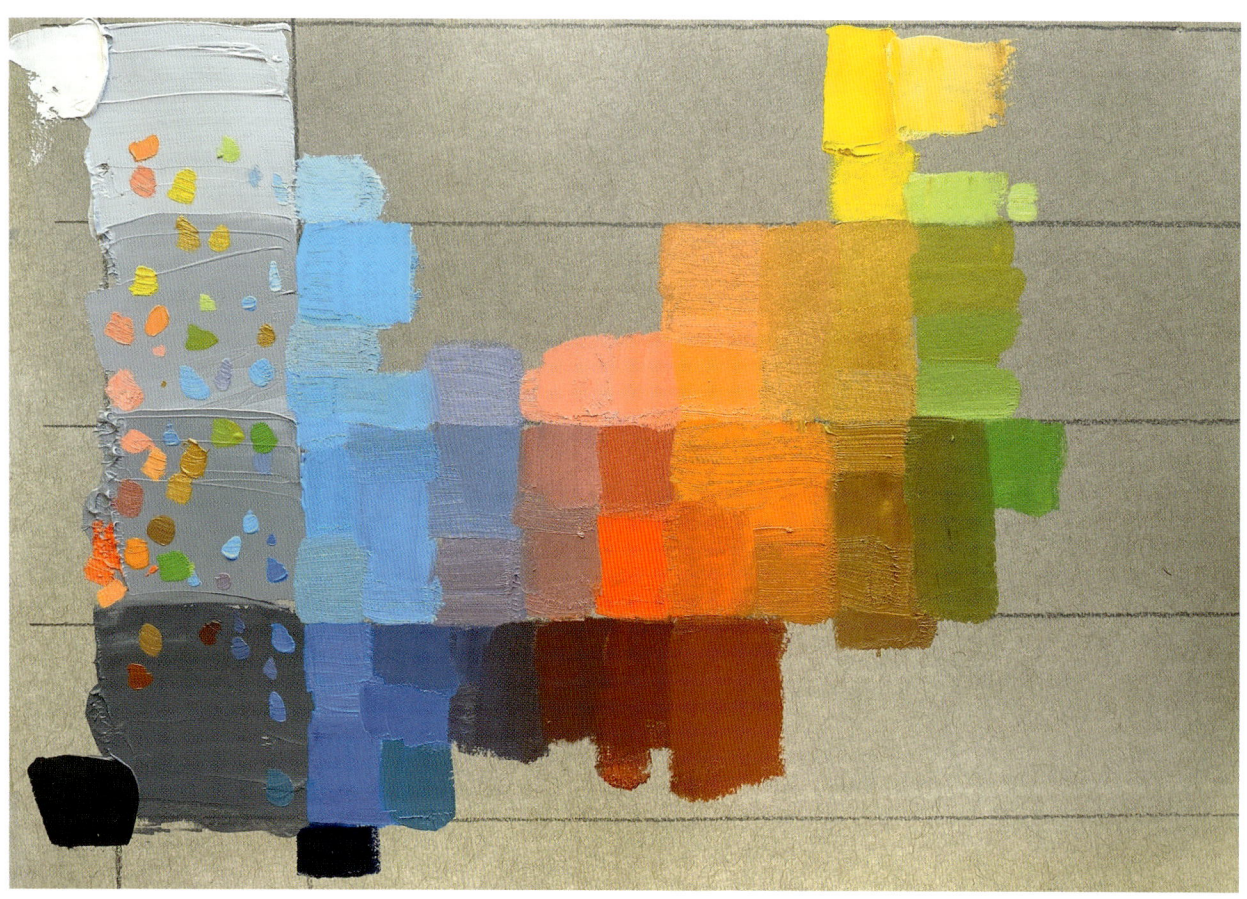

EXERCISE:
COLOR LADDERS

A color ladder is similar to a value scale, but with an important difference. Working in color means there are many hues possible at any given value. Every time you go up a rung in value, you can shift around a bit in hue and chroma using other pigments on your palette.

In plein air painting, this process of going lighter and then adjusting chroma and hue happens *all the time*. Here we just isolate it for practice.

Color ladders also help us understand how to solve a common problem with opaque pigments, that of "chalking out." This unpleasant phenomenon—colors looking chalky or too whitish—results from the mixture being too cool or too low in saturation, often because it's been lightened with white only. Even if the value is correct, the color looks flat and washed out.

continued ▶

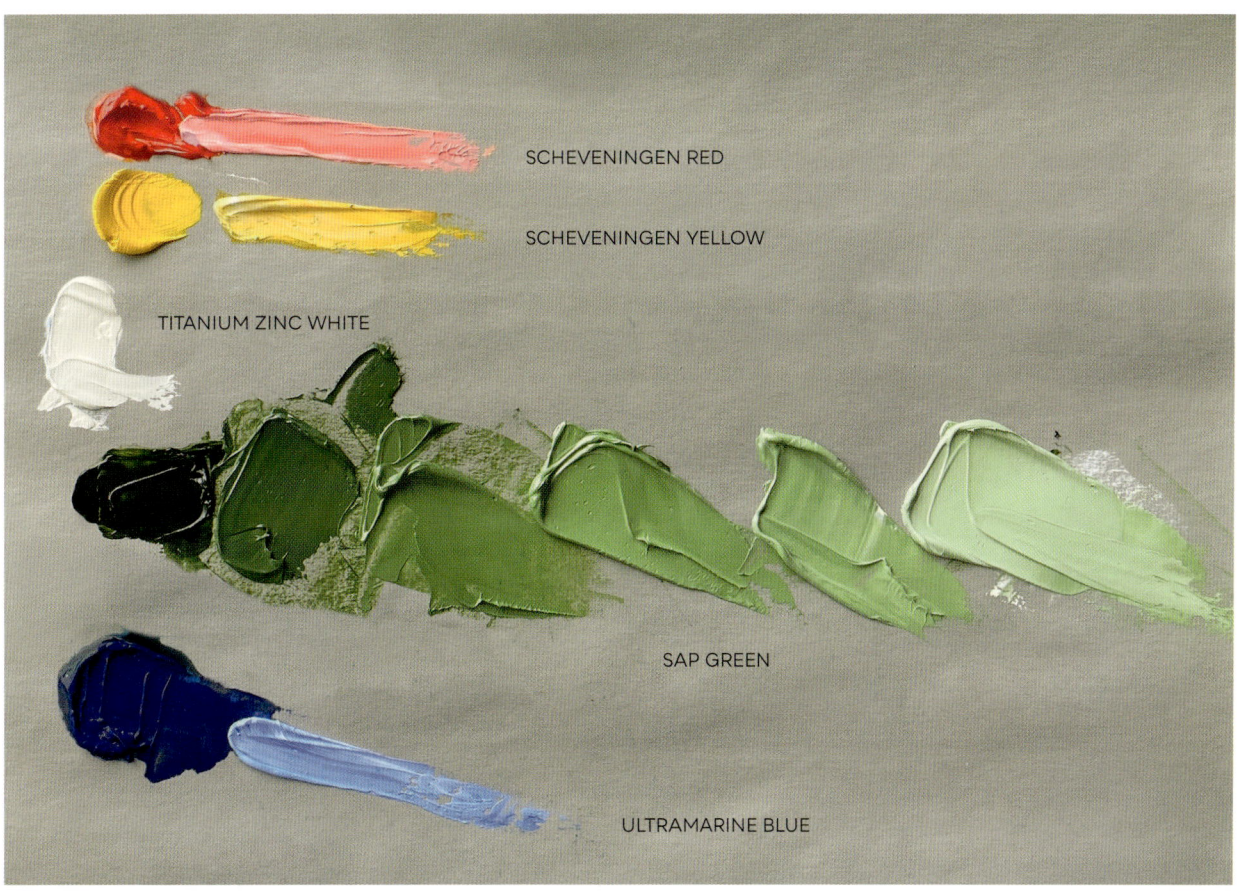

SCHEVENINGEN RED

SCHEVENINGEN YELLOW

TITANIUM ZINC WHITE

SAP GREEN

ULTRAMARINE BLUE

Pigments used in the examples.

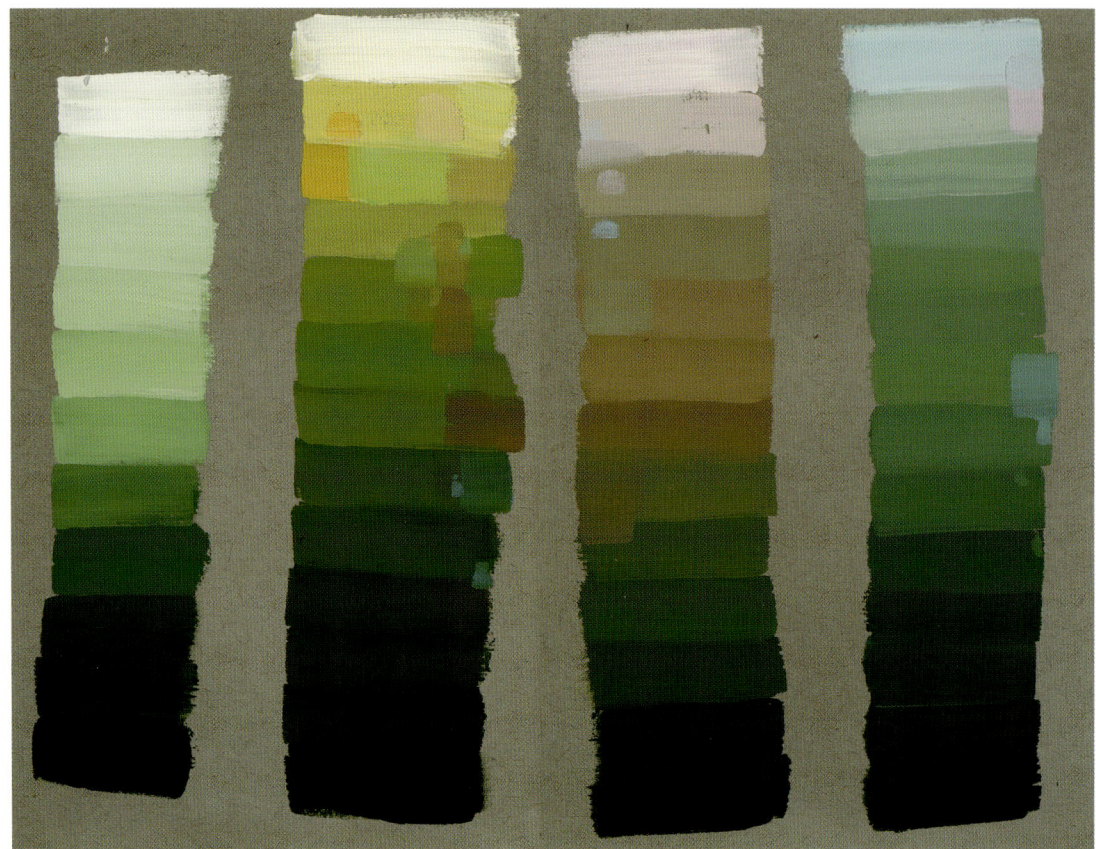

SAP GREEN + WHITE

SAP GREEN + OTHER PIGMENTS LEANING YELLOW

SAP GREEN + OTHER PIGMENTS LEANING RED

SAP GREEN + OTHER PIGMENTS LEANING BLUE

1. Premixing: Start with a dark (a tube color or a mixture, mine is Sap Green) and white. Mix two or three intermediate values so you can see where you're going and have something to work with.

2. First is the control scale: Sap Green + Titanium Zinc White. Lay down the dark as the lowest rung of the ladder and then work your way up.

3. Now for the color-adjusted variations. Again, lay down the dark first and then add white to make it lighter for the next rung up. Spot-check the value with a dab of paint on the chart and then decide whether you want to change the hue using other pigments.

So, the thinking is: How much lighter do I want this rung to be? Then, do I want to shift the hue at all? First value, then hue and chroma.

CHROMATIC PEAK

Any time you make a color-plus-white scale like the control scale above, you'll be able to observe where in the scale the color is at its highest saturation. Each pigment has a peak chroma at a value particular to itself. In theory, a pigment is at its strongest right out of the tube, but some pigments, particularly dark or transparent ones, increase in chroma as they are lightened, to a point.

Sap Green out of the tube is strong in chroma and very dark. As the value steps up, its chroma increases, then levels off, and then decreases and starts to look chalky.

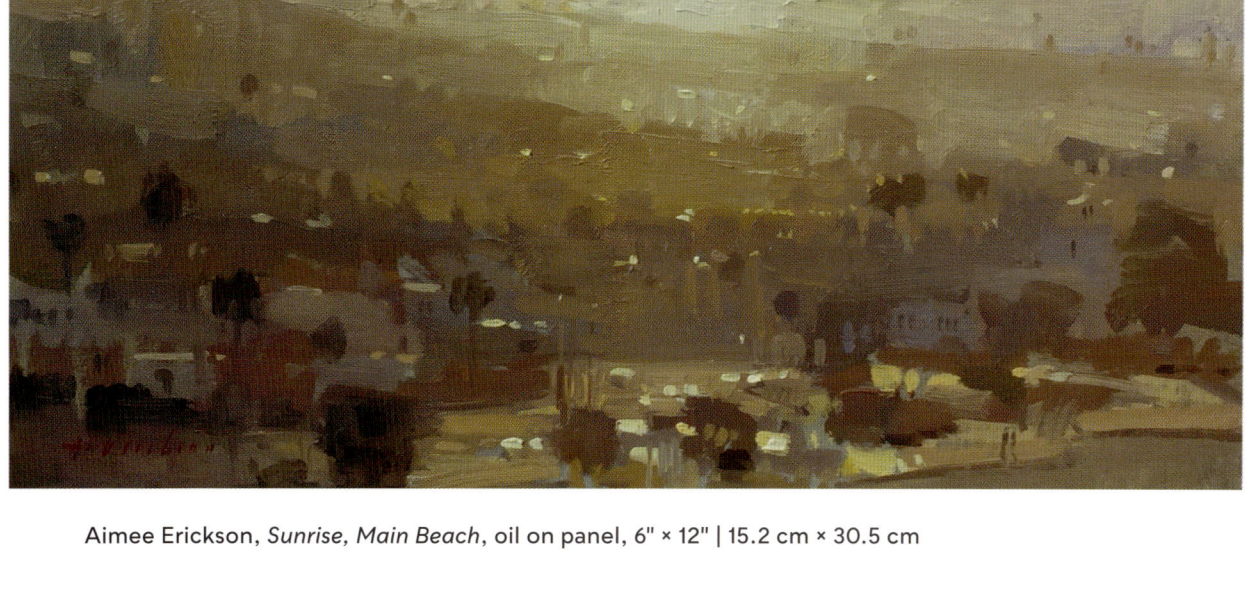

Aimee Erickson, *Sunrise, Main Beach*, oil on panel, 6" × 12" | 15.2 cm × 30.5 cm

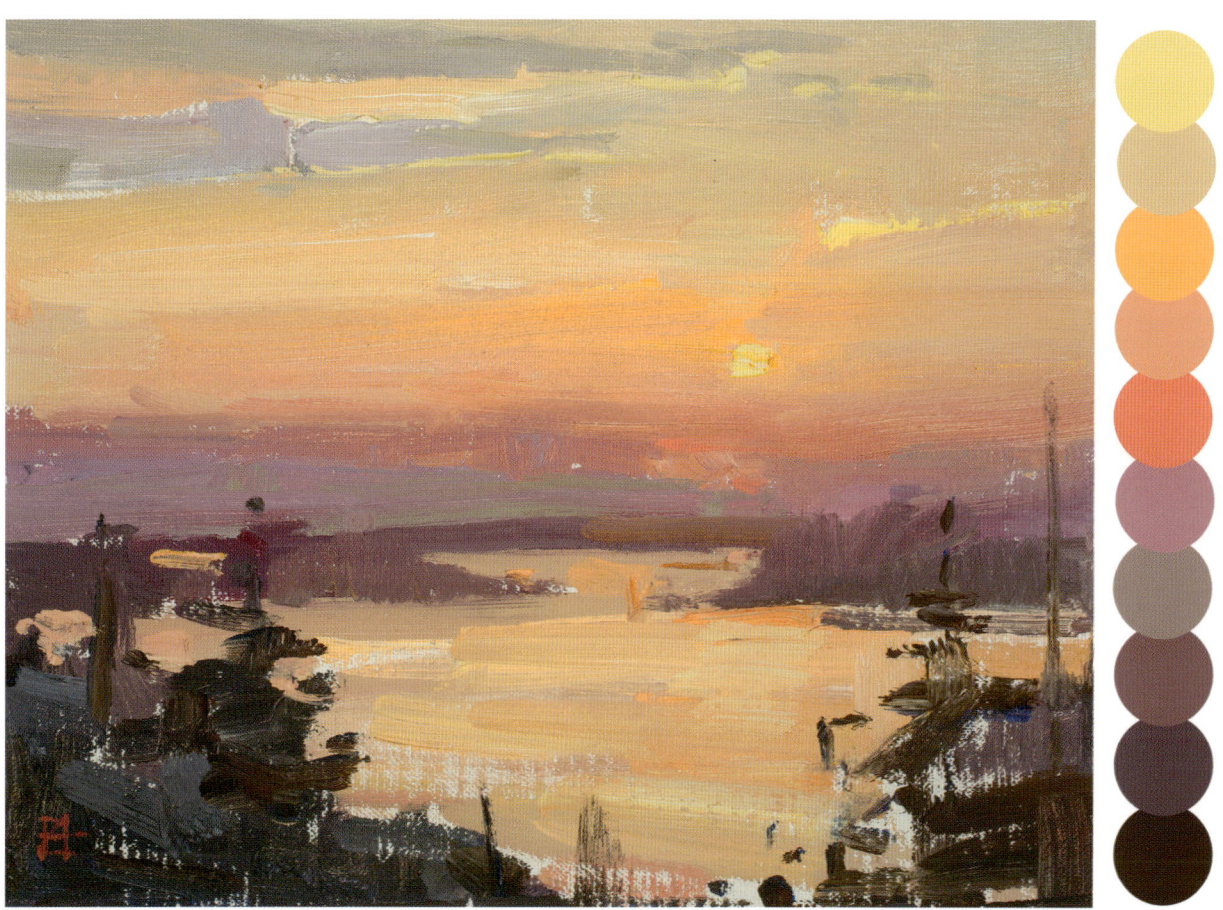

Aimee Erickson, *Menucha Sunset*, oil on canvas panel, 9" × 12" | 22.9 cm × 30.5 cm

A progression of color shifts can be the main idea for a painting. Color harmony is achieved here by intermixing pigments so that they are related and by adjusting the mixtures for hue or chroma shifts at different values.

LIMITED PALETTES

Creativity thrives within constraints. Painting is essentially a process of problem-solving, and limiting the parameters of the project is not a limit to creative thinking, but the foundation of it.

There's no strict number of colors that determines a limited palette, but generally, it's fewer than four or maybe five (plus white, usually).

TRUE SINGLE-COLOR PALETTE

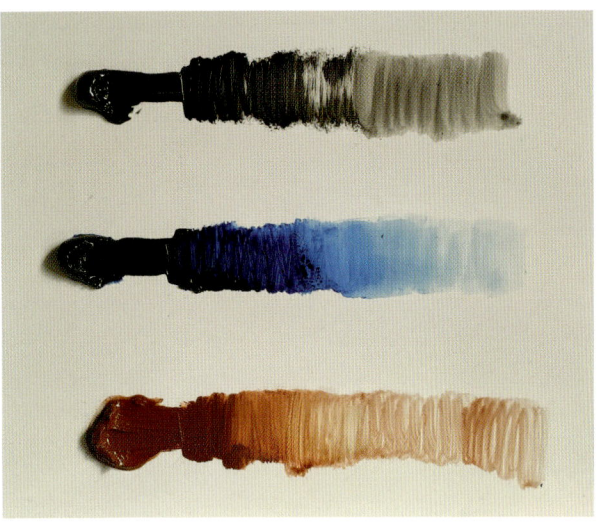

SINGLE-COLOR PALETTE (PLUS WHITE)

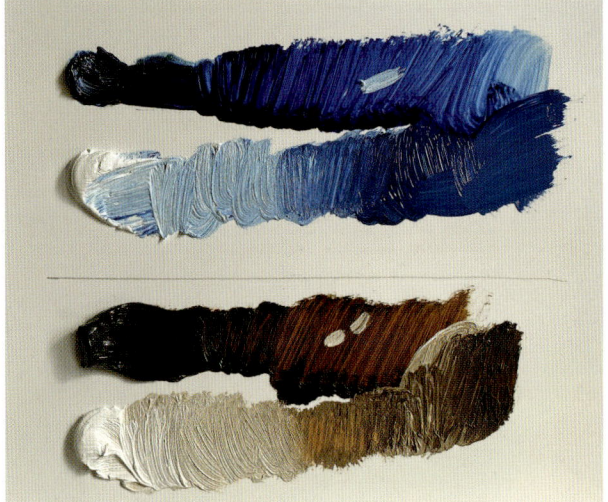

Using a single paint color is the most limited palette possible. Value changes are achieved by applying more or less paint and letting the (usually white) ground show through. Even with opaque pigments, the effect is similar to watercolor, which also uses the white of the paper and transparent paint to achieve lighter values. In this image are three examples: Sennelier Ivory Black, Rembrandt Prussian Blue, and Richeson Venetian Red.

In a palette using one tube color plus white, opaque lights can be made using white, in addition to controlling value with transparency. Transparent lights tend to have a warmer quality and in traditional methods, are better suited to describing shadow than opaque lights.

(We sometimes call this a single-pigment palette, but it's more accurate to say "single color" since some paint tubes contain more than one pigment. Most manufacturers list the pigments on the tube using a universal code. Asphaltum, for example, contains PR101 Transparent Mars Red and PBk9 Bone Black.) Colors shown: Rembrandt Prussian Blue and Gamblin Asphaltum, both mixed with Gamblin's Titanium Zinc White.

WARM-COOL PALETTE

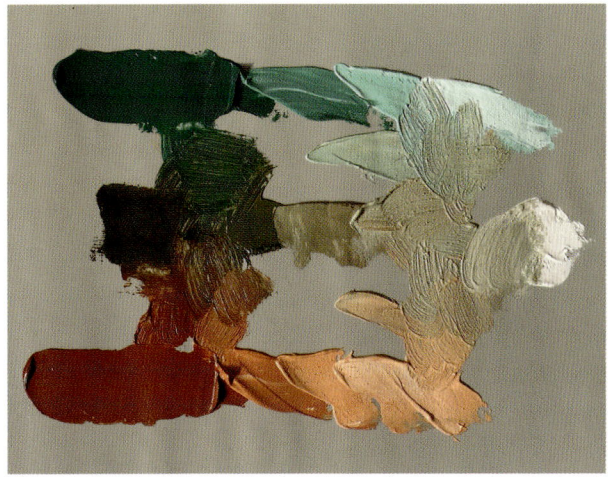

The idea here is to use two colors—one from the warm side of the color wheel and one from the cool side, so that combining them makes a neutral—plus white. Warm colors include anything from the red or earth family: Burnt Sienna, Venetian Red, Indian Red, Transparent Earth Red (or any of the other iron-based pigments), or less commonly, a Cadmium Red or Orange or Alizarin Crimson. Choose a cool from the blue range—any black is good, or Viridian, or any blue. The interaction between the two colors gains particular importance—try out pairs of colors and look for appealing neutral interactions. Shown here: Michael Harding Viridian, Burnt Sienna, and Stack Lead White.

TRIAD PALETTES

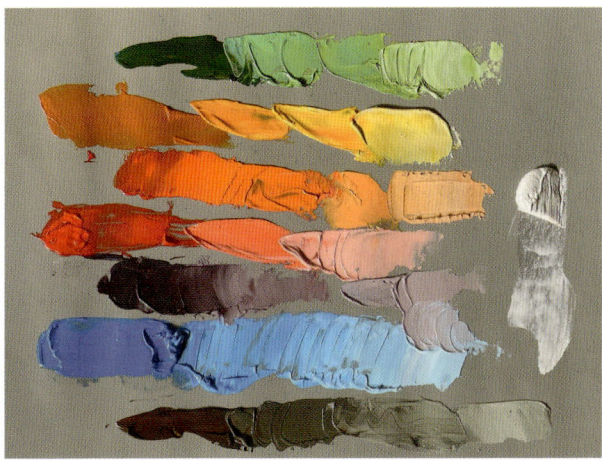

A triad palette uses three colors, which moves us suddenly into a world of color. Choose a red, a yellow, and a blue for the widest range. Purple, orange, and green are also a worthy group. Colors in a triad palette are generally spaced somewhat equally on the color wheel. Shown here is Gamblin Indian Yellow, Gamblin Napthol Red, Rembrandt Sèvres Blue, and Gamblin Titanium Zinc White.

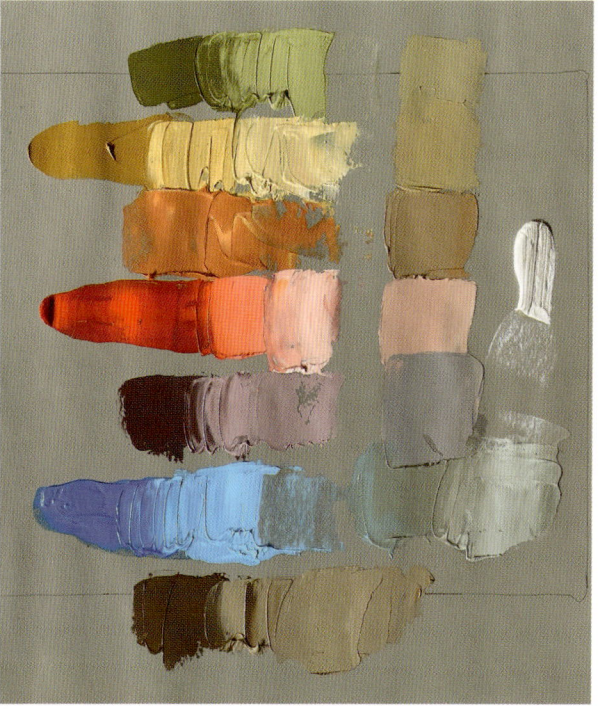

One way to pull in the gamut of a triad palette is to replace one of the three high-chroma colors with a lower-chroma version of the same hue. Here, Yellow Ochre replaces Indian Yellow.

PALETTE-DRIVEN COLOR

Choosing a palette that cannot arrive at what you see invites the practice of translating color. The thinking is: There's what I see. Now, what's possible within my palette? In this instance, there wasn't anything particularly compelling about the light or location—as you can see in the photo at right, everything was green. At random, I chose Ultramarine Blue, Cadmium Orange, and Manganese Violet (plus white: You always get white). I used the value structure from the scene and experimented with the range of color possible in my palette.

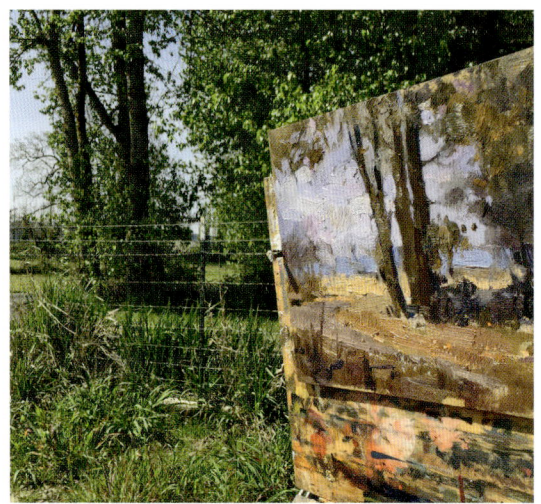

On location, Sauvie Island, Oregon, USA.

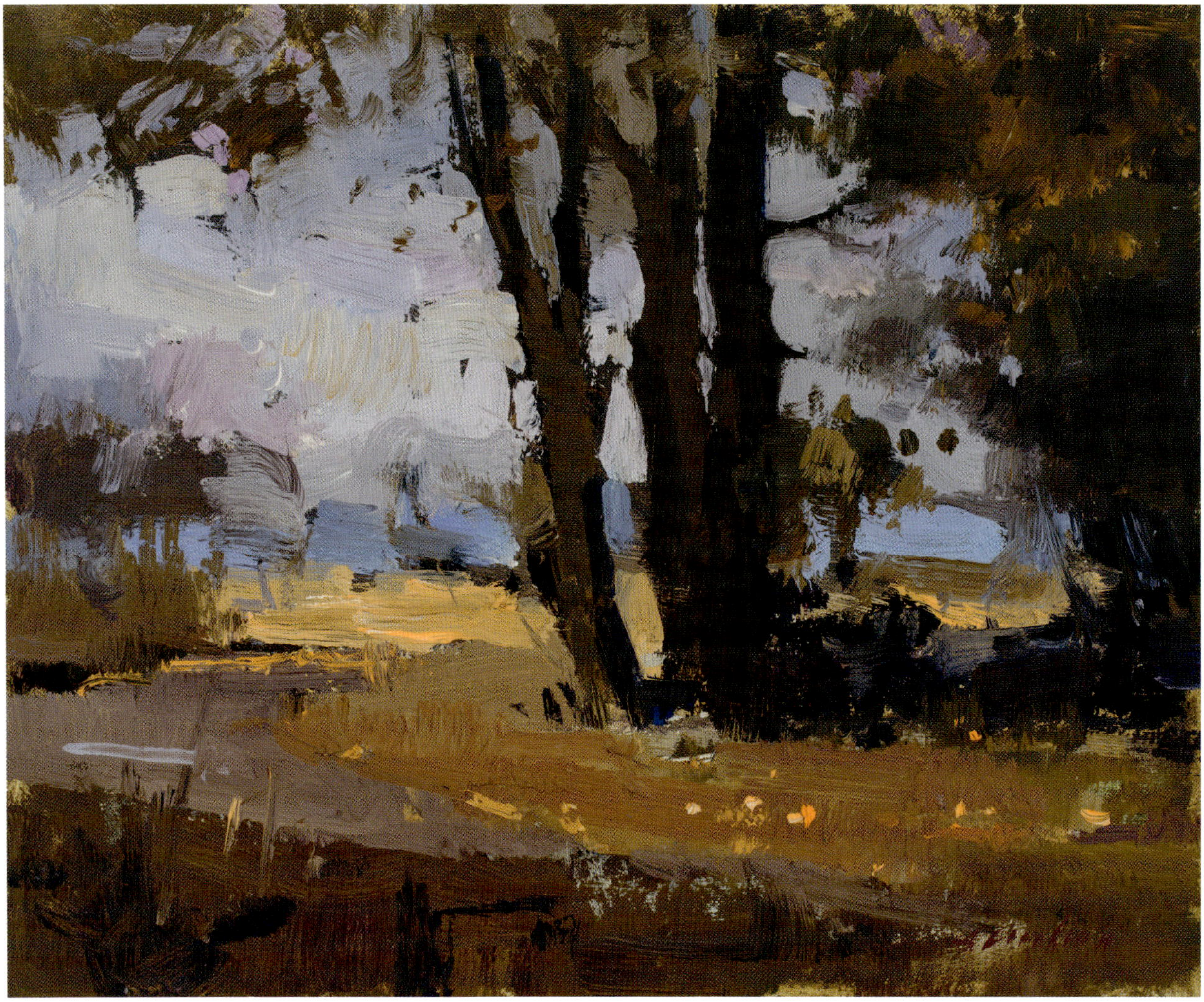

Aimee Erickson, *Untitled*, oil on muslin panel, 8" × 10" | 20.3 cm × 25.4 cm

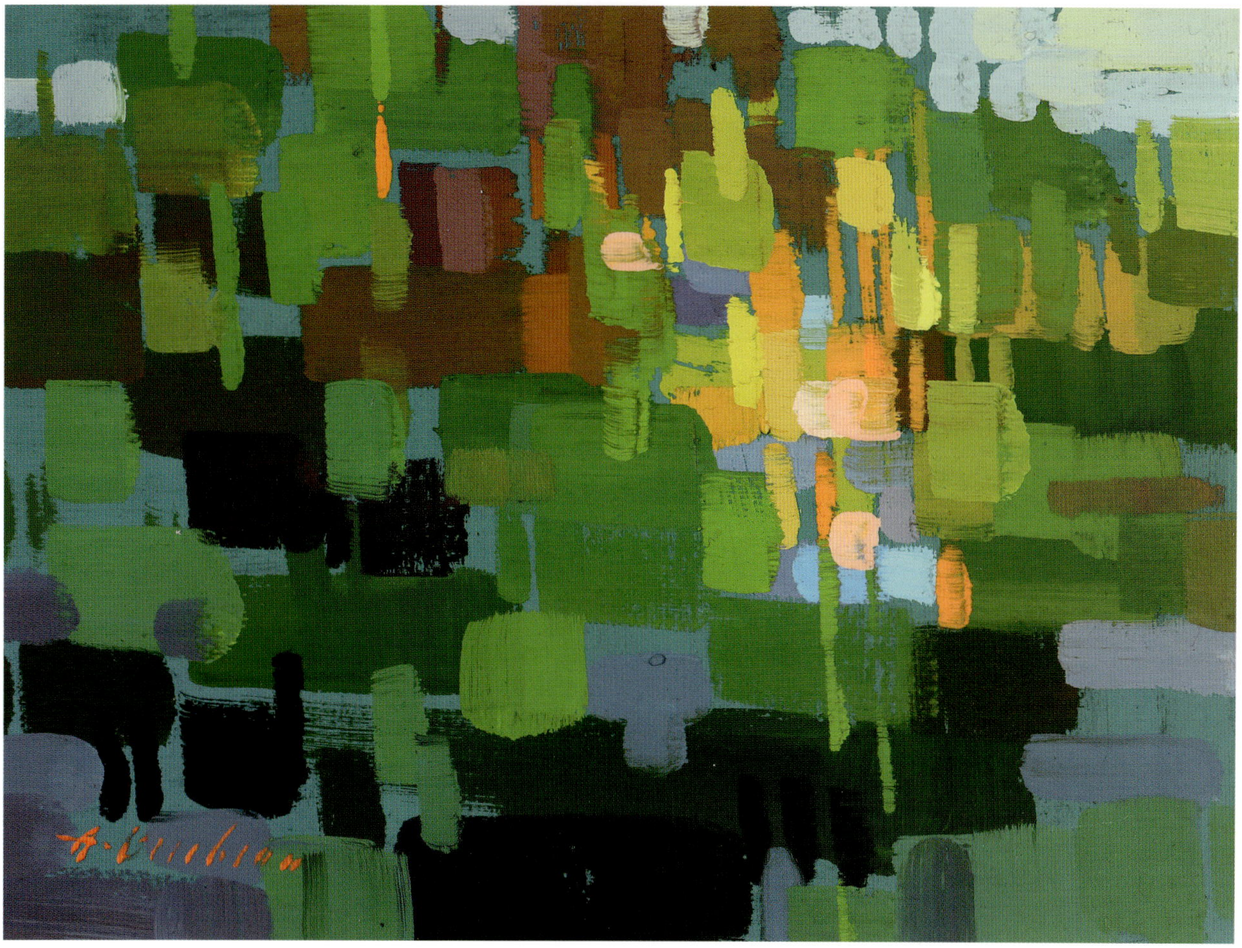

Aimee Erickson, *Wetlands Study*, oil on masonite, 6" × 8" | 15.2 cm × 20.3 cm

COLOR SPOT STUDIES

Color spot painting is the practice of observing color relationships in nature, mixing one color at a time, and laying it down—essentially abstracting the color from the subject. It's a way to observe color and not concern oneself—at least at the start—with subject matter or drawing.

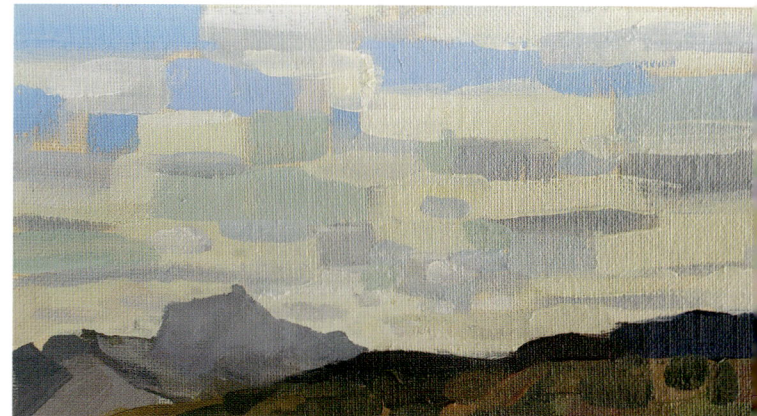

Agustina Hein, *Clouds over Red Mountain*, oil on canvas panel, 5" × 8" | 12.7 cm × 20.3 cm

Color spot study by a beginning oil painter—her second ever oil painting.

"Painting is just getting one spot of color in relation to another spot . . . Let color make form, do not make form and color it."

—CHARLES HAWTHORNE

COLOR DEVELOPMENT
OF VALUE STUDIES

To build and reinforce your understanding of value as a component of color, do limited value studies of your subject first and then use them as a basis for color. These are ridiculously fun to do. The immediate challenge occurs when we realize the number of colors that are possible at a given value. Herein lies opportunity! A successful value study can be realized in easily a dozen different color schemes.

If you're doing these in the studio to work out color ideas, there's a shortcut you should know about. Once you have a composition you like, you can print copies of the sketch and try out different color ideas without having to redraw the whole thing. If you're working on location, do your value study first and refer to it, or do your notan in acrylic and then paint over it in oil.

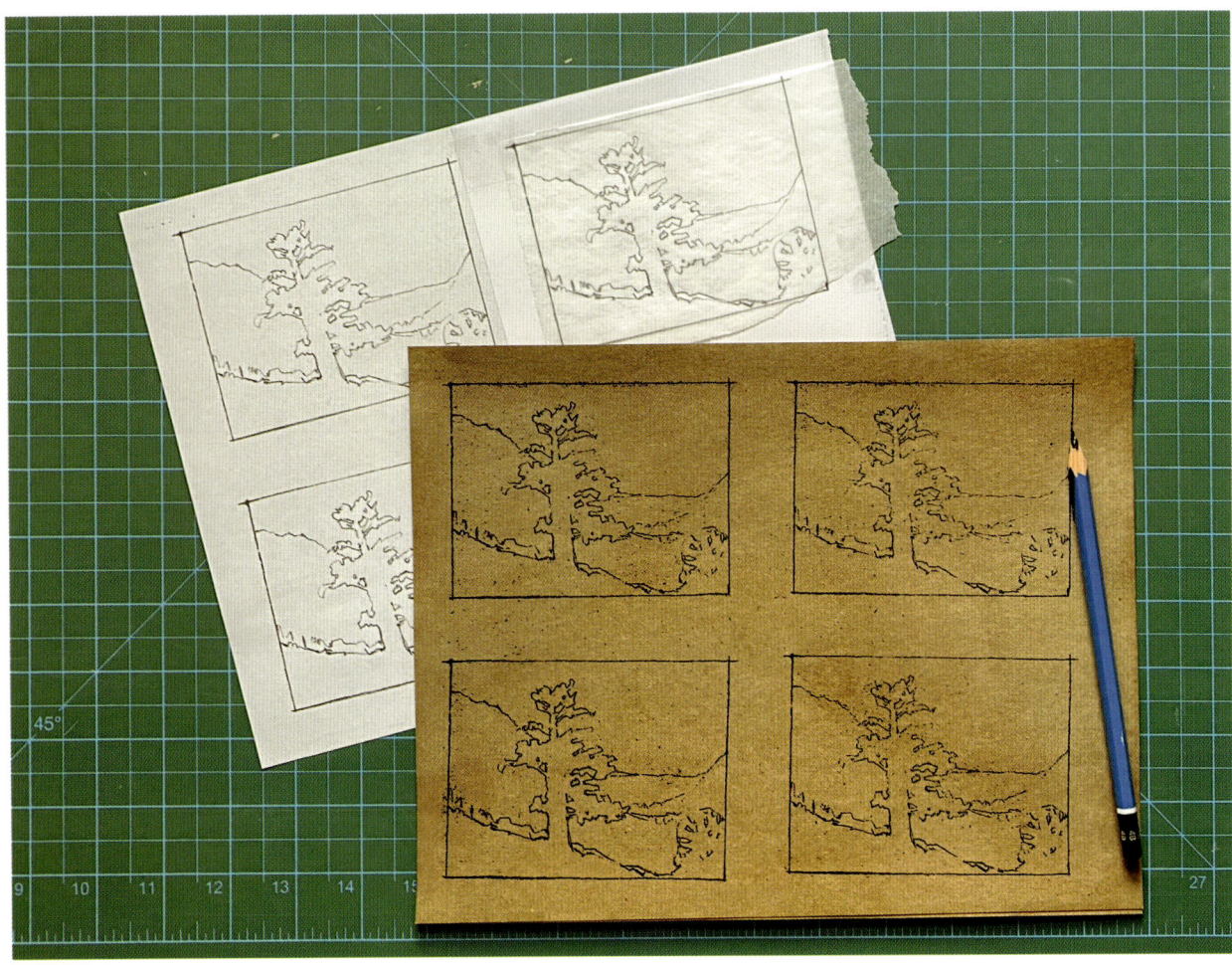

COLOR VERSIONS OF
THE BRISTLECONE PINE

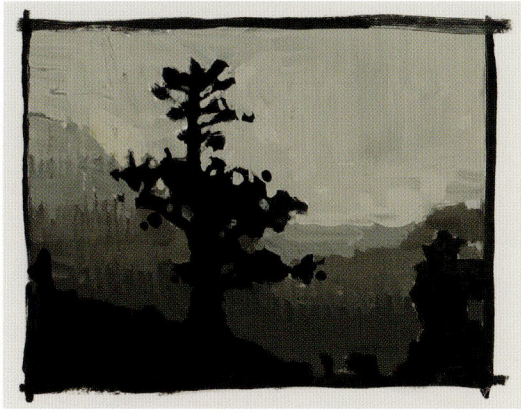

The value comp these are based on. Two value areas with a dark-to-light gradient.

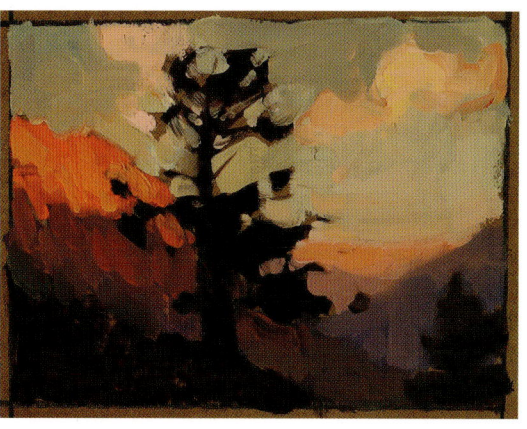

Intense color at sunset.

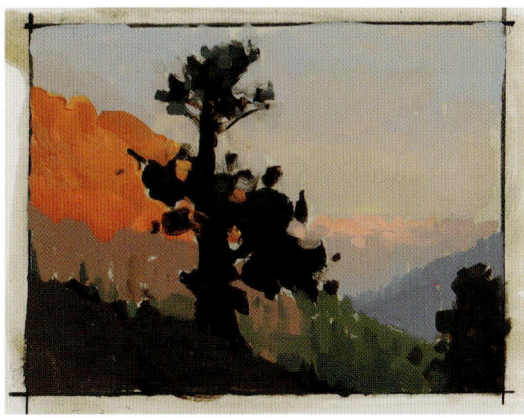

Late afternoon light with shadowed foreground.

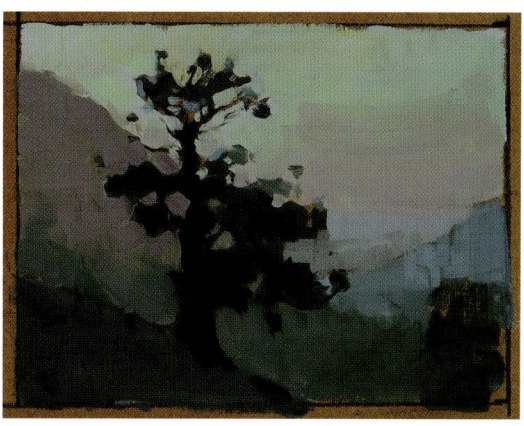

The blues of dusk.

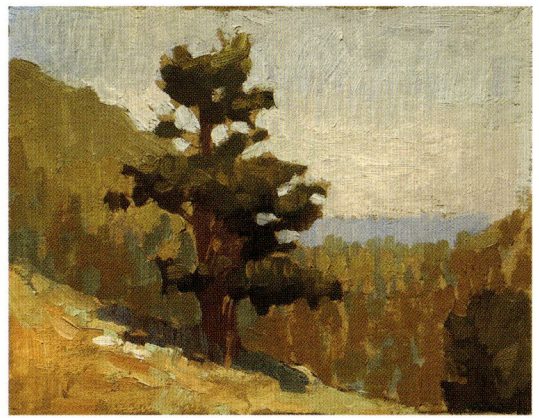

Experimenting with a different value structure to show broad daylight.

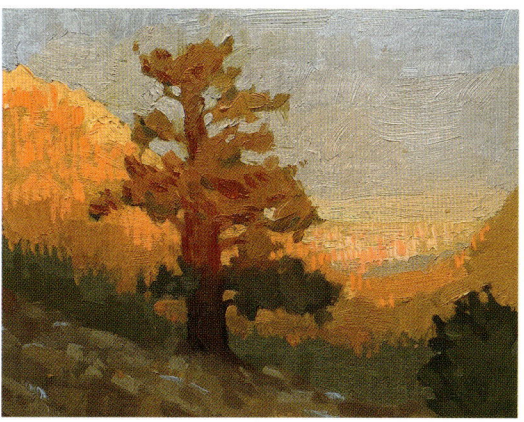

Another experiment, this one in half-light.

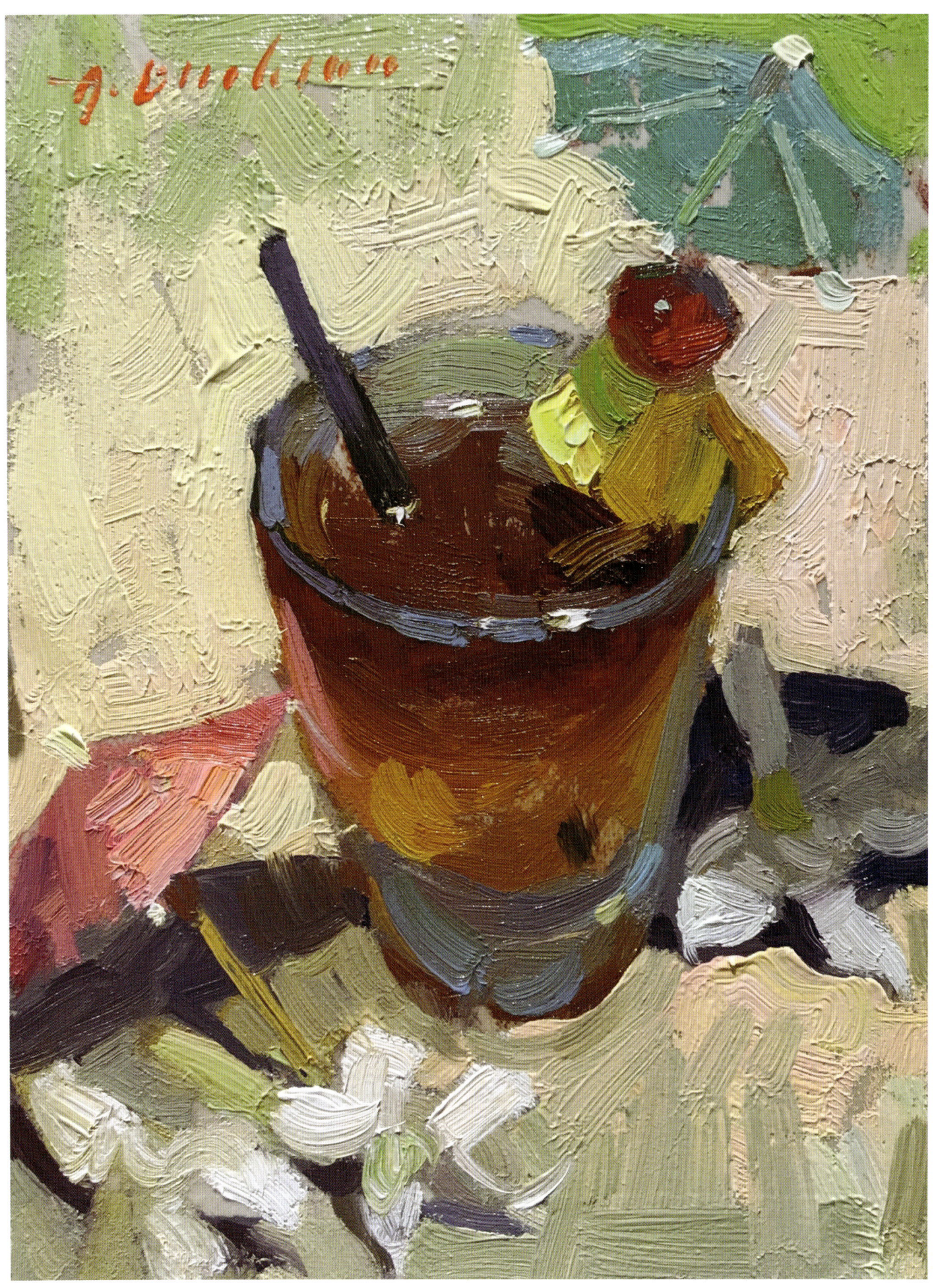

4

SUNLIGHT
AND SHADOW

The conditions of the day affect everything we see. How much light is there and of what quality—soft, diffuse, golden, harsh, pale, or dusky—this is where our interest lies. Everything changes with the light.

As artists, we are limited by what we can and can't see. The eyes are an extension of the brain, which processes visual input. Our (learned) default is to identify local color: The flowers are white, the pineapple chunk is yellow, the little paper umbrella is pink. This is good for survival but restricts artistic decisions—*knowing* the pineapple is yellow means you may not be able to see the green in its shadow side. To alter our perception, we must slow down, take a longer look, and learn some new ways of seeing.

This chapter addresses broad daylight, when we see objects as mostly lit, with some shadow. In general, the land itself is lit. Fields, valley floors, and all the broad, flat, sky-facing surfaces of the earth receive sunlight. Upstanding features or objects, like trees and buildings, are partly lit and partly in shadow, depending on the angle of the light and which direction we look.

◄ Aimee Erickson, *Mai Tai*, oil on muslin panel, 8" × 6" | 20.3 cm × 15.2 cm

SEEING SKILLS:
SHIFT YOUR PERCEPTION

You can't paint what you can't see. Artists use visual information in artistic ways, so we need ways to see differently and take in more of our surroundings. Here are some techniques.

Soften your gaze. Sometimes we want so much to understand something visual that we look sharply at it, as if to grab it with our eyes. This isolates the object in our macular vision, and we lose the relationship to the context. Here's how to soften your gaze: Close your eyes for a moment, put your hands gently over your eyes, take about ten seconds, and let yourself relax. Imagine the muscles around your eyes letting go and the area behind your eyes softening. Then open them and allow your gaze to float around softly as you observe your subject matter.

Turn your head sideways. Your perception of colors will shift right away.

Make a loose fist and look through it with one eye, like a telescope. The dark tunnel puts the subject in a different context and you'll perceive it differently.

Move your eyes from one thing to another. You can use this to measure a color difference in the landscape, for example, dry grass that extends into the distance. Look first at the near grass and then the distant grass a few times. The differences will become more evident.

Squint. Very nearly closing your eyes has the effect of reducing color contrast in areas of similar value.

Look in a mirror, or use your smartphone screen next to your eye to see a reverse image of the landscape.

Take a brief glance. Look away or close your eyes, then glance briefly at the scene.

In Nature, light reveals color.
In painting, color describes light.

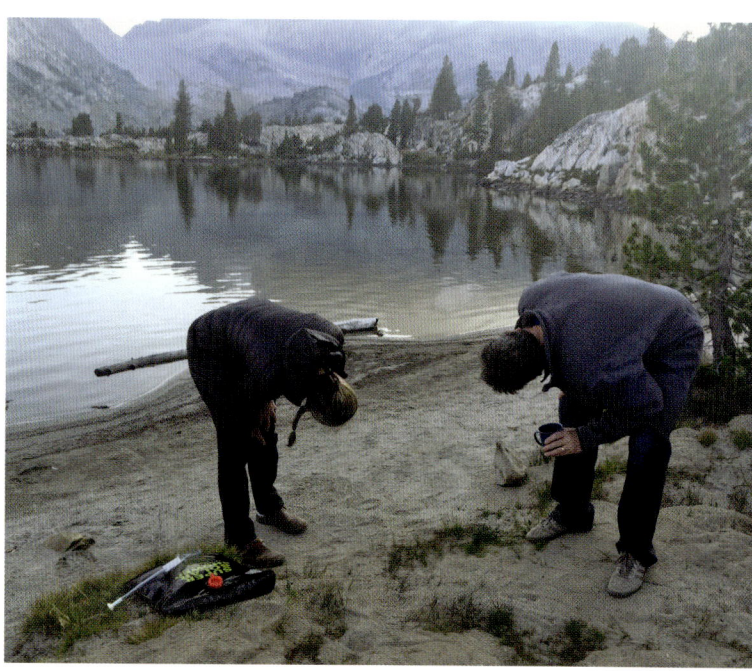

The author and Bill Cone observe the landscape at Garnet Lake in the Eastern Sierra region of California, USA. Photo by Suzie Baker.

LIGHT, SHADOW, AND COLOR

Since we're used to thinking in terms of local color, we need a different paradigm in order to see color in a new way. Consider this: Color is something that *happens* rather than *is*. Without light, everything is dark: There is no color happening. With a little light, a little color happens. In broad daylight, a full spectrum of color is activated.

Color is a function of light—a reaction between the object, the light falling on it, and our eyes. When sunlight—electromagnetic radiation—falls on an object, some of that light-energy is reflected (as color we see) and some is absorbed as heat. Just as a flowerpot "is" (or "does") one color in light and another in shadow, it would need another color altogether in moonlight (which, parenthetically, is sunlight that has traveled past the earth and reflected off the moon back to us).

So ask yourself: what color is happening? What's the light doing to things? What's the contrast (or interval) between light and shadow? Is there a color difference as well as a value difference? Can I start with mixing one color for the lit part and another one for the shadow? Can I see it as one color, next to another color, next to another?

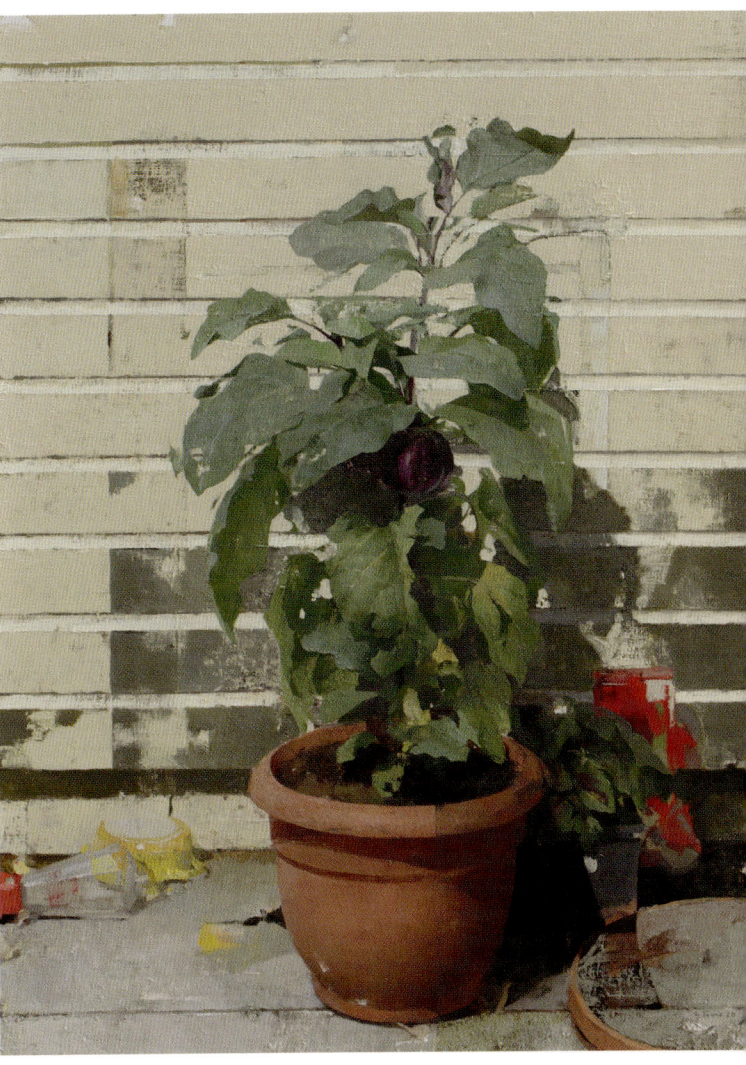

Zoey Frank, *Eggplant*, oil on linen on panel, 40" × 31" | 101.6 cm × 78.7 cm

DEMONSTRATION:
LIGHT AND SHADOW
ON ARCHITECTURE

AIMEE ERICKSON:
BACK DOORS

DEMONSTRATION NOTES
- Palette: Titanium Zinc White, Cadmium Yellow Deep, Yellow Ochre, Indian Yellow, Transparent Earth Red, Old Holland Scheveningen Red Medium, Ultramarine Blue, Sap Green, and Ivory Black.

My panel was toned ahead of time with the Old Holland Raw Umber and white mix, and I had rubbed out the middle to lighten it, figuring the most lit part of a painting often happens in the middle and this could give it a head start. It had a really nice lit quality that I missed once I painted over it, and I made some adjustments to regain a bit.

1. Setting up. I use an 11-inch × 14-inch (28 cm × 35.6 cm) Open Box M easel. Big clouds are passing overhead, so the lighting alternates between diffuse and direct sunlight.

2. The sun comes out, and things become far more interesting.

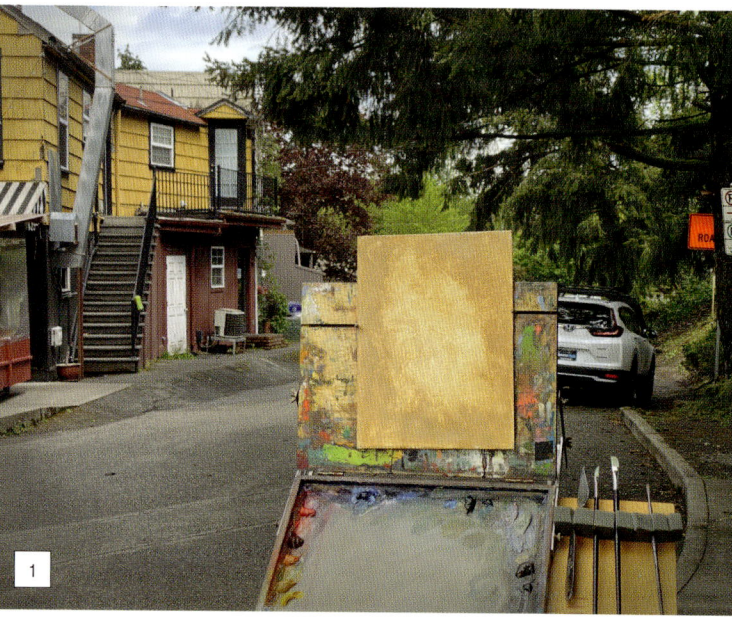

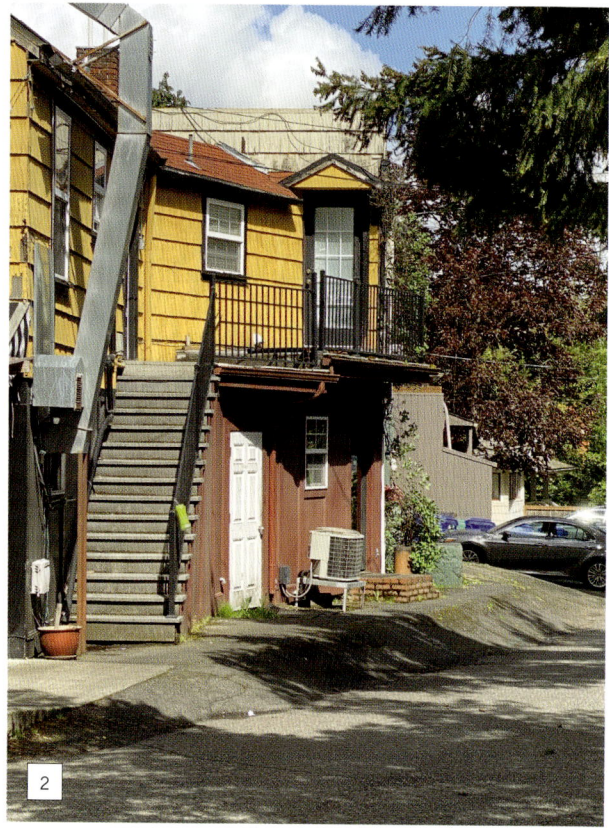

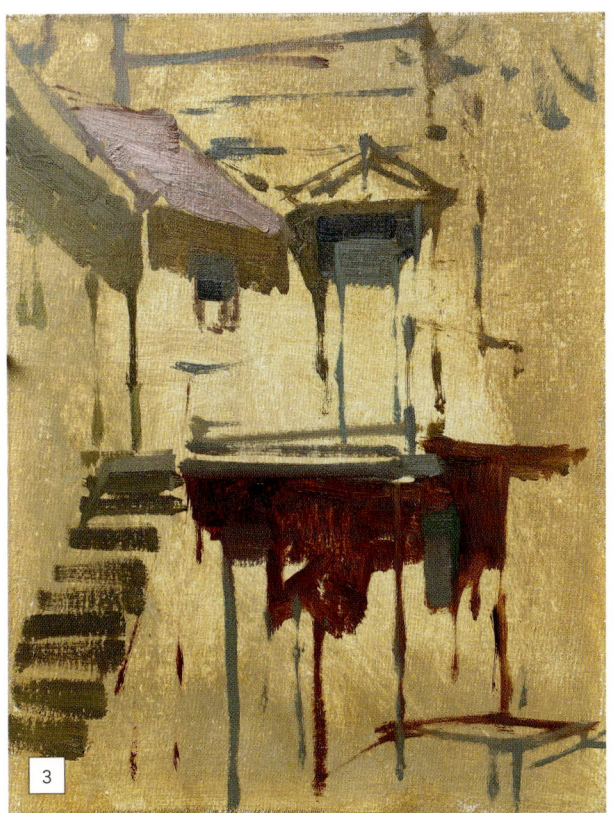

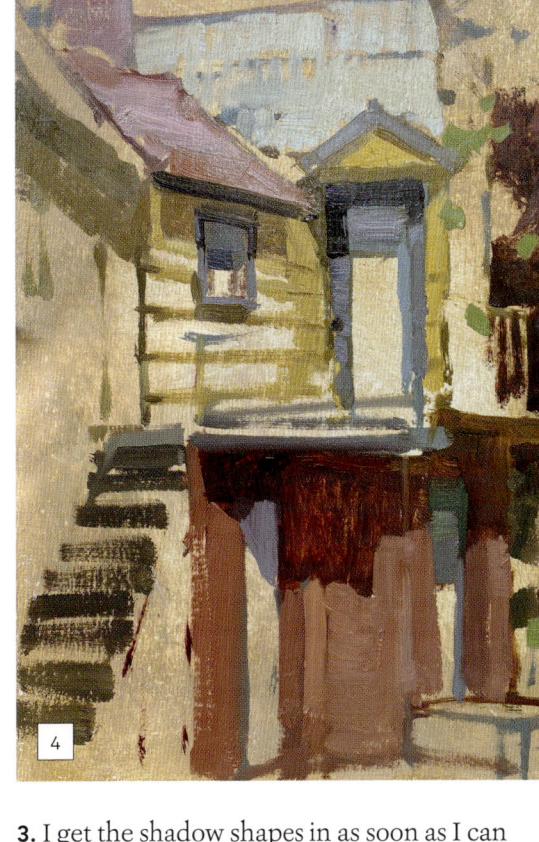

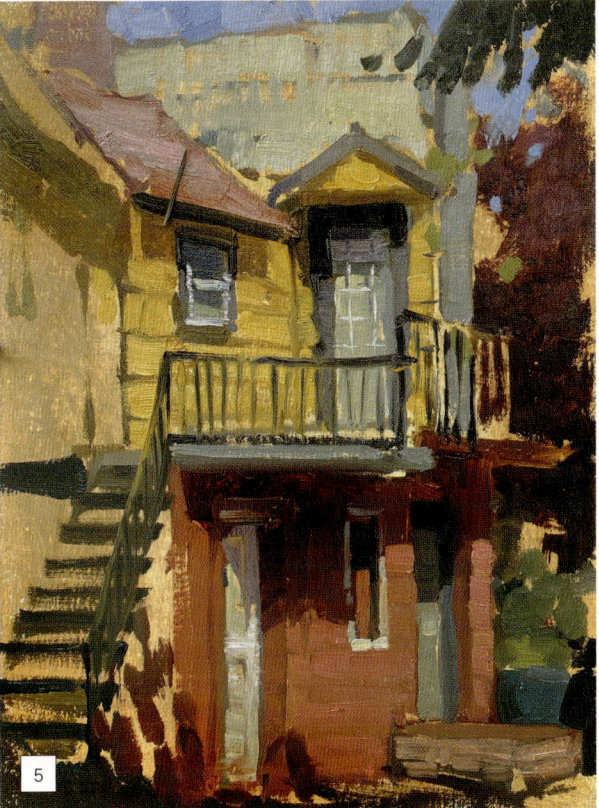

3. I get the shadow shapes in as soon as I can see them. I love the painting at this stage. The building feels sun-bleached because all the lit areas are unified in color, and there's a sense of possibility when things aren't all defined.

4. Building in some lit areas. I aim to nail the color the first time, but it doesn't always work out. Here, you can see that I have blocked in the light *as I see it* on the red wall of the ground floor.

5. Developing the light areas. That red wall gets reworked a couple times as I try out a little pinker color. If the paint builds up too much—this is an oil painting problem specifically—and I can't lay any more paint into it, I'll take my knife and scrape it, then paint back into it. I also put the lit color of the yellow siding in, but the sun was not out at this point and it's a little rich—a little too dark and too much chroma.

continued ▶

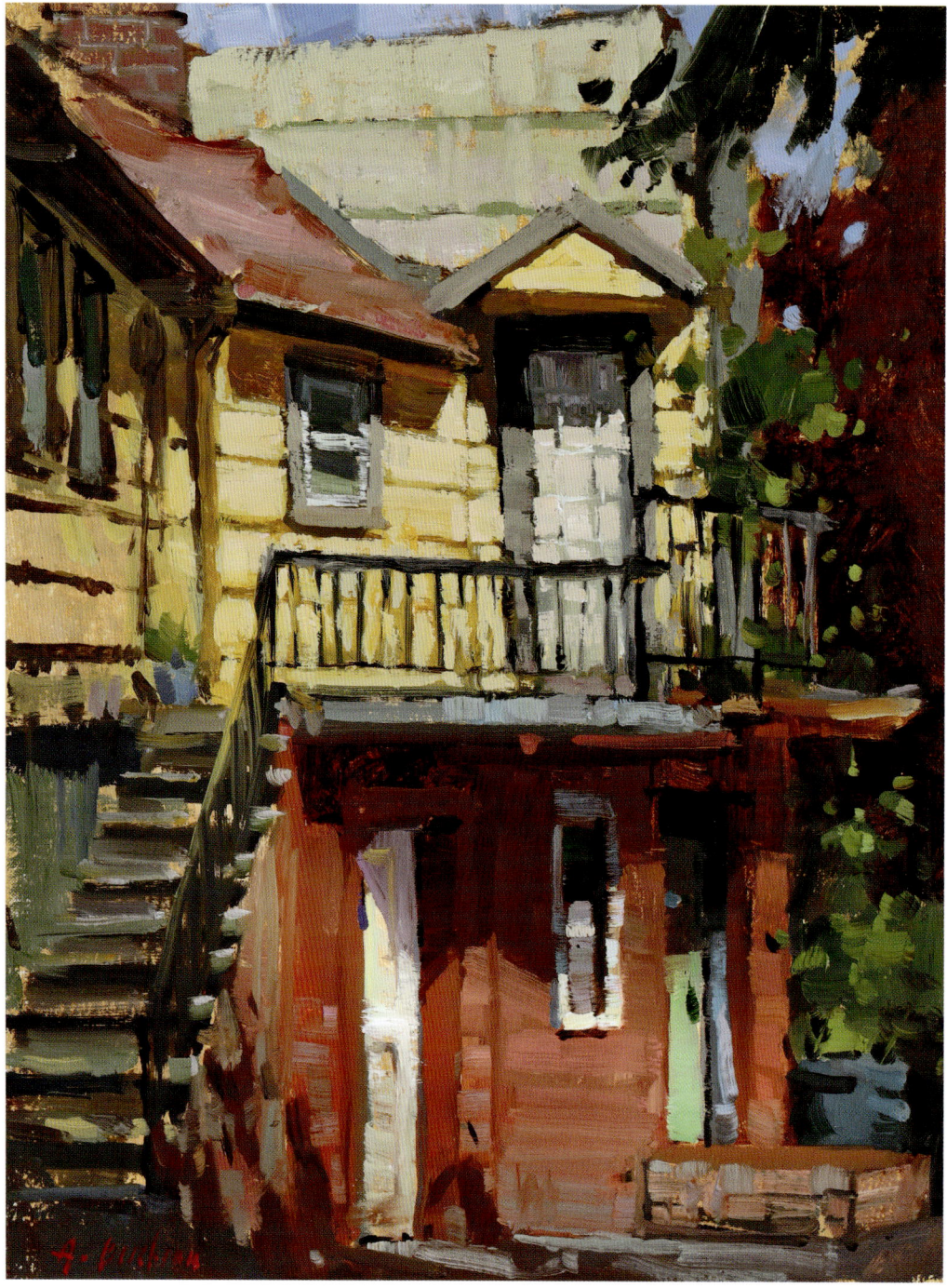

Aimee Erickson, *Back Doors*, oil on muslin panel, 12" × 9" | 30.5 cm × 22.9 cm

In the yellow siding area, I want to have more of that bleached sunlit feeling again, so I mix a color that is a little lighter and has a little more pink in it and lay that on top. I also lighten the black trim where the light hits it—that color I mixed out of Titanium Zinc White, Scheveningen Red Medium, and Sap Green. So many of the interesting things in a painting happen in needing to solve how light or dark to make a black object with strong light hitting it or just the opposite, when it's a white object in the shadows.

"Start somewhere and make a series of corrections."

—DEANE KELLER

WHERE TO START

Your painting can happen in any order that makes sense to you. You can start with a pencil drawing, some loose "drawing" brushstrokes, or with an allover tone; by massing in the big shapes, putting in the highlight, by laying in finished brushstrokes *alla prima*—Italian for "at first attempt"—or you can start by painting solid shapes you know you'll paint into and over.

Start by putting in your best guess of what you do know, to see what you need to see and to find out what you need to know to take the next step.

"If I can see it at nine o'clock, I can see it at ten o'clock."

—DAVID LEFFEL,
when asked if he ever put a drawing in first

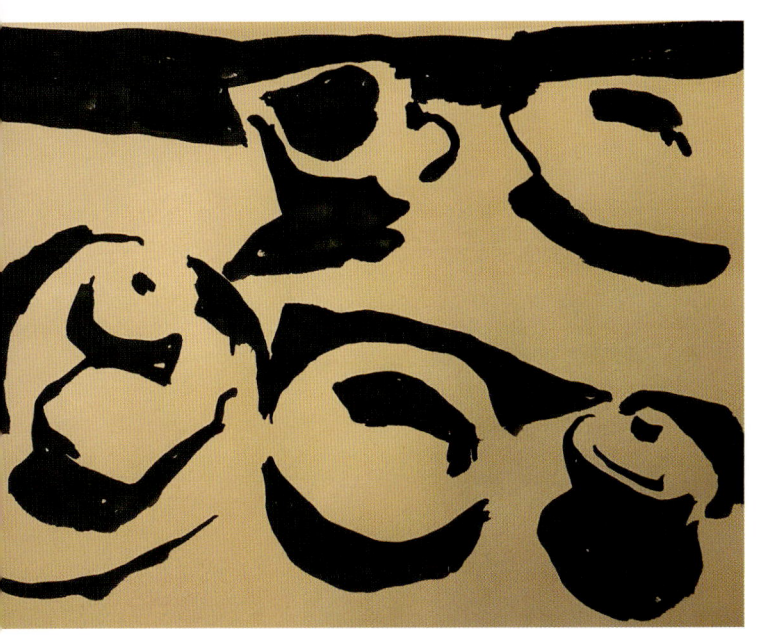

Peggi Kroll Roberts, *Light and Shadow*, India ink on pastel paper, 8" × 10" | 20.3 cm × 25.4 cm

Peggi Kroll Roberts being very matter-of-fact about what's lit and what's in shadow. Here, she has stated all shadow in black and allowed the paper to hold all the lit areas. Note that she does not use any lines to separate lit objects from each other. The shadow shapes do all the work.

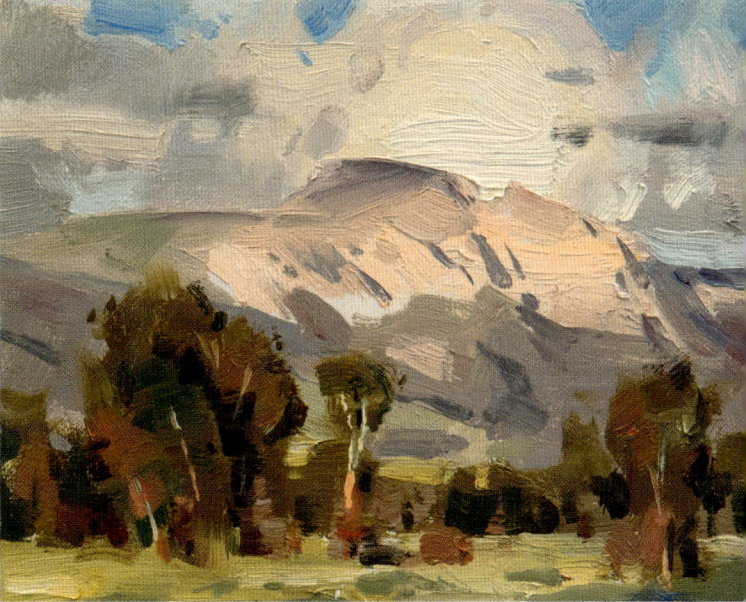

Mitch Baird, *Sleeping Indian Study*, oil on linen panel, 6" × 8" | 15.2 cm × 20.3 cm

A much more complex study of light and shadow affecting the colors in the landscape.

SHADOW SHAPES AND CHANGING LIGHT

ERIC JACOBSEN:
MORNING AT VERMILION CLIFFS

The angle of sunlight changes as the earth turns, so be prepared for the shadows to change. Even small differences in shadow shapes can dramatically change the look of the landscape. Side lighting gives us that strong sculptural look.

Morning at Vermilion Cliffs is a plein air study in acrylic. As the morning progresses and the sun moves south and higher in the sky, the shadows on the cliffs change from big unbroken shapes to shapes broken up and made busy by sunlight. A good strategy is to define the shadow shapes first and then do not observe the breakup in your painting.

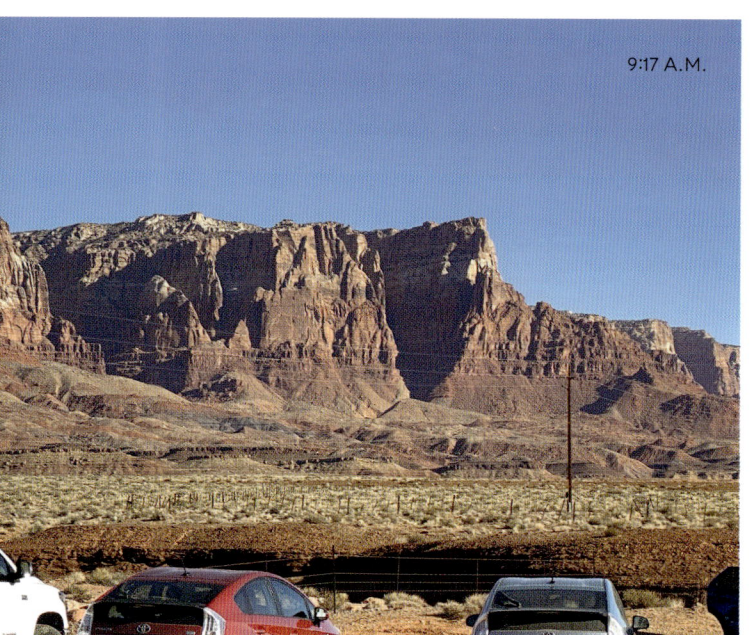

9:17 A.M.

At 9 a.m., the western faces of the cliffs are in shadow, and these big shapes are part of the appeal.

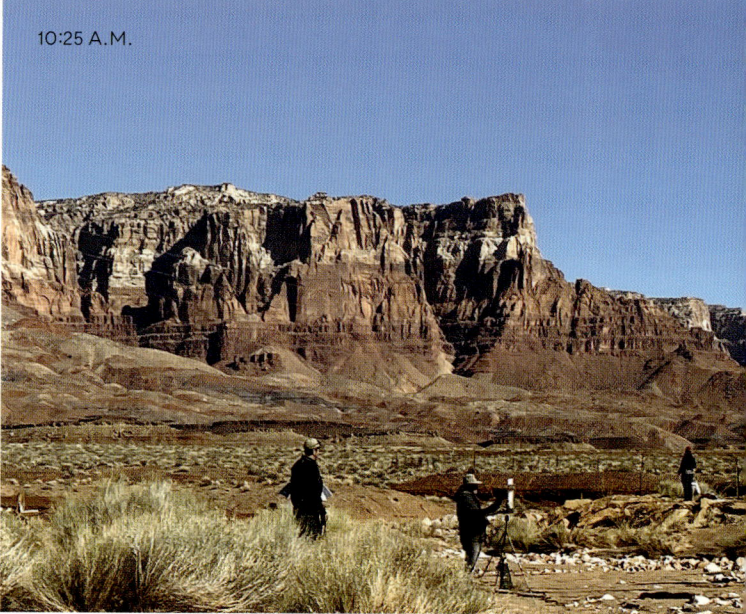

10:25 A.M.

In just a little over an hour, everything looks very different. The big shadows are gone, and the colors have shifted.

"The trick to this kind of thing is to drop your shadow shapes in first, if you like them. Then, stick to it instead of chasing that stuff."

—ERIC JACOBSEN

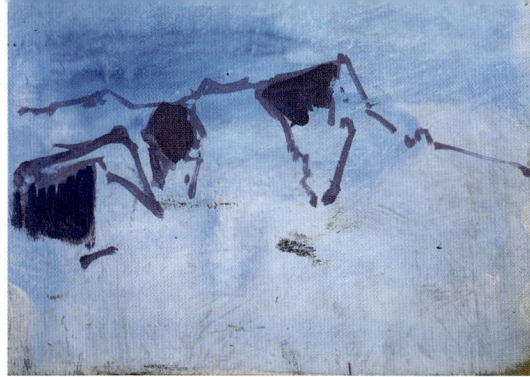

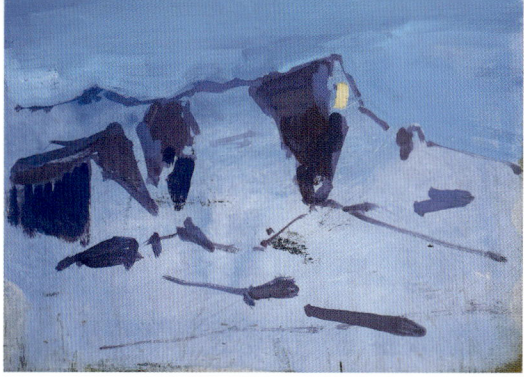

9:11 a.m. Having drawn in the primary shapes, Jacobsen drops in an average shadow color.

Spot check: a test dab on the painting to gauge the color in context.

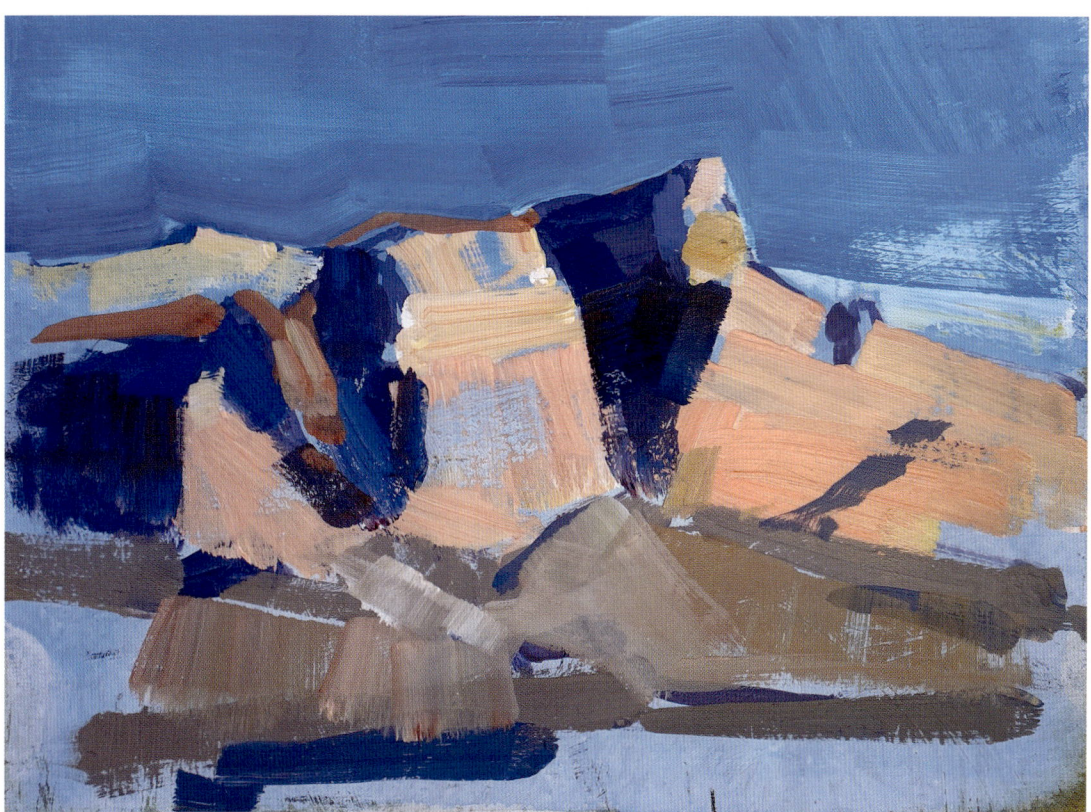

10:02 a.m. At this point, the sun is hitting and revealing all kinds of forms that were previously in shadow. Jacobsen does not get distracted by these shenanigans. He likes his shadow shapes and is now mostly making decisions based on comparing the painting to itself, rather than looking at the cliffs for information. His goal is to achieve dynamic balance within the painting.

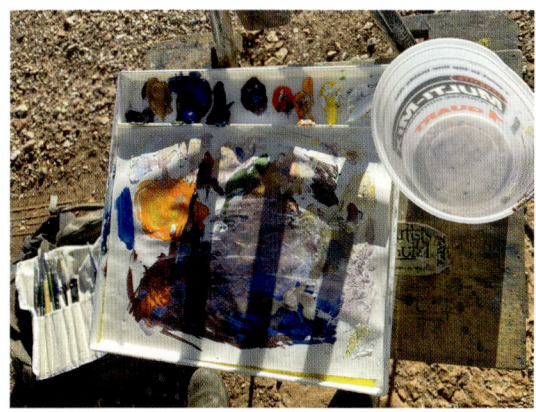

Jacobsen's palette. He's painting in acrylics because on this outing, he wants his paintings to dry for easy handling and transport (and to keep his friend's car clean). This is a Sta-Wet Palette, and the pigments are Yellow Ochre, Ultramarine Blue, Phthalo Blue, Alizarin Crimson, Cadmium Red, Cadmium Orange, Cadmium Yellow, and Titanium White.

EXERCISE:
THE COLOR OF LIGHT

We tend to see sunlight as neutral, just "light," and color as belonging to *things*. But if we *can* discern a color to the light, we can use it to unify the painting and heighten the effect of light.

At the end of the day, in the "golden hour," it's easy to see a shift in the color of the sunlight as it passes through more of the earth's atmosphere and makes *every color in the scene* a golden version of itself. Likewise in moonlight, every color in the scene is a darker, bluer version of itself (or greener, or however you see moonlight). Learning how to "lean" your palette toward a color, to convey the color of light, is an important skill.

This is a plein air exercise, to practice letting a single color influence the entire scene. Choose a simple subject, and as you set up, pay attention to the conditions of the day. See if you can discern a color to the light. (If you can't tell, start with pink.) Then, lean all the colors in the painting toward that color, using one or both of the following methods:

Use a mother color. On your palette, mix red with white to make a string of four or five tints and then use these to influence every color to some degree as you proceed. The *more lit* something is, the *more pink* it takes on. Shadows are unified by a narrow value range and are affected by the conditions of the day, but they will not be where the strongest pink happens.

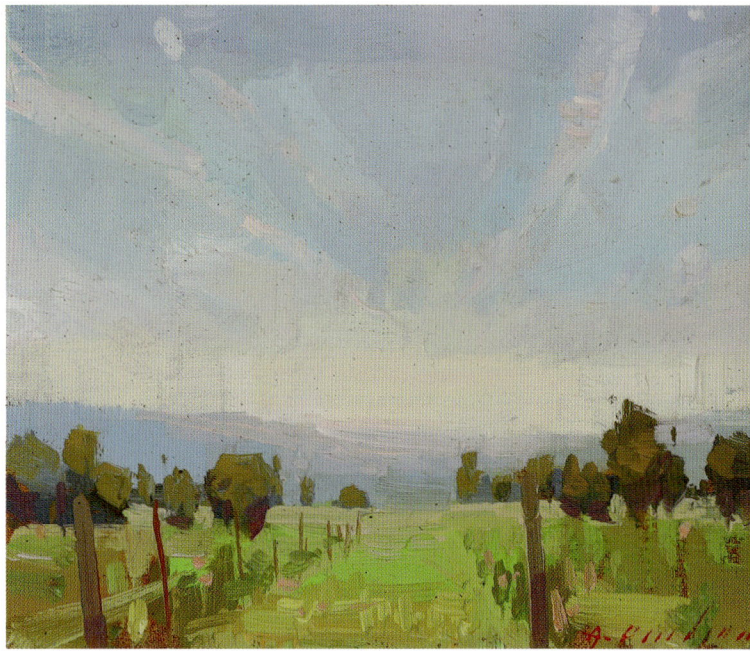

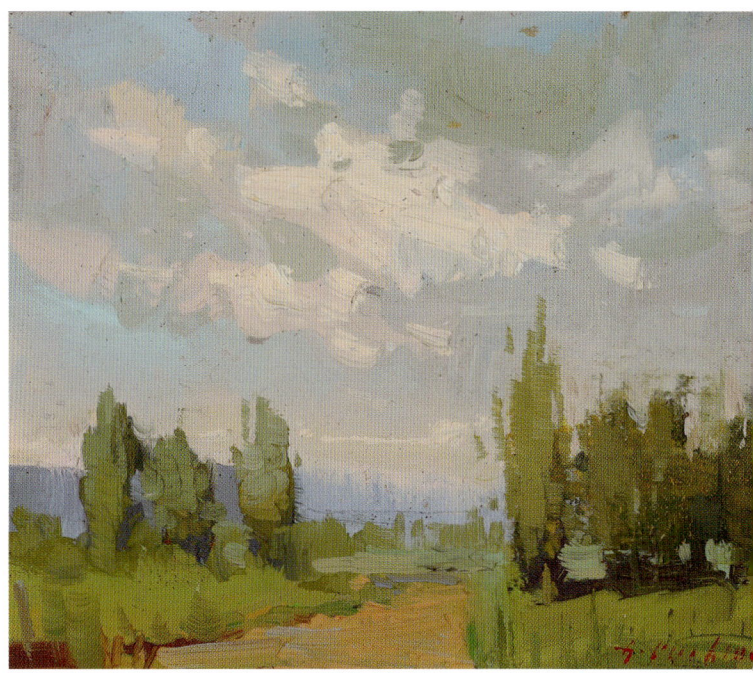

Shift colors. The second method is more complex and involves shifting color around the color wheel toward the identified color of the light. (This approach is most effective with a full palette, not a limited palette.)

For example, consider a grassy field in rosy orange light. Green needs some yellow, but because of the color of the light, you have to move chromatically in the direction of the more orangey yellows, or even some orange-reds.

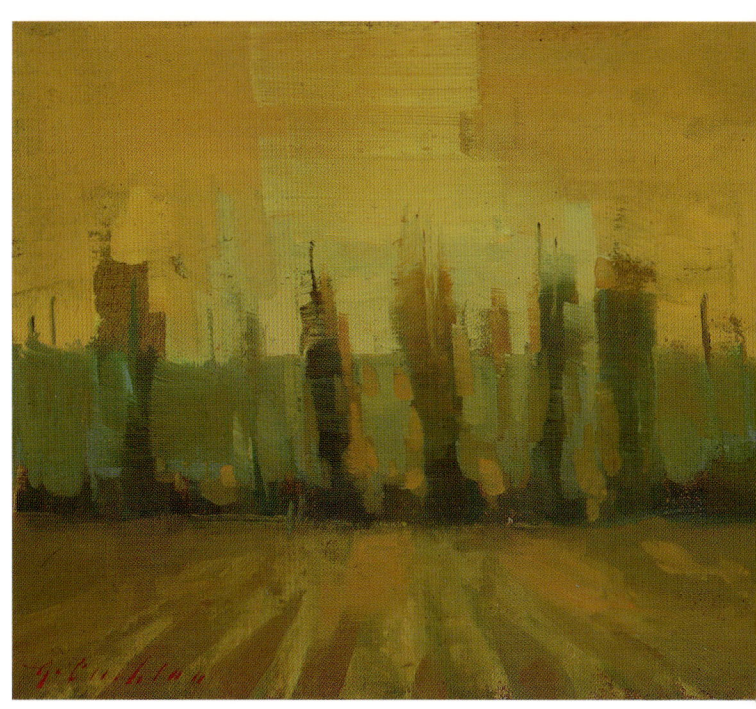

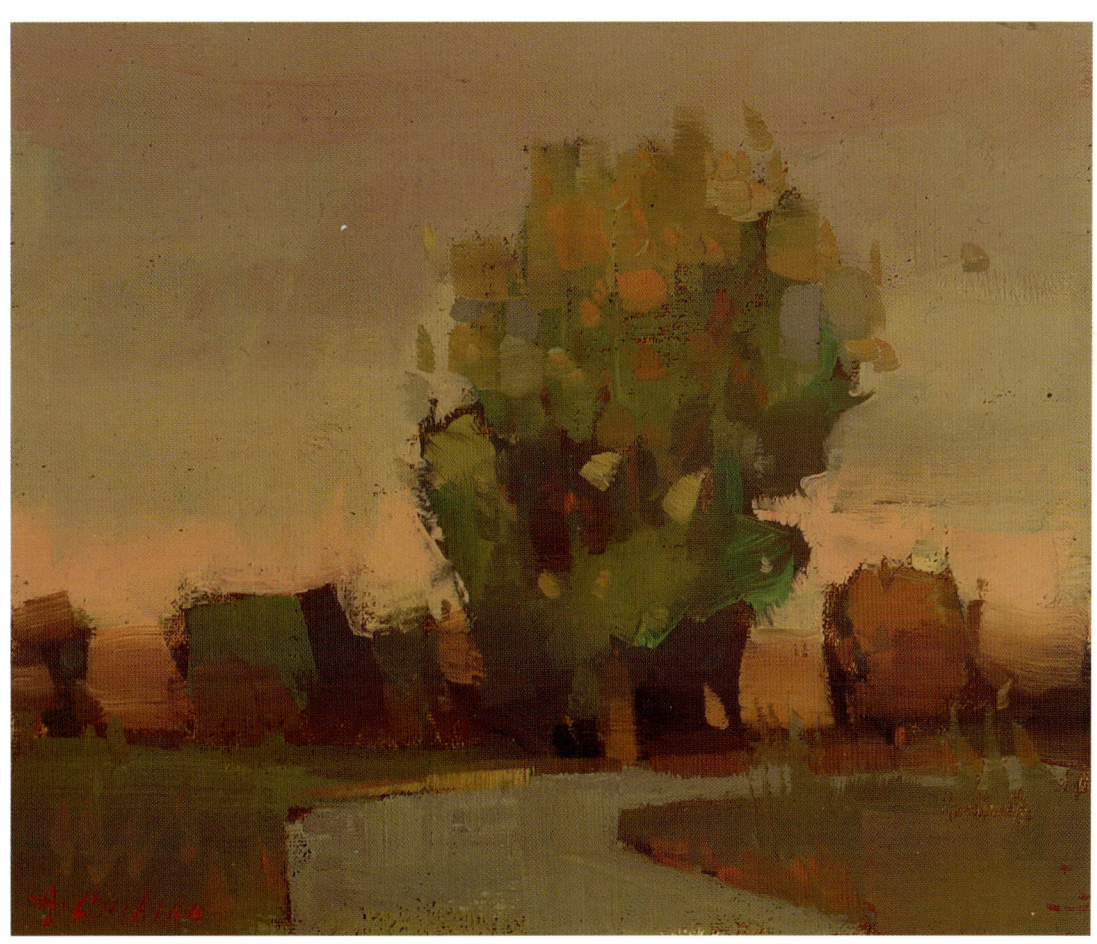

On-the-spot color studies from an afternoon on Sauvie Island.

RAKING LIGHT

EARLY OR LATE IN THE DAY, LIGHT COMING FROM THE SIDE

Raking light happens when the sun is low and to the side, and the light "rakes" across the scene. It creates light and shadow within each object. If you're looking toward the horizon, shadows fall laterally, parallel to the top and bottom of the canvas or close to it.

A general rule about cast shadows is that we use them to indicate the direction of the light as well as the contour of the surface onto which the shadow falls.

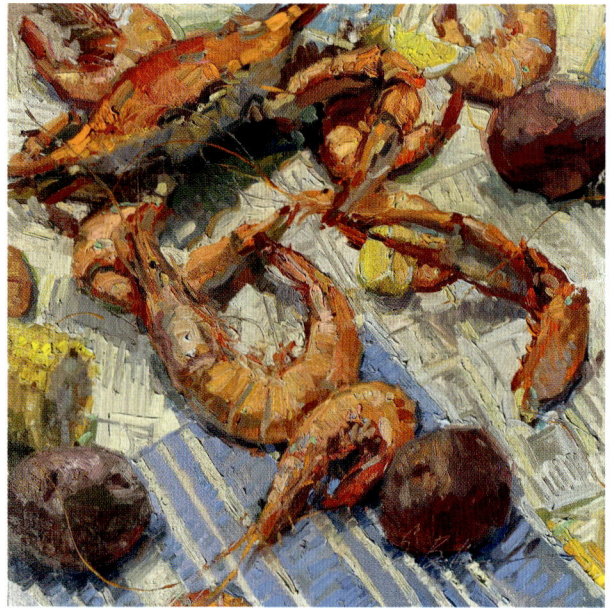

Suzie Baker, *Galveston Meat and Potatoes*, oil on canvas panel, 20" × 20" | 50.8 cm × 50.8 cm

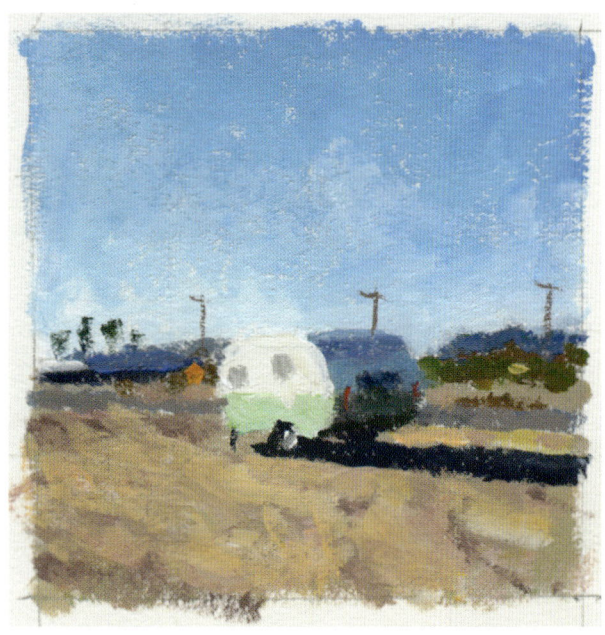

Tim Horn, *Nowhere*, oil on paper, 4" × 4" | 10.2 cm × 10.2 cm

A small study of raking light. The trailer has a lit side and a shadow side, and the shadow is cast horizontally. Its length tells us how high the sun is in the sky.

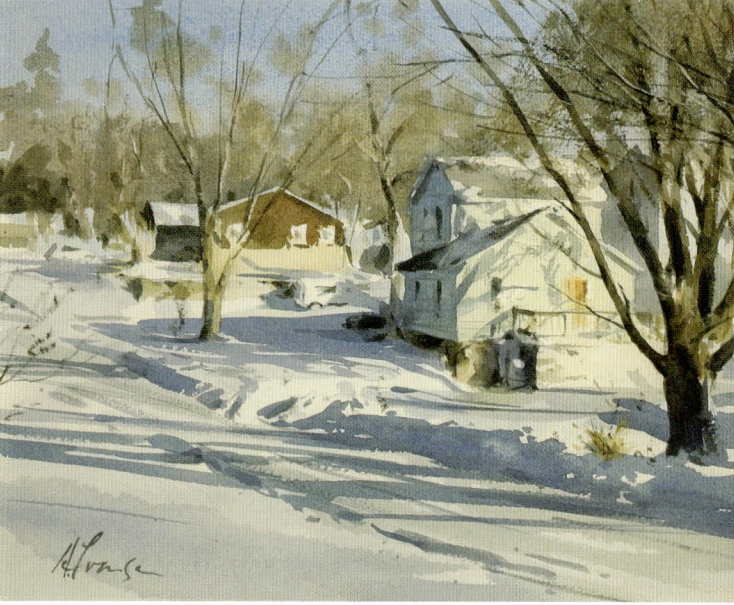

Andy Evansen, *Fresh Snow*, Hastings, watercolor, 11" × 15" | 28 cm × 38 cm

TECHNIQUE:
STAIN IT, DRAW IT, PAINT IT

COLIN PAGE:
WINTER ON SPRING STREET

Here's a tried-and-true approach to painting on location: Stain it, draw it, and then throw a bunch of paint at it.

- First, stain (or tone) the canvas with a thin layer of color.
- Second, draw the main shapes to establish your composition.
- Finally, load up your brush and go for the color.

DEMONSTRATION NOTES

- Canvas panel, 16" × 20" | 40.6 cm × 50.8 cm.
- Palette (oil paints): Winsor & Newton Phthalo Blue, Ultramarine Blue, Titanium Zinc White, Cadmium Lemon, Cadmium Yellow Medium, Quinacridone Red, Cadmium Red Medium, Burnt Sienna, and sometimes, Alizarin Violet, Alizarin Yellow, Radiant Turquoise, and Cadmium Green.

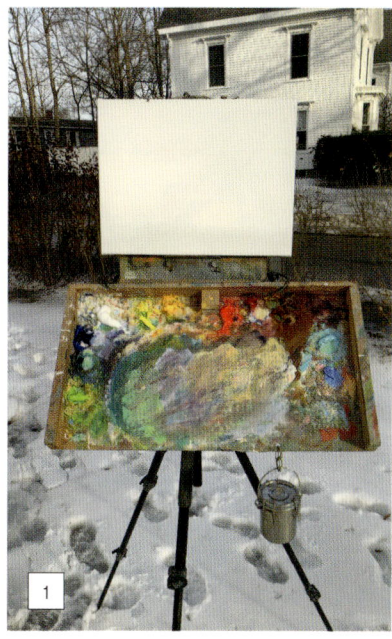

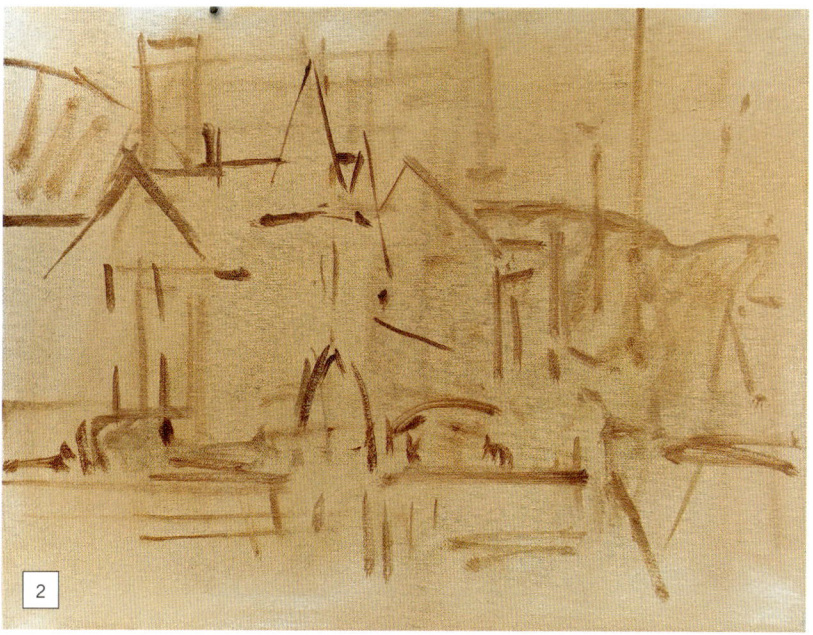

1. Page's setup, with blank panel and palette.

2. Burnt Sienna canvas tone (the "stain") and a loose sketch (the drawing) to work out size and placement.

continued ▶

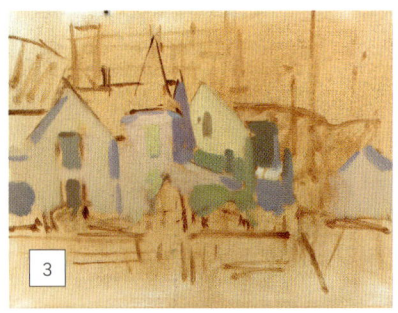

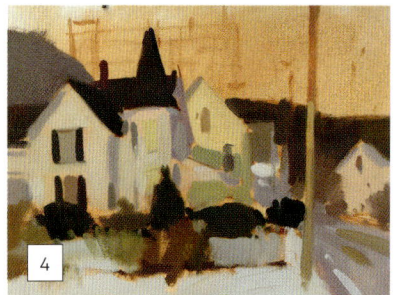

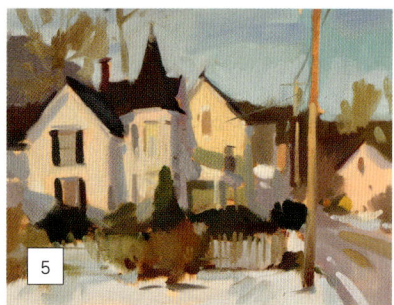

3. Blocking in a series of related lit and shadow areas on the white houses.

4. Laying in the darks with shifting hues.

5. Snow and sky. Just lay it in.

"The key to simplifying and making better plein air paintings is to lose as many edges as possible and merge shapes."

—COLIN PAGE

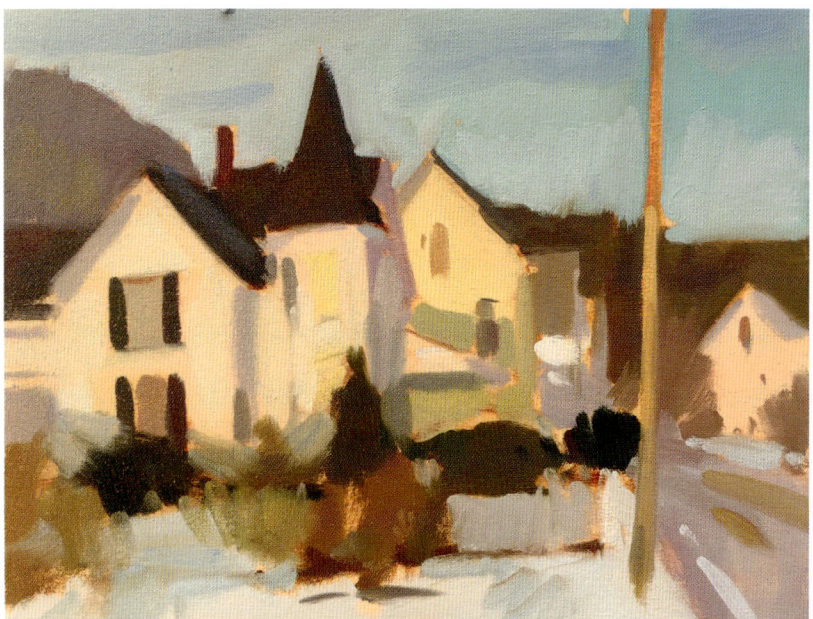

Colin Page, *Winter on Spring Street*, oil on canvas panel, 16" × 20" | 40.6 cm × 50.8 cm

Finish. That original Burnt Sienna canvas tone influences all the color. A snow scene can easily become frigid, and a warm undertone counteracts that from the start.

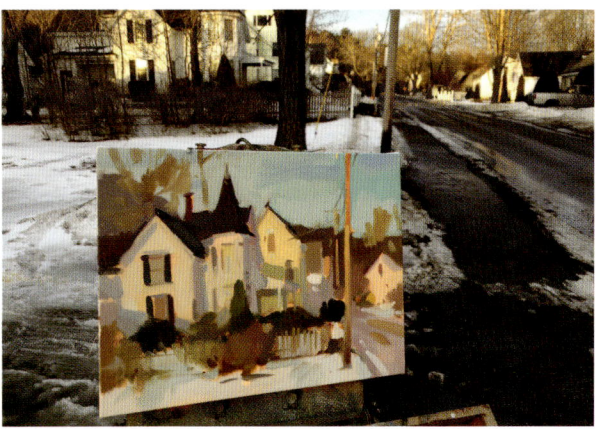

The scene behind the easel.

"I look for places to lay color next to color— it has to be the exact same value and has to be one touch so it doesn't get muddy—but it gives it that shimmer, that vibration, which adds energy to the painting. If you copy the colors in nature, things are pretty gray."

—COLIN PAGE

PERSPECTIVE

A canvas is a flat, two-dimensional surface. We need to use certain visual clues to imply distance. The general principle is this: *Less* recedes and *more* advances. Of course, there are many ways an element in a painting can be more or less than another. As with so many other aspects of painting, judgment is required. We usually employ multiple strategies together to imply distance, often subordinating one strategy to another.

Size and placement. In reality, perceived size changes drastically with distance (a brush or pencil held at arm's length is a good measuring stick). In paintings, we make things bigger to appear closer and smaller to appear farther away.

Placement matters. Proximity to the horizon line indicates distance. In the sky, a large cloud placed higher in the picture will appear closer than a smaller cloud placed nearer the horizon. On the ground, a puddle placed near the horizon will appear farther away than one located at the bottom of the picture plane. (When we see this in a picture, we tend to think of the objects being "closer" and "more distant," when in actuality they are in the same two-dimensional plane, and distance is an illusion. It's useful to realize that in a landscape painting, every ½ inch [1.3 cm] you move up the canvas, you're much farther away in the actual landscape.)

One other tool to show distance is overlapping: Place one of two objects slightly "behind" the other to show which one is closer.

Atmospheric perspective. Faraway objects are lighter and take on the color of the atmosphere.

Development. Development has to do with detail, contrast, and paint handling. Adding more detail and descriptive paint quality is a way to indicate proximity. Simplified forms, flatter paint, less contrast, and less detail allow an object to recede.

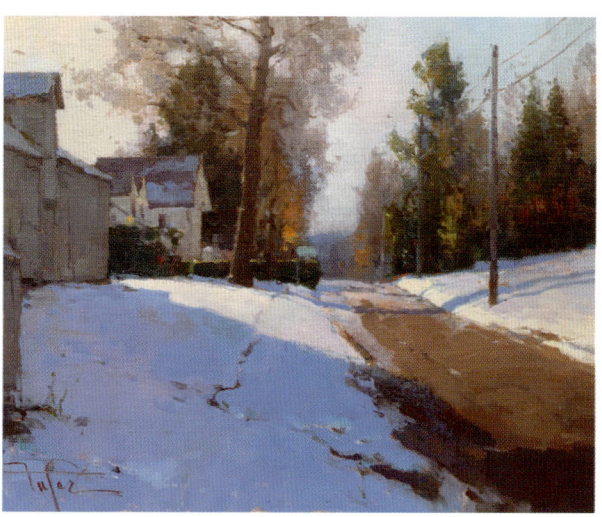

Zufar Bikbov, *Winter Farm Road*, oil on linen panel, 11" × 14" | 28 cm × 35.6 cm

The largest shape is the closest: A shadow occupies the near ground and fills maybe a quarter of the picture. The flat ground appears to recede (instead of looking like a wall). All the drawing elements indicate distance: The road's edges converge; buildings get smaller; the tree "closest" to us is the one that exits the frame; rooflines converge; and lit and shadow shapes on the ground are organized to become smaller (less vertical space) moving toward the horizon.

The foreground shadow is an excellent compositional device. It functions as a lead-in because we tend to look past it toward the light.

ATMOSPHERIC PERSPECTIVE

The principle of *atmospheric, or aerial, perspective* addresses the visual effect of the earth's atmosphere on distant objects. The farther away something is, the more air we are looking through to see it. This means there's a visible color shift that we can take advantage of to describe distance in paintings. We can change value (lighter implies more distant), chroma (stronger color advances, weaker color recedes), and hue (dependent upon the conditions of the day). The biggest value shift happens in shadow areas, and lit areas are where chroma shifts the most. In terms of value *contrast* between lit and shadow areas, distant objects have less contrast and proximate objects have more.

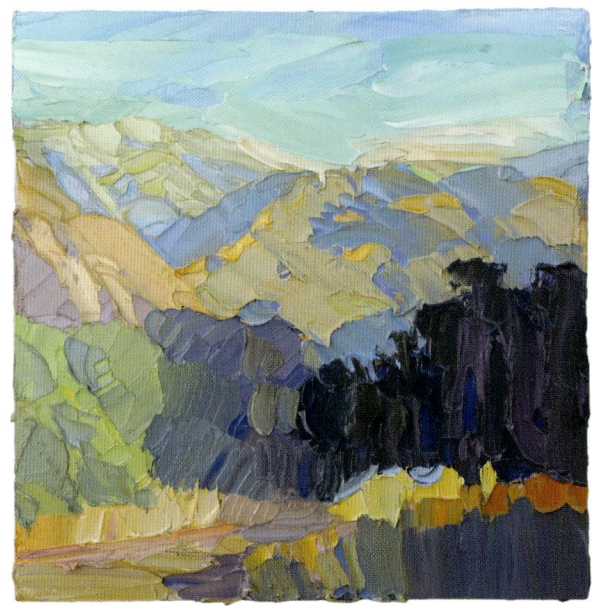

Carole Gray-Weihman, *Late Afternoon at Almaden*, oil on panel, 6" × 6" | 15.2 cm × 15.2 cm

A beautiful study of atmospheric perspective executed in impasto paint. Carole has not copied the values exactly (although the photograph probably didn't record them perfectly either) but has shifted them into a lighter range to express a mild summer afternoon.

MORE/LESS

- Darker/Lighter
- More colorful/ More gray
- More contrast/ More similar
- Bigger/Smaller
- Thicker paint/ Flatter paint
- More developed/ Simplified

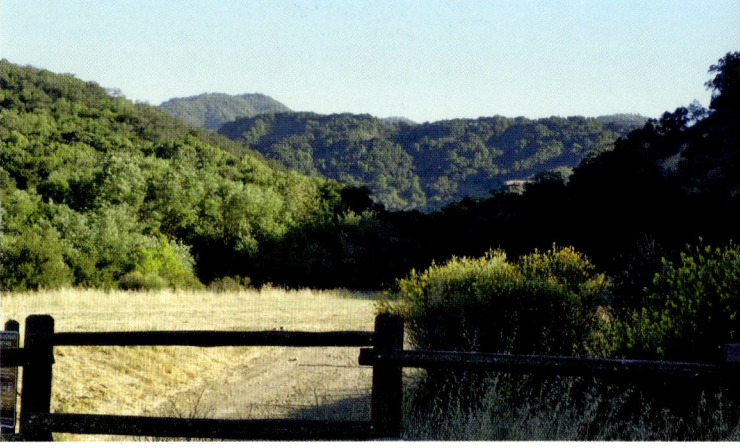

The scene: raking afternoon light in the hills of California, USA, with the blue atmospheric effect clearly visible in the shadows.

FOREGROUND SOLUTIONS

The foreground of a painting plays an important role in the picture and merits attention. Most significantly, a foreground that is in dialogue with the rest of the picture will make more sense than one whose role has not been considered.

Just as the placement of the horizon line is a design decision, elements in the foreground should be designed to contribute, not detract.

If the main focus of the painting is in the foreground, it should be developed and made of primary importance, while maintaining the play of elements throughout the picture. In this case, the more distant part of the landscape would be subordinated—even just a little—to play a background role.

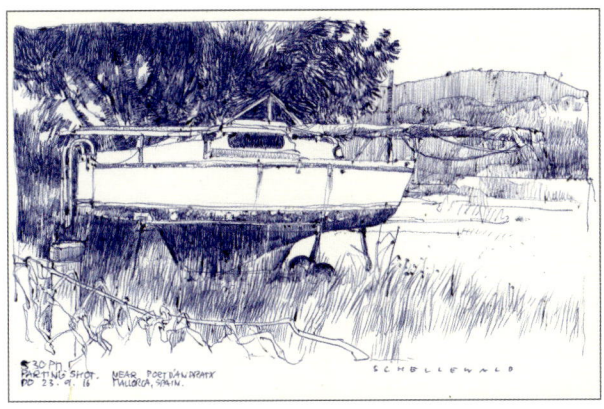

Christian Schellewald, *Parting Shot*, Andratx, Mallorca, Spain, LAMY ballpoint pen on paper, 8" × 5" | 20.3 cm × 12.7 cm

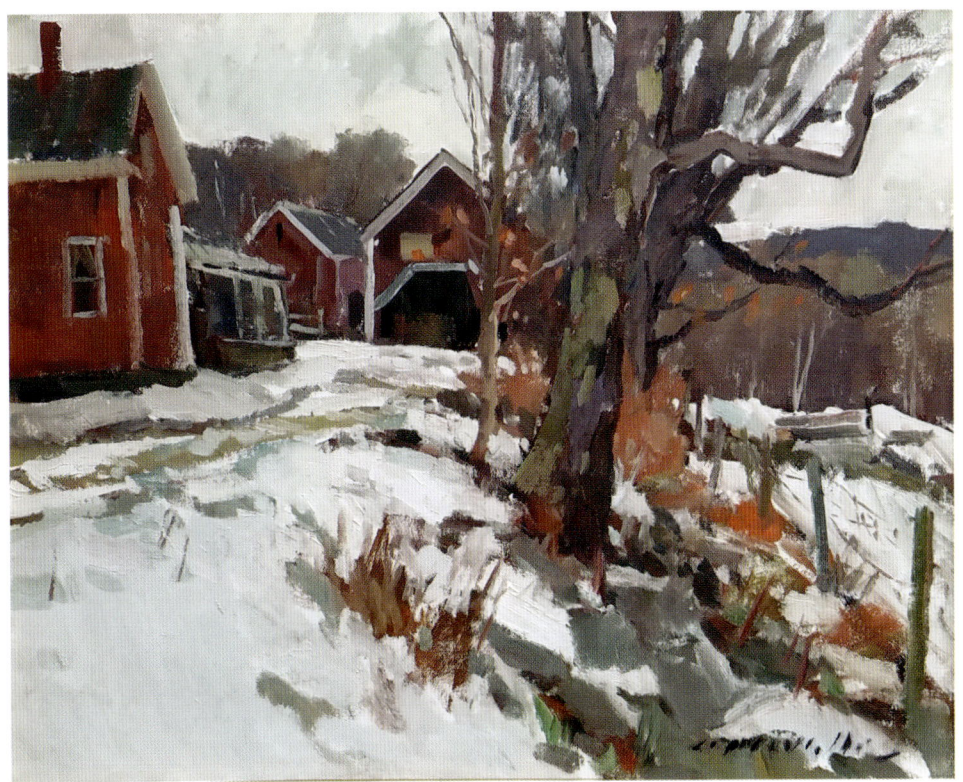

Charles Movalli, *Red Farm*, oil on canvas, 16" × 20" | 40.62 cm × 50.8 cm

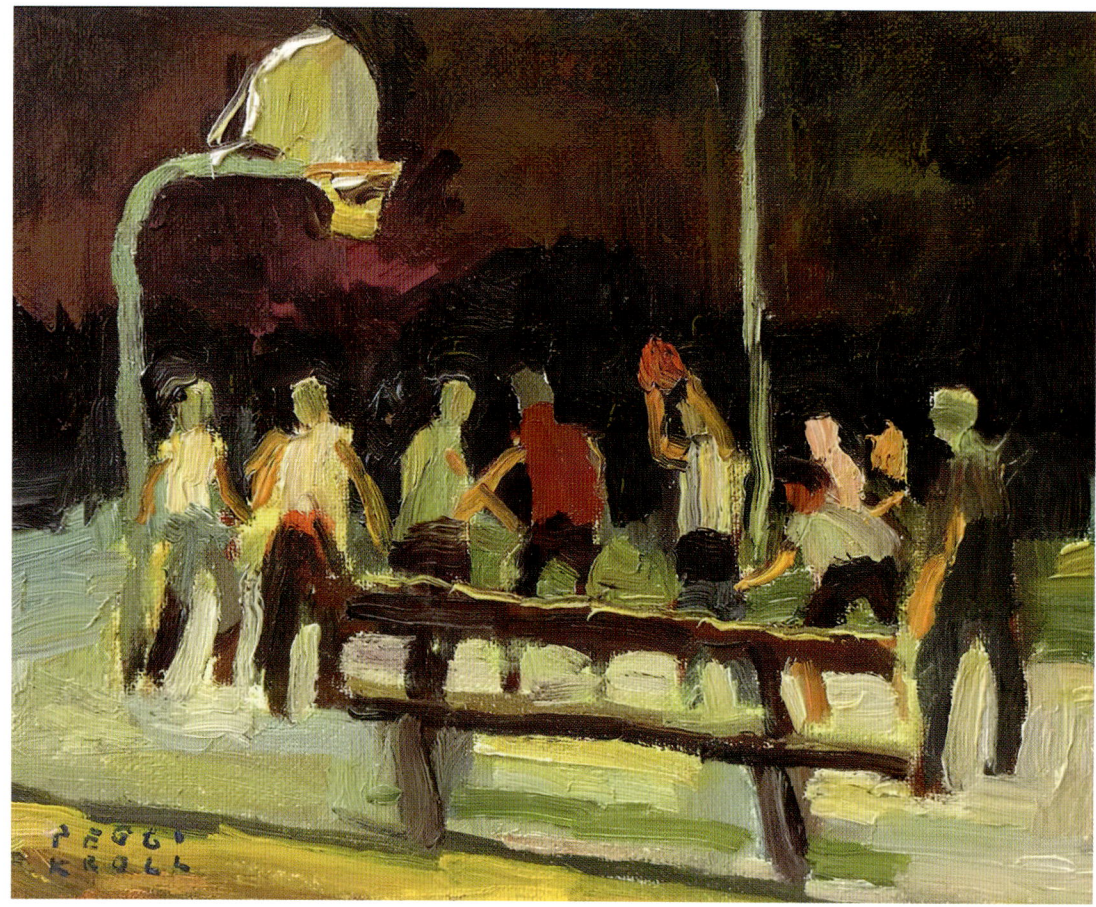

Peggi Kroll Roberts, *Night Basketball*, oil on canvas, 8" × 10" | 20.3 cm × 25.4 cm

Foreground lit by artificial light. Beyond the basketball court is the darkness of the ocean at night.

If the main subject of the painting is in the distance, the foreground steps into a supporting role, a lead-in to the subject. What we do *not* want in this case is a barrier, either a literal one like a wall or fence, or an implied one. We want the foreground to provide a way in, the beginning of an "eye trip," where we are led in and around the picture—not an "eye trap," where we get stuck in one place and the picture feels confining.

If the foreground is rendered as a flat plain, it can function just like a wall with a KEEP OUT sign. Make a way in. Look for zigzag or "S" shapes in the features of the land—they can be used as a way to subtly create a path in. A creek or a road provides a natural lead-in, as long as it is constructed to relate to the rest of the picture.

Lighting can be an effective way to direct attention. Think like a theater director and shine a spotlight on the soloist. We tend to look past shadows toward the light, so a foreground shadow is an effective device, even if you have to make it up.

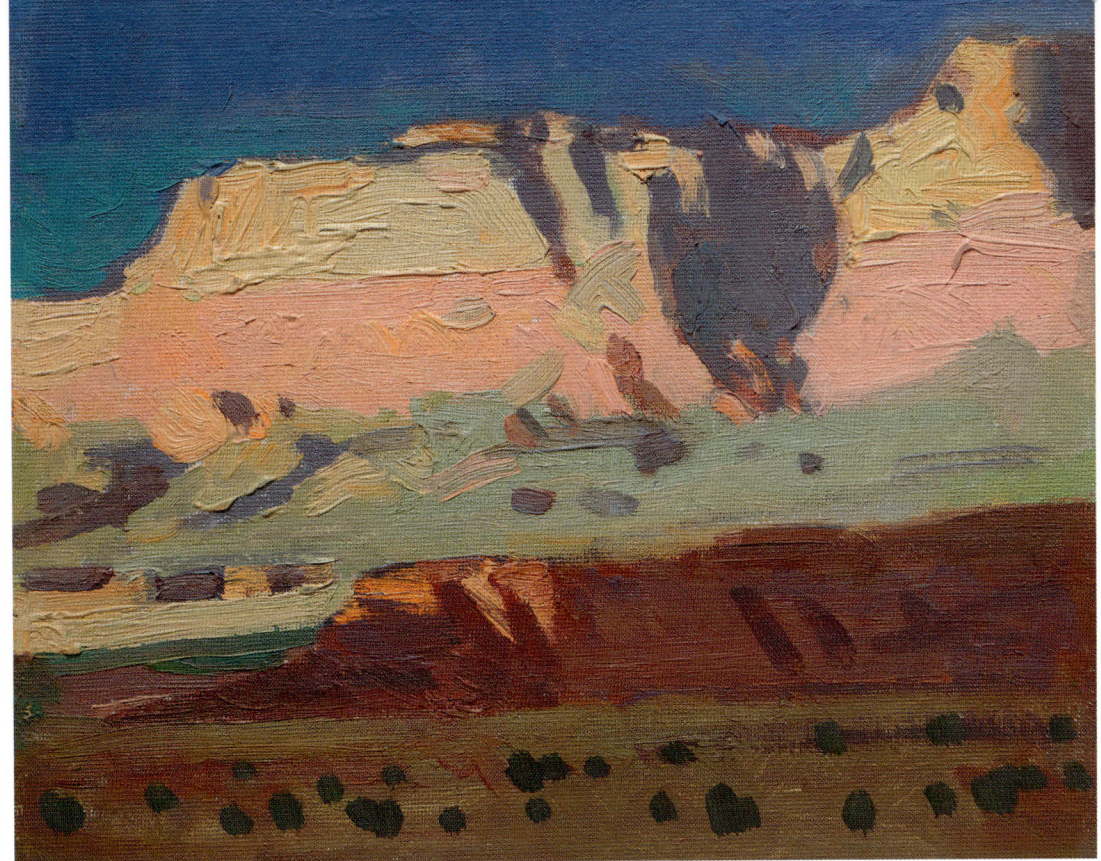

Ray Roberts, *Vermilion Cliffs, Northern Arizona*, oil on canvas, 8" × 10" | 20.3 cm × 25.4 cm

Here the foreground shadow serves as a way to ground the composition and advance the foreground. Note also the use of warm and cool in the light, and warm and cool in the shadow.

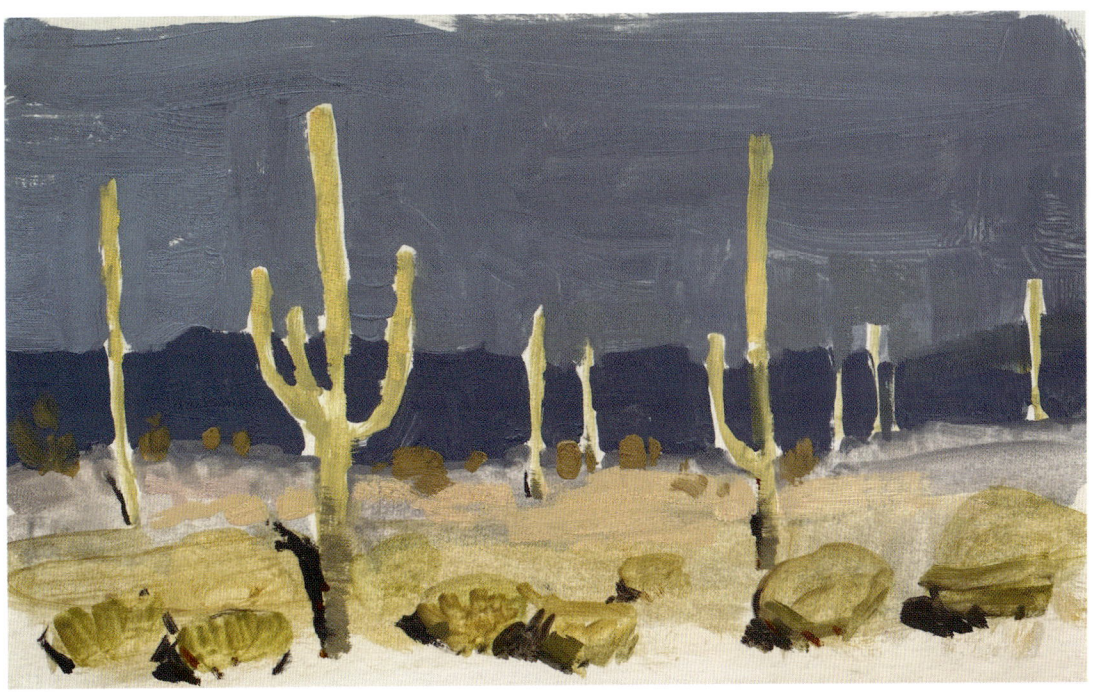

Aimee Erickson, *Lit Up Saguaro Study*, oil on sketchbook paper, 5" × 8" | 12.7 cm × 20.3 cm

Lit foreground in daylight, with storm clouds darkening the sky and hills in the distance. The little cast shadows under the foreground shrubs are darker than the hills. Note the simplicity of the shrubs: a single lit color with brushstroke direction indicating form, an in-between color where the form turns toward shadow, and a shadow color.

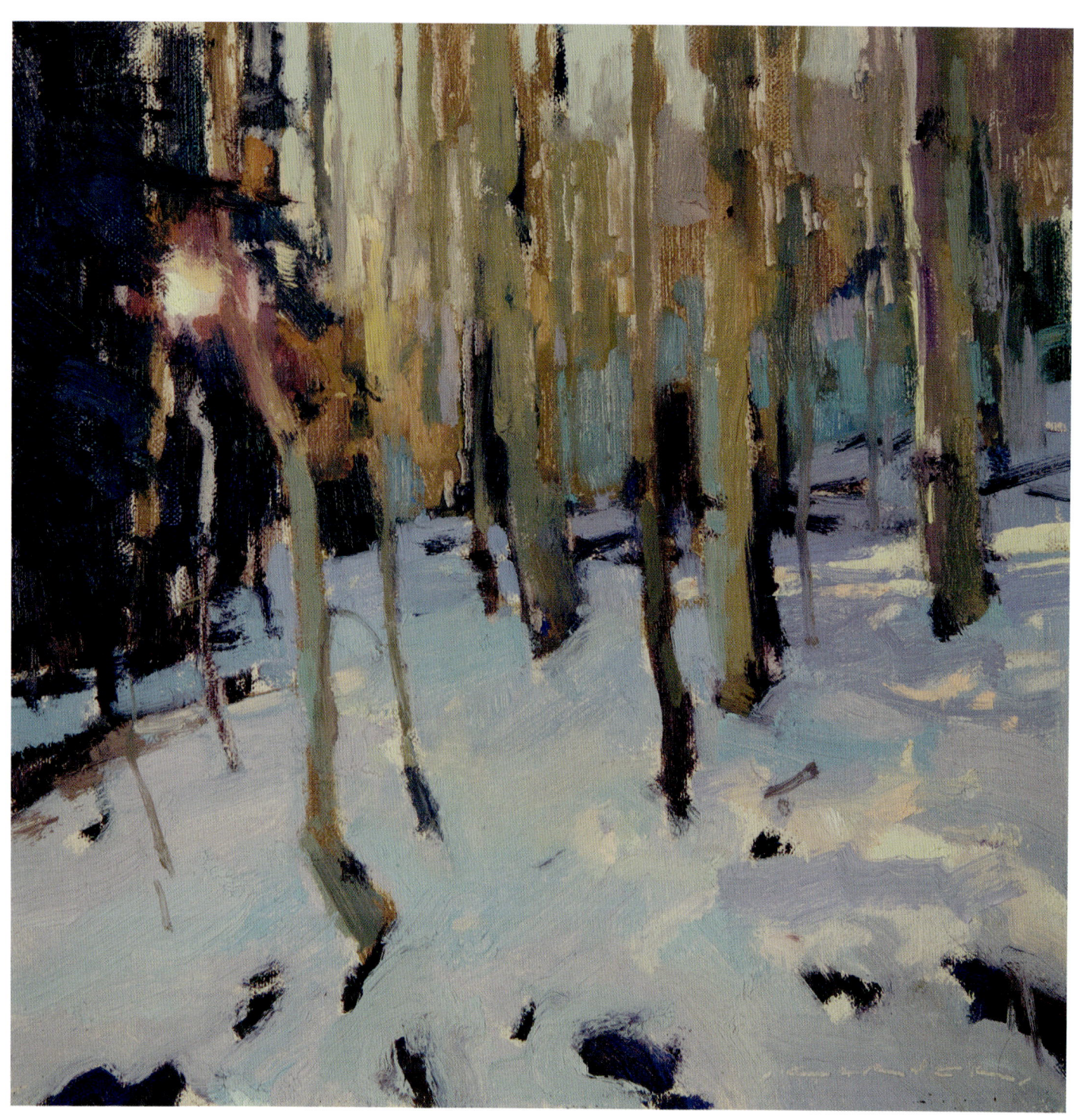

Jill Carver, *Last Light*, oil, 10" × 10" | 25.4 cm × 25.4 cm

5

INDIRECT LIGHT

Anything other than direct sunlight counts as indirect light: overcast light, light filtered by a tree canopy or by an umbrella, or reflected light in the shade.

A high cloud layer scatters the light and cools it, absorbing heat as well as color. A forest canopy filters the sunlight, catching most of it and creating a green, dappled world in the understory. A tree—not at all an impenetrable solid—casts an imperfect shadow full of holes. These are conditions without the obvious light and shadow of direct sunlight, but instead a range of other possibilities.

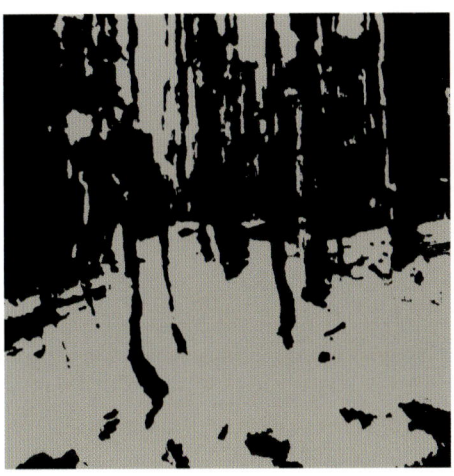

A two-value study of *Last Light*.

A three-value study of *Last Light*. Often, a painter is thinking in terms of a major division of value first and then a secondary division of value within one of the primary areas.

DAPPLED AND FILTERED LIGHT

Light passing through the imperfect canopy of a tree creates a pattern of dappled light and shadow. But the shadow is full of filtered light, too. This scenario offers the artist a challenge—how to make sense of a scene without the clear light and shadow that we often use as an organizing principle. Every situation is a little different, but the most important thing is to remember that *you* are the designer and that *you* have to find a way to make sense of things.

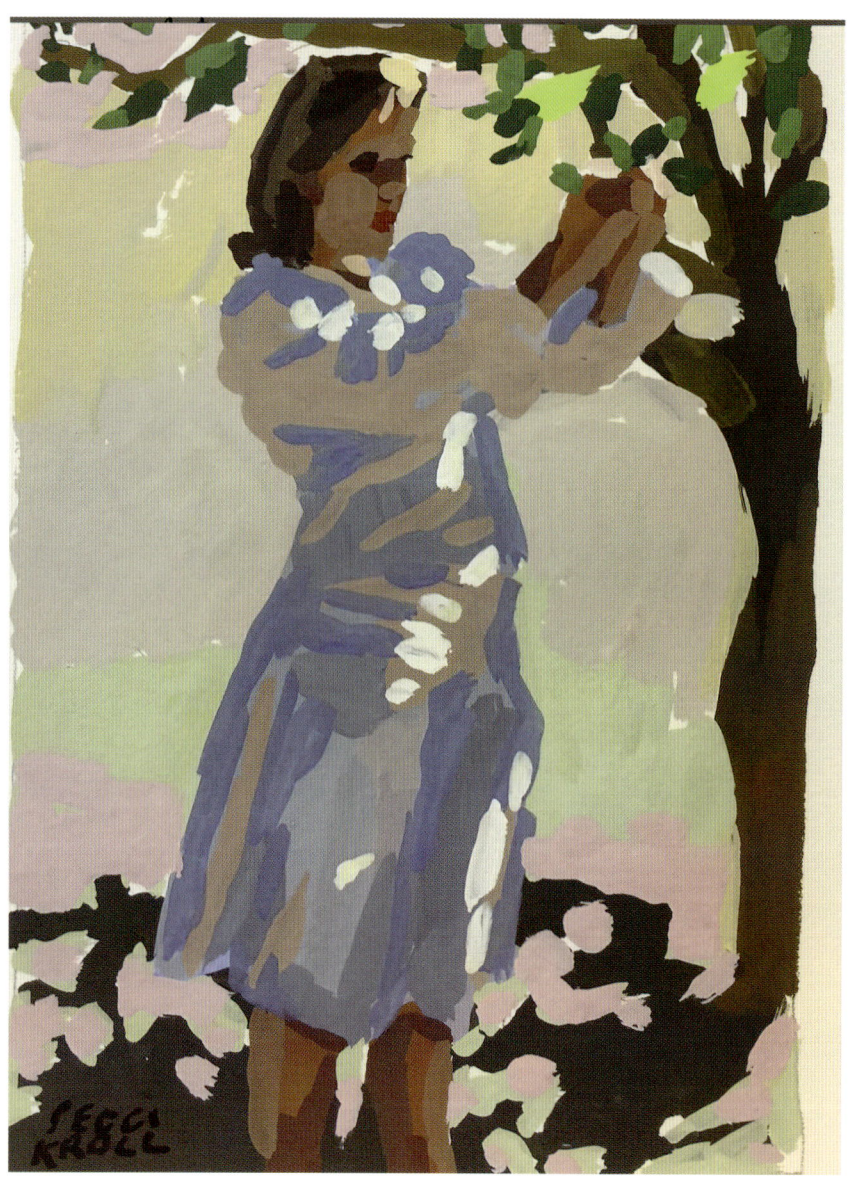

Peggi Kroll Roberts, *Apple Tree*, gouache on acid-free paper, 8" × 6" | 20.3 cm × 15.2 cm

TECHNIQUE:
STARTING WITH A MID-TONE CANVAS

THREE-VALUE THINKING

Painting in a forest on the Oregon coast. My panel isn't new and has a gray tone and various value and color scales, all dry. It holds the middle ground while I look for the high and low values and makes for some interesting color relationships right off the bat. The light is coming through the trees, a combination of backlighting and filtered light. The distinction between light and shadow is not well defined and doesn't naturally separate into clear big shapes. There's also a confounding layering instead of a clear figure-ground relationship. Here's how I understand it: The deeper we are in the forest, the more the trees can hold darkness. Foliage and tree trunks—especially narrow ones—that are farther up the hill are more affected by the light. Combine with that the shafts of light slicing vertically between the trees.

Walking away from the easel isn't quitting. There's something to be said for working at it for a while, and there's something to be said for taking a break.

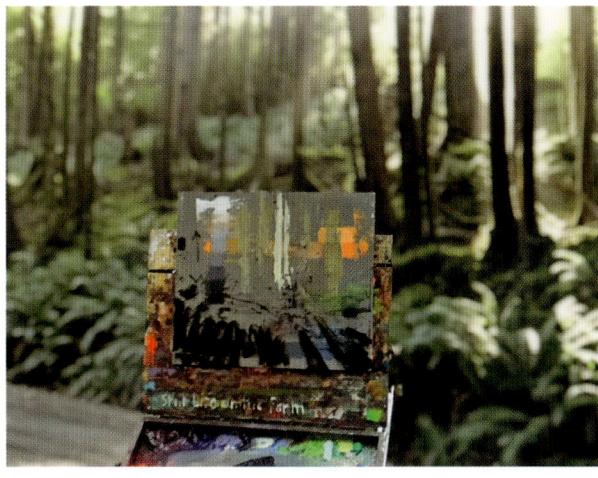

A start, and the scene.

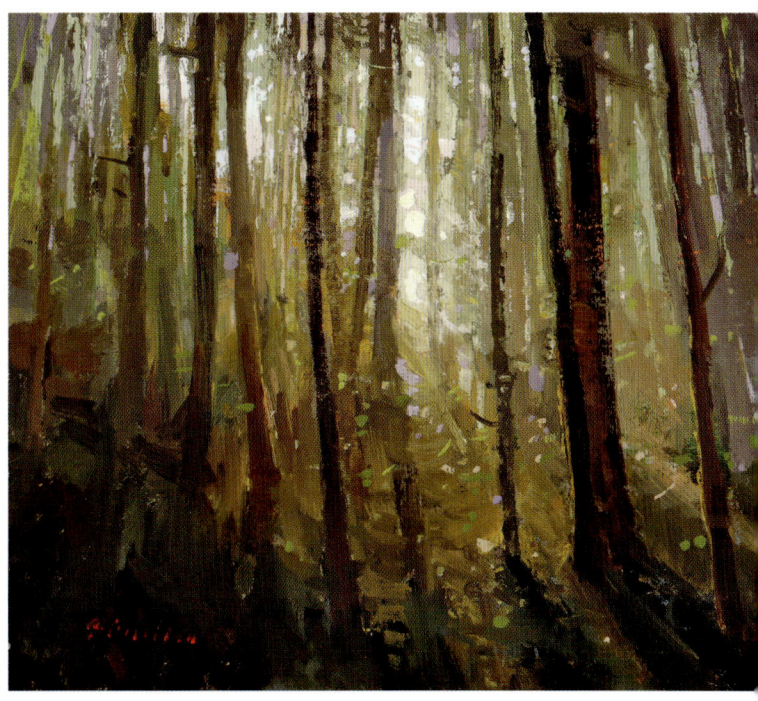

Aimee Erickson, *Cove Beach Road*, oil on canvas panel, 10" × 12" | 25.4 cm × 30.5 cm

DEMONSTRATION:
LARGE-SCALE WORK

MARY TONKIN:
RAMBLE, KALORAMA

The difference between small paintings and large-scale paintings is more than simply having more real estate to cover. More time and effort are needed, and more paint, as well as more knowledge, since the problems inherent in a big picture are, well, bigger than those in a small one. There's also the question of transportation. One advantage to a big painting is that it makes its presence known—it has a visual power.

I know many contemporary painters who work big—which in the plein air world usually means 18-inch × 24-inch (45.7 cm × 61 cm) and up. This multi-panel work is in a class by itself. Painting on location in the Australian brush over a period of eighteen months, Mary Tonkin made a series of large-scale paintings that create a continuous image spanning a breathtaking 59 feet (18 meters).

It is not a panoramic view, but a linear representation of looking up and around and back in a space.

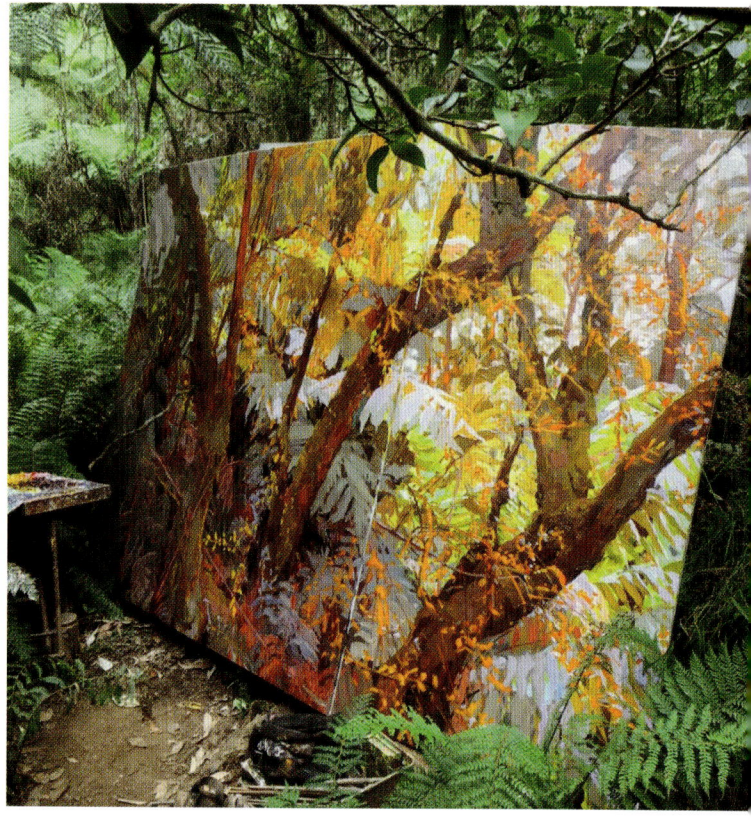

Mary notes: "Might need a larger easel, shifting things about across three panels. Work in progress in the 'studio.'" Each canvas is 5' 11" (1.8 m) tall.

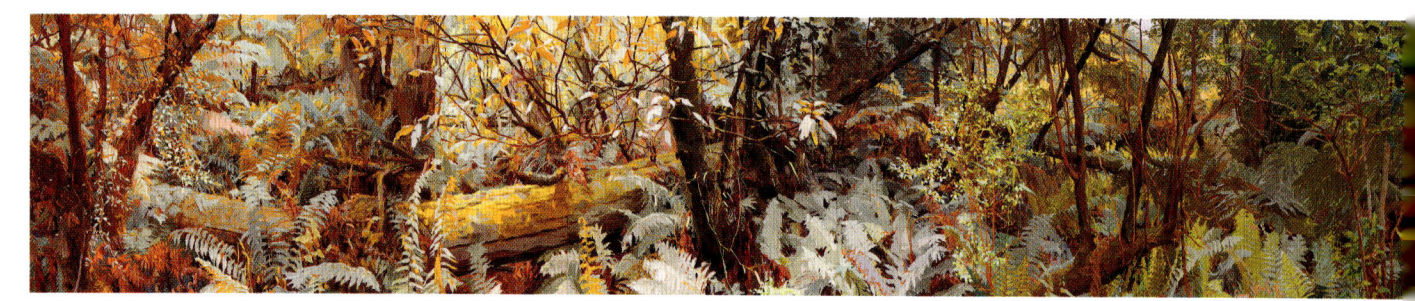

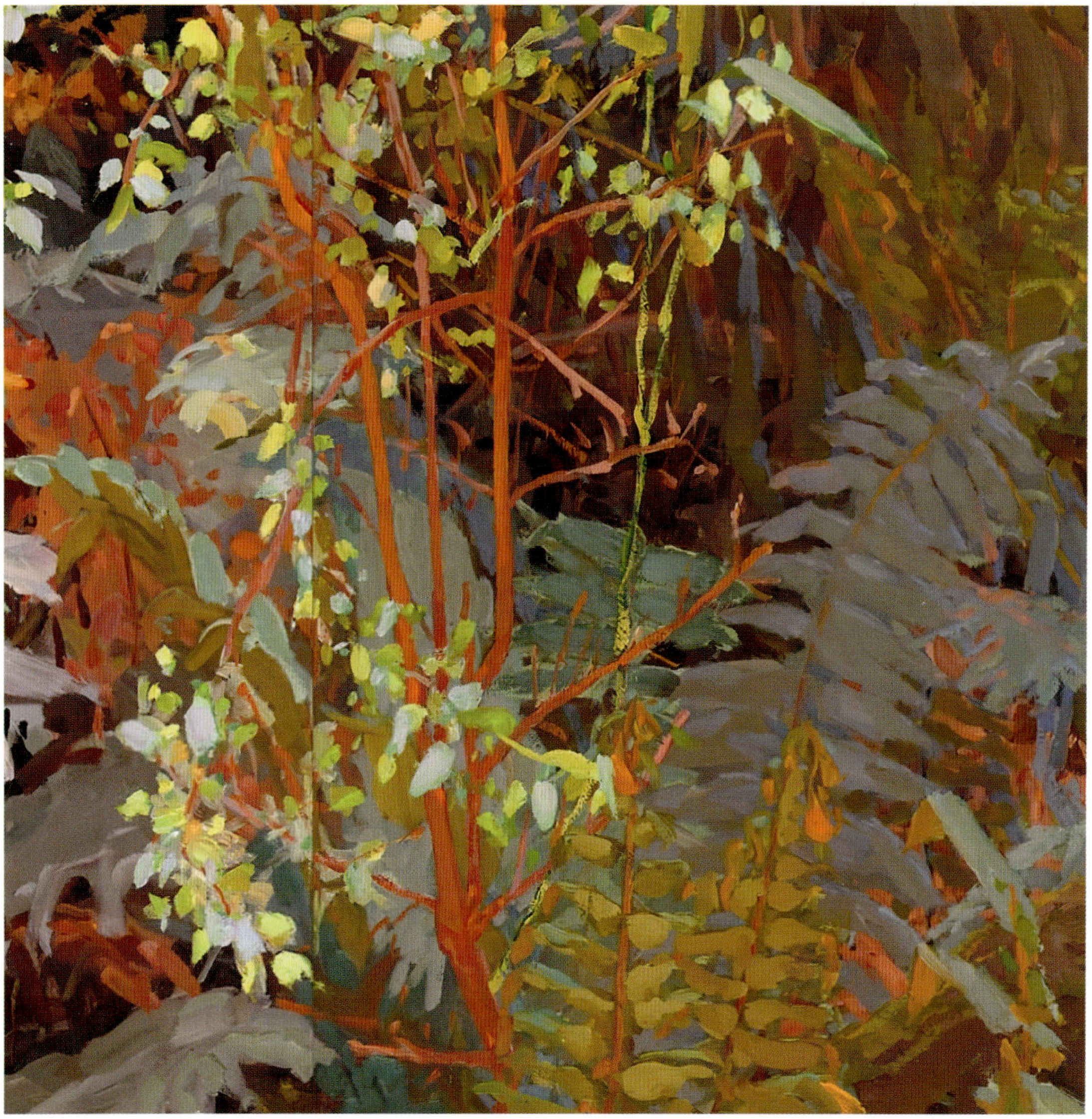

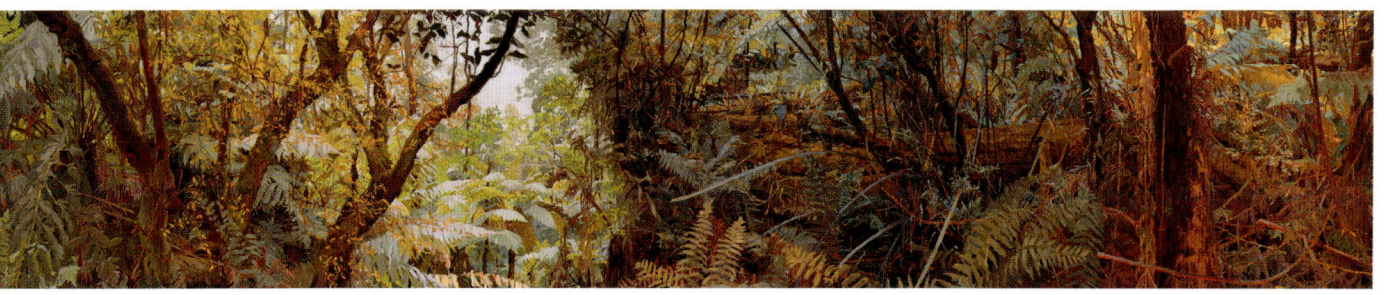

Mary Tonkin, *Ramble, Kalorama* (detail), (approximately 29½" × 29½" | 75 cm × 75 cm shown)

Mary Tonkin, *Ramble, Kalorama*, oil on linen, 71" × 744" | 180 cm × 1,890 cm. Photo by Matthew Stanton

DEMONSTRATION:
DAPPLED AFTERNOON LIGHT

TIM HORN:
SUMMERTIME WHEELS

DEMONSTRATION NOTES

- Canvas panel, 16" × 20" | 40.6 cm × 50.8 cm.
- Palette (oil paints): Permanent Alizarin Crimson, Cadmium Red Light, Cadmium Orange, Cadmium Yellow Medium, Cadmium Yellow Light, Ultramarine Blue, Cobalt Blue, Sap Green, Cerulean Blue, Phthalo Blue, and Titanium White.

In this lovely afternoon scene at a lake, an out-of-frame tree casts its shadow across the lawn and onto the house and its roof. The development of the roof is shown in detail at right, from initial wash and block-in of average light and shadow colors, to the working of the edge and adjustment of color to achieve the character of a tree shadow.

Horn uses this same approach throughout the painting: general to specific, building layers, modulating color, and adjusting edges.

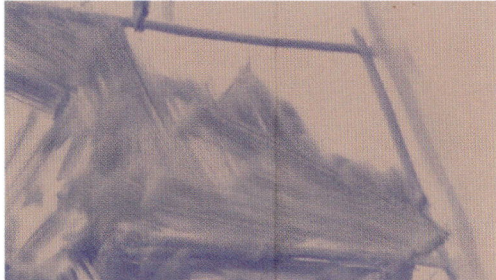
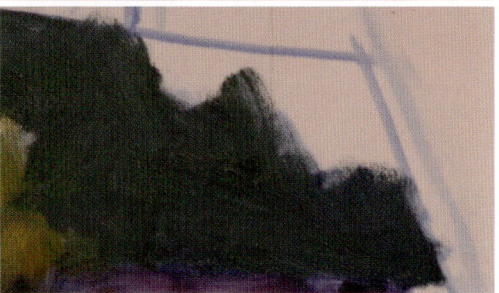
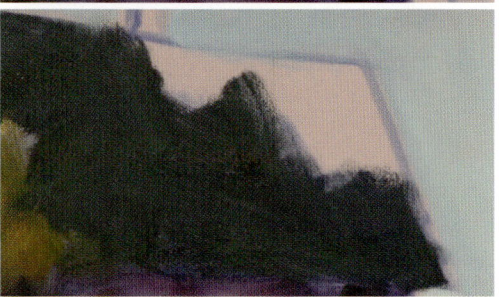
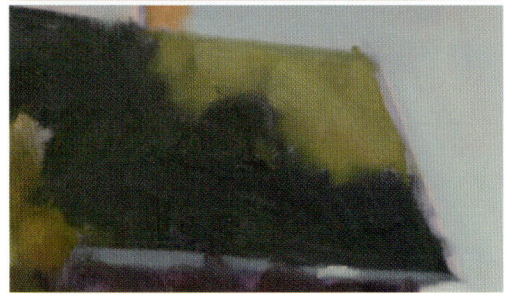
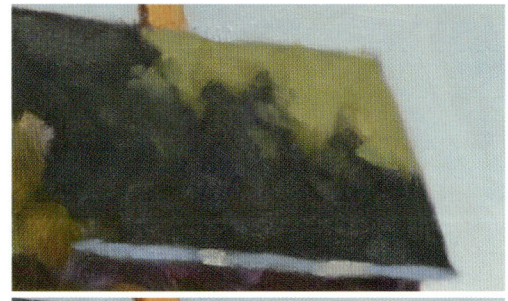
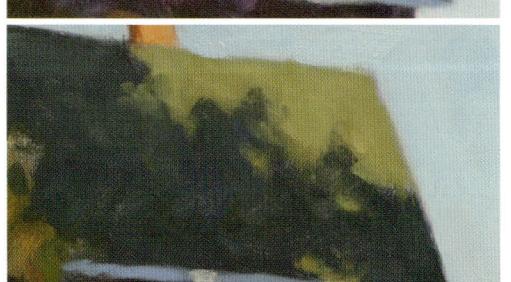

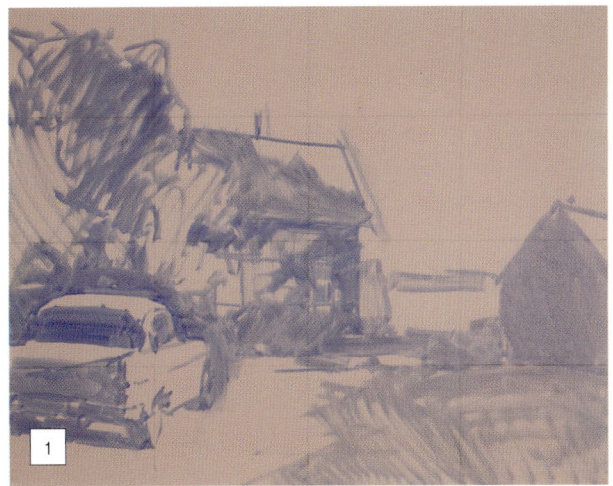

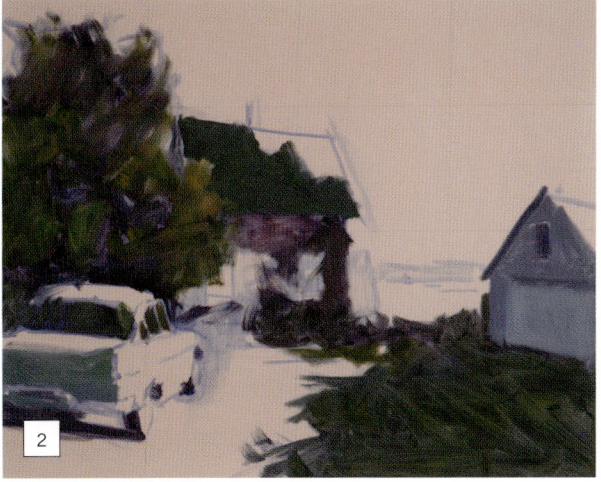

1. Starting with a pink-toned panel, Horn has used a ruler to mark out a grid, lightly, with a pencil. The initial thin blue wash establishes the shadow areas and still lets some pink come through so that light and shadow are automatically related.

2. Shadows are built dark first, with a unifying color. Later in the process, more color is built into the shadows. The pink of the panel holds the lit areas.

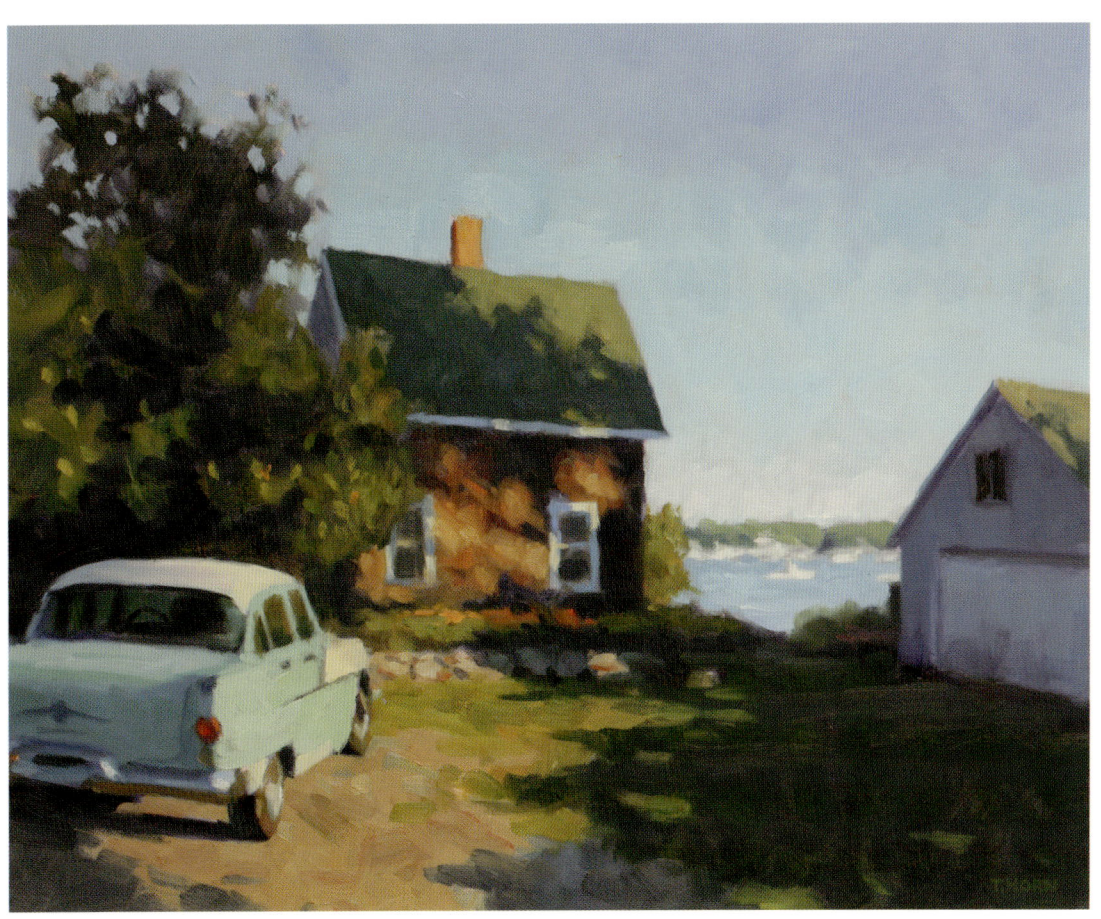

Tim Horn, *Summertime Wheels*, oil on canvas, 16" × 20" | 40.6 cm × 50.8 cm

OVERCAST LIGHT

On a gray day, everything is softer. The interval between light and dark is lessened and there are no clear shadow shapes. The sky tends to be very pale and flat. There are no cast shadows at all, only occlusion shadows that occur where two objects meet and the light can't get in. So, instead of having a painting driven by light and shadow, it can be driven by color or by subtle changes within a narrowed value range.

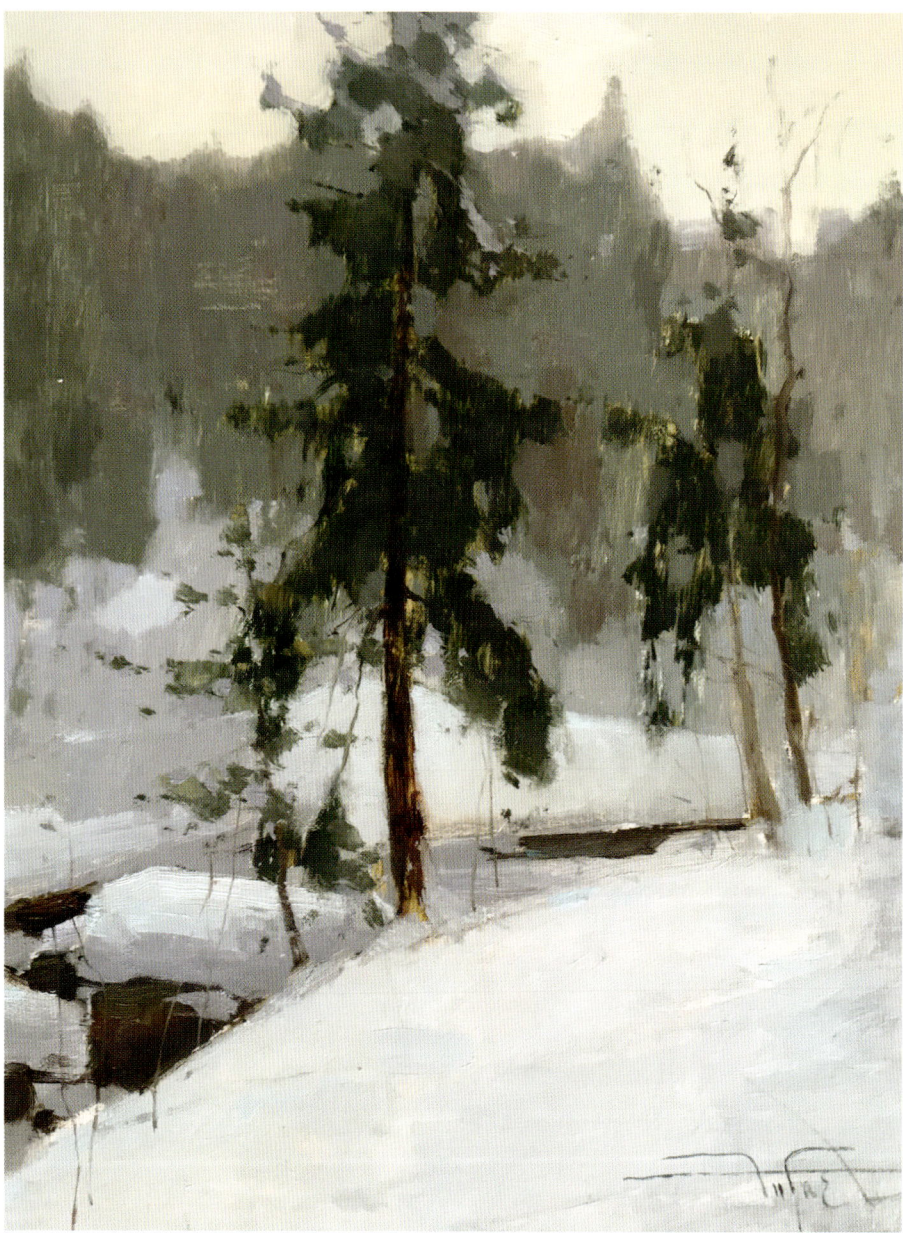

Zufar Bikbov, *Winter in New England*, oil on canvas, 14" × 11" | 35.6 cm × 27.9 cm

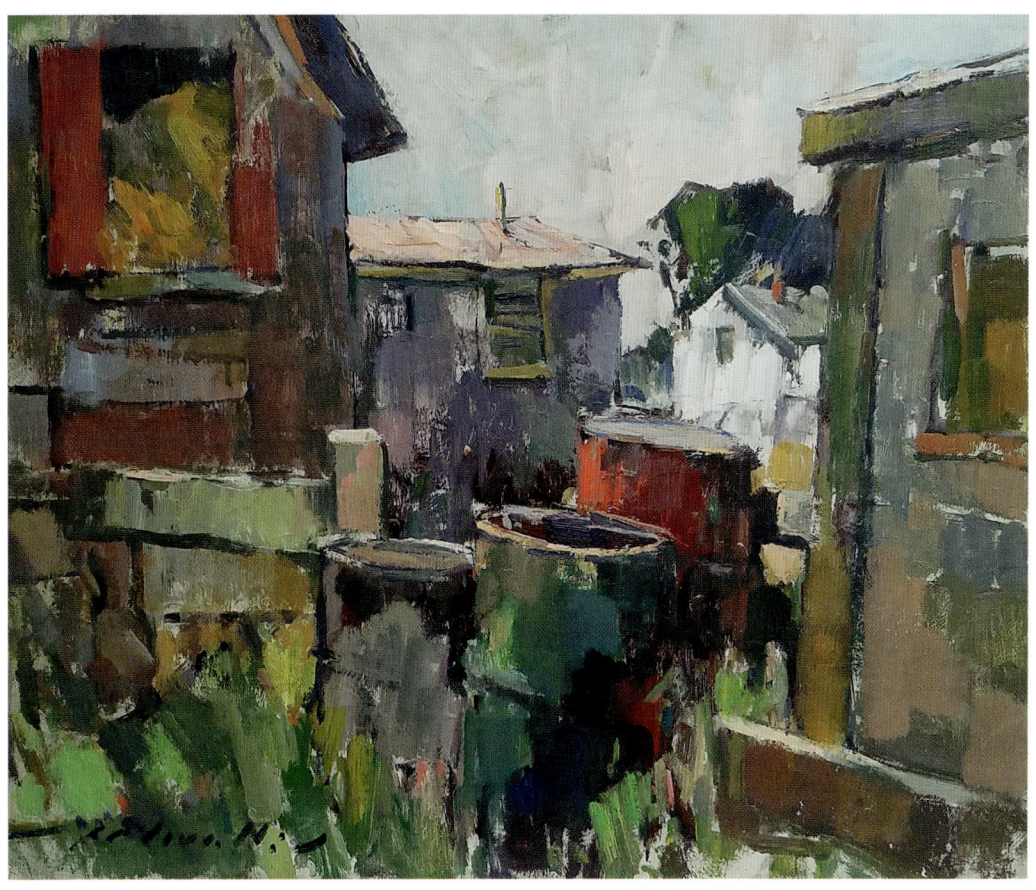

Charles Movalli, *Barrels*, oil on canvas, 16" × 20" | 40.6 cm × 50.8 cm

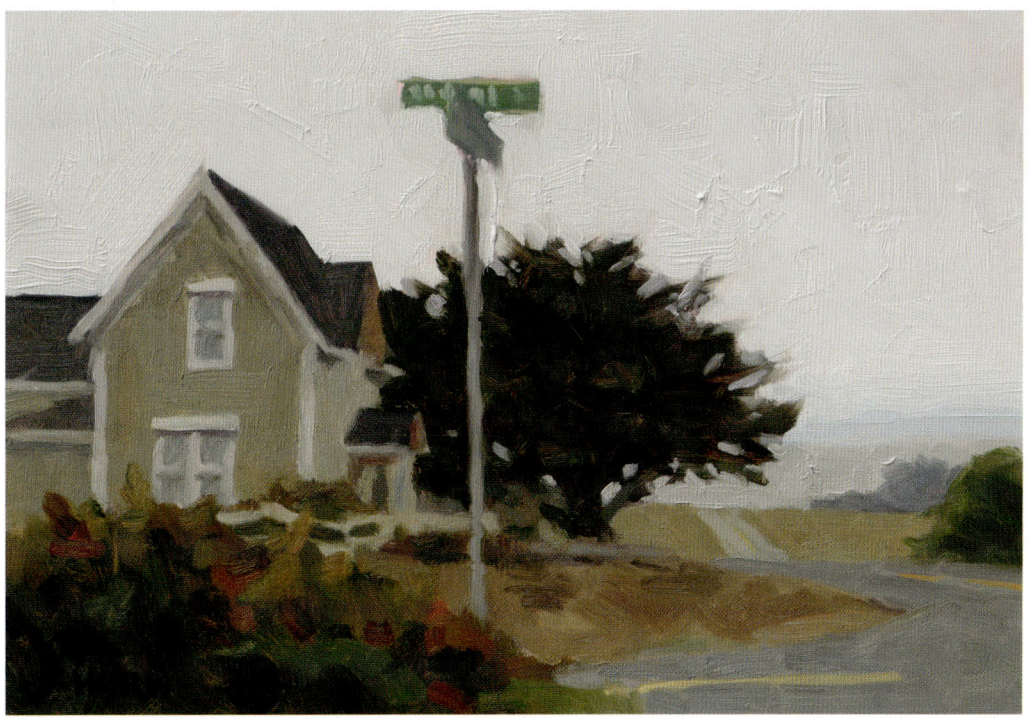

Tim Horn, *William Street*, oil on panel, 8" × 12" | 20.3 cm × 30.5 cm

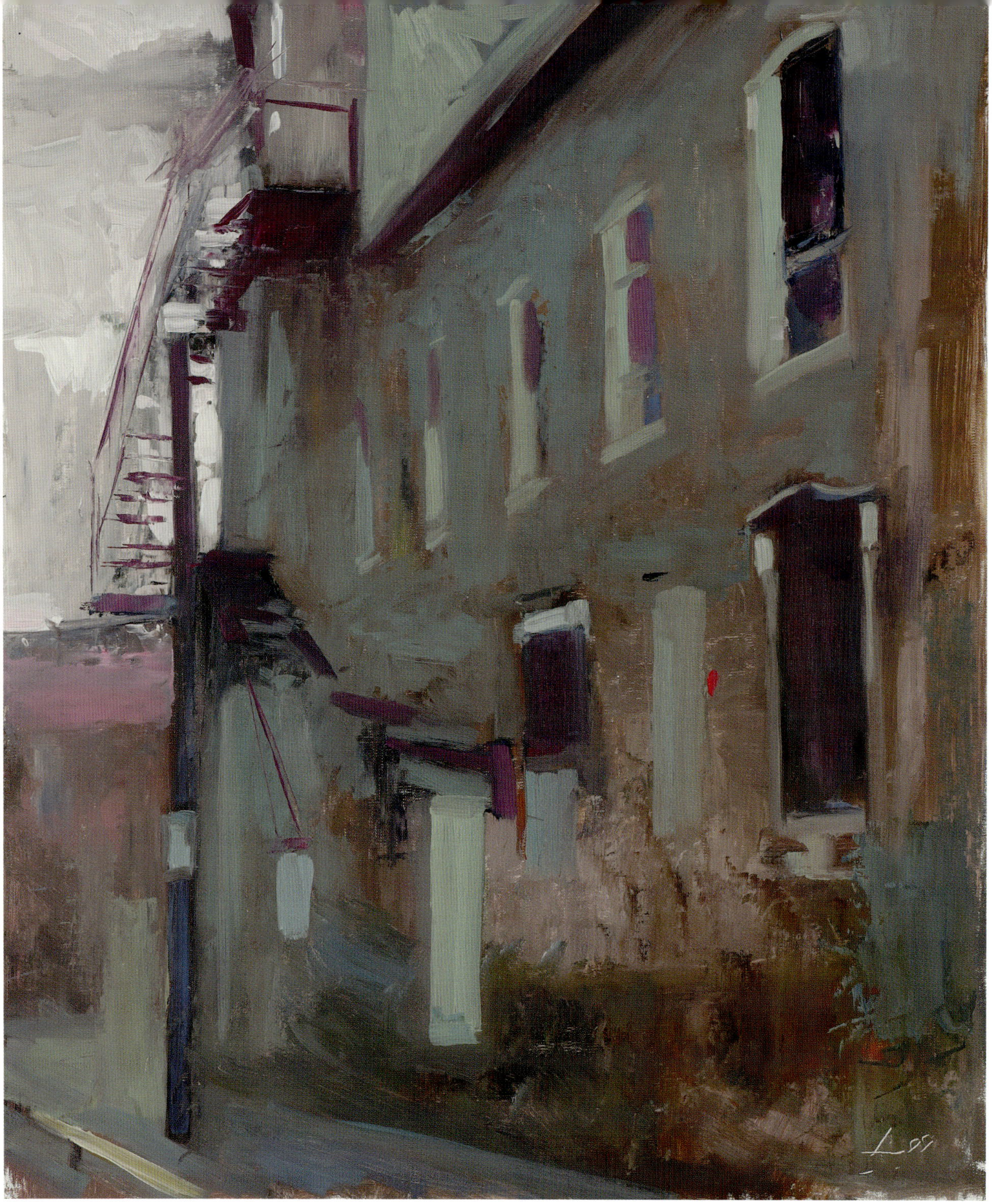

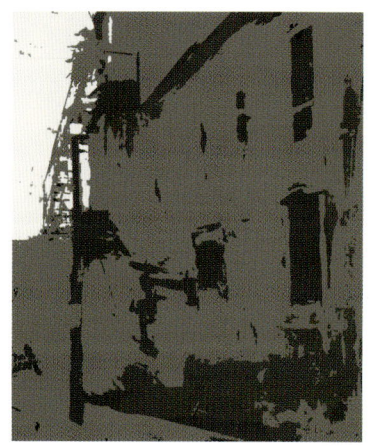

Patrick Lee, *The Street Outside my Studio*, oil on linen panel,
24" × 20" | 61 cm × 50.8 cm

With no direct sunlight or even a clear sense of direction of light, the entire subject is described in a compressed value range. Compositionally, we have a big expanse of building, with the sky and fire escape taking up maybe an eighth of the real estate.

A digitally rendered three-value study confirms the strength of the 70-30-10 formula—mostly middle value, some dark, and a little light.

DEMONSTRATION:
A TWO-SESSION PAINTING

NICHOLAS O'LEARY:
OSSEUS

DEMONSTRATION NOTES

- Canvas: 43½" × 27½" (110 cm × 70 cm).
- Palette (oil paints): Michael Harding Titanium White, Williamsburg Montserrat Orange, Old Holland Cadmium Yellow, Old Holland Brillant Yellow, Michael Harding Yellow Ochre, Sennelier Chinese Vermilion, Williamsburg Dianthus Pink, Old Holland Cadmium Orange, Williamsburg Persian Rose, Rembrandt Permanent Madder Deep, Old Holland Ultramarine Blue, Michael Harding Cerulean Blue, Michael Harding Cobalt Blue, Williamsburg King's Blue, Williamsburg Teal.

1. Starting loose and fast, with thinned-out paint over a thin ochre tone. Size and placement of the subject are the main concern at the start—fitting the composition into the format. The color also acts as a block-in color, which cuts out a step later.

2. Blocking in colors to establish the tonality, value, and composition of the painting.

3. Working from foreground (trunk and branches) to background (twigs, initially stated as a mass, and sky), the general image emerges. At this point, the sun came out and ended the session.

continued ▶

> *"I use a mix of brands depending on prices/stiffness/concentration of pigment, but mostly availability. My palette changes at a whim. I insert colors and take them out again if I don't use them."*
>
> —NICHOLAS O'LEARY

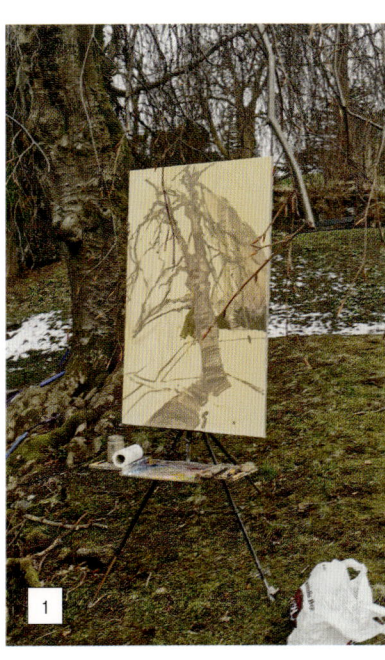

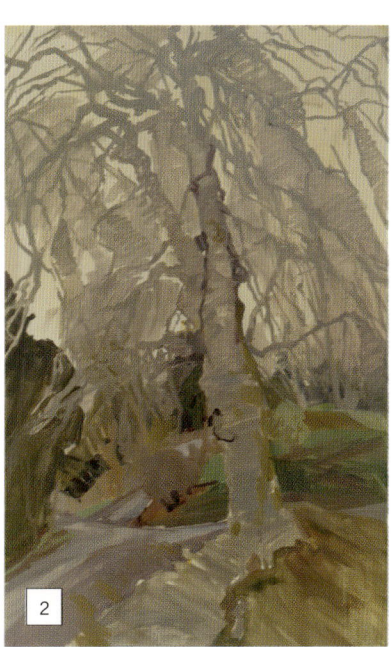

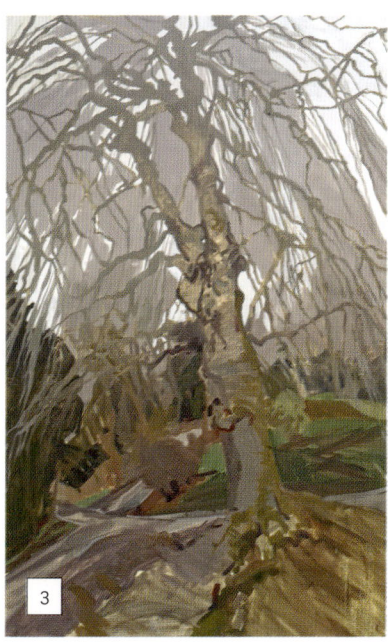

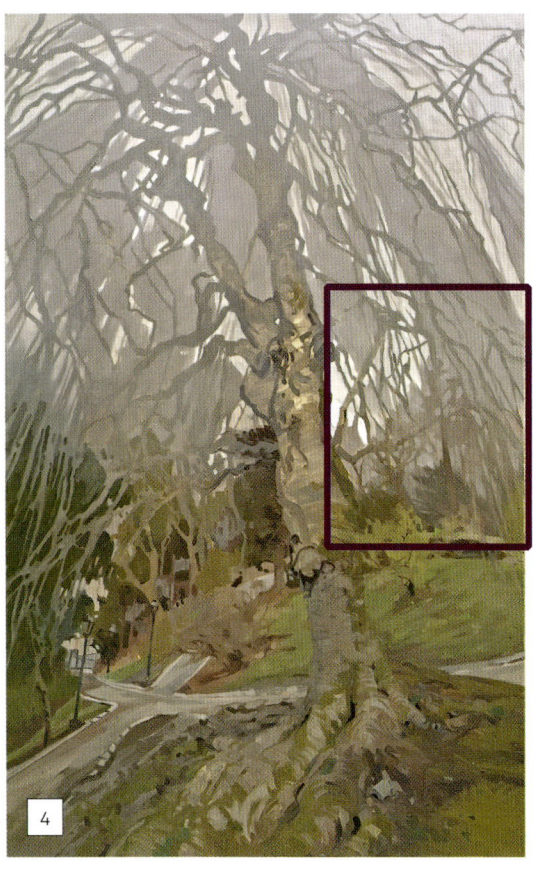

4. Start of the second session. A week later, the paint has dried, so O'Leary starts with a cool-color scumble over the branches to push them back and then adds detail into the background and the roots in the foreground.

5. Details showing how the sky is cut in to define the branches and twigs. This section is about 12 inches (30.5 cm) across.

"Cutting in just looks sharper, and I like it that way. It can be problematic as you need to constantly make sure your brush is clean before each stroke; otherwise, it can become quite muddy."

—NICHOLAS O'LEARY

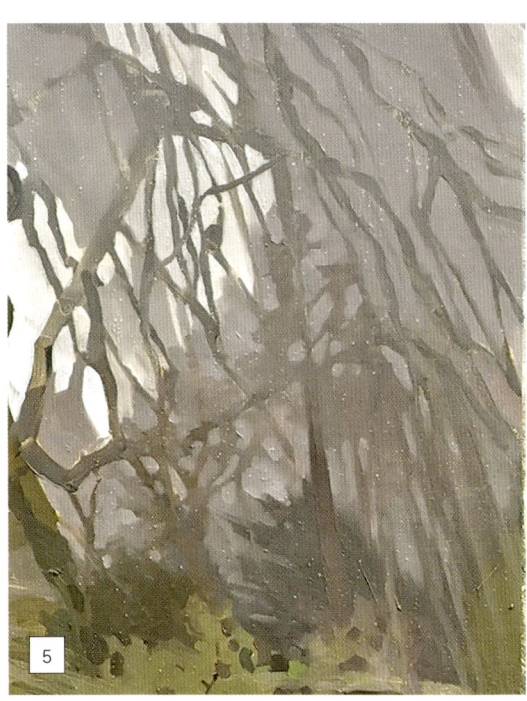

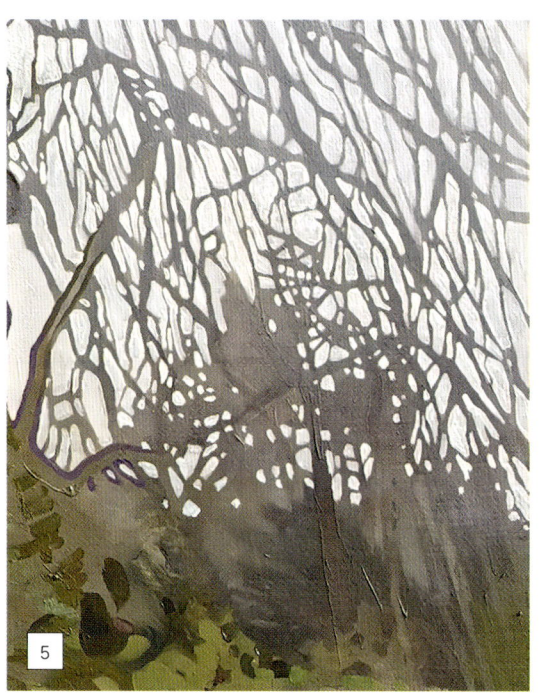

▸ Nicholas O'Leary, *Osseus*, oil on canvas, 43¼" × 27½" | 110 cm × 70 cm

Finish, after development of the tonality and shapes within the trunk, cutting in the sky with more precision, and getting all the parts to work harmoniously with each other.

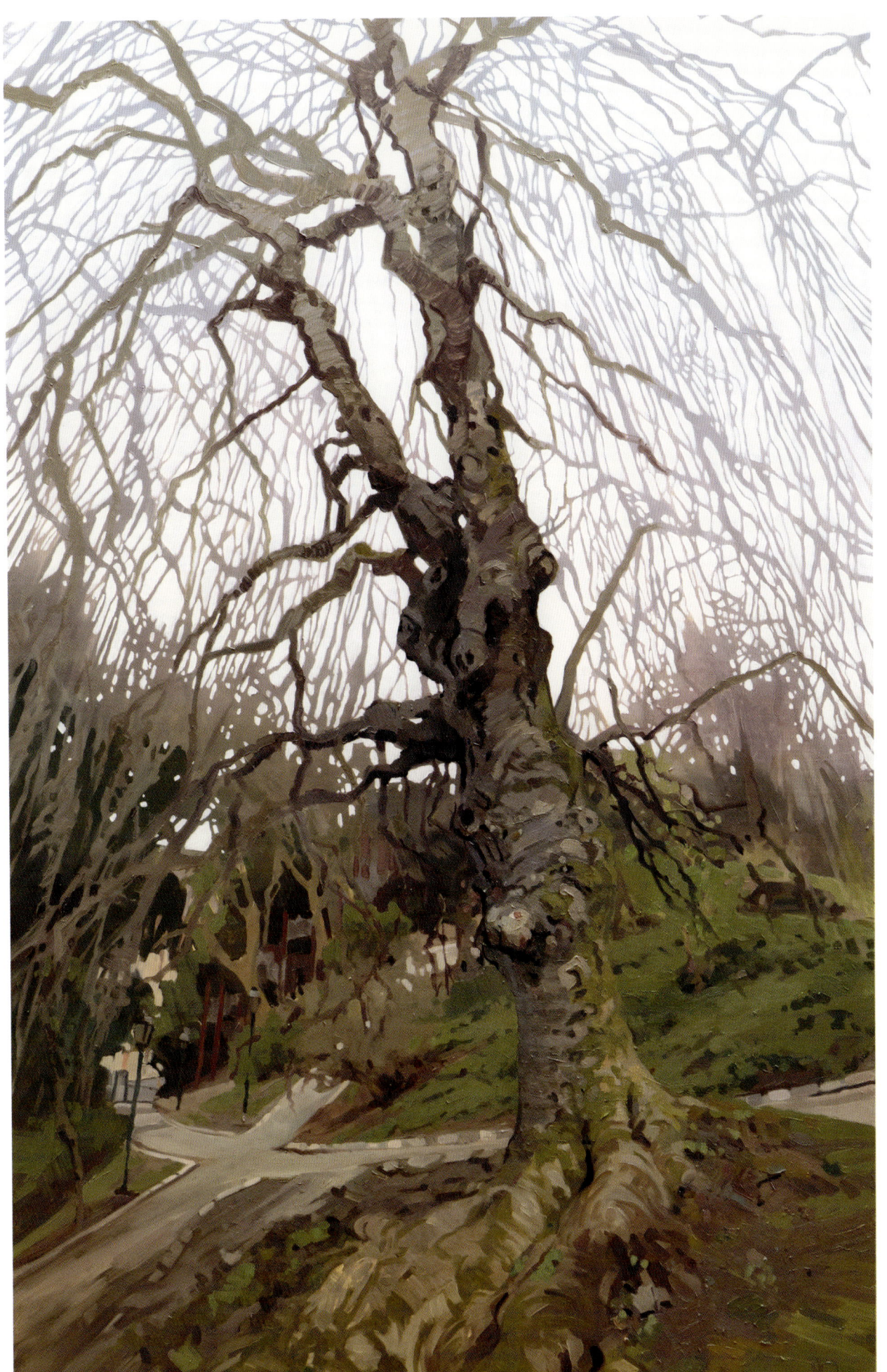

TECHNIQUE:
CUTTING IN

Cutting in means putting the foreground shape in first and then refining its shape with the lighter background: painting the sky after the tree. There are a couple of good reasons to consider cutting in. It reflects general-to-specific thinking: You can generalize the tree shapes (or buildings, or a portrait subject's hair, or whatever the thing is) and then define them with the background (rather than hitting your edges from both sides—not a painterly approach). It allows complexity and connectedness in foreground shapes without complexity in paint quality. It also makes sense when the background is much lighter than the object because paint more thinly applied describes shadow and opaque impasto paint describes light.

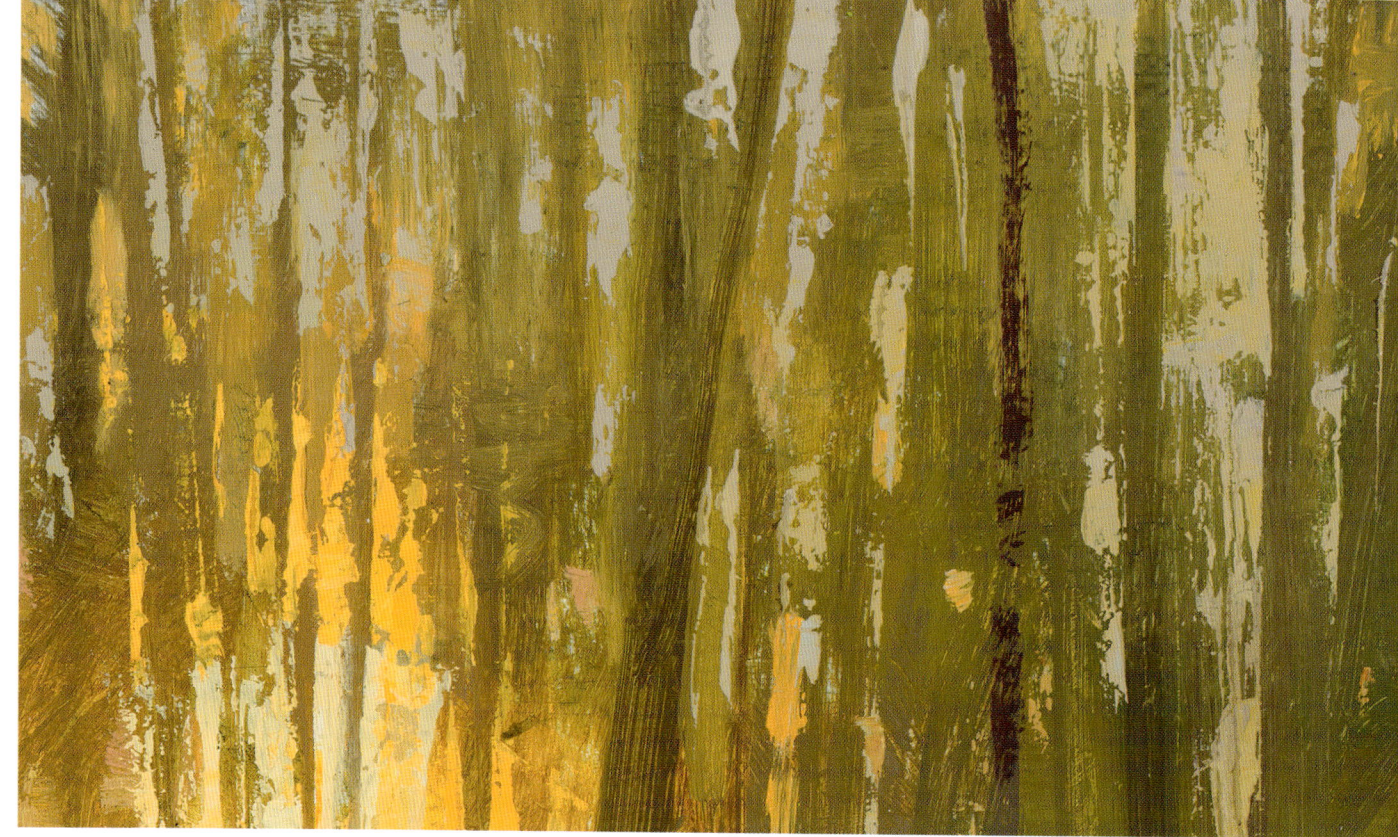

Aimee Erickson, *Sunset at the Falls* (detail), oil on panel, 14" × 18" | 35.6 cm × 45.7 cm

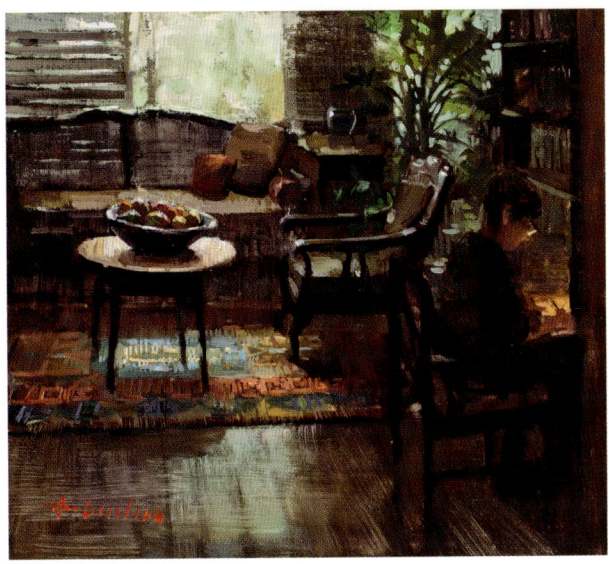

Aimee Erickson, *The Writer*, oil on muslin panel, 16" × 18" | 40.6 cm × 45.7 cm

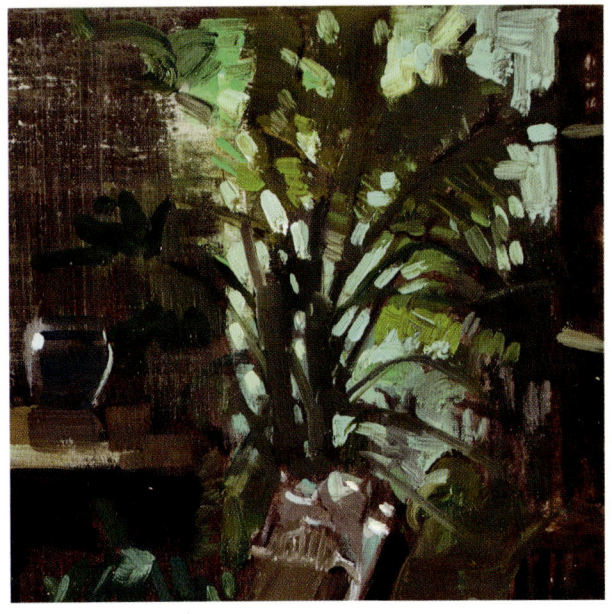

Aimee Erickson, *The Writer* (detail), oil on muslin panel, 16" × 18" | 40.6 cm × 45.7 cm

Another good thing about cutting in is that the sky holes take on positive, blobby shapes, which indicates brightness of the light. Dimmer light is respectful of twigs and lets them remain intact, but bright light takes on its own shape.

CUTTING IN, SIMPLIFIED FOR FIRST-TIMERS

1. Paint a solid, roughly triangular shape in a thinly applied dark color.

2. With a lighter color and using more paint, paint a background around and into the triangle, cutting into it to make it into a letter A (or whatever letter your name starts with).

A tree is more organic and complex, but the technique is the same.

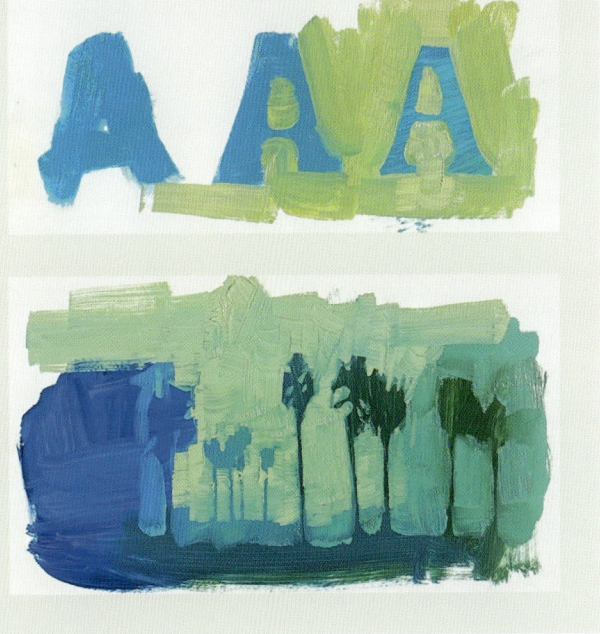

PAINTING MAKEOVER:
LIGHT AND SHADOW RELATIONSHIPS

STILL LIFE IN RAKING LIGHT/ WHITE WITH LEMONS

Correcting student paintings is one of the most effective teaching methods (if the student agrees to it, of course). It introduces solutions for problems to which the student has already given thought. In the "painting makeover" activity, students submit paintings that they couldn't solve to their satisfaction—paintings that they are willing to sacrifice for education. We discuss the original intention, problems that arose—painting problems belong to all of us—and possible solutions, and then as the instructor, I make changes to the painting.

- Palette: Raw Umber, Indian Yellow, and Ultramarine Blue. I use the Old Holland Raw Umber, which is much less gray and more golden in its tints than other raw umbers, and interestingly, it's the reddest color in this palette.

DEMONSTRATION NOTES
- Intention: Capture beautiful late afternoon light.
- What's working: Good setup and nice play of light across white objects.
- What isn't working: Insufficient organization of shadows; absence of any effect of light on the lemons— they are simply bright yellow.
- Goal: Improve feeling of being outdoors; organize shadows and light to create more of the beautiful feeling of late-afternoon light.

Notes. The lemons could be arranged better: We have an unintentional halo situation where one object is directly behind another, which is awkward visually. I pushed the whole lemon further back— if I had the actual setup, I might have found a better solution, but this works okay.

On the tabletop, I emphasize the flatness of the surface and the direction of the light, both horizontal, over the verticals and diagonals of the tablecloth's shadows and wrinkles. Just like clothing, drapery *conceals and reveals* the form underneath. To me, this is akin to telling the fundamental truth rather than the superficial truth. It also settles the painting down, making it a little more static.

The background in the *Before* version just isn't developed—no problem there, sometimes laying in a value is all you have time for. Bringing that value up a little and putting in a little color makes it feel more like outdoors, where there's lots of light. Very dark backgrounds can happen outside, but they are much more common indoors.

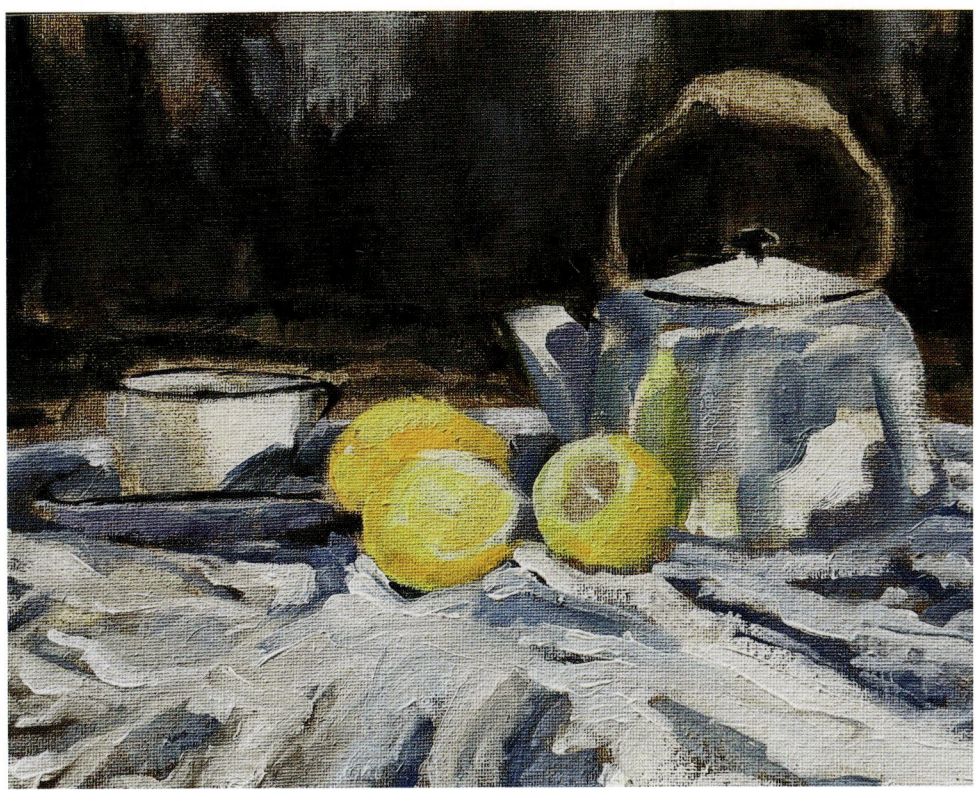

A. Hauser, *Tea with Lemons Outside*, oil on canvas panel, 9" × 12" | 22.9 cm × 30.5 cm

Before.

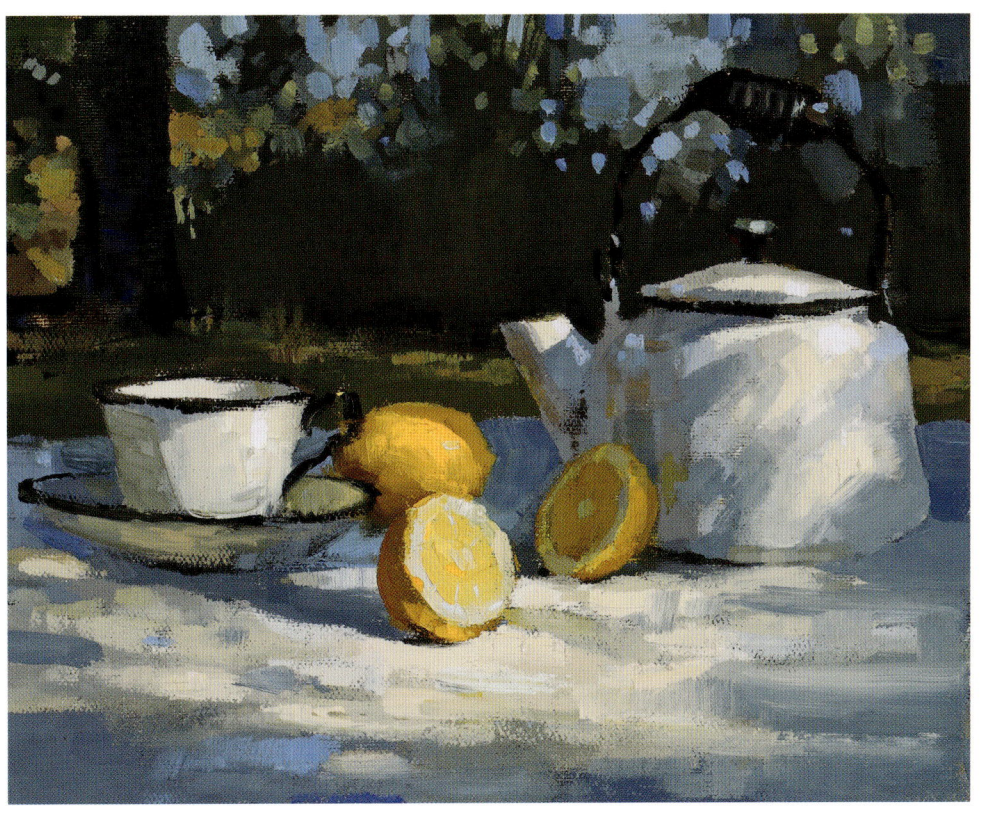

After.

TECHNIQUE:
USING A BROAD BRUSH

This painting demonstrates the efficient use of a very broad brush. I had very little time before dinner, but I'd been passing these birch trees daily and the moment had come. I had with me a 6-inch (15.2-cm) wide hardware-store paintbrush with soft bristles. Looking at the complex patterning on the tree trunks, I figured I could use that wide brush, in a horizontal stroke, to put in all the darks at once, as a broken pattern, maybe even with a single stripey brushstroke, and then add grass and white birch bark to make an illusion of different-sized trees. It worked! I tend to not be a detail painter, and all those dark markings on the birch trunks would be mighty discouraging if I had to paint them with a rigger.

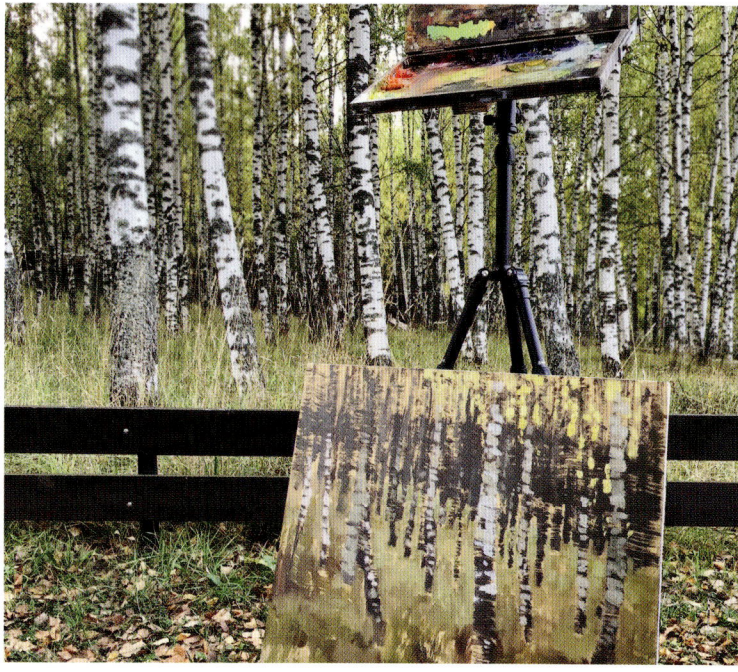

Somewhere in the middle of things.

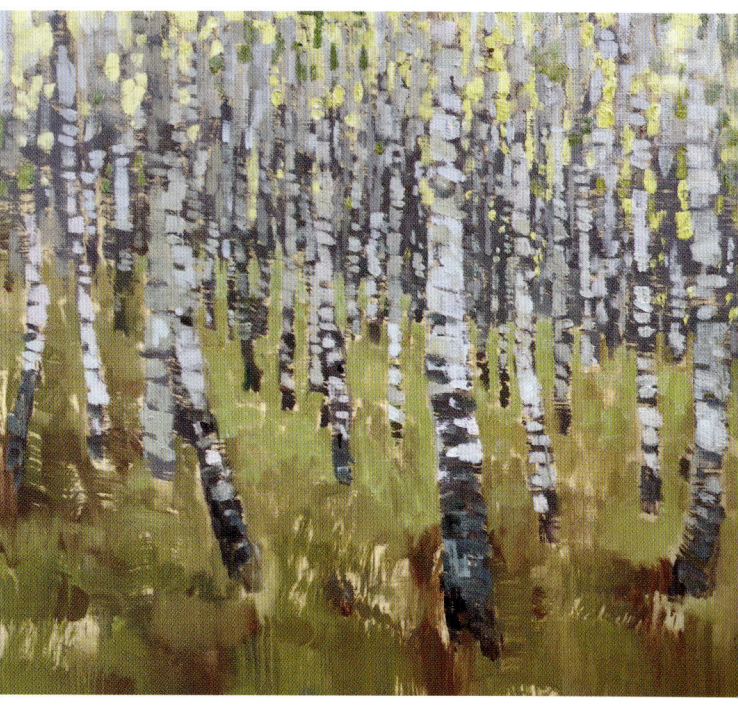

Aimee Erickson, *Birches of Volzhkiy Priboy*, oil on linen, 15¾" × 23⅔" | 40 cm × 60 cm

SHADE AND REFLECTED LIGHT

There's a difference between deep shadow, where darkness reigns and nothing can be seen, and shadow in an area of bright light. Since the light is bouncing around, even the shadows—while still darker than the lit areas—start to fill with color. If the shadow shapes are descriptive of the objects or scene, it's important to maintain a value separation between light and shadow.

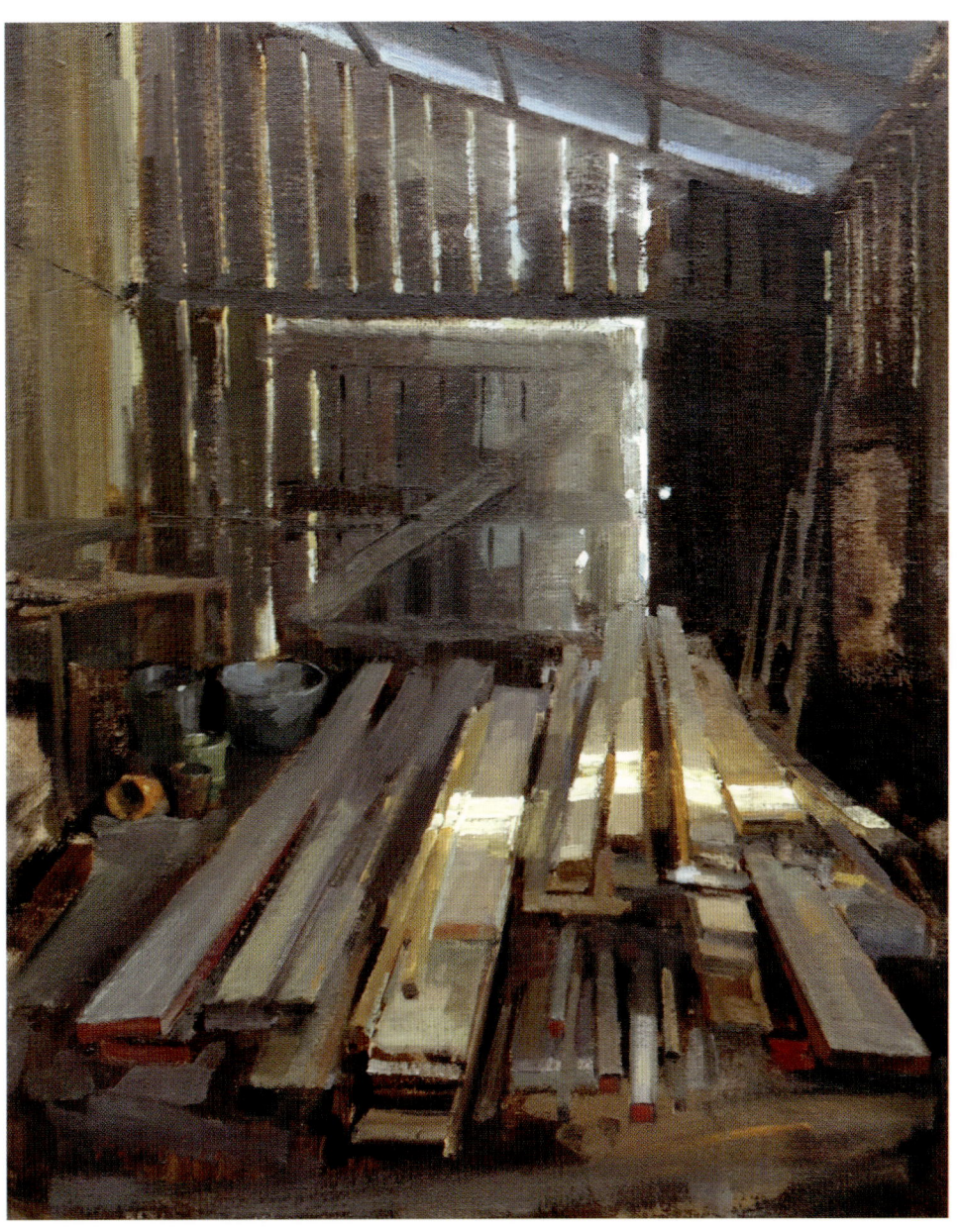

Aimee Erickson, *Shaft of Sunlight*, oil on canvas panel, 20" × 16" | 50.8 cm × 40.6 cm

Below is an example of shadow shapes being first stated as a single dark value, paying particular attention to how the shapes interact. Color modulation is added in a second stage.

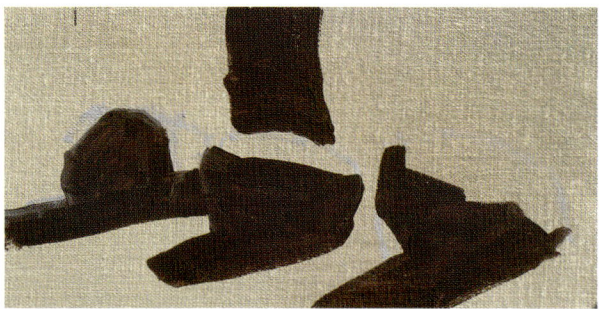

A simple statement dividing light from shadow. The lit tops of the rocks disappear against the lit earth behind them—light against light is no definition. The tree trunk is there as a shape to relieve the lit side of the middle rock.

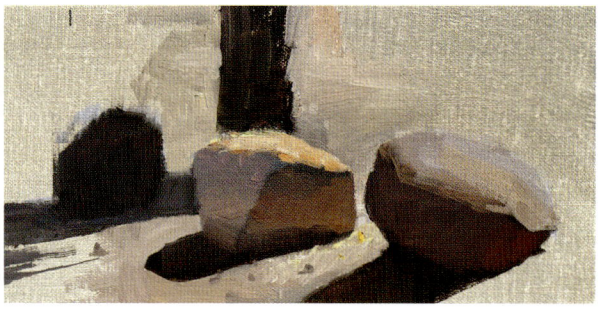

Modulating the shadows without crossing into the lit value range. Where the light from the warm sand reflects onto a downward-facing plane, the color is a little warmer. Where the shadow plane of the rock turns toward the sky, the color is cooler because its source is light from the blue sky. Looking for a warm-to-cool shift within shadow areas can add a lot of interest to a painting.

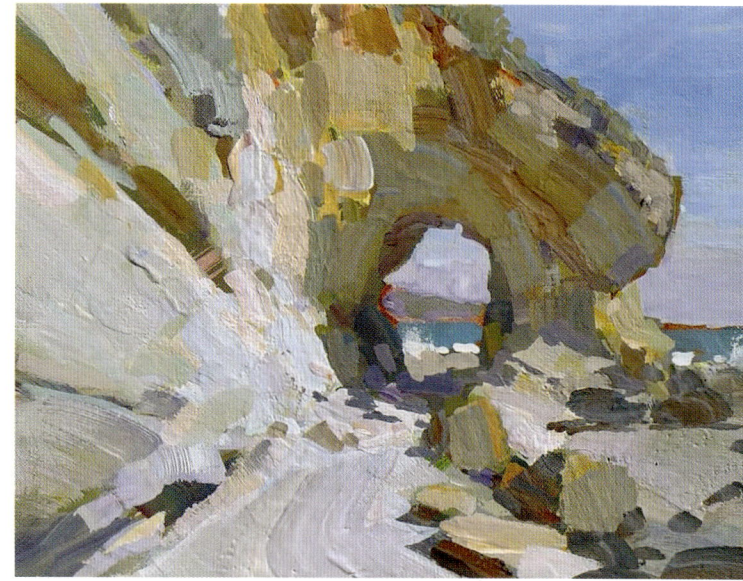

Mike Hernandez, *Keyhole Arch*, gouache on illustration board, 6" × 8" | 15.2 cm × 20.3 cm

Here's a much more complex (and interesting) iteration of light and shadow on rocks, with a symphony of color both in light and in shadow. You can see the cool-to-warm shift right around the keyhole: Reflected light from the ground warms the shadow in the overhead arch, and the floor in shadow is much bluer. Hernandez applies the later stages of gouache in thick impasto strokes.

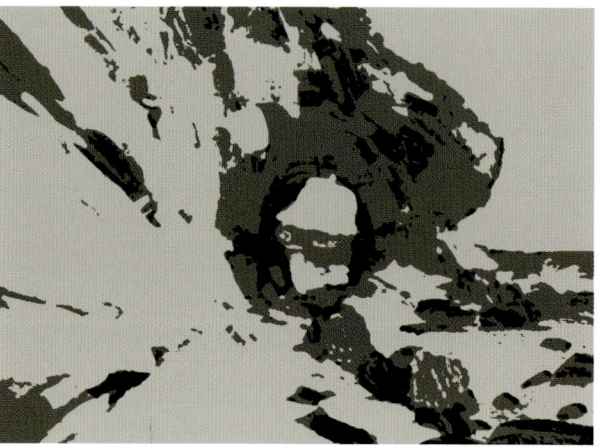

Value analysis of *Keyhole Arch*.

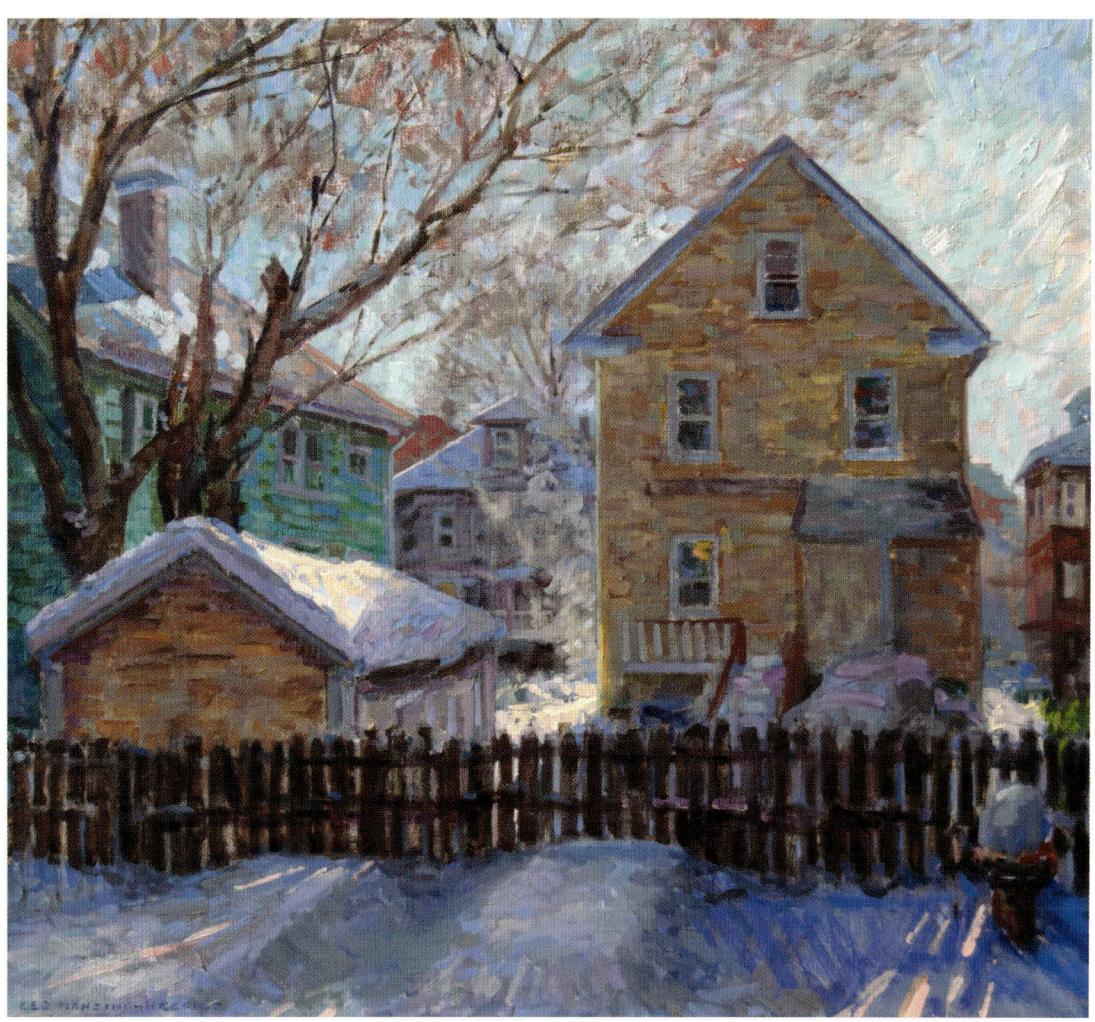

Leo Mancini-Hresko, *January*, oil on canvas, 26" × 29" | 66 cm × 73.7 cm

Broken color in the shadows, as well as the value range in shadow, indicates the amount of light in this winter scene.

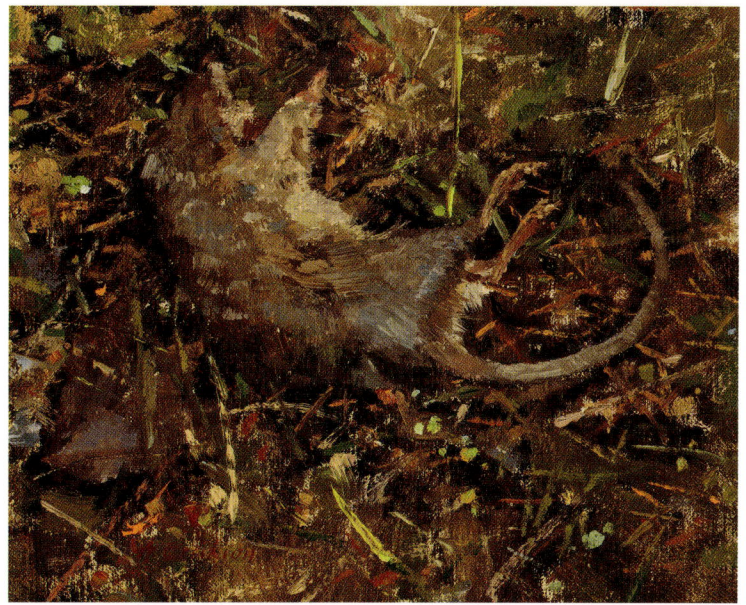

Aimee Erickson, *Rat*, oil on muslin panel, 8" × 10" | 20.3 cm × 25.4 cm

This painting has an overall low key, as the subject is in deep shade. The form turns into warm shadow; the most-lit areas are cooler.

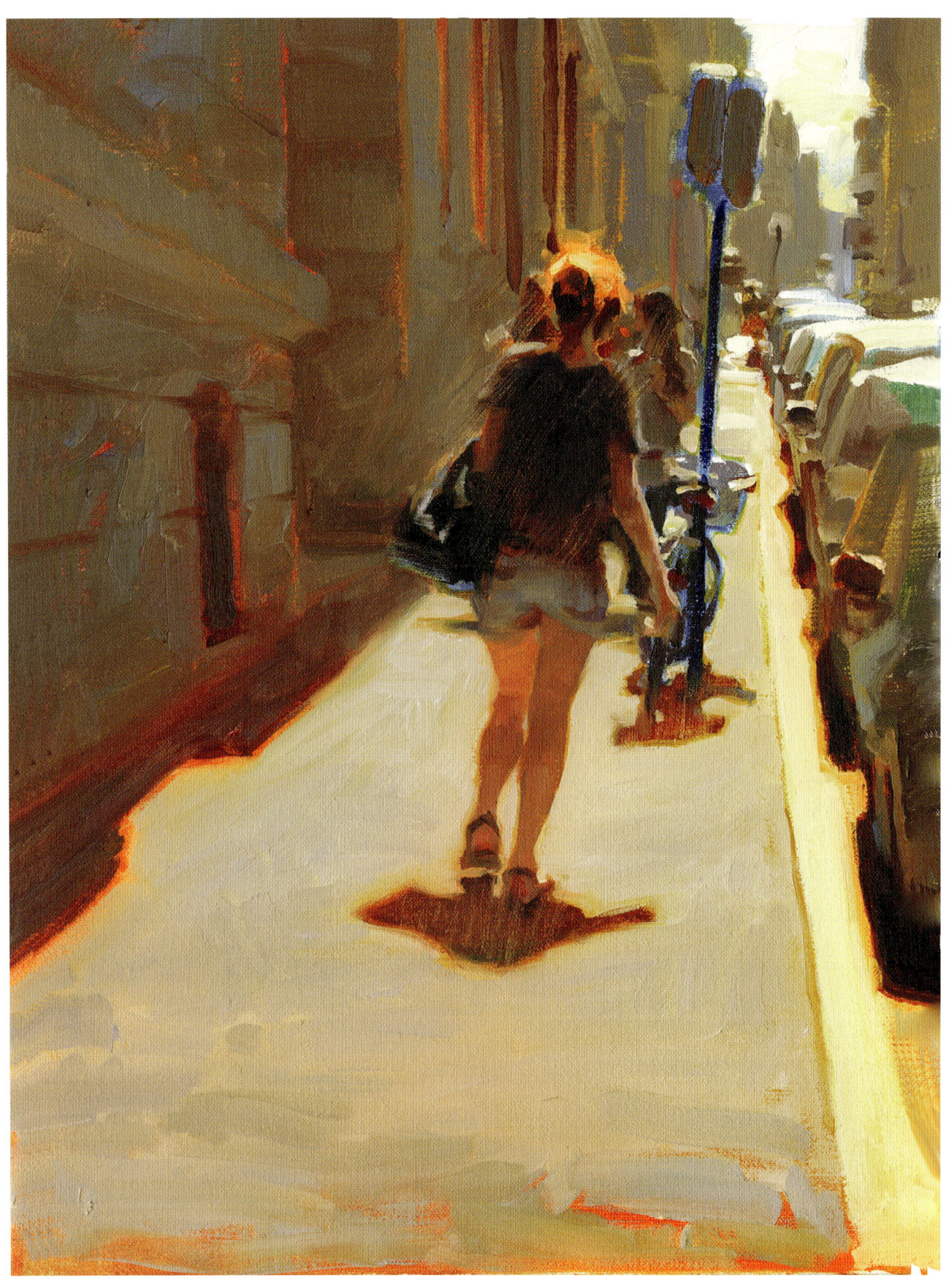

Kim English, *Walk through Paris*, oil, 16" × 12" | 40.6 cm × 30.5 cm

Within the shadow, downward-facing planes catch light reflected from the pavement.

6

BACKLIGHT

Backlighting occurs when the light is coming toward you. The best times are early or late in the day, facing the sun. Objects rise up against the light, silhouetted and unified by shadow. Any color happening within the shadow comes from reflected or ambient light. The ground plane tends to be lit, along with the edges of form turning toward the light. It's helpful to distinguish between rim light, when the background is in shadow and only the rim of the object is lit, and *contre-jour*, or "against the light," when the background is a field of light that merges into that lit rim. Cast shadows come toward us on the ground and can be used as a perspective device. Objects that are solid and opaque, like buildings, block the light. Semitransparent objects, like the sails on a sailboat, laundry on a clothesline, or even trees in some circumstances, transmit light like stained glass. Understanding the phenomenon helps you know what to look for.

Painting into the sun has some challenges that need to be worked out, starting with the sun in your eyes. Obviously, you can't look into the sun for two hours. Find a shady spot, wear a hat, and consider facing away from the subject, glancing over your shoulder to get information.

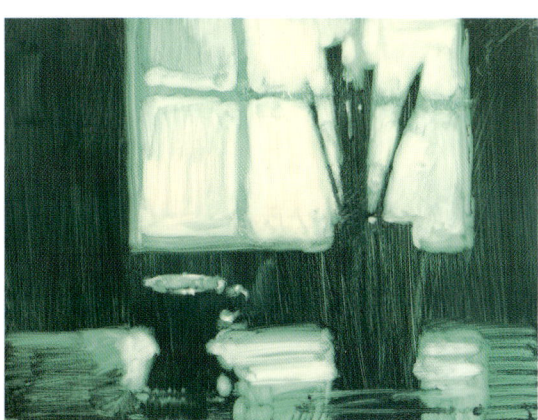

A straightforward study of backlighting, dividing light from shadow using the rubout technique. The teacup is rim-lit; the paintbrushes are contre-jour.

RIM LIGHT

FACING THE LIGHT WITH BACKGROUND IN SHADOW

Rim light is a scenario that is mostly shadow. The background is shadow, and the object is all shadow except for its rim. Reflected and ambient light are the source of any color in the shadow areas.

In *Coffee Cup*, at right, the cup and saucer are lit by an out-of-frame window. This is fundamentally a three-value composition, built on a color idea of warm shadows and cool light. On the table, the light concentrates where the saucer sits (because I like it that way, not because it always happens).

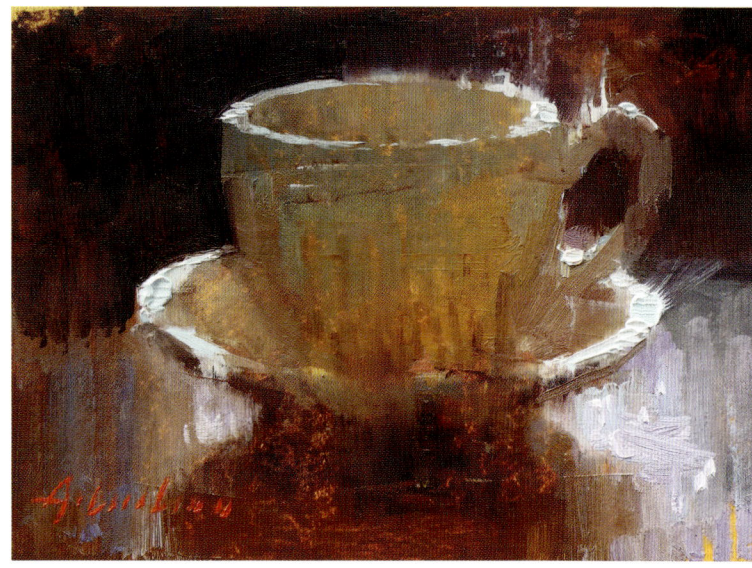

Aimee Erickson, *Coffee Cup*, oil on panel, 6" × 8" | 15.2 cm × 20.3 cm

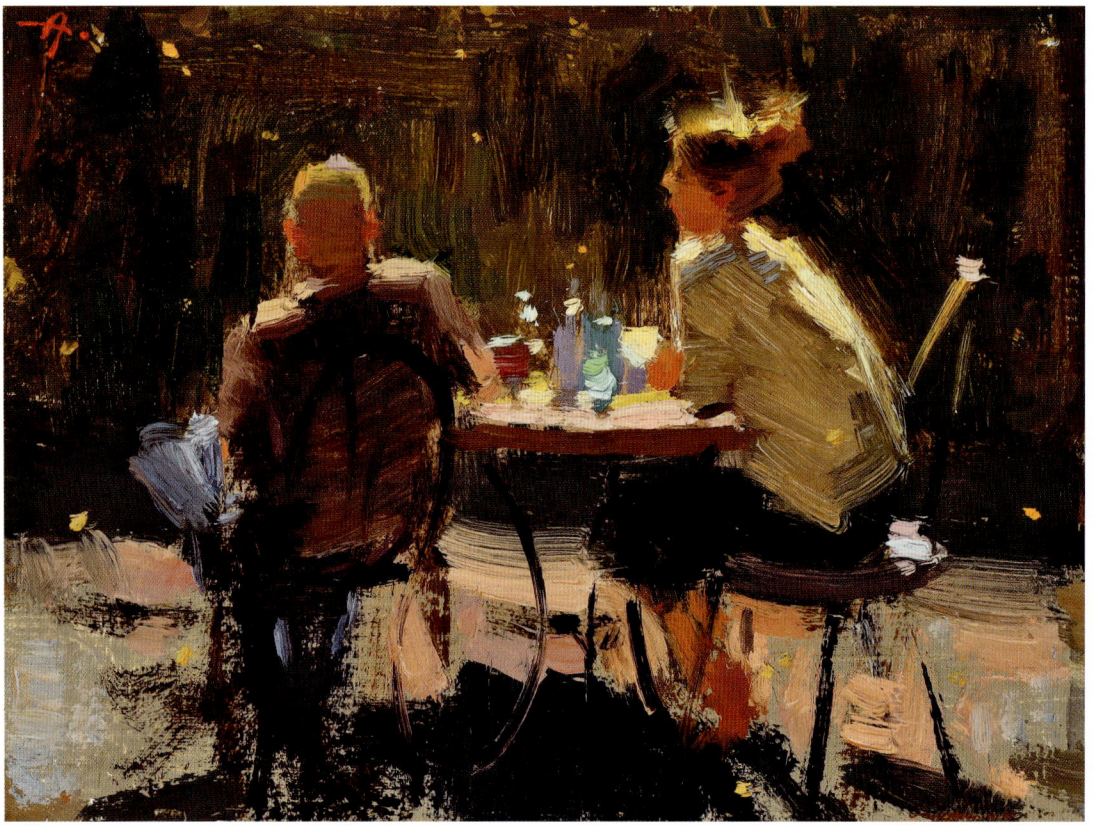

Aimee Erickson, *Wine-Tasting Couple*, oil on panel, 4" × 5" | 10.2 cm × 12.7 cm

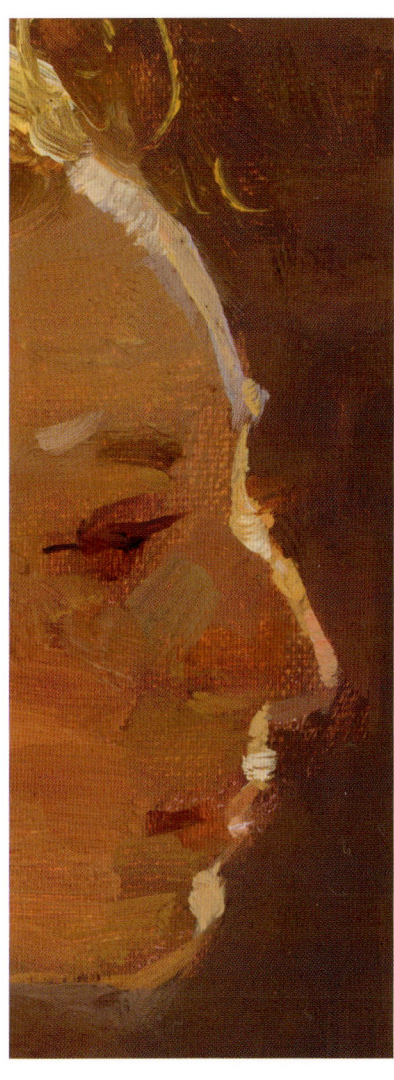

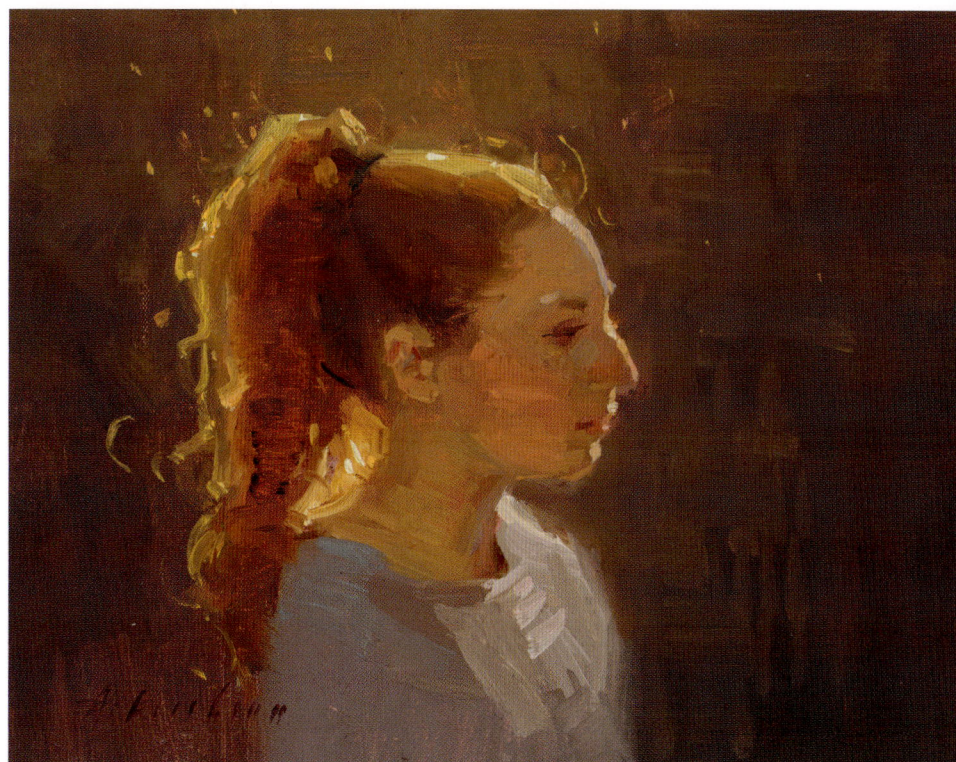

Aimee Erickson, *Backlit Redhead*, oil on canvas panel,
9" × 12" | 22.9 cm × 30.5 cm

Light on the rim is not just a stripe. A plane that turns more gradually or
flatter can hold more light; the underside or a swifter turn holds less. Here,
the rim light varies in color, width, and value to describe the planes of the
face—bone is hard, flesh is soft, hair is like smoke.

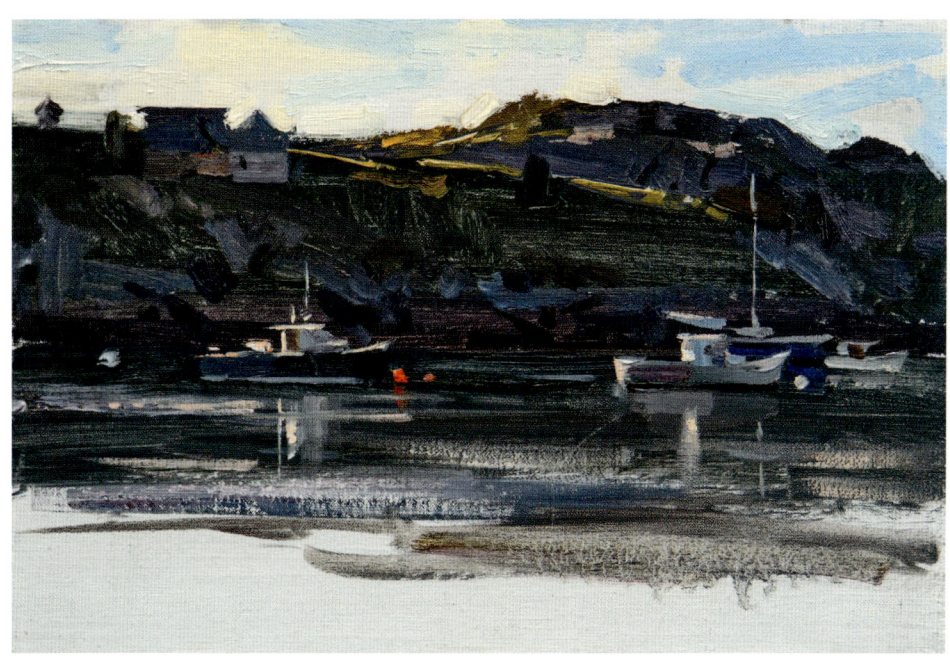

Mitch Baird, *Monhegan
View (unfinished)*, oil
on linen panel, 8" × 12" |
20.3 cm × 25.4 cm

Raking light can take
on the qualities of
rim light.

CONTRE-JOUR:
AGAINST THE LIGHT

BACKLIT OBJECT AGAINST LIGHT

Contre-jour (pronounced "contra-zhoor") is backlighting where the figure is set against the sky or a lit surface. The rim lighting is still there, but merges with the background value, so we look for the silhouette to hold the shape. (A similar scenario is a figure in shadow, silhouetted against the sky.)

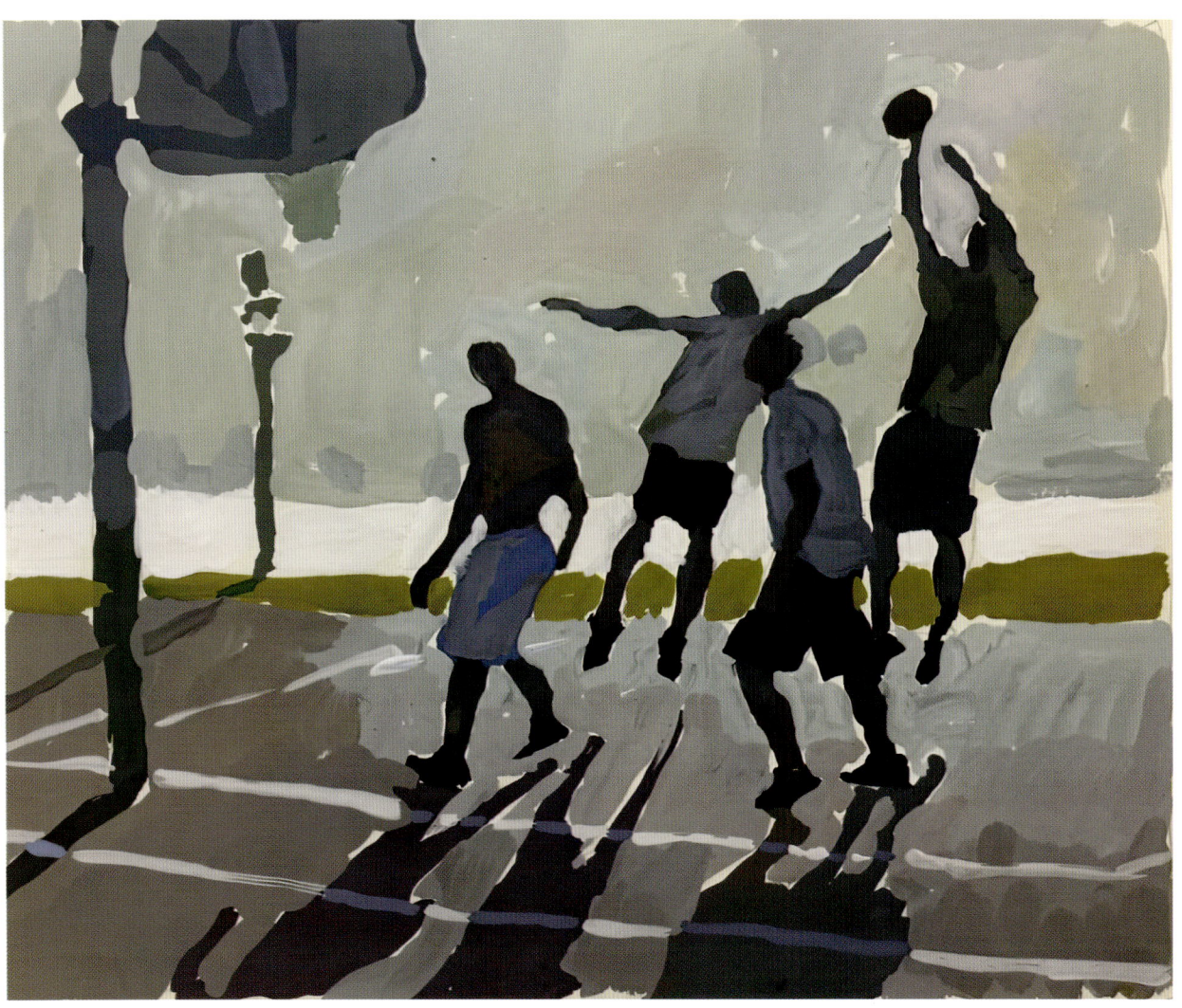

Peggi Kroll Roberts, *Laguna Beach Basketball*, gouache on acid-free paper, 9" × 12" | 22.9 cm × 30.5 cm

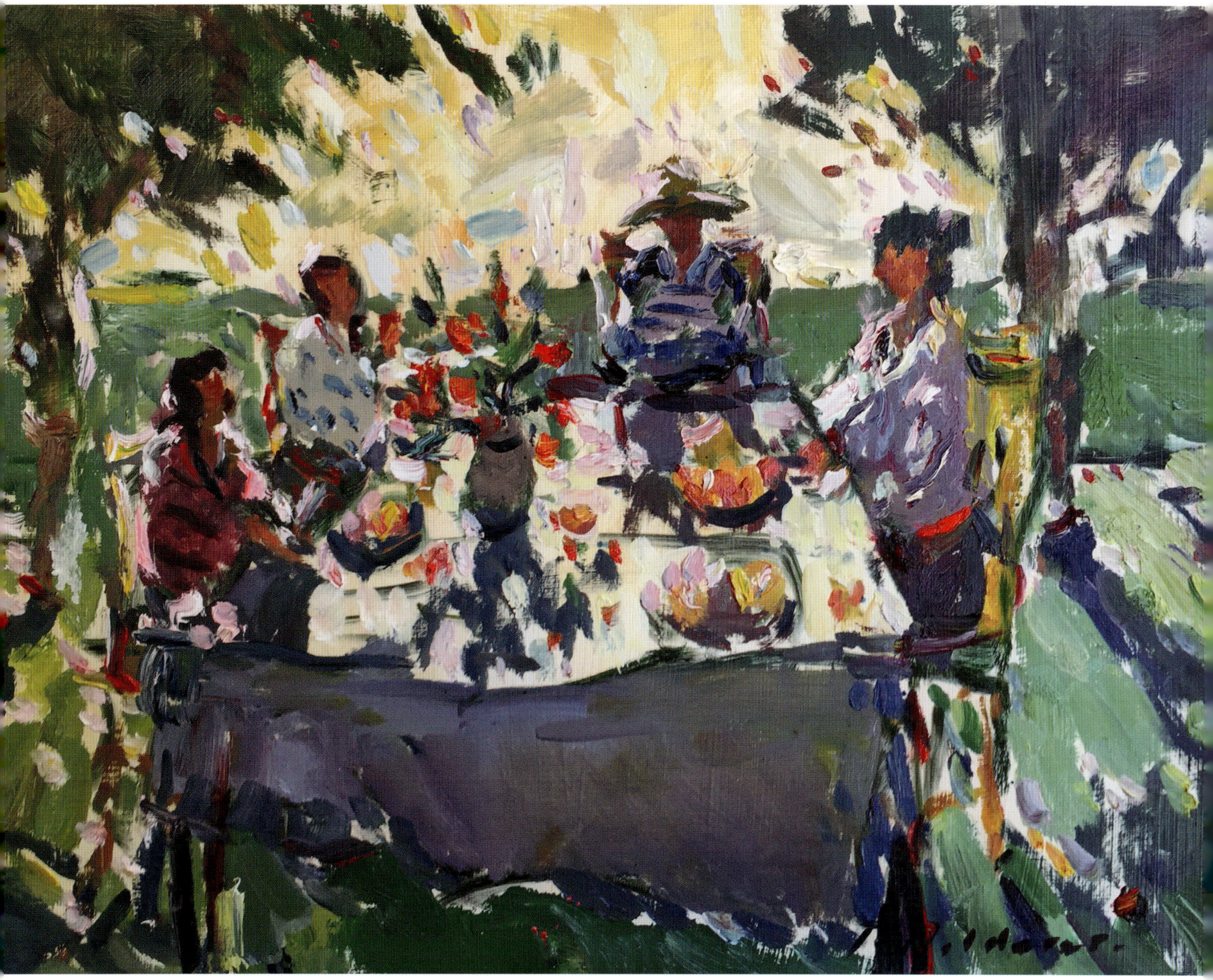

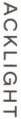

Tom Balderas, *Figures at a Table*, oil on canvas, 16" × 20" | 40.6 cm × 50.8 cm

Often, contre-jour and rim light will occur in the same scene. For the sake of simplicity, the artist may decide to leave out a lit rim and state the object as silhouetted: dark against light.

If you want to understand something, don't look for exceptions. Look for circumstances where the principle applies.

TRANSMITTED LIGHT

LIGHT COMING THROUGH AN OBJECT

A phenomenon that often accompanies backlighting is *transmitted light*. When an object is semitransparent and the light is bright, some light passes through, causing an effect like stained glass. This is an opportunity for color. In shadow, since it's less lit, we look for color to be less revealed, so the chroma will be lower. But transmitted light takes on a warmer, more saturated color than you would otherwise see in shadow. Be careful not to raise the value too much or you'll destroy the form by breaking up your shadow shapes.

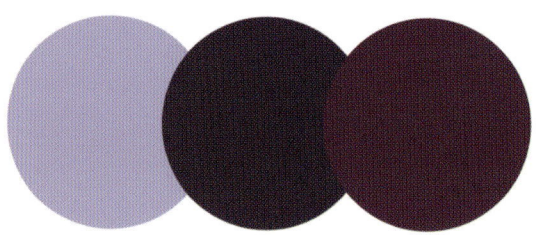

Average lit color, shadow color, and transmitted light color of the purple lawn chair.

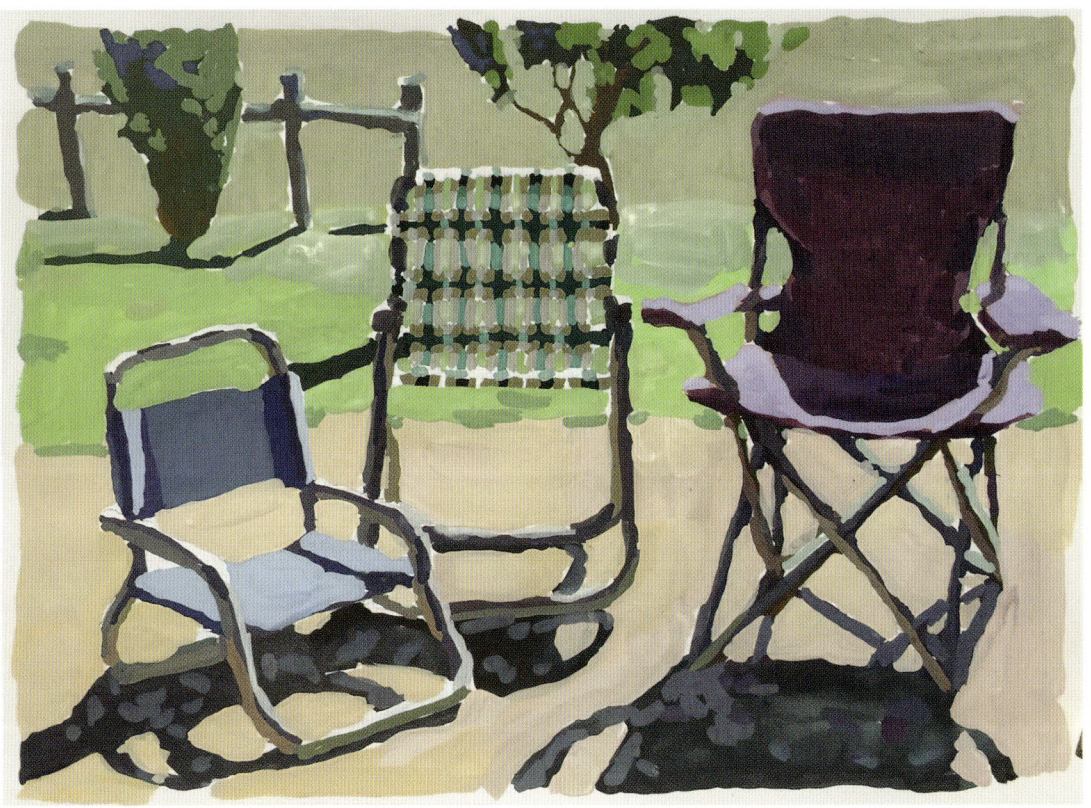

Peggi Kroll Roberts, *Three Chairs*, gouache on paper, 9" × 12" | 22.9 cm × 30.5 cm

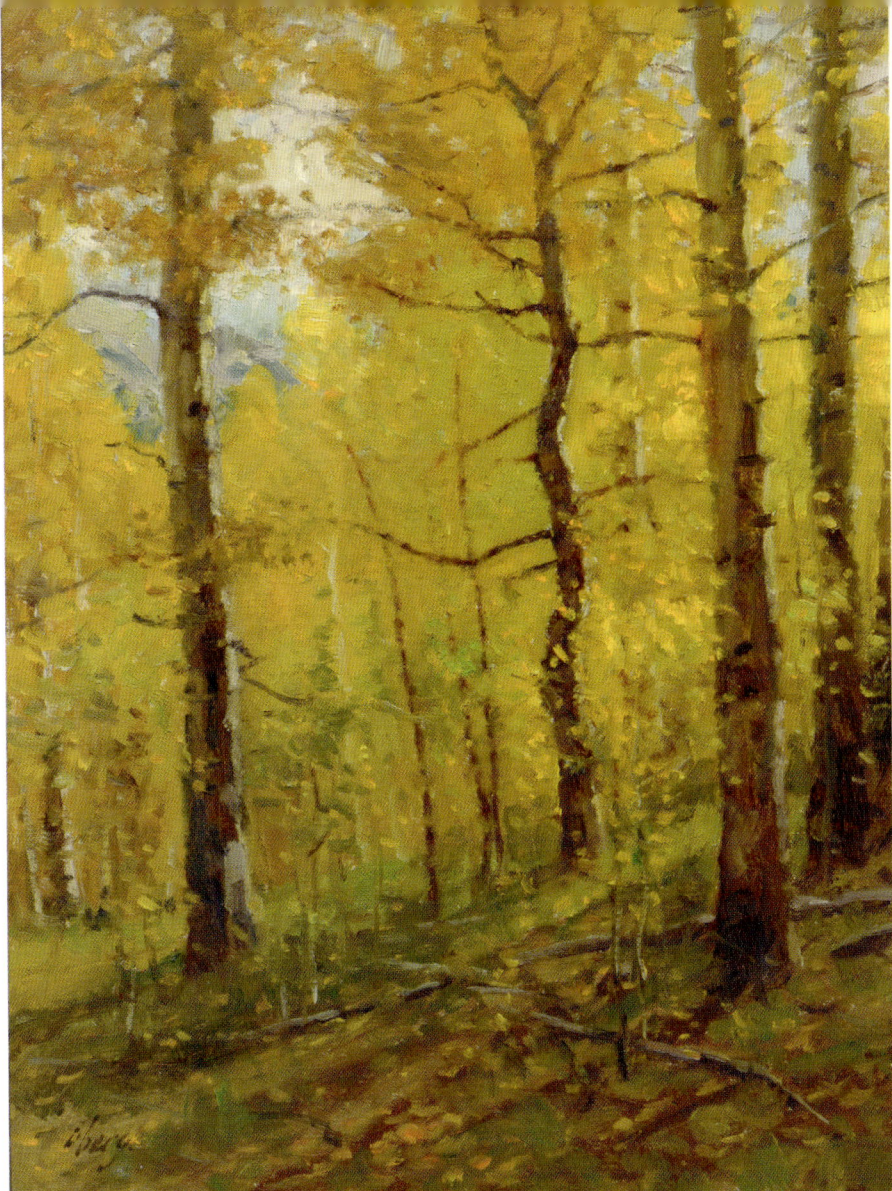

Ralph Oberg, *La Plata Aspens*, oil on linen, 16" × 12" | 40.6 cm × 30.5 cm

An entire grove of aspens glowing with transmitted light, or, in other words, the aspen leaves block all but the yellow light.

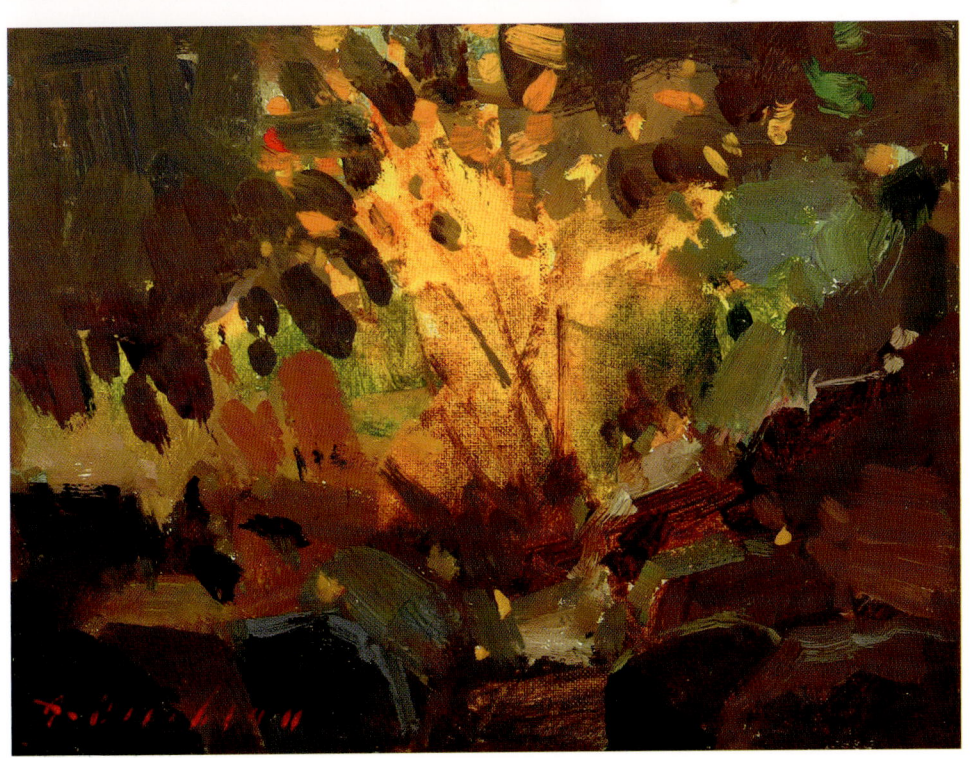

Study of a shrub transmitting light.

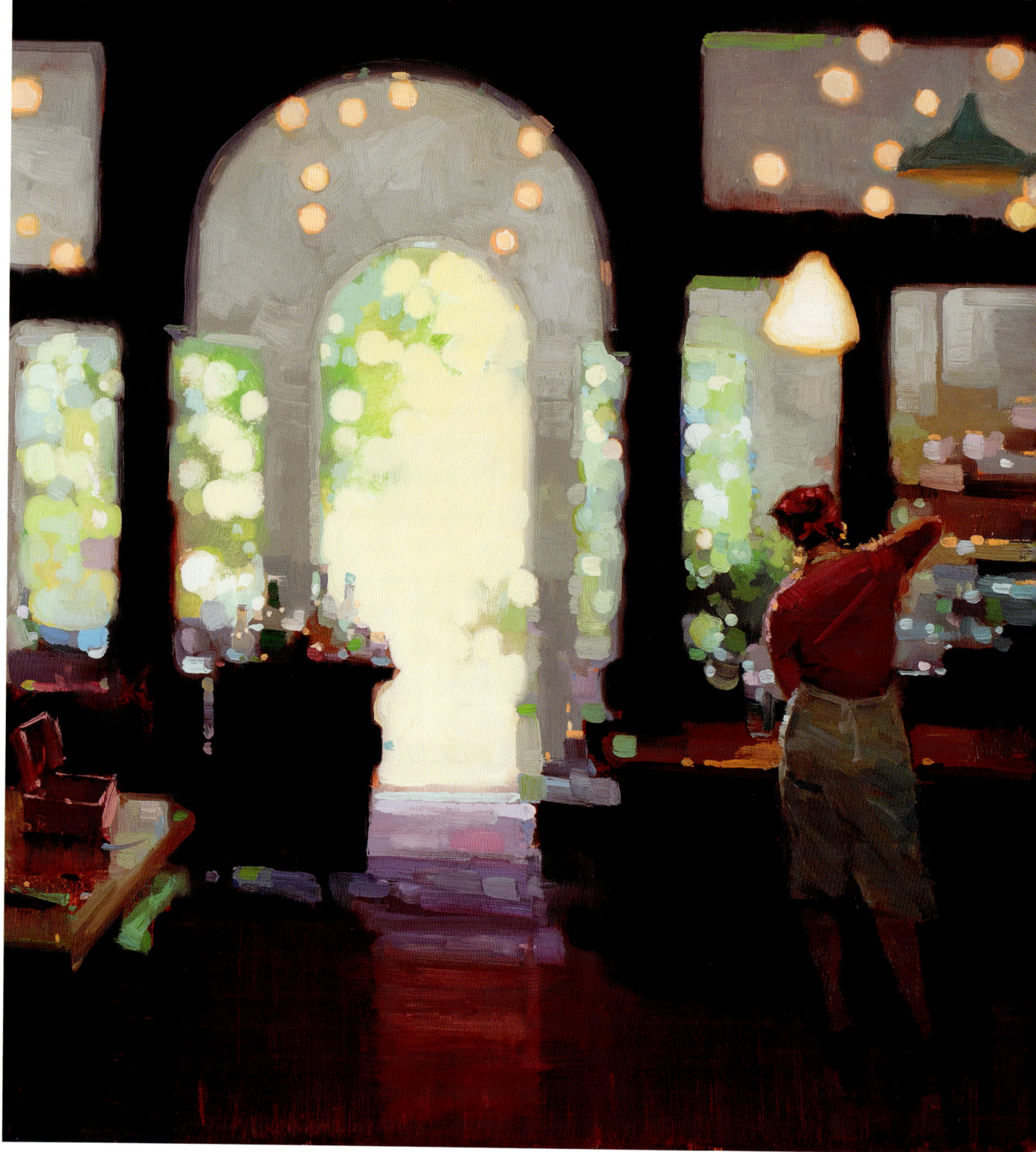

Aimee Erickson, *Interior, Cake Shop* (detail), oil on panel, 23" × 32" | 58.4 cm × 81.3 cm

INTERIORS AND BACKLIGHTING

One place where we commonly encounter backlighting is in an interior looking toward a window. In this scenario, a good strategy is to limit the world outside the window to a very high, narrow value range.

TECHNIQUE:
A LOOSE START

PATRICK LEE:
UNDER THE BIG BARN AT WINTERSPRING

Here's a demonstration of an interior with a window, using a general-to-specific approach rather than starting with a linear division of the canvas. In this painting, Patrick Lee starts very loosely, then works to gradually build color relationships and resolution of shapes. The canvas is 30 inches (76.2 cm) tall and white to start with.

- Palette: Alizarin Crimson, Cadmium Red Deep, Cadmium Orange, Cadmium Lemon, Cobalt Teal, Ultramarine Blue, and Titanium Zinc White.

"This painting might not work. You know? You're just working. You just go with the flow. It doesn't always work. Basically, you don't know."

—PATRICK LEE

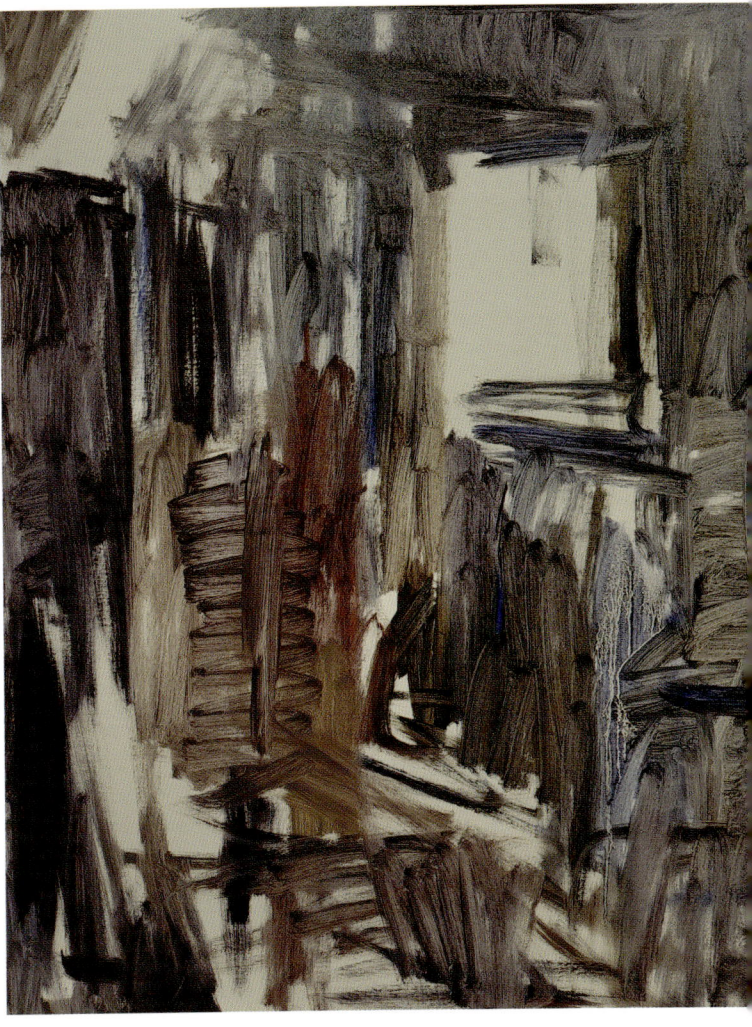

1. Start. No drawing—Lee just starts tossing paint on there, moving from one color to another, sticking with transparent pigments for the most part. Transparent pigments best describe deep shadows.

continued ▶

BACKLIGHT

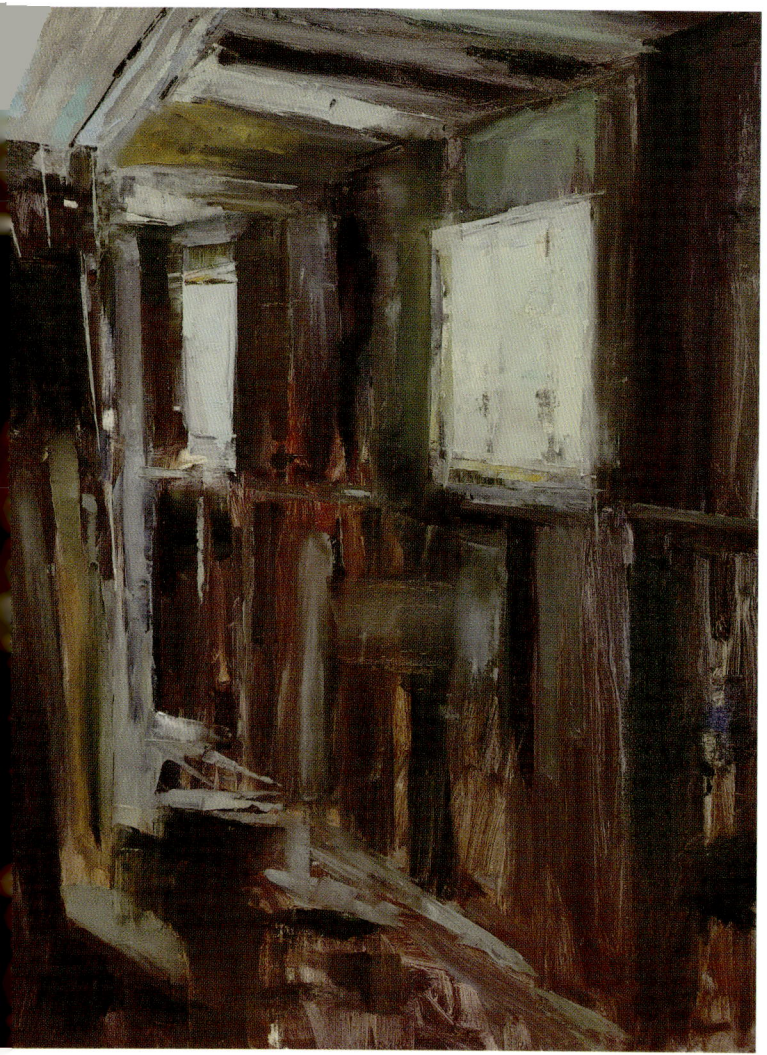

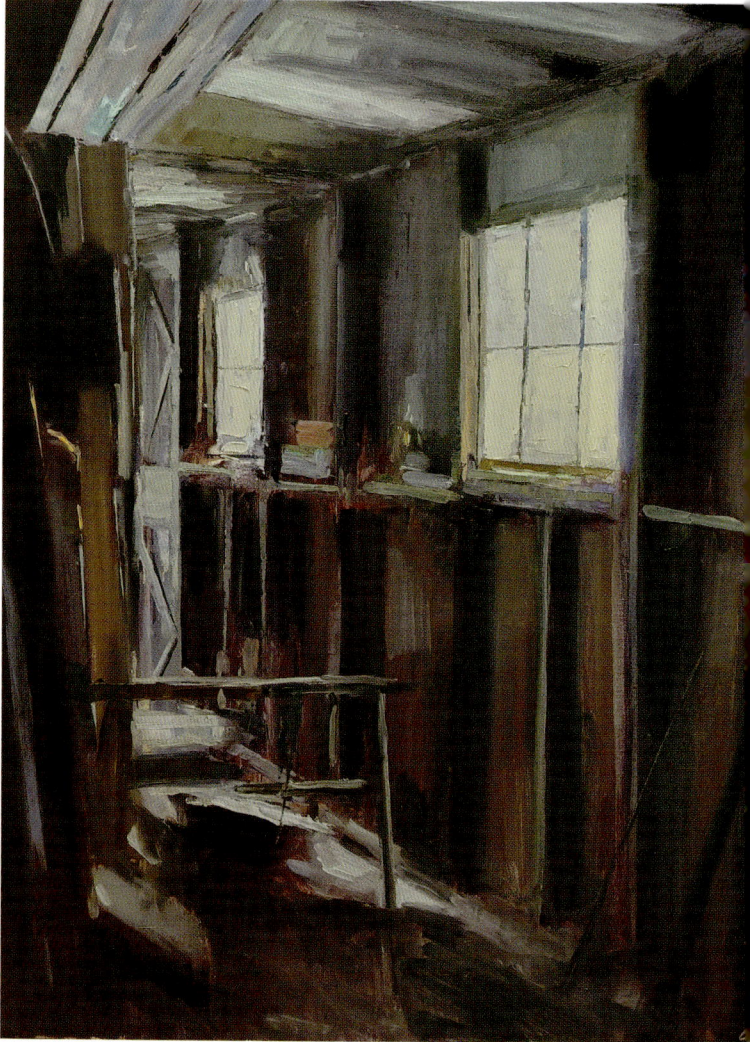

Patrick Lee, *Under the Big Barn at Winterspring*, oil on canvas, 30" × 24" | 76.2 cm × 61 cm

2. Gradual development. Bouncing light around the interior by building some opacity into those shadows.

3. The finished painting. Consistent with a general-to-specific approach, Lee works the larger relationships first and saves tiny elements, like the window mullions, for the end. This painting took about five hours.

"I like it to look like a dream or a memory. Like you're driving away and glance over your shoulder."

—PATRICK LEE

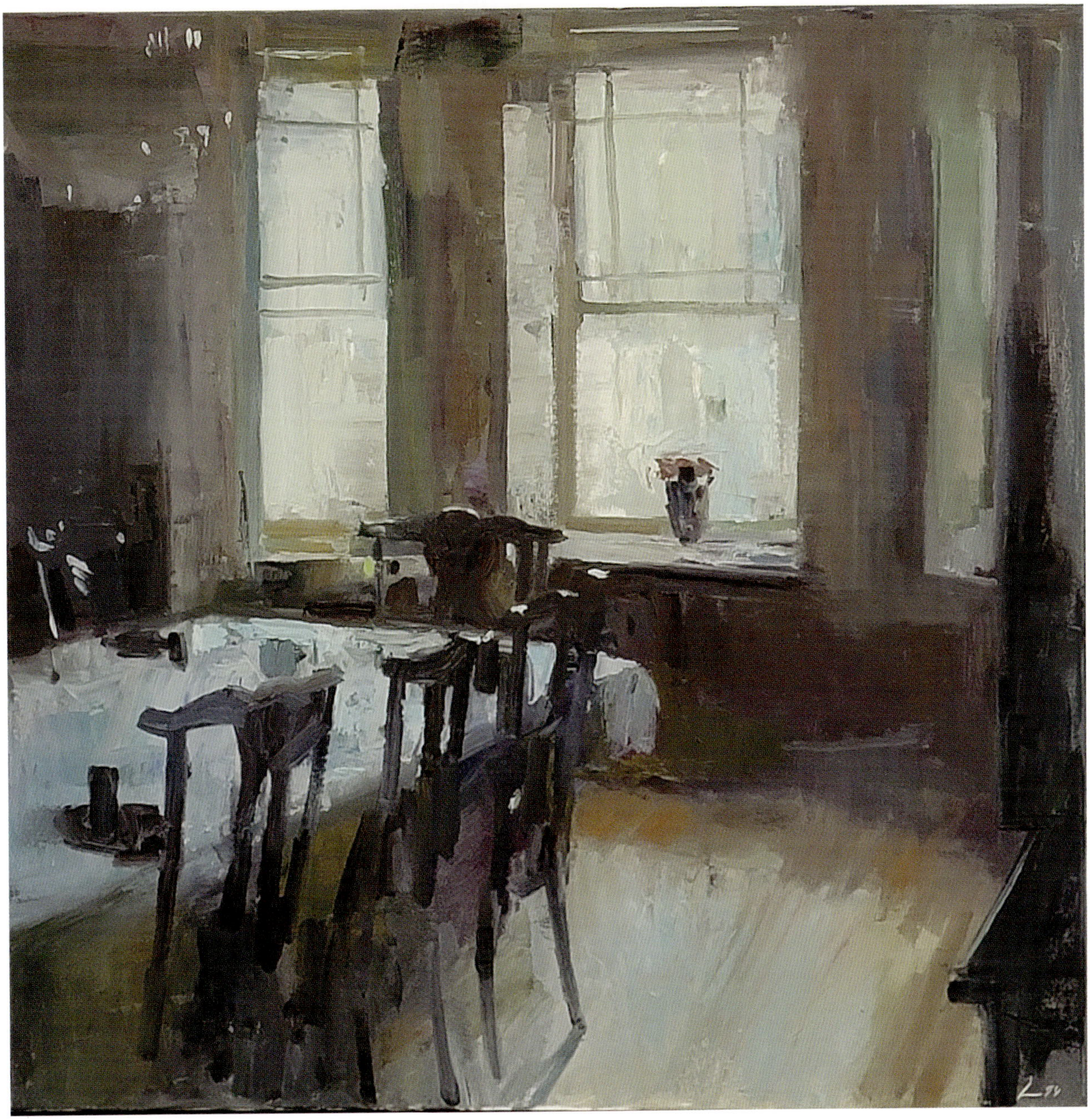

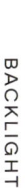

Patrick Lee, *Breakfast Table*, oil on canvas, 24" × 24" | 61 cm × 61 cm

A different room, but the same process and lighting phenomenon: in a dark interior looking toward a window.

PAINTING MAKEOVER:
PERSPECTIVE

This makeover is of a student's painting of a red rock mountain in Arizona, United States of America. Original intention: show the striking beauty of a remarkable mountain-shape across the desert.

What's working well: Overall, the color harmony is lovely, and there's a nice feeling of desert plants and climate. But what could be done to make the mountain look bigger, more impressive, and also distant? What principles can be applied to make more of the idea?

- **Aerial perspective.** The mountain needs to be significantly lighter in value than the foreground. Comparing shadows to shadows, the mountain shadows need to be much lighter and bluer than the foreground shadows, which should be dark and lean more red/yellow (warmer). In the flat, lit, shrubby plain of the landscape, the distant colors should be grayer/less colorful than the foreground colors.

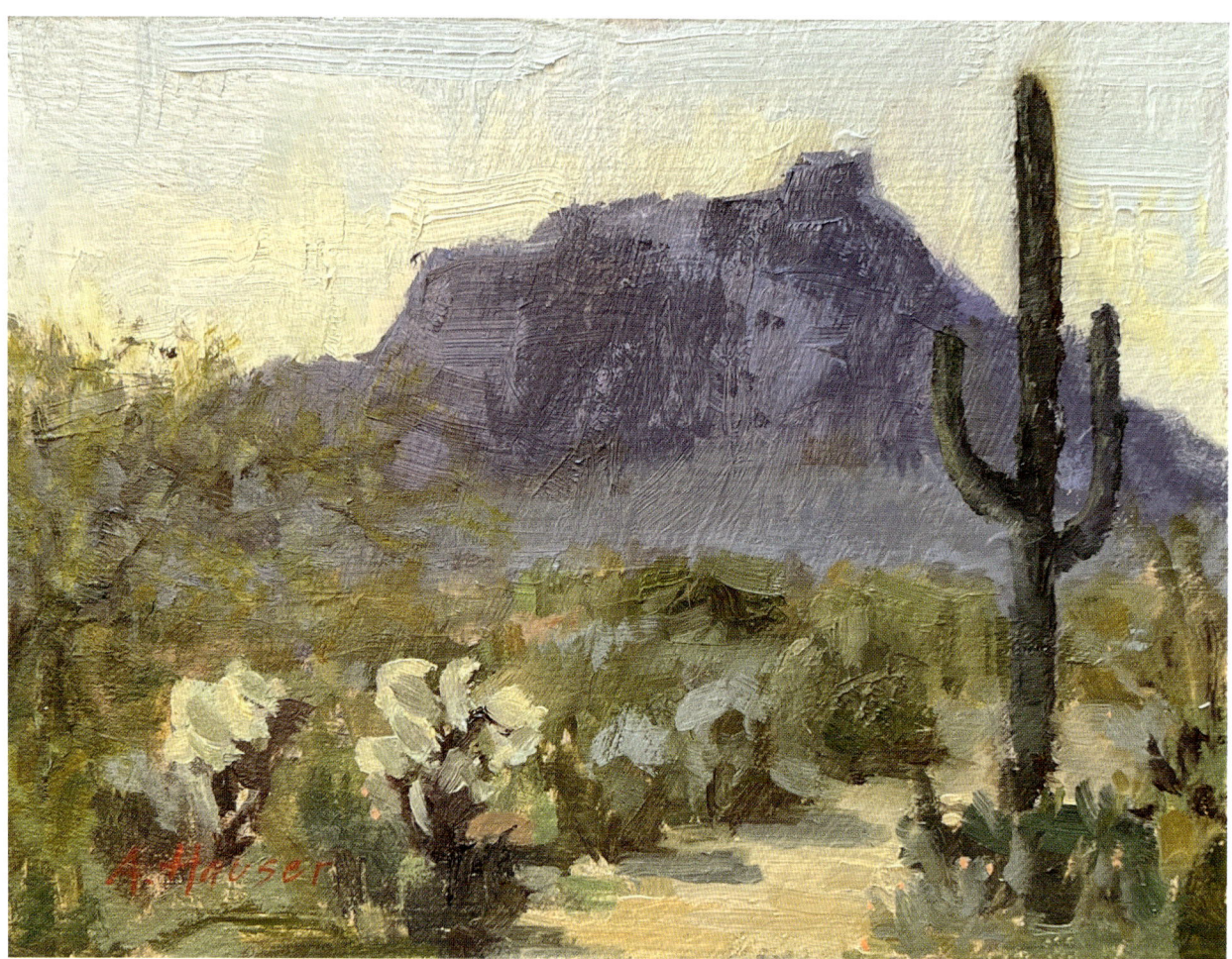

A. Hauser, *Red Rock Mountain*, oil on canvas panel, 9" × 12" | 22.9 cm × 30.5 cm

Before.

- **Size and placement.** We want it to be clear that the mountain is the main attraction and that the shrubbery and cacti are there to lead in and frame it. In the original, there's some tension between the saguaro and the mountain. A little more space between them might do the trick, so I move the mountain a little toward the center of the picture.
- **Advancing the foreground with more development.** Those cholla are such interesting shapes and developing them should give more character to the scene as well as doing more to advance the foreground. I'm also reinforcing and defining the foreground shadow areas. Darker shadows advance.
- **Scale.** Adding more saguaro—tiny vertical elements—in the middle distance give a greater sense of how vast the landscape is, how the land extends across the desert floor before the mountain rears up. These little guys made a big difference—the mountain suddenly felt enormous by comparison.

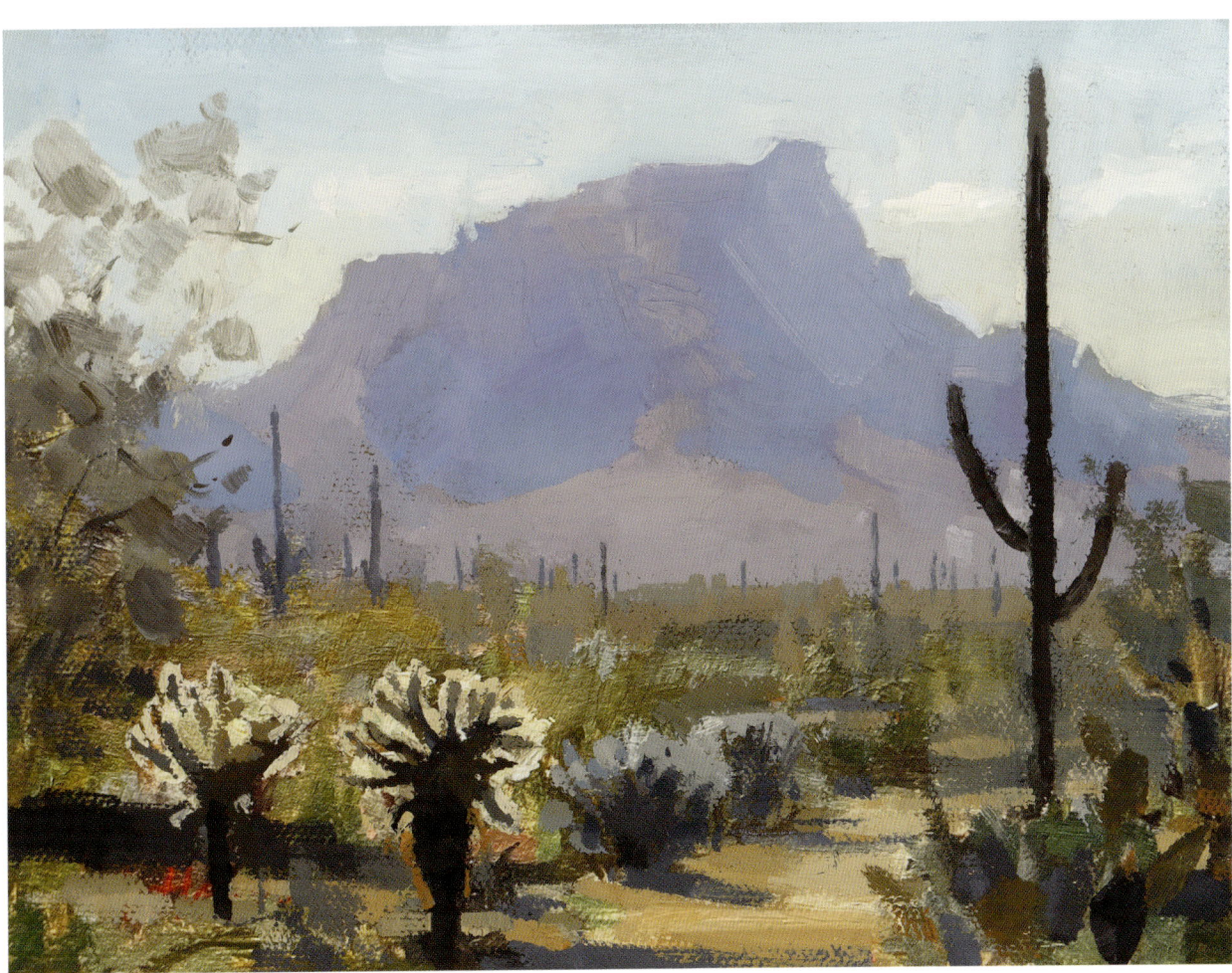

After.

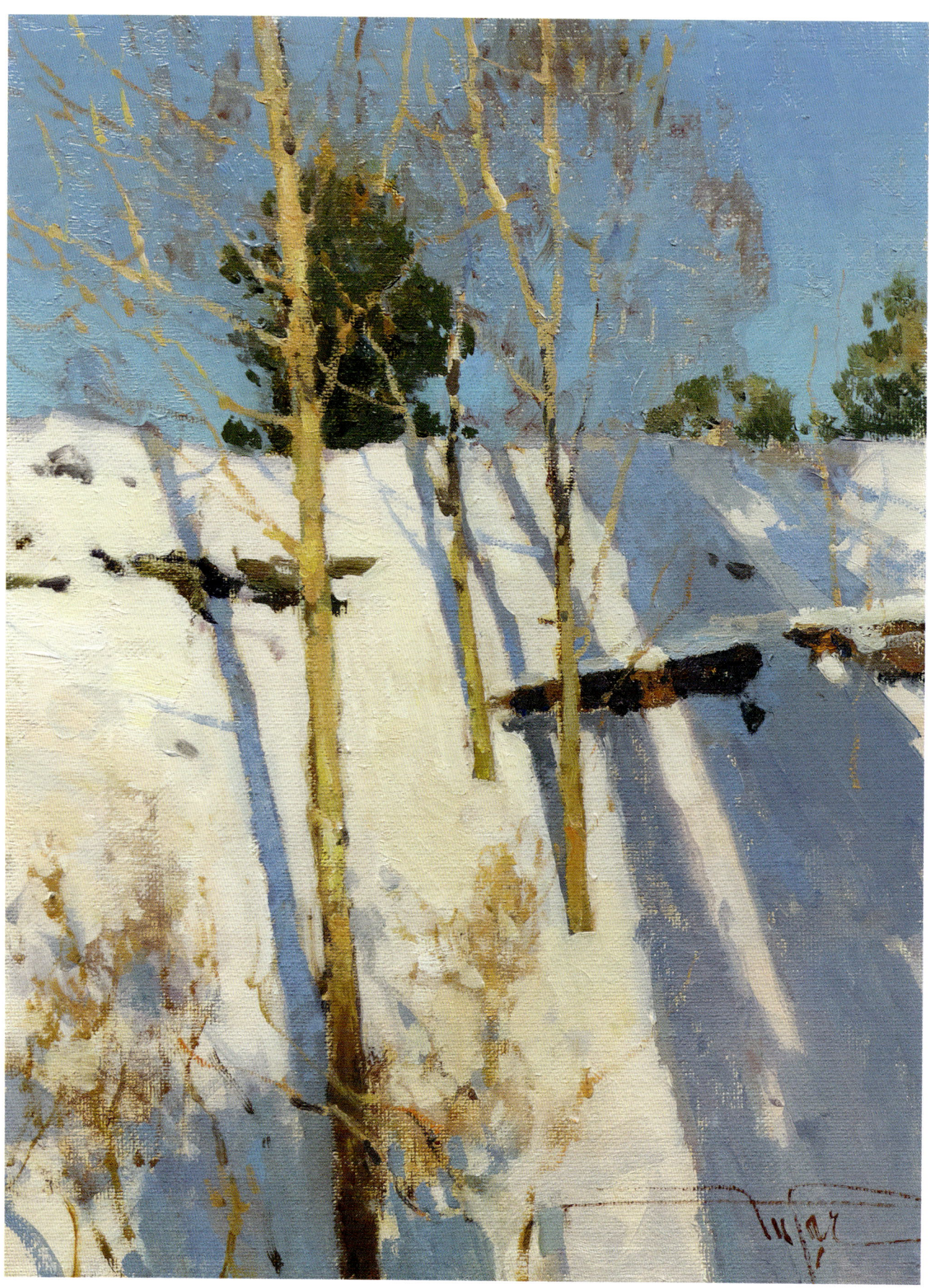

Zufar Bikbov, *Golden Light on Trees*, oil on panel, 12" × 9" | 30.5 cm × 22.9 cm

7

FRONT LIGHT

Front light happens when the sun is low in the sky and you turn your back on it. Any upright form before you rises up to face the sun: The entire form receives light. Highlights occur in the center of the form. Surface contours diminish or disappear, and the object looks flat (as opposed to in raking light, where every bump and wrinkle is revealed). Everything facing us is facing the light, and shadows fall away from us. (If you turn slightly to one side or the other, you'll see objects that are three-quarters lit. True front lighting means that the sun, the painter, and the subject are lined up.)

In the example opposite, with the sun behind us and the shadows falling away from us, everything before us is front lit. The direction of the cast shadow tells us the steepness of the hillside.

Below are three value analyses, made digitally, which demonstrate the strength of the value patterns in the finished painting.

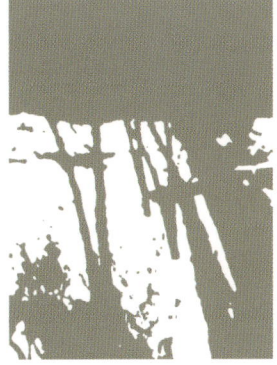 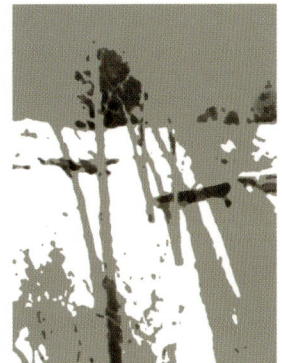 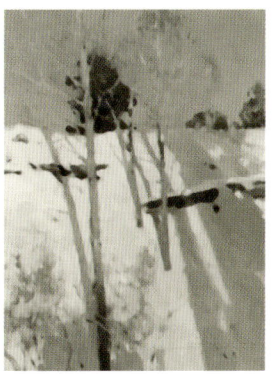

(Left) A two-value analysis of *Golden Light on Trees*, making the distinction between lit snow and everything else. **(Center)** With the darks added in. **(Right)** A desaturated version of the painting shows the modulation in a strong three-value structure.

FRONT LIGHT: A DRAMATIC FULLY LIT EFFECT

A good strategy for front lighting is to use a narrow value range to describe each object and to push all lit areas into a high key.

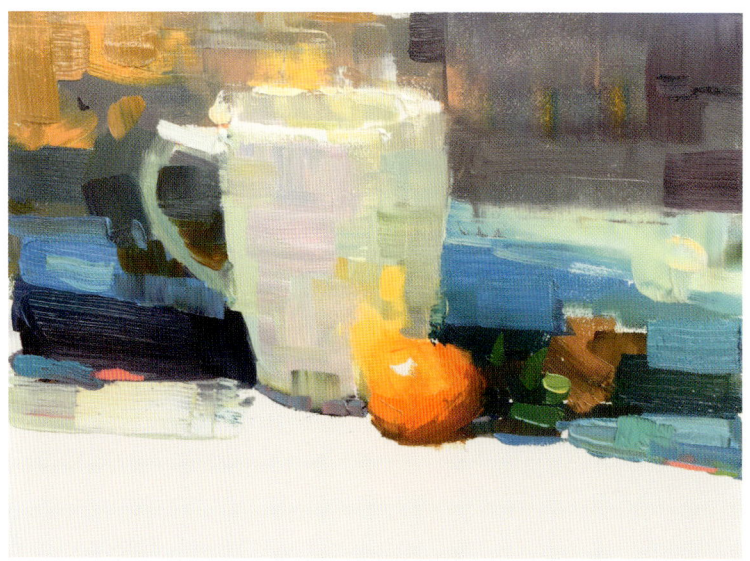

Aimee Erickson, *White Cup and Clementine*, oil on panel, 8" × 10" | 20.3 cm × 25.4 cm

A simple iteration of the front-lit phenomenon.

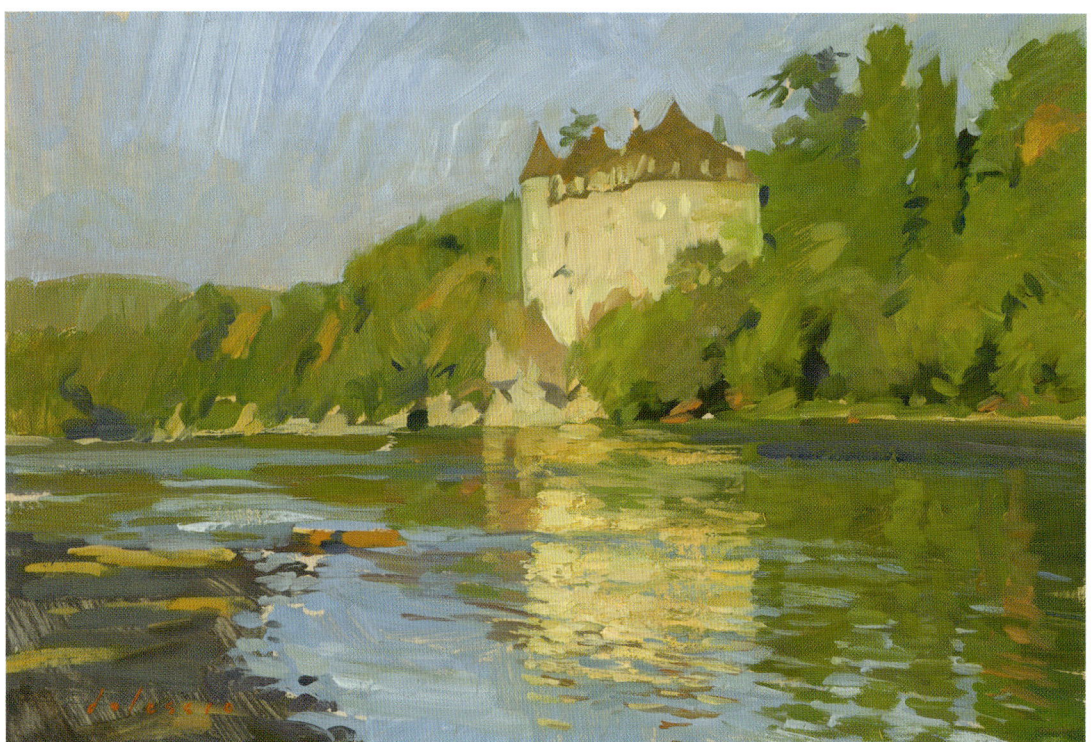

Marc Dalessio, *Afternoon Light, Château de la Treyne*, oil on panel, 7⁹⁄₁₀" × 11⁴⁄₅" | 20 cm × 30 cm

Same phenomenon—where the sun is low and behind the artist—but more complex. Note that local colors are used to distinguish between lit areas, and we get only little pockets of shadow.

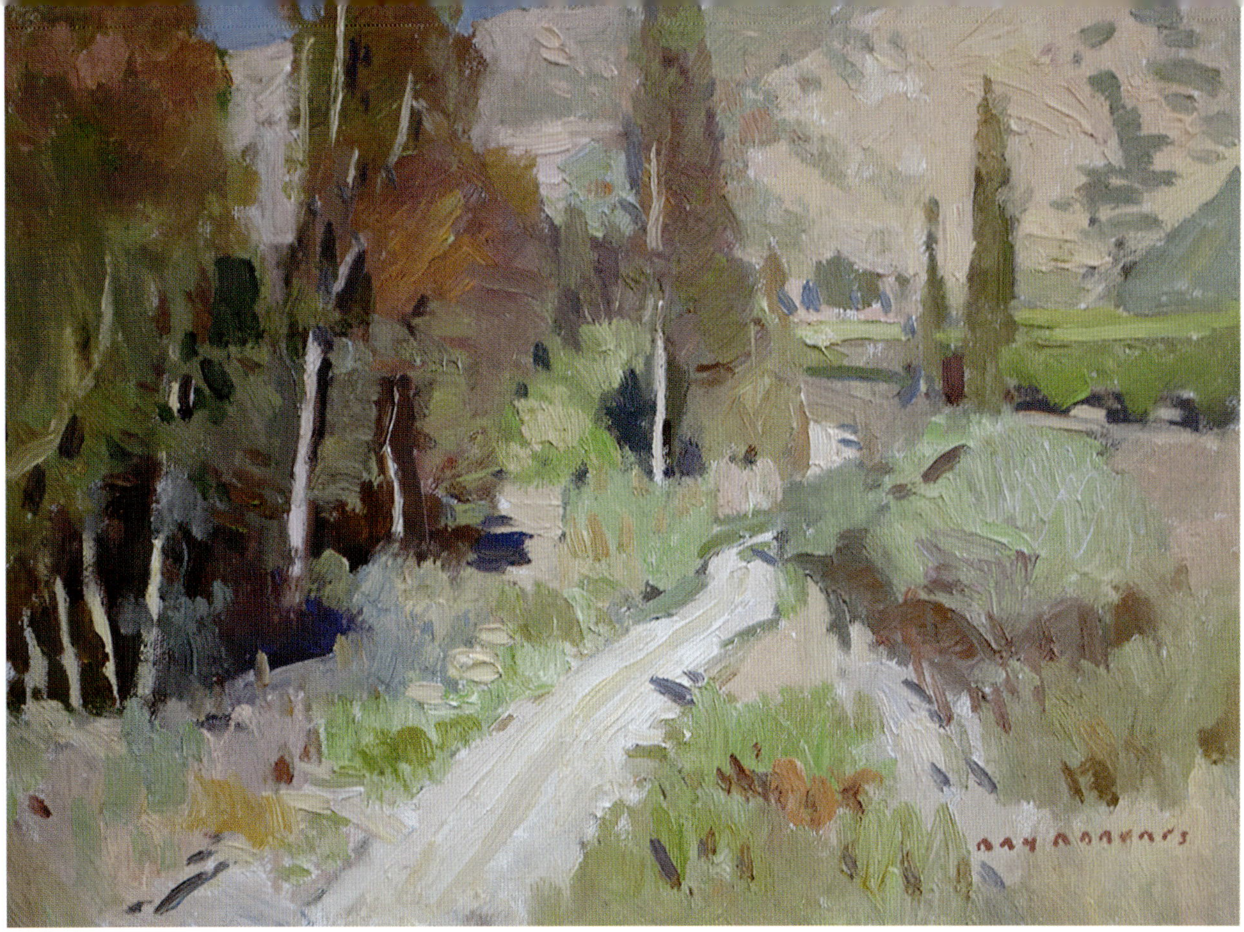

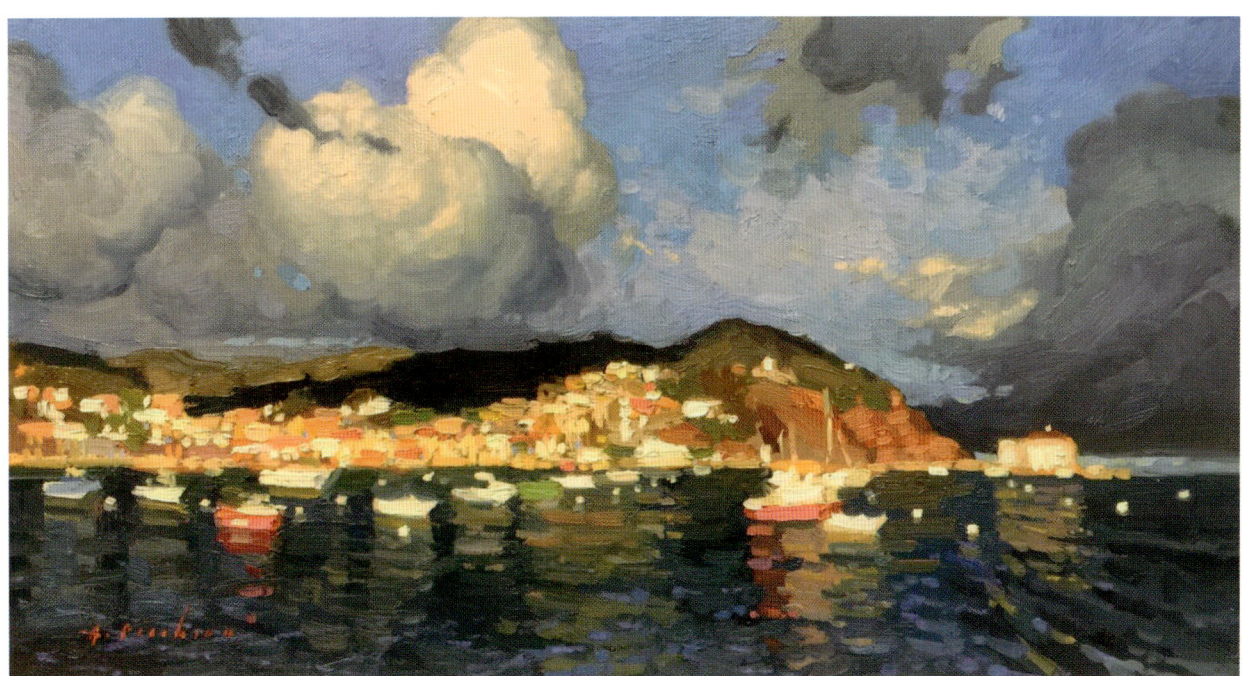

Ray Roberts, *East of Escondido*, oil on canvas, 12" × 16" | 30.5 cm × 40.6 cm

Aimee Erickson, *Winter in Avalon*, oil on linen panel, 8" × 16" | 20.3 cm × 40.6 cm

The lower the sun is, the more the angle of the light approaches horizontal. This means that the flat surface of the water is in grazing light. The boats and hillsides rise up to face the sun. Reflections go straight down.

SAME SUBJECT, DIFFERENT LIGHTING

NICHOLAS O'LEARY AND THE OAK TREE

Varying conditions of light have an enormous effect on the relationship of an object, or figure, to its surroundings, or background. In studio painting, this is the figure-ground relationship, and the idea applies in plein air painting as well. Is the figure lighter or darker than the background? More dramatic paintings result from this relationship being the product of light, rather than of local value.

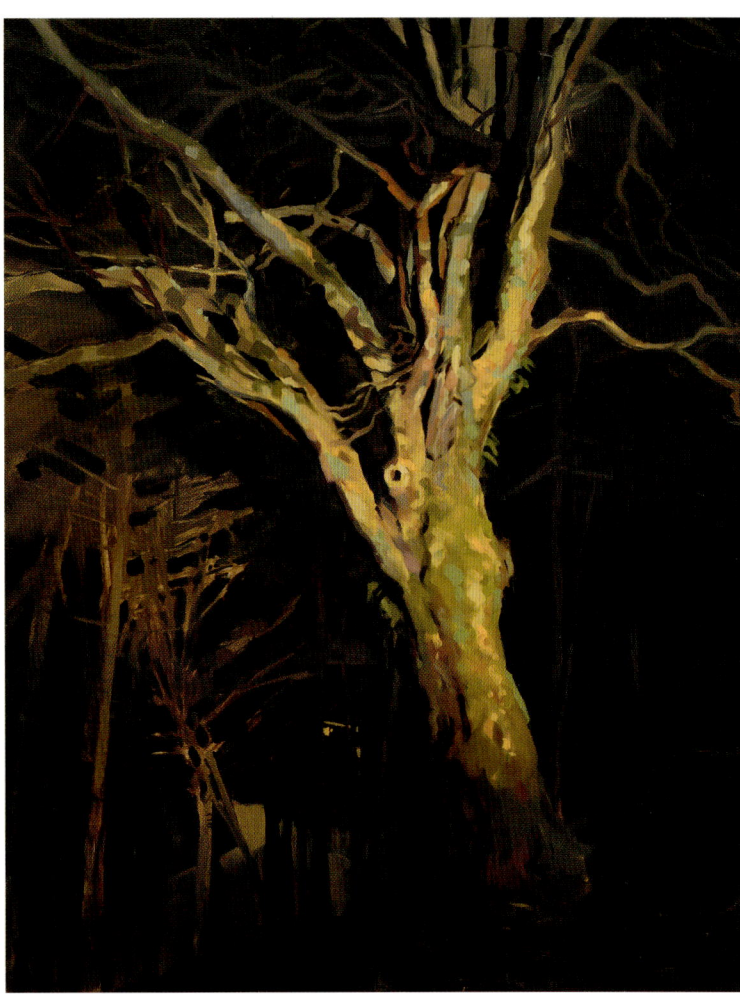

Nicholas O'Leary, *Great Oak, Night, Isdalen*, oil on canvas, 23 3/5" × 19 7/10" | 60 cm × 50 cm

Light figure against dark background. In this spectacular nocturne, the oak tree is lit up—front lit—against a nearly black background.

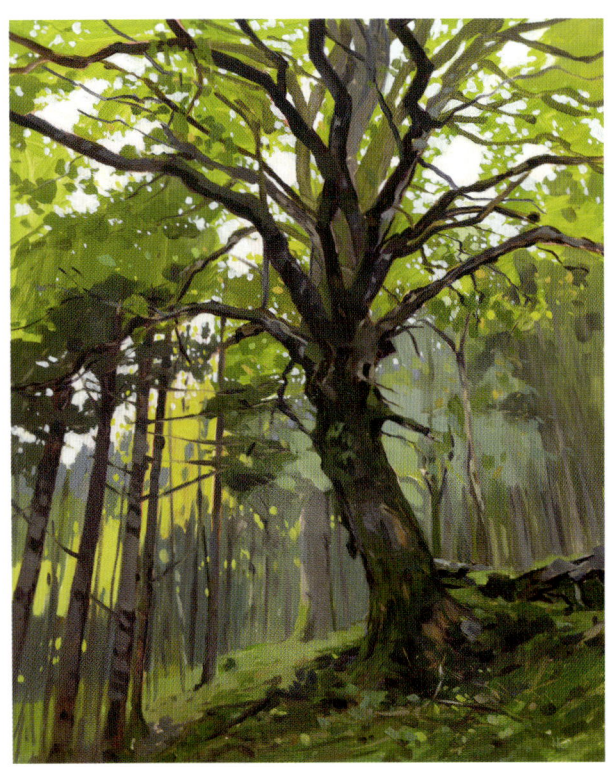

Nicholas O'Leary, *Great Oak, Autumn, Svartediket*, oil on canvas, 23 3/5" × 19 7/10" | 60 cm × 50 cm

Dark against light. The oak tree is in shadow against a backdrop of forest, which has been intentionally rendered in a value range lighter than the oak.

In each case, it's likely that these figure-ground relationships existed to some degree in nature. However, it is one hundred percent certain that Nicholas O'Leary decided how to structure these relationships in each painting.

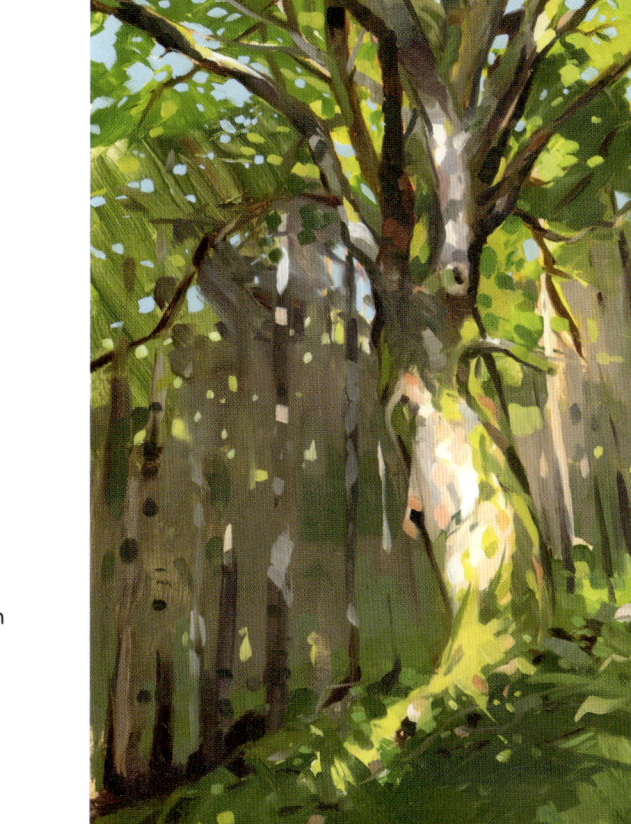

Nicholas O'Leary, *Great Oak, Summer*, oil on canvas, 23 ⅗" × 19 ⁷⁄₁₀" | 60 cm × 30 cm

Dappled light. Here, the foreground oak is not distinguished from the background by a simple value relationship. Its darks are darker than the trees behind, its lights are lighter, and the middle values exist in both the figure and the ground.

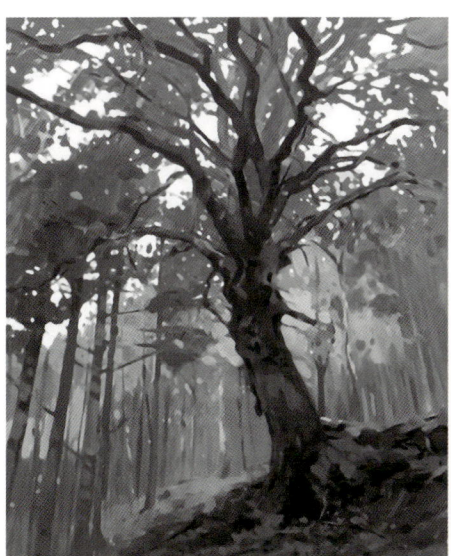 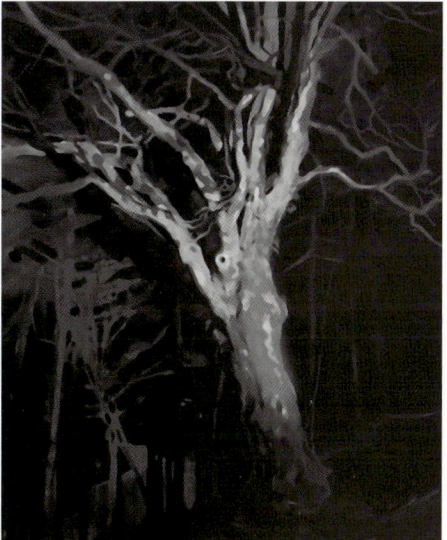 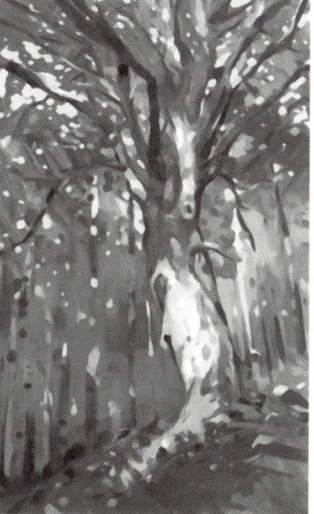

Value analyses of the three oak tree paintings.

TECHNIQUE:
DIRECT IMPASTO BRUSHWORK

ERIC JACOBSEN:
SUNLIT DESERT

Jacobsen is a very direct painter. In this demo, we see one of his common working methods: direct and rapid impasto paint application. This approach has some commonality with color-spot painting. Essentially, it's observe, decide, load the brush, lay down the paint. The first stroke has the same quality as the last.

- Palette: White, Cadmium Yellow Light, Yellow Ochre, Cadmium Orange, Cadmium Red Light, Alizarin Crimson, Ultramarine Blue, Cerulean Blue Hue, and Phthalo Blue.

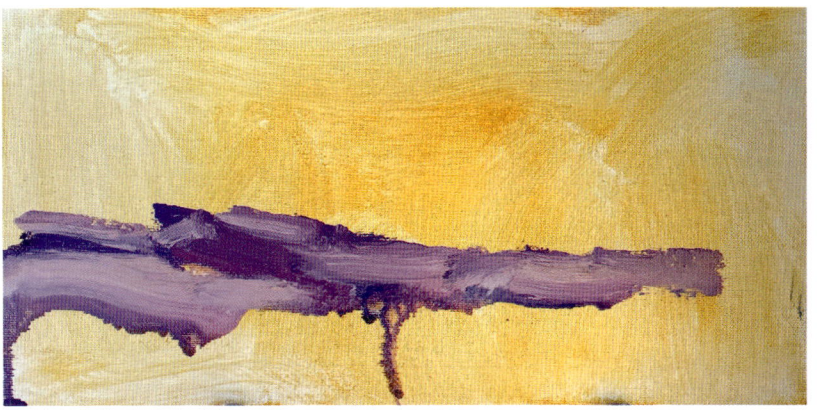

1:08 p.m. First, some Yellow Ochre is scribbled on and wiped off to tone the canvas. Mixing with his brush—the first strokes show several colors going down at once and unmixed turps dripping.

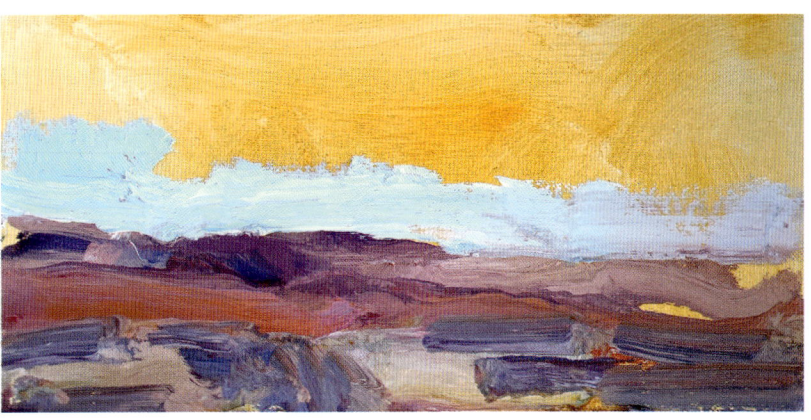

1:12 p.m.

"We are not merely allowed to make changes to what we see; it's my belief that, as artists, we are required to."

—ERIC JACOBSEN

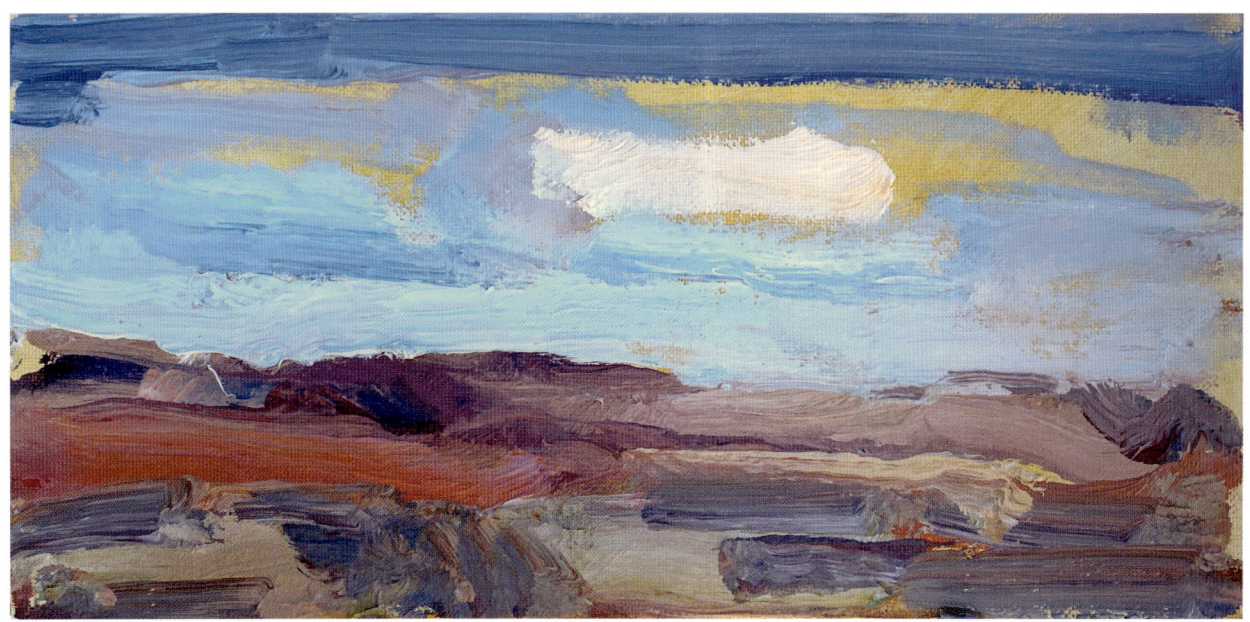

1:17 p.m.

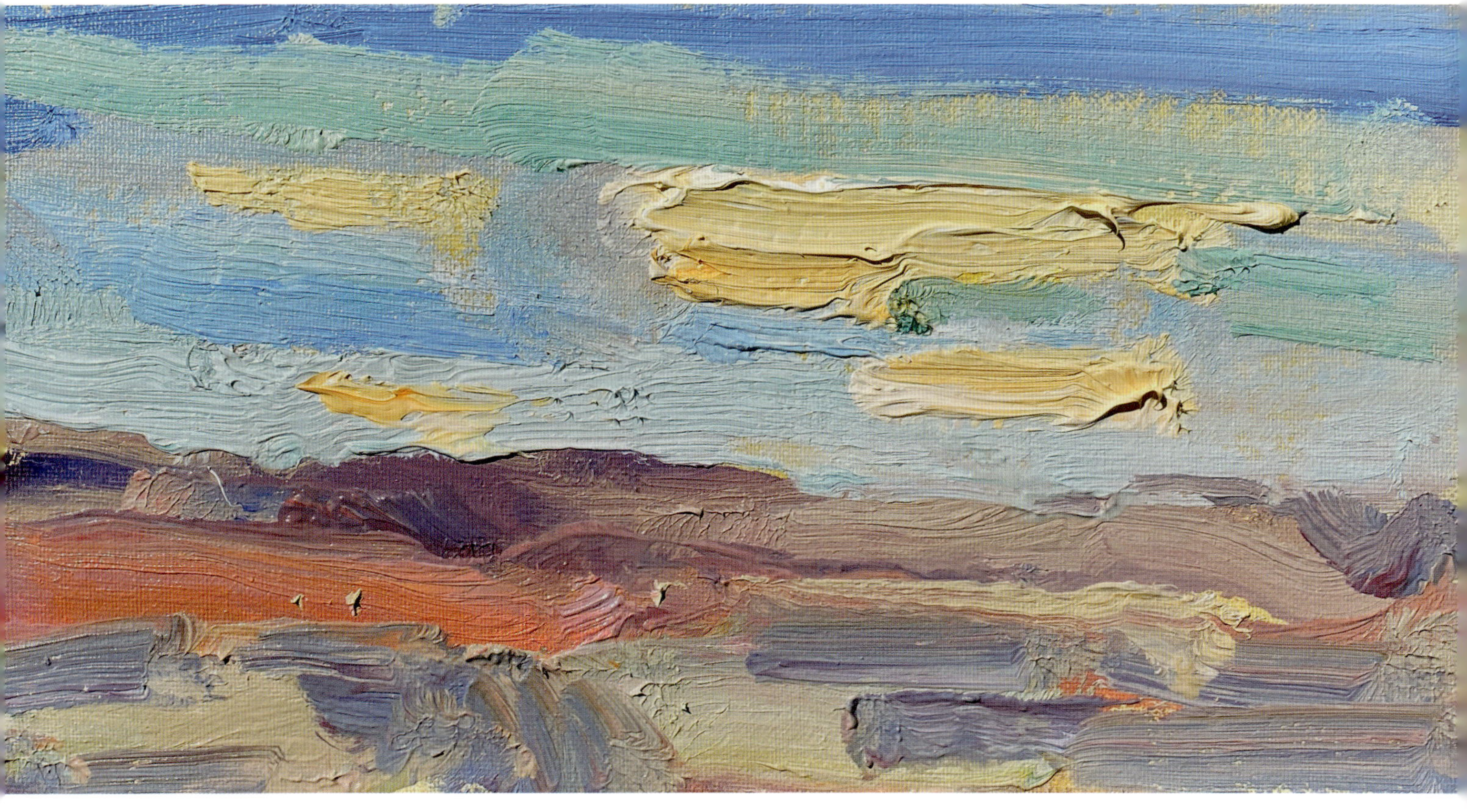

Eric Jacobsen, *Sunlit Desert*, oil on Masonite panel, 6" × 12" | 15.2 cm × 30.5 cm

1:21 p.m. The last strokes are the same as the first in terms of load and application. "Finish" is when the painting is balanced in an energetic sense. (Color differences from one of these images to the next are due to the camera's response to changing light.)

PAINTING MAKEOVER:
MORE COLOR

This painting was made late in the day, as the sunlight cast warm light on Mt. Adams and shadows began to creep up its flanks.

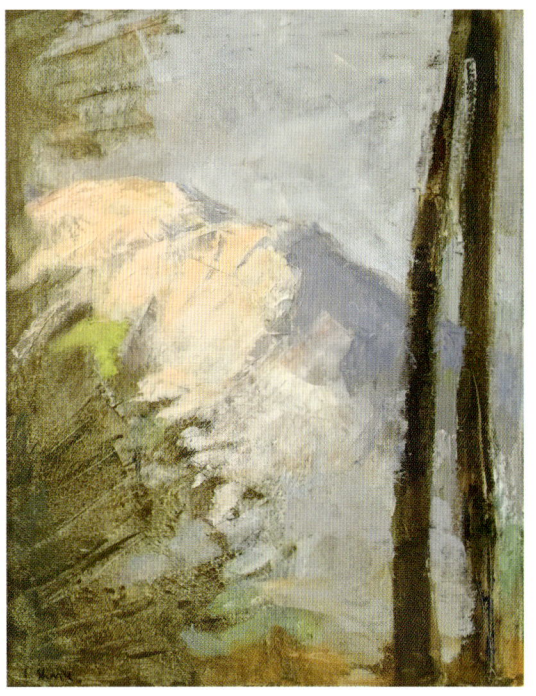

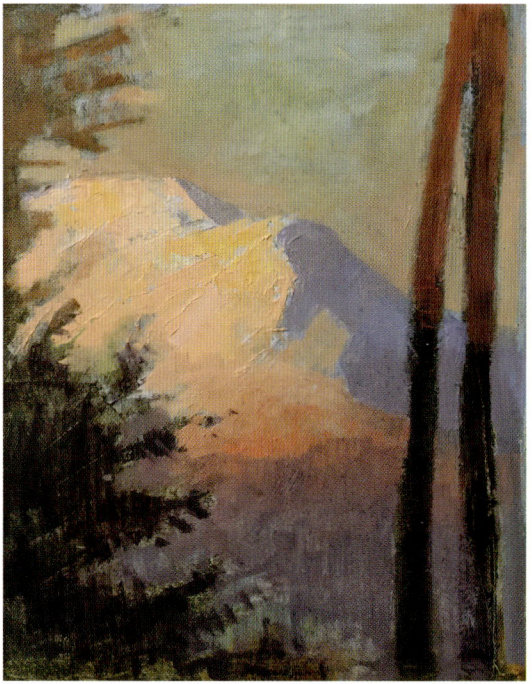

L. Sharpe, *Mt. Adams*, oil on panel, 12" × 9" | 30.5 cm × 22.9 cm

Original. There's not enough color. There are the beginnings of a rosy glow and purple shadow on the mountaintop, but it doesn't do enough to indicate the color of the light. The difficulty of moving away from local color is real.

In order for the lit snow to hold more color, it has to be darker, but since it's really well lit and its local color is white, it still has to be the lightest thing in the picture. Which means everything else has to get darker, too.

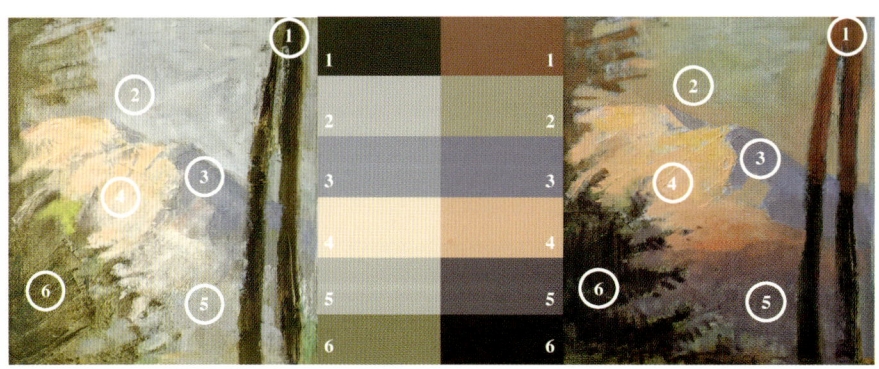

Showing side-by-side color changes.

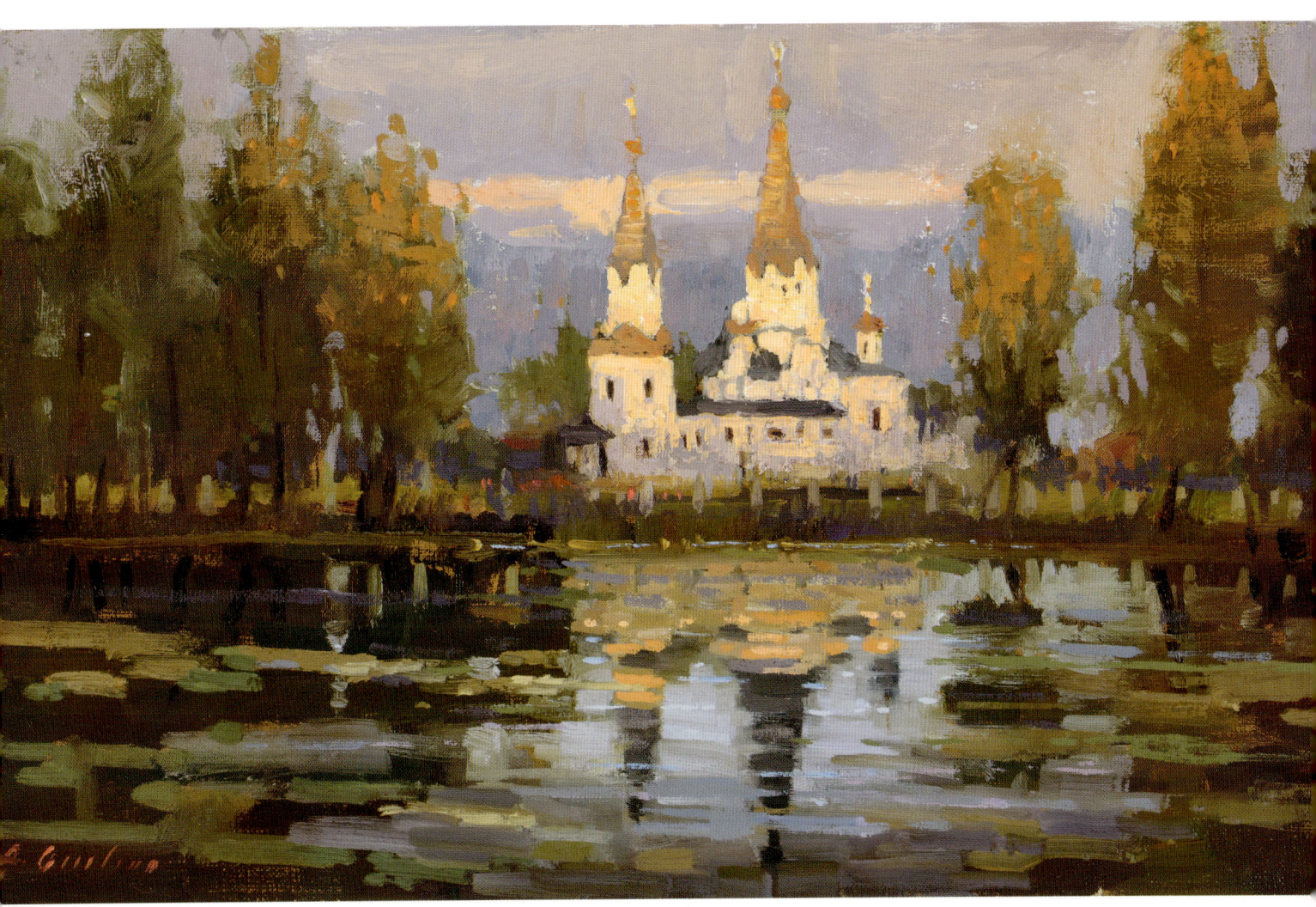

Aimee Erickson, *Russian Church at Dusk*,
oil on canvas, 12" × 17" | 30.5 cm × 43.2 cm

HALF-LIGHT

The dramatic phenomenon of half-light
occurs late in the day (or early) when the top
half of the scene is bathed in warm frontal
light, and long shadows cast the lower half
into shadow. Colors tend to be rich.

SEPARATE OBJECTS OR CONNECTED SURFACE

Either/or thinking in painting means seeing things as discrete objects, clearly distinct from their surroundings. The opposing and complementary approach is to view the canvas as a continuous, connected surface. We can even see things as being more than one thing at once: sky *and* cloud. Or consider a tree, for example–it's solid *and also* transparent. Our thinking affects how we represent things.

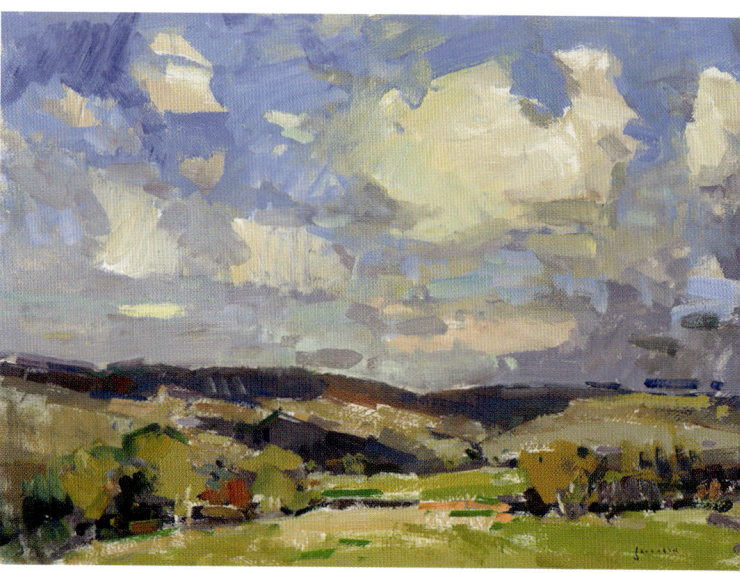

Eric Jacobsen, *Rolling Hills*, oil on canvas, 18" × 26" | 45.7 cm × 66 cm

Thinking about the skyscape as a continuum of brushstrokes, clouds, and sky moving together. Some parts are clearly sky, some are clearly cloud, and many places are both.

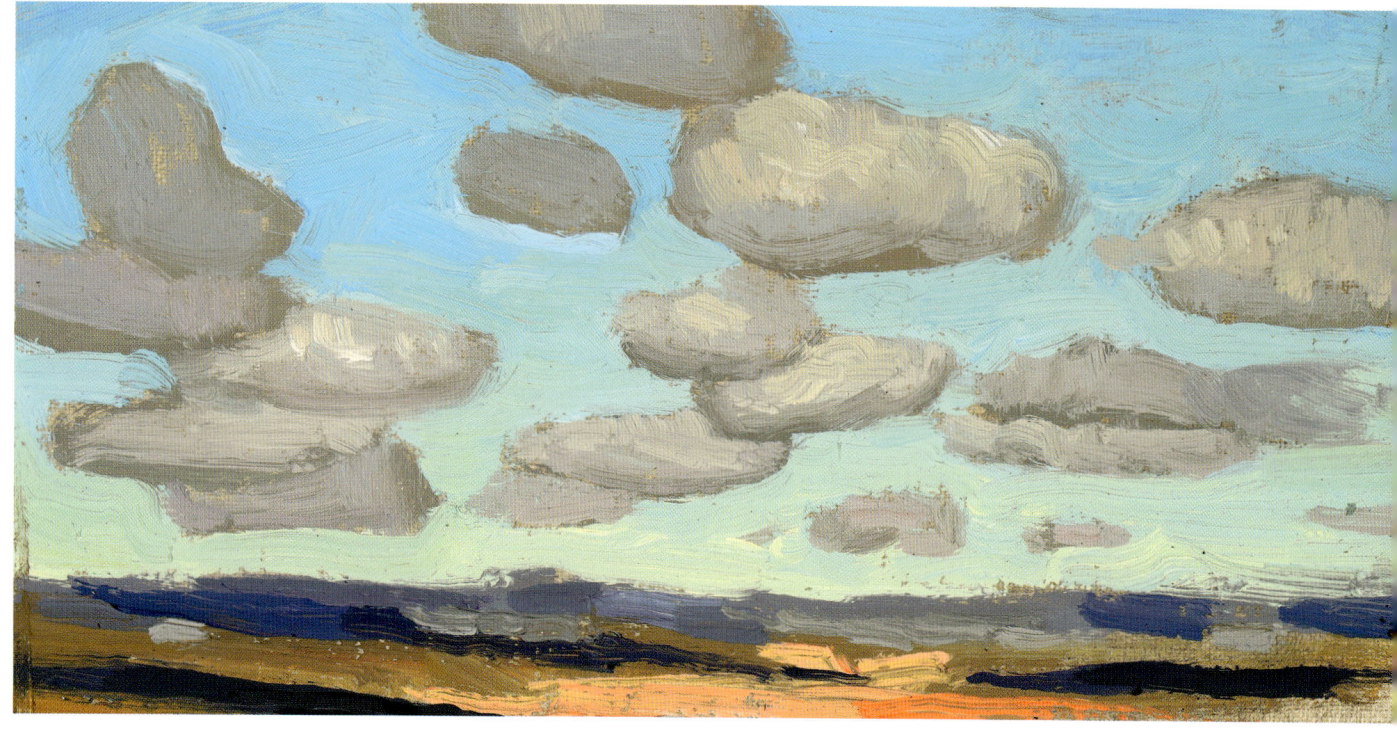

Aimee Erickson, *Cloud study*, oil on muslin panel, 4" × 8" | 10.2 cm × 20.3 cm

Thinking about the clouds as distinct from the blue yonder: *either* clouds *or* sky. Figures against a background.

A REASON TO EXPAND YOUR PALETTE

Countering the principle that you can paint any subject (no matter its color) with a limited palette is the truth that certain colors cannot be mixed—they have to come out of a tube. In *theory*, all colors can be made out of three primaries—mix your red and your blue and you'll get violet. In *practice*, the violet you get from mixing Ultramarine Blue (PB 29) and Cadmium Red Light (PR 108) will never achieve the high chroma of Quinacridone Violet, a single pigment transparent color (PV 19).

- Palette: Old Holland Alizarin Crimson Lake Extra, Gamblin Quinacridone Magenta, Richeson Quinacridone Violet, Gamblin Titanium Zinc White, Sennelier Red, Michael Harding Permanent Orange, and Gamblin Radiant Blue.

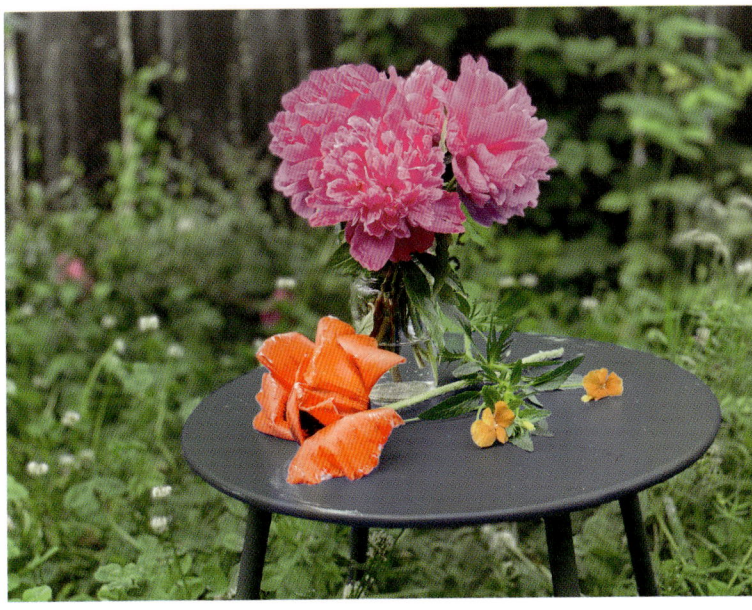

Peonies and a poppy. The peonies are a zingy high-chroma red-violet, and the poppy (it was battered by rain) is a high-chroma red-orange. If I were to paint either of these with the aim of achieving the intensity of color that I see, I would organize my palette around pigments that can achieve those colors.

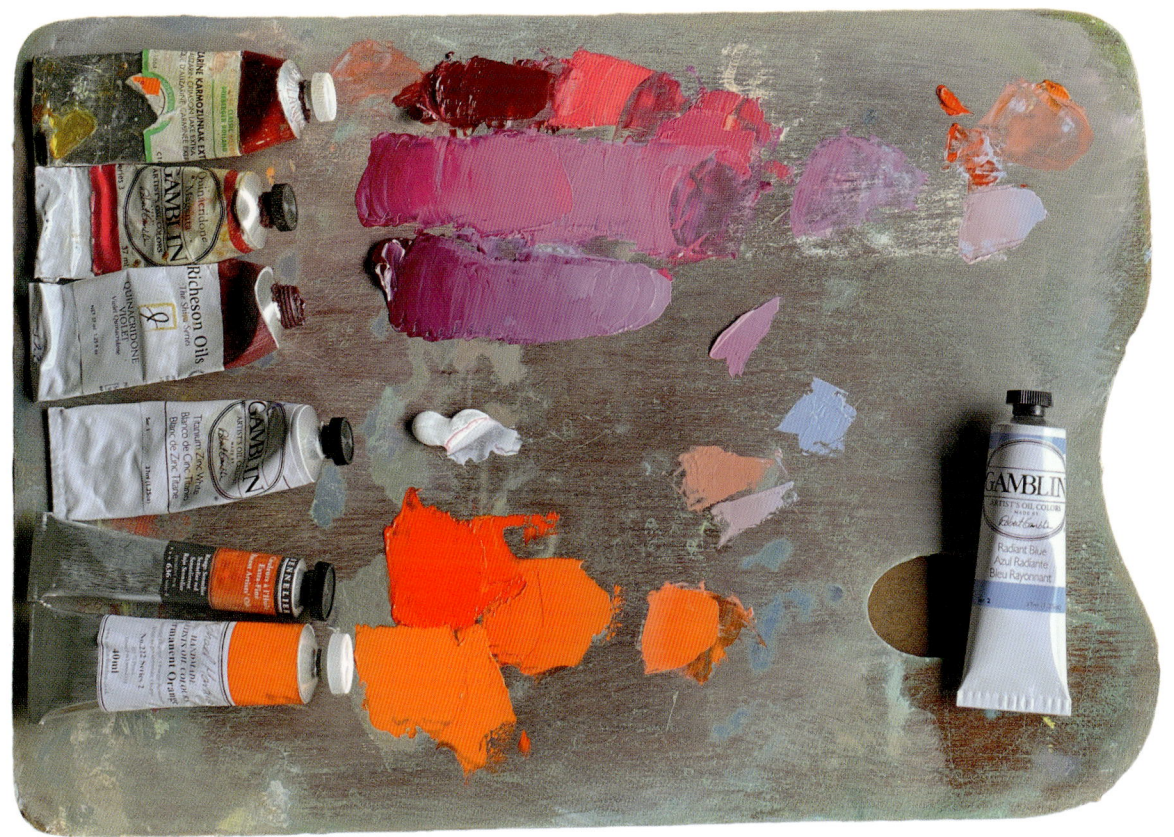

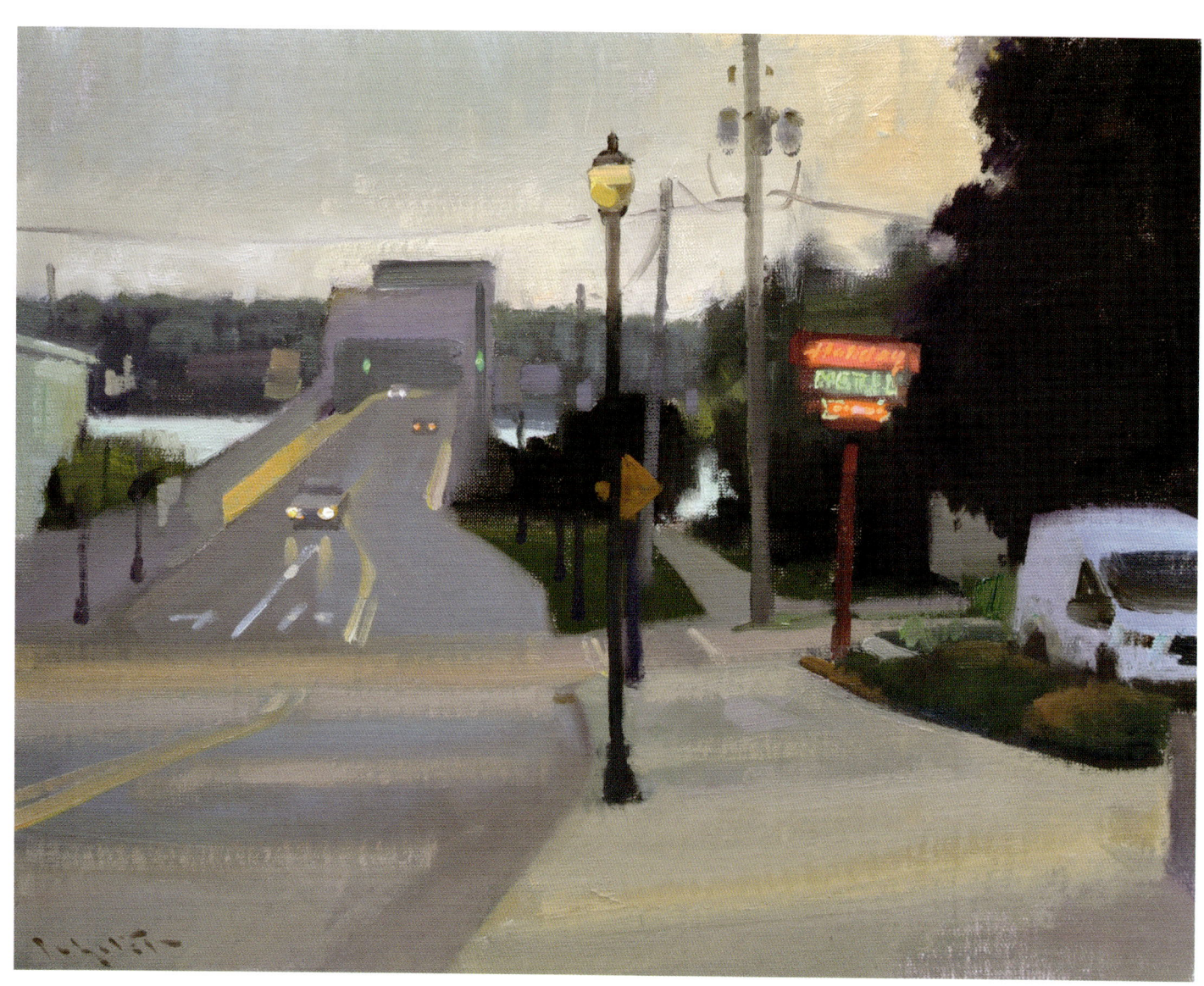

John Lasater, *Visual Holiday*, oil on panel, 14" × 18" | 35.6 cm × 45.7 cm

8

NOCTURNES

Less light in the sky and no direct light from the sun creates so many beautiful soft effects, all naturally fleeting.

After sunset, we see immense changes in the landscape. The light decreases, the sky changes color, and the landscape relaxes into softness: There's an ease of seeing in the gentler light. Twilight lasts until the sun is eighteen degrees below the horizon, the light lessening with each minute. Night means a dark sky and dark earth. In nighttime paintings, the value structure is mostly dark, some medium value, and a touch of light. The running joke is that a good formula for value structure is a 70-30-10 percentage split, reminding us that no formula is too reliable.

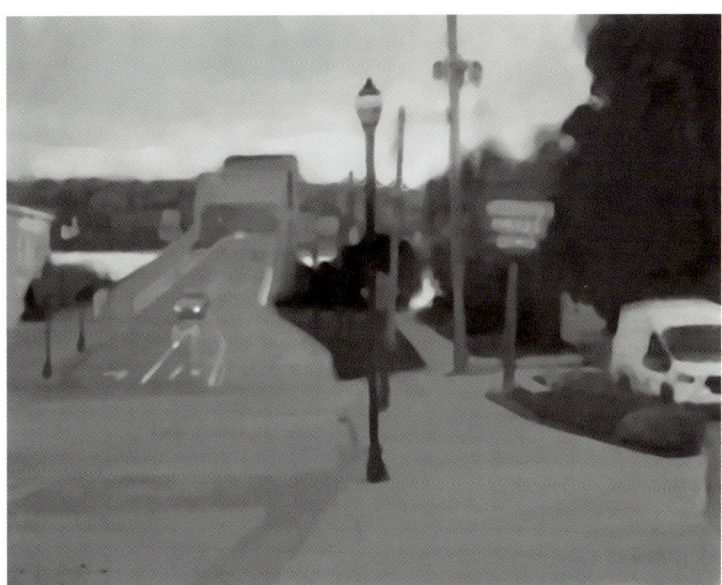

Value analysis of
Visual Holiday.

TWILIGHT

There's still light in the sky, fading fast and shifting colors at the same time. We have passed the cusp, at sunset, when the sun's rays are traveling essentially parallel to the land, and we have moved into the shadow side of the planet. But the sunlight is still illuminating the air and scattering down to the darkening land. Colors are richer, contrast is lessened, and everything softens. Shadows gather under trees and in pockets of the landscape, but without the crisp edges of daytime. Streetlamps and kitchen windows glow in the landscape. The moon, if it's up, grows brighter as the sky darkens.

Establish a hierarchy of values to organize the scene. Which is brighter, artificial lamps or the sky? How much darker are the distant hills? What value are the open planes of the earth?

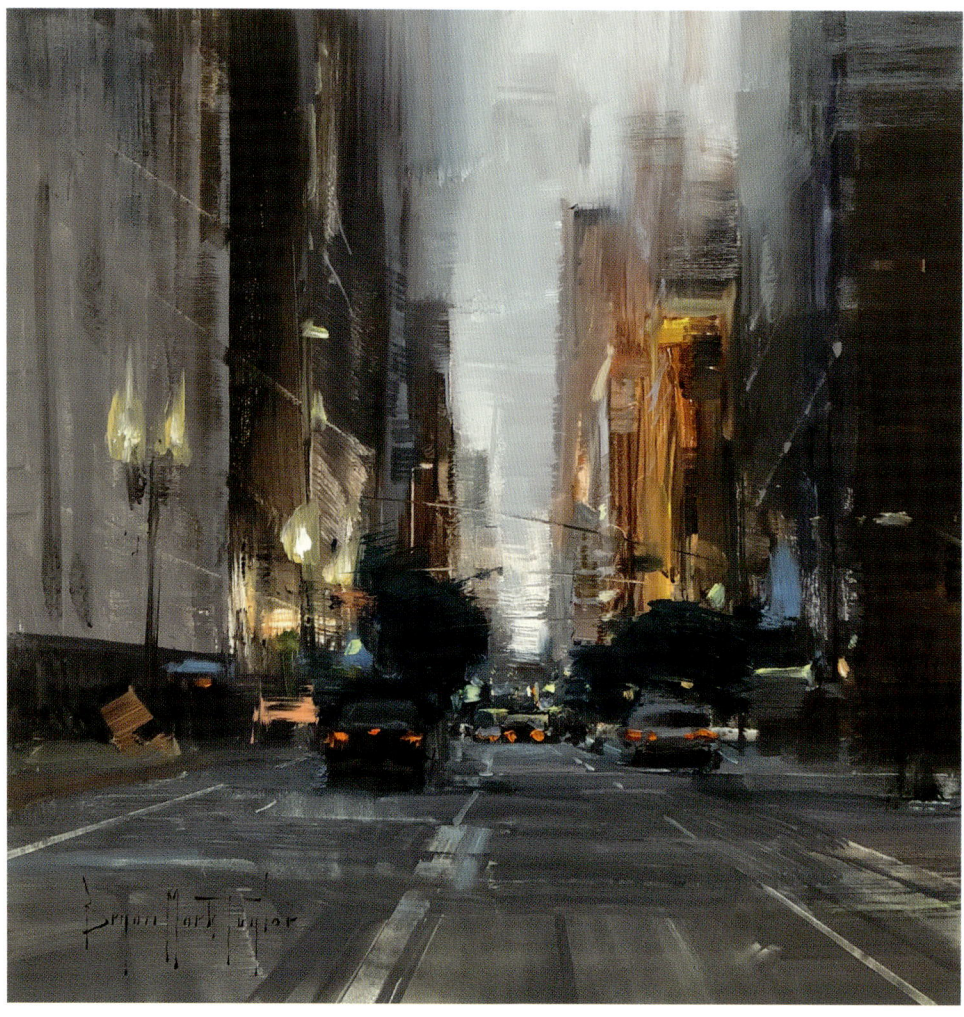

Bryan Mark Taylor, *Downtown L.A.*, oil on panel, 12" × 12" | 30.5 cm × 30.5 cm

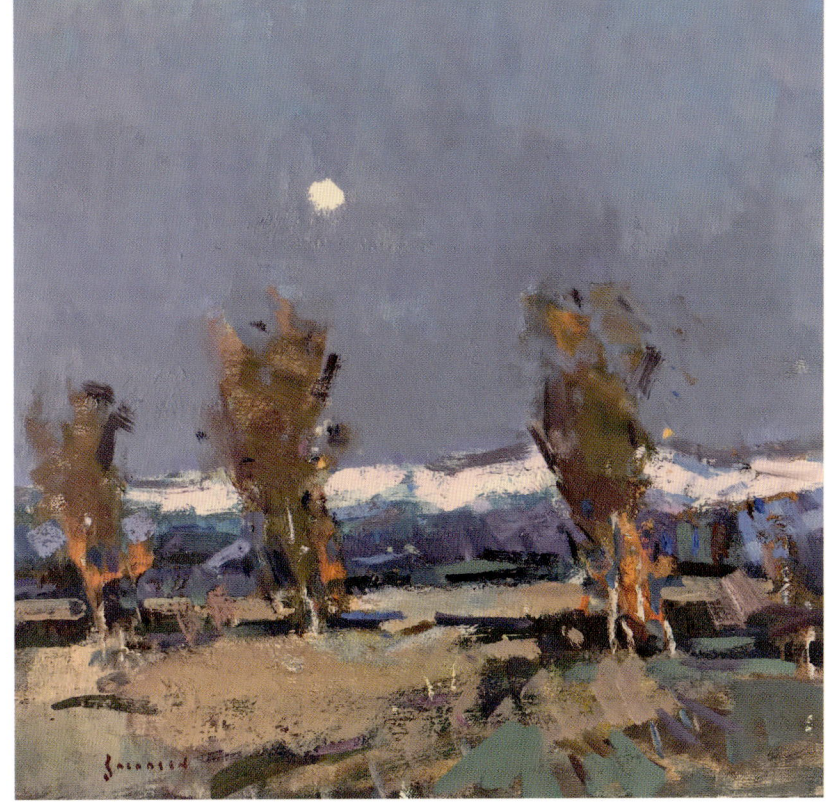

Eric Jacobsen, *October Moon*, oil on canvas, 18" × 20" | 45.7 cm × 50.8 cm

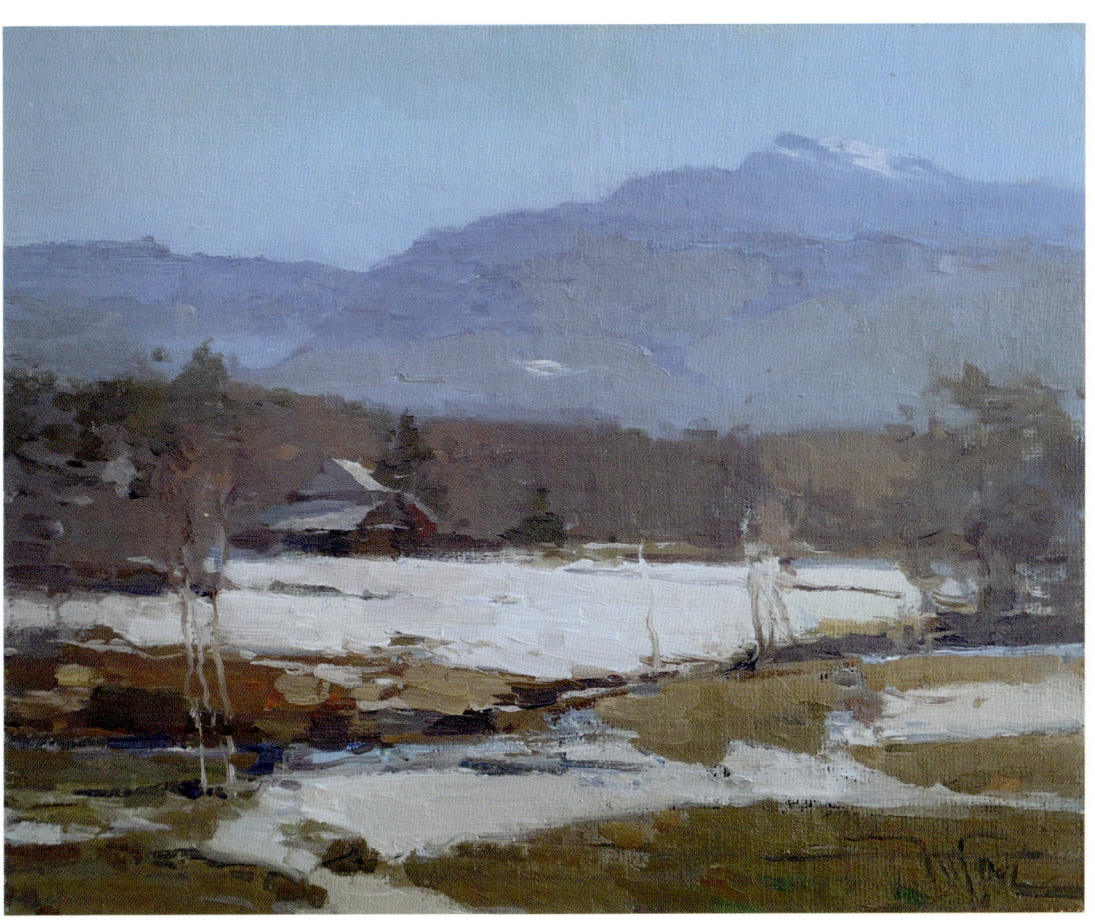

Zufar Bikbov, *Mansfield Mountain View Study*, oil on canvas panel, 8" × 10" | 20.3 cm × 25.4 cm

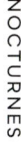

NIGHTTIME

Once the sky is dark, the light source in a painting is either moonlight or artificial light—a streetlight, a light in a window, or a string of party lights.

Unless you're painting right under a streetlamp or by a storefront, you'll need a battery-powered easel lamp or a music stand lamp. Look for one with adjustable brightness and color temperature, so you can adjust the settings for the conditions you find yourself in.

▸ Christian Schellewald, *Franklin*, LAMY Ballpoint Pen, Holbein Watercolor, and Prismacolor Colored Pencil on sketchbook paper, 8" × 5" | 20.3 cm × 12.7 cm

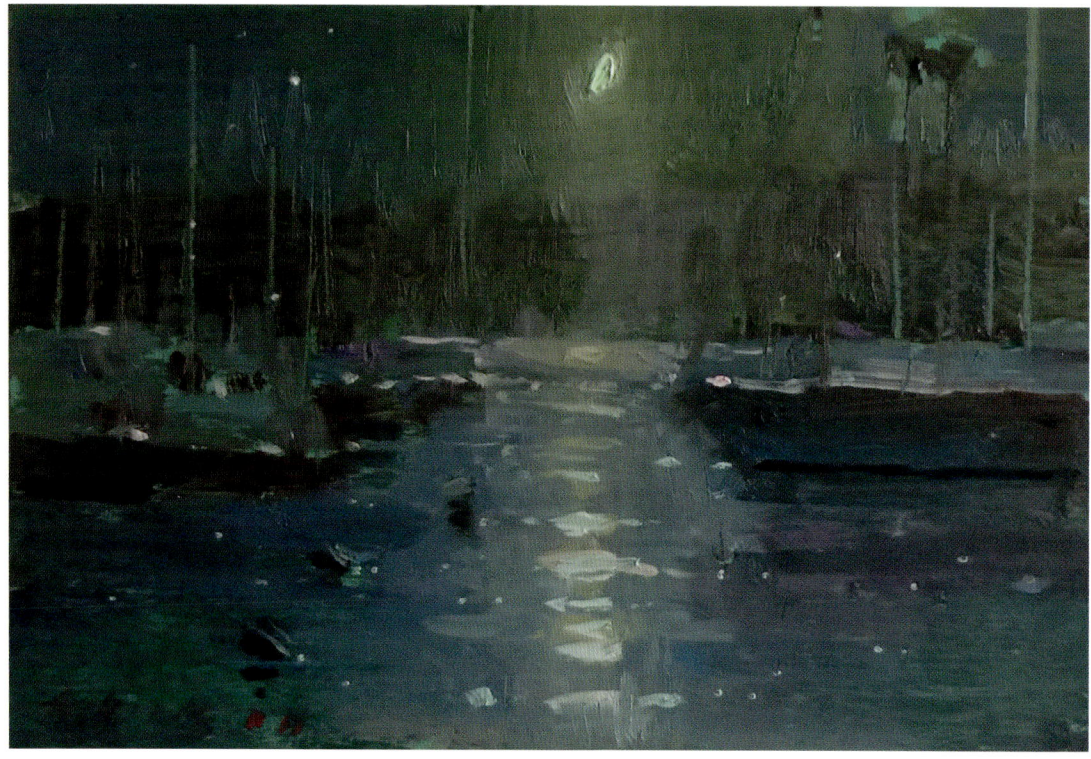

Aimee Erickson, *Night*, oil on matboard, 3" × 4½" | 7.6 cm × 11.4 cm

DEMONSTRATION:
NOCTURNE

CARL BRETZKE:
THE AC TAP BAR

DEMONSTRATION NOTES

- Canvas panel.
- Palette (oil paints): Any Titanium White, Old Holland Cadmium Yellow Light, Winsor & Newton Cadmium Yellow, Winsor & Newton Cadmium Scarlet, Winsor & Newton Cadmium Red, Winsor & Newton Permanent Alizarin Crimson, Old Holland Manganese Blue Extra, Winsor & Newton Cobalt Blue, Winsor & Newton French Ultramarine, Winsor & Newton Ivory Black, Winsor & Newton Winsor Violet (Dioxazine), Winsor & Newton Winsor Green (Phthalo), Winsor & Newton Transparent Brown Oxide, and Sennelier King's Blue.
- Brushes: mostly Princeton Aspen flats.

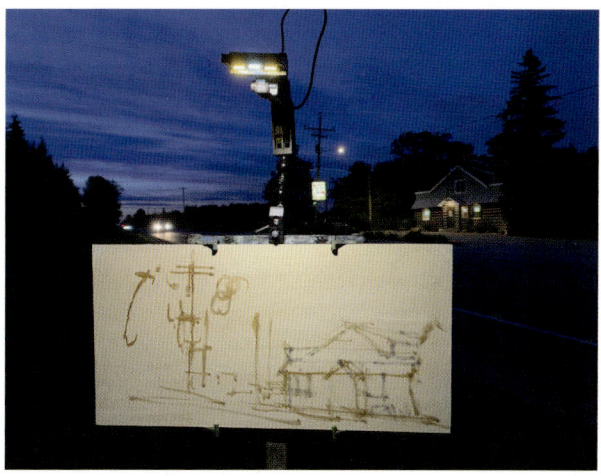

Soltek Easel with an easel light. Setting up at dusk, across the street from the bar, knowing the light in the sky will fade.

1. Bretzke draws in all the major shapes first on a white canvas. The late stage of the drawing dovetails with the early stage of the color. Picking up a new color is a good way to make changes to the drawing and composition and segue into the blocking in of major color areas.

continued ▸

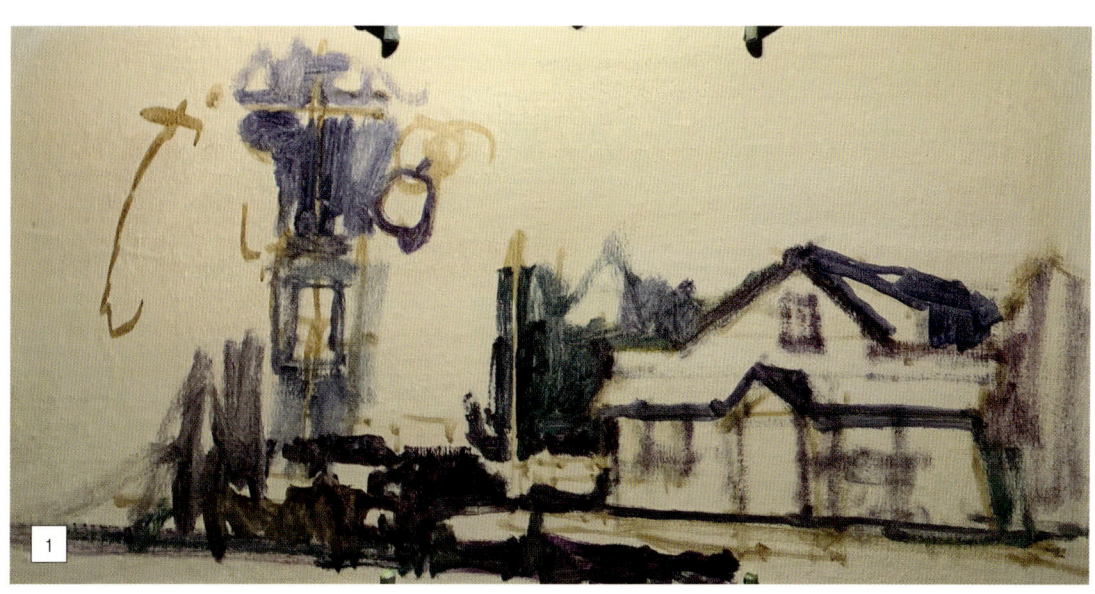

1

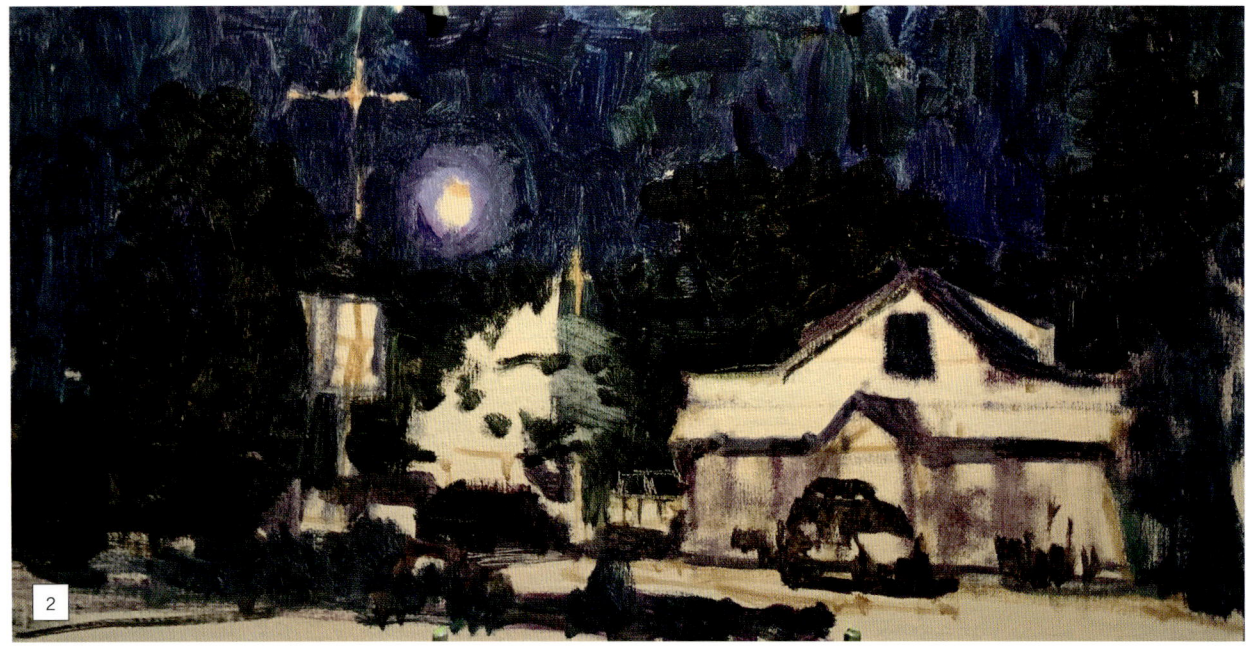

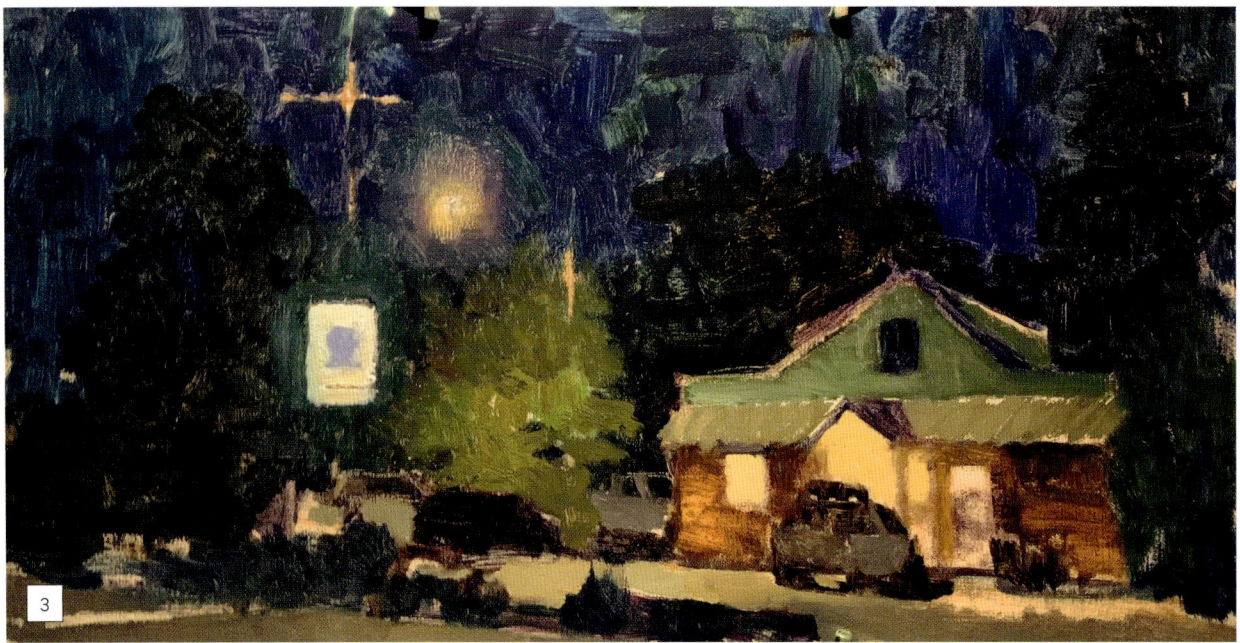

2. Bretzke fills in and connects as many darks as possible, leaving gaps for lights and illuminated areas, then paints light sources, starting with their haloes.

3. He paints illuminated surfaces with proper light and color gradation, then touches up all areas.

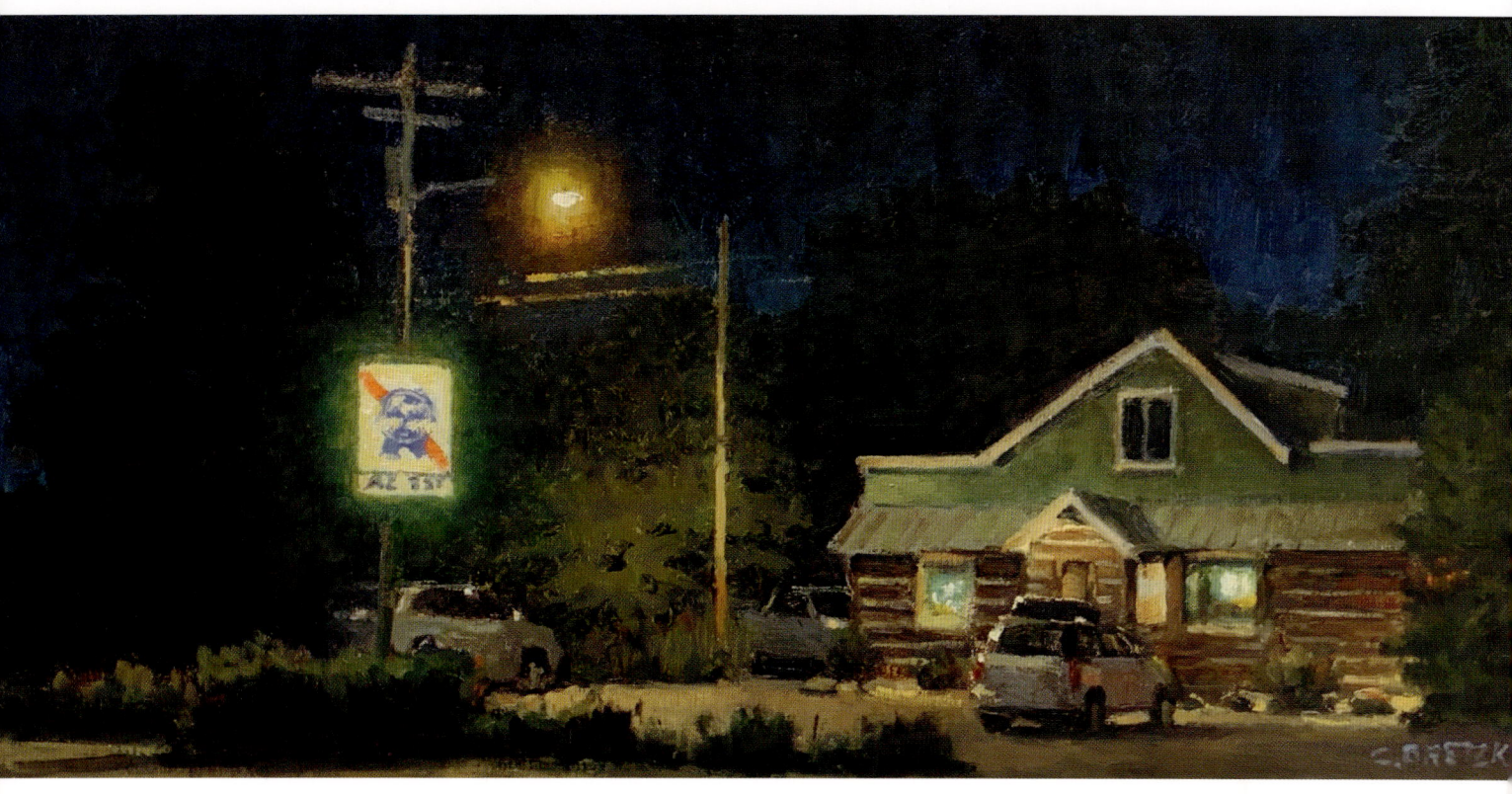

Carl Bretzke, *The AC Tap Bar*, Door County, Wisconsin, USA, oil on canvas panel, 10" × 20" | 25.4 cm × 50.8 cm

- **Darks and Glare.** Your darks can get destroyed by reflecting ambient light if the stroke direction is horizontal and the paint is too thick. In general, dark passages read as dark if the paint is flat and the brushstrokes are vertical (or smoothed with a fan brush to remove ridges). Light passages are built up and catch the ambient light, which reinforces their lit quality.

- **Layering Outdoors.** Starting with a white panel means you may need two passes to get darks to feel solid. Dark colors tend to be more transparent and may not cover as well. A great solution for this is to do your first pass very thin, using a little rectified turpentine. It'll tack up in 20 minutes or so depending on the weather, and you can paint over it and achieve better coverage.

"I like when there's one warm light and one cool light."

—CARL BRETZKE

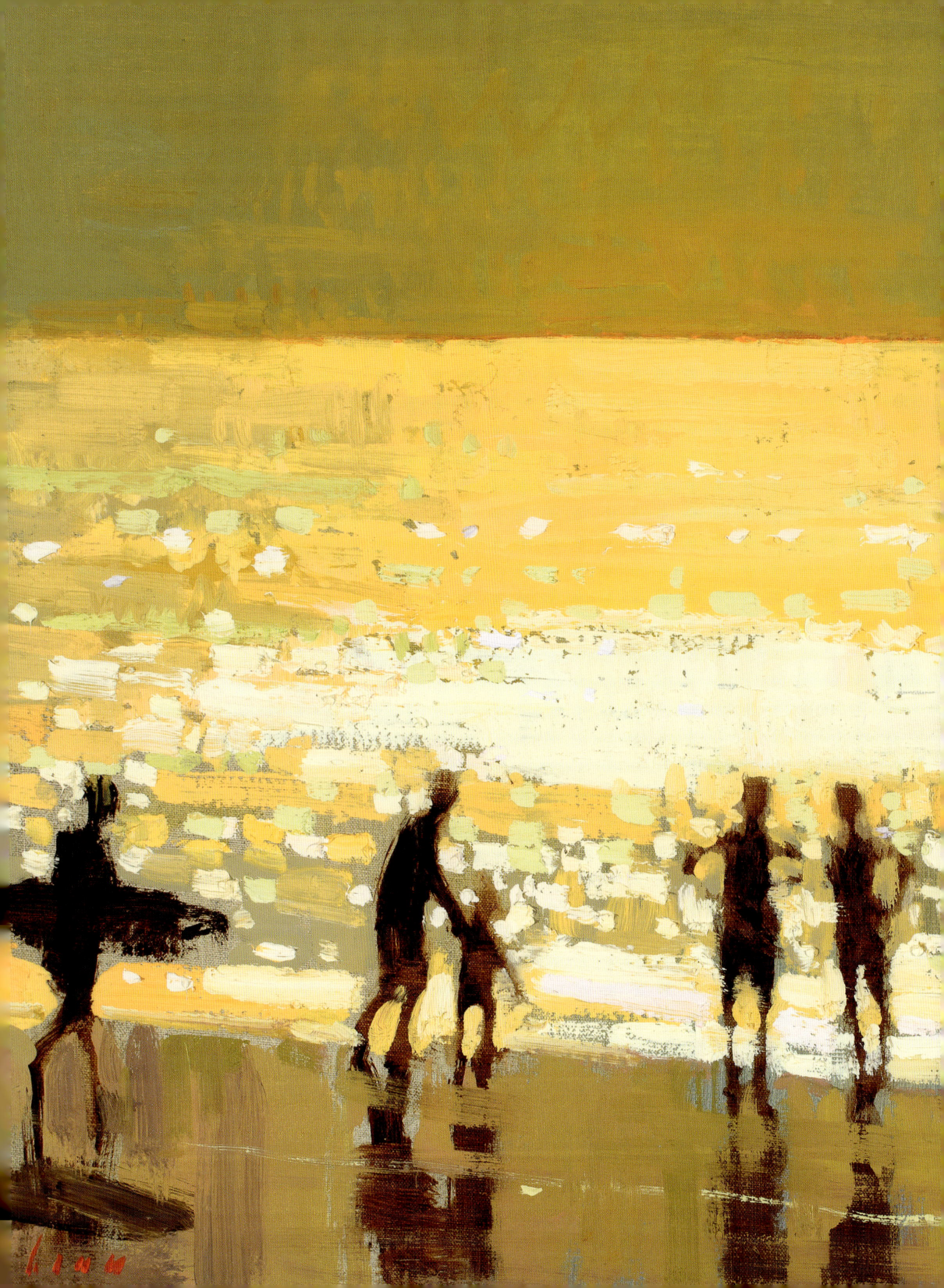

9

SPECIAL EFFECTS

Once we have the understanding and skill to render the effect that light has on objects, we can start to learn how to go a step further and discover how paint can describe certain other effects of light. Some of the concepts that come into play are these:

Because light reveals color, we associate saturated color with a lit quality. If a color is too pale, that is, so *light in value* that it contains very little color, it may look like white paint rather than something bright in the picture. Likewise, if a color in shadow is too saturated, it appears to glow in the dark. Therefore, in addition to using a higher value to communicate a lit quality, we have a second tool of higher chroma or saturation. And, of course, this is all context-dependent.

Very bright light has something in common with the complete absence of light: We can't see anything in it. We represent absolute darkness with a flat (dark) color. Similarly, we represent a very bright light with a flat, high-value color, because *we do not describe form* within the shape of a very bright light source.

The air holds light: In outer space, the sky is always black because there is no atmosphere to be lit up. Aerial perspective takes this into account, but we see it even more when aerosols—particulate matter in the atmosphere—scatter the light.

Bright highlights take on their own shape, reflecting their source, the sun. This means that bright light doesn't have corners or spikes. It turns into a blob that does not necessarily stay within the lines.

◄ Aimee Erickson, *Glow* (detail), oil on panel, 18" × 24" | 45.7 cm × 61 cm

GLOW

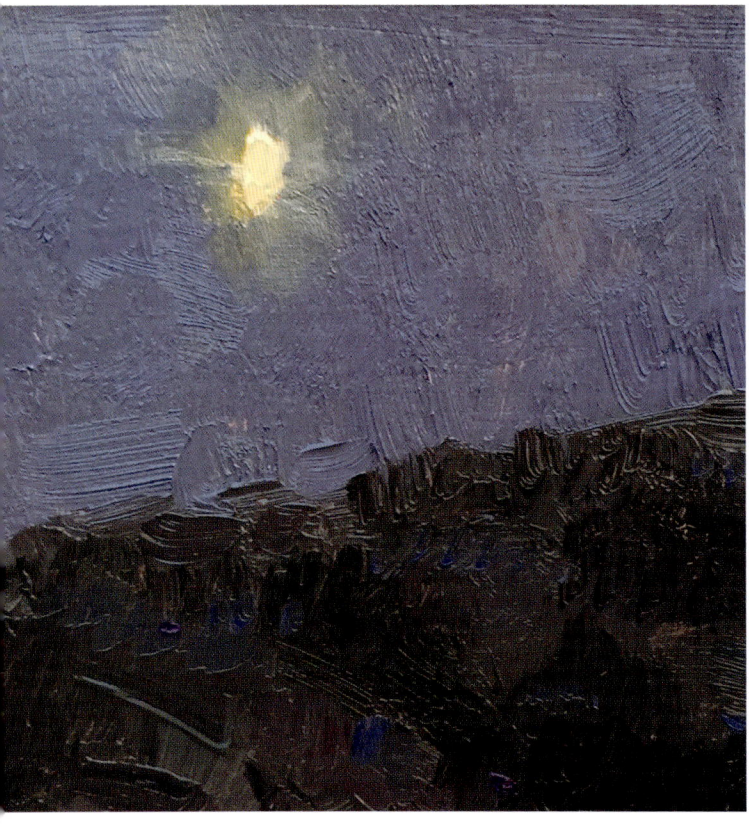

The first thing you need is enough darkness in the background. Then, lessen the darkness as it approaches the light. Glowing light is not contained within the bounds of *things*. Glow happens *off the object*, in the air and in the surrounding objects.

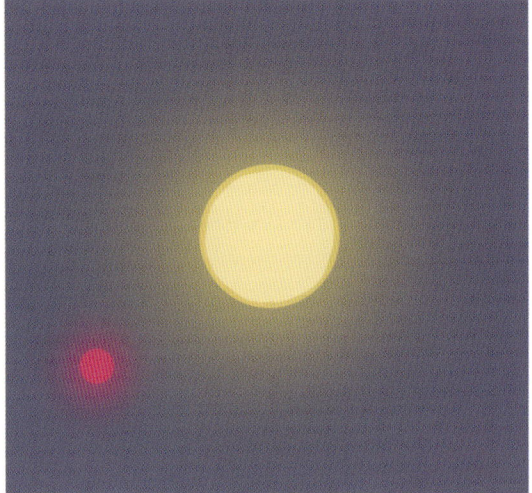

Aimee Erickson, *Back Bay Moonrise* (detail), oil on linen panel, 6" × 12" | 15.2 cm × 30.5 cm

The moon in the night sky is the loveliest natural example of a glowing object. In broad daylight, the moon does not glow—its light is not bright enough—and it appears as a pale chip in the blue. At night, though, it's the brightest thing in the sky—so bright that, depending on the weather, it has a halo of light around itself, which lessens with distance.

The background, or air, or whatever stuff surrounds the light source, needs to diminish to some degree in darkness as it approaches the light source.

So the phenomenon is that the light source or lit object—in this case, the moon—is lightest in value. Its edges are where we look to see the value drop a tad and the chroma increase. The background is dark, then moving away from the moon it gets darker still. In other words, the sky is dark, but it can't hold its darkness as it approaches the moon.

Here it is as a digital illustration, a yellow moon with more color at the edge and a background moving from yellow-purple to purple at pretty much the same value. The hot pink dot glows not because it is light in value, but because it is high chroma, and its color moves off it into the background.

Kathleen B. Hudson, *Out of Time and Memory*, oil on linen panel, 20" × 20" | 50.8 cm × 50.8 cm

Here, we have a slightly more complex glow phenomenon because we have clouds, which make it more interesting—instead of straight glow, you get glow held by cloud shapes. Still, you can see the general phenomenon of everything falling in value from the brightest part and places near the light source that have more color.

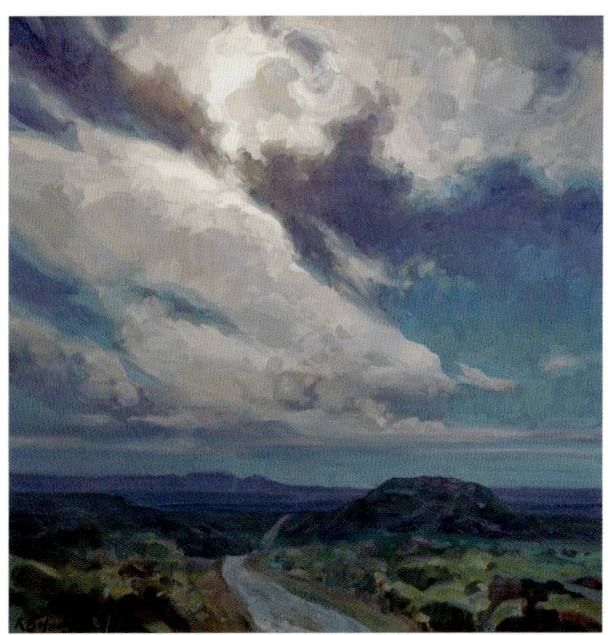

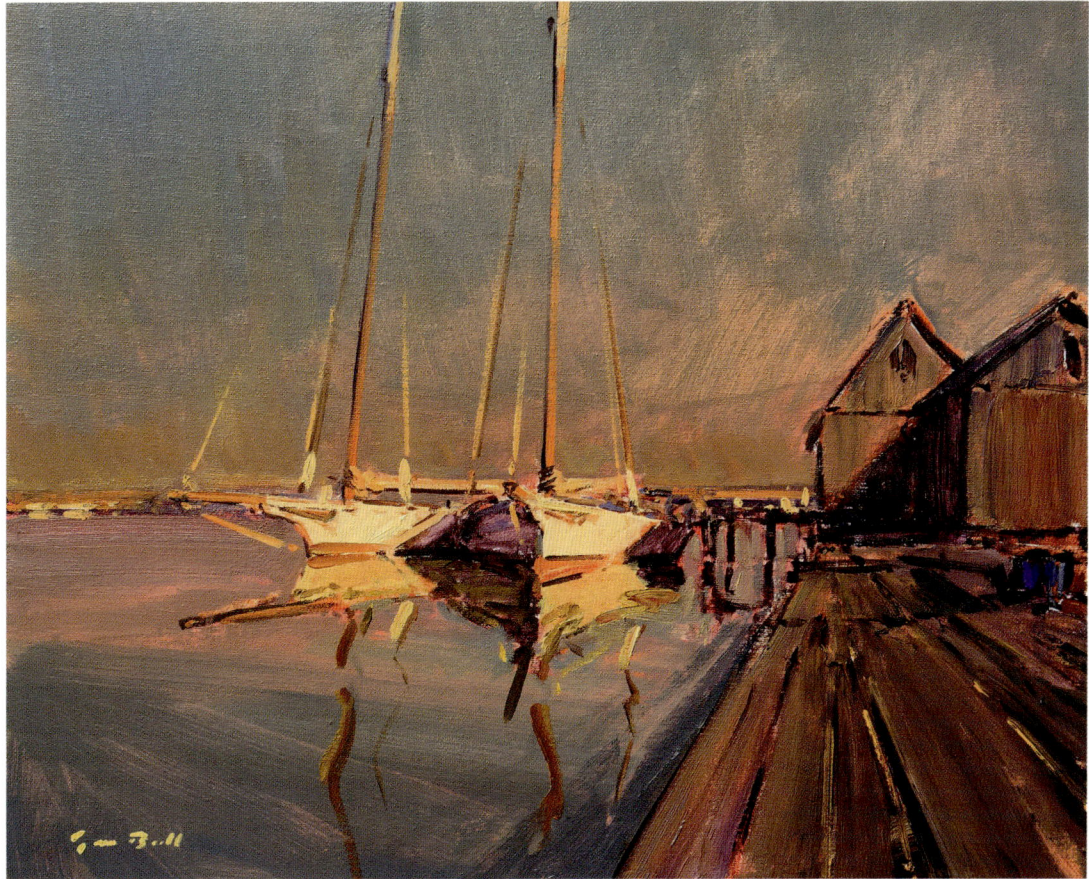

Tim Beall, *Two Boats*, oil on linen, 16" × 20" | 40.6 cm × 50.8 cm

Two boats glowing like hot coals. Look how the areas of most color are right in that area around the boats and how the sky and water fade to a scruffy gray.

It doesn't matter if the object actually generates light, like the sun or a light bulb, or reflects light, like the moon or a boat at sunset. What matters is the conditions—the color of the light and its surroundings, how bright the light is, and, of course, how you want it to look in your painting.

DEMONSTRATION:
MULTIPLE LIGHT SOURCES

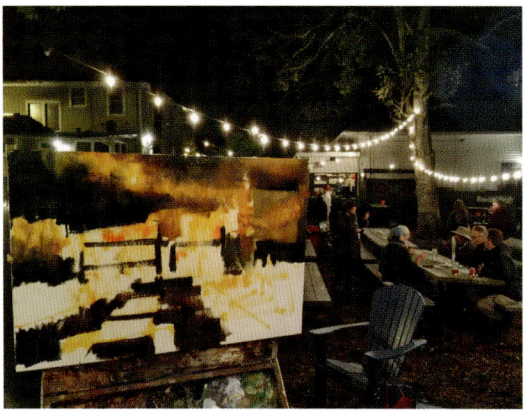

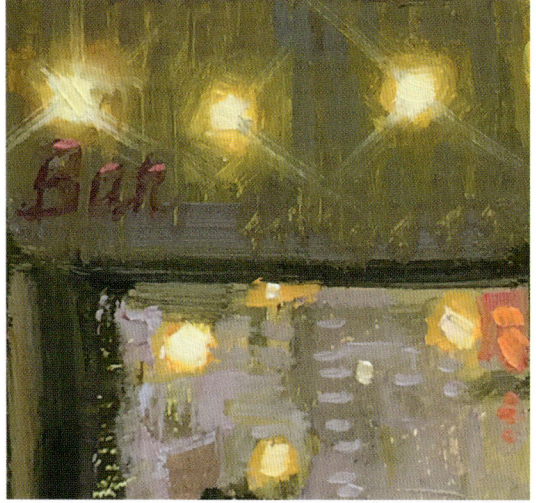

Starting a painting during a party. The event organizers planned this after dark (at an excellent restaurant called Reunion), assuming we would all be finished painting. I had a white panel and started with Indian Yellow to find my composition, wanting to keep the areas that would become light bulbs clean of dark paint. I was interested in the warm and cool of the different light sources and in the play of the string lights. The halo around the light bulb tends to have more color (higher chroma) than the bulb itself.

Detail of *Reunion* showing cooler colors—blue-purples and grays—laid down on top of warmer colors—greenish golds and pinkier purples—and also showing several variations of glowing lights. In photos of outer space, we are used to seeing stars with crosshairs glow, a threadlike plus sign in addition to the radial glow. This is an artifact of the telescope—light hitting the four rods that suspend the secondary mirror. I like to put them in sometimes.

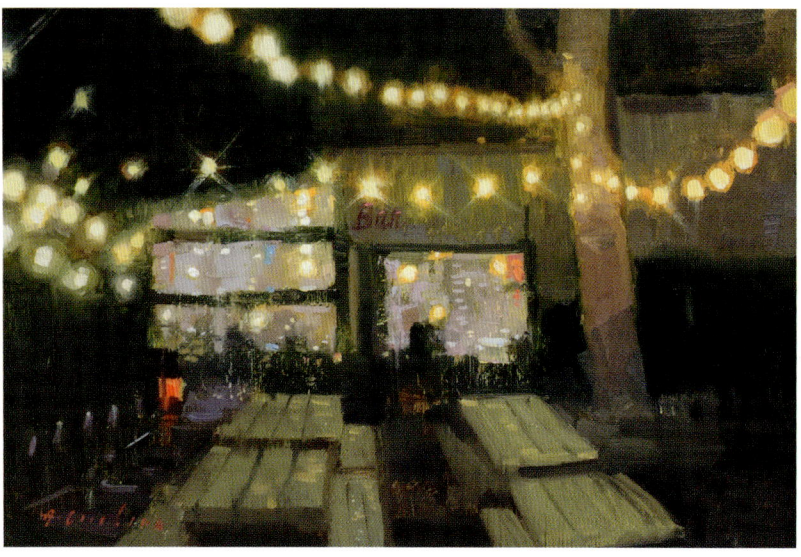

Aimee Erickson, *Reunion*, oil on muslin panel, 12" × 18" | 30.5 cm × 45.7 cm

No matter the motif, every picture is a design project.

GLARE

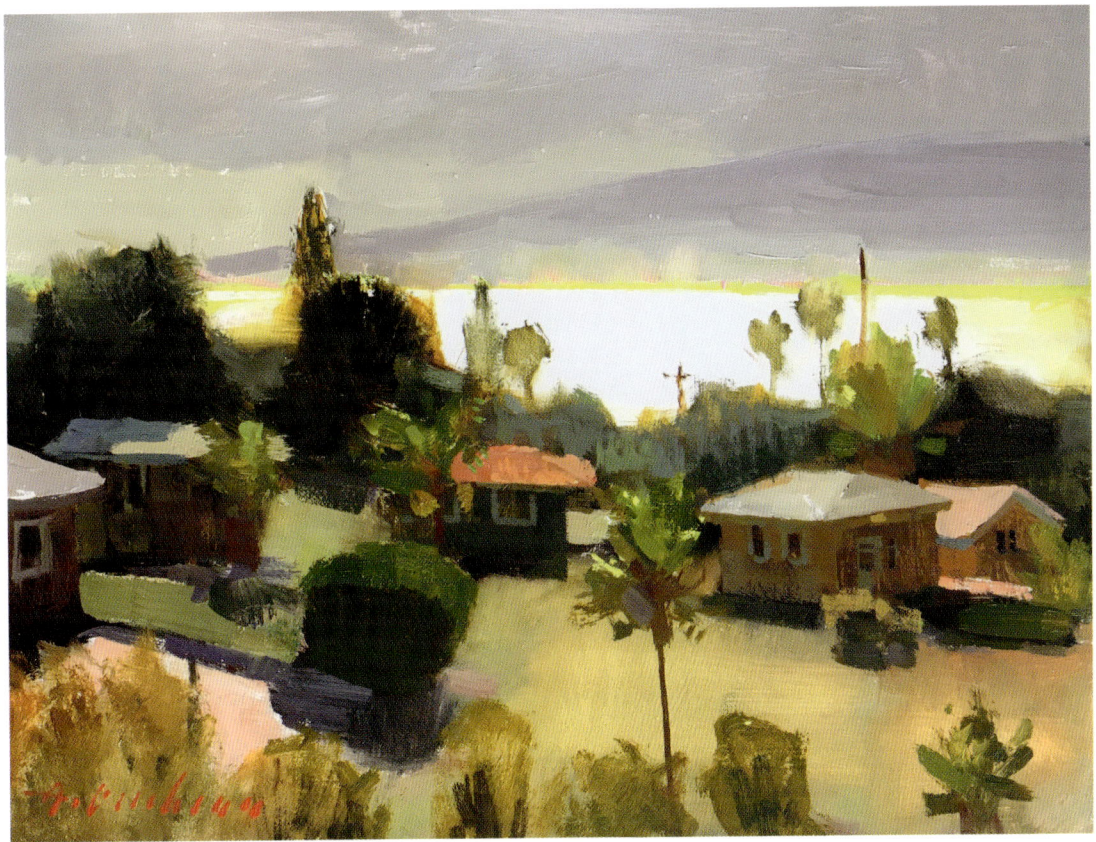

Aimee Erickson, *Maui Glare*, oil on panel, 11" × 14" | 28 cm × 35.6 cm

The light on the water is too bright to look at. I put my hat over my face and look through the fabric. The sea is a mirror reflecting the sun. Trees standing up against the glare are weak— they barely hold their form. The light swims through them; their edges are obliterated. The distant island loses its shore to the light. The land mass fades and shimmers behind all the light in the air. Up on this hilltop, the trees and houses and I are safe, shadows intact, color held easily in the lit planes.

I started with a white gessoed panel. Leaving the gesso untouched somehow conveys the blank, blinding quality of the glare. Nothing happens in glare. It's flat, and its edges glow, often a lot. I put in some pale bright yellow marks to indicate the limits of the glare: the island shoreline at the top, edges of trees, and structures below. I put a little more paint in the obliterated palm trees and then wiped it mostly off—there's too much light for them to be solid.

Working outward from there, I kept the island and sky pale, stepping down gingerly from the white, saving darks for the foreground. I sketched in the foreground shapes—tree, structure, field, another tree, and driveway—rearranging them to get a decent arrangement since they weren't laid out that well in reality. On the far left and right where the glare on the water lessens, trees recover and hold their own values.

I've found there's a limit to the amount of real estate you can devote to glare in a painting before it becomes an unpleasant "I need sunglasses" experience instead of a happy "Ooh, the light" moment.

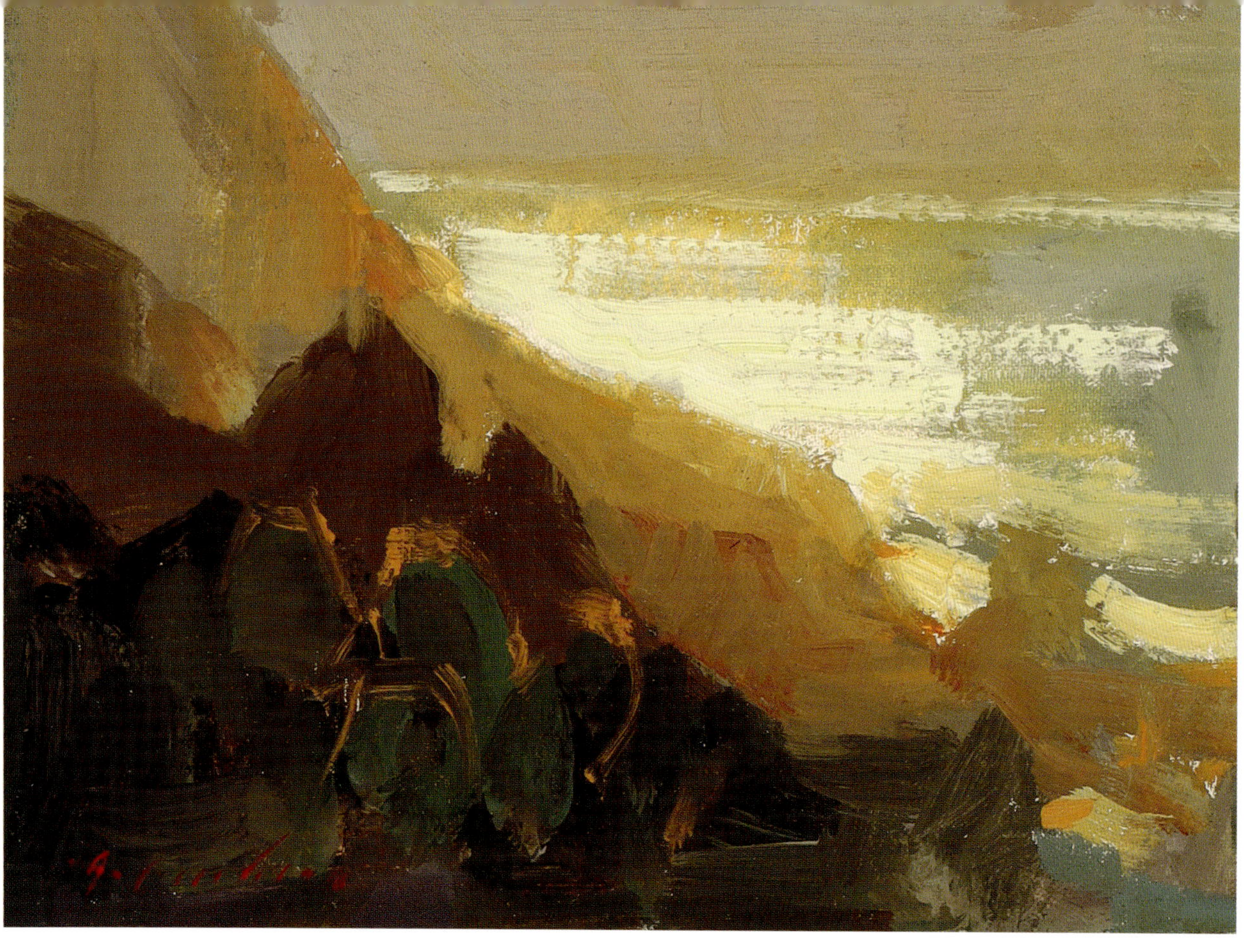

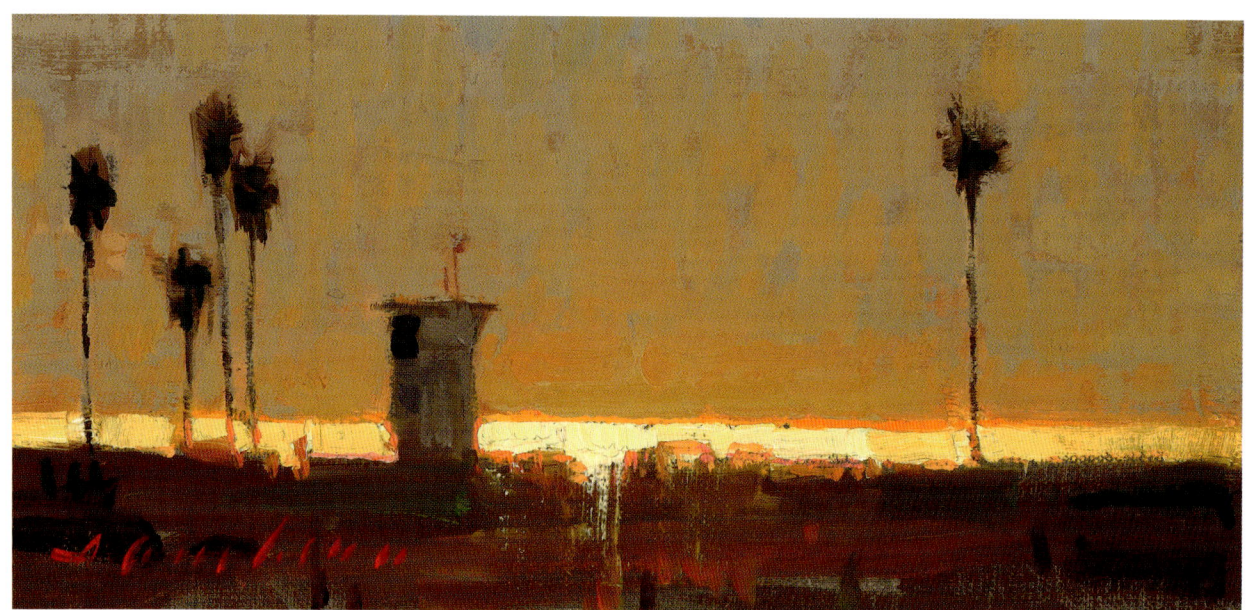

Aimee Erickson, *Pacific Glare Study*, oil on muslin panel, 4½" × 6" | 11.4 cm × 15.2 cm

From high on the back side of Catalina Island.

Aimee Erickson, *Study of Laguna main beach in the afternoon*, oil on muslin panel,
3" × 5½" | 7.6 cm × 14 cm

The fading of objects near the light source is sometimes called *burnout*. Note the warm and cool in the sky.

REFLECTIONS

A general approach to reflections is this: The reflection should somehow be *less than* the object—less developed, flatter, simpler, broken up, or dimmer. If it's reflecting a light source, the reflection is never as bright as the source. After all, it is a mere reflection.

Any visible object is reflecting light. That's how we see it: Light hits it and bounces off. The more reflective the surface, the less we see of its own color and the more we see of its surroundings. A mirrored surface reflects all the light.

On location, compare a reflection to its surroundings. How does it differ in terms of color? Is it lighter or darker (if you had to pick one)? In two-dimensional thinking, what's greater, its width or its height?

On flat, open reflective surfaces like wet pavement, the surface of water, or a glossy tabletop, look for the reflection directly below the object. It should be drawn not as a mirror image, but as a second object stacked underneath. Its character should be painted to describe the surface: clear and crisp for smooth surfaces, broken for choppy surfaces.

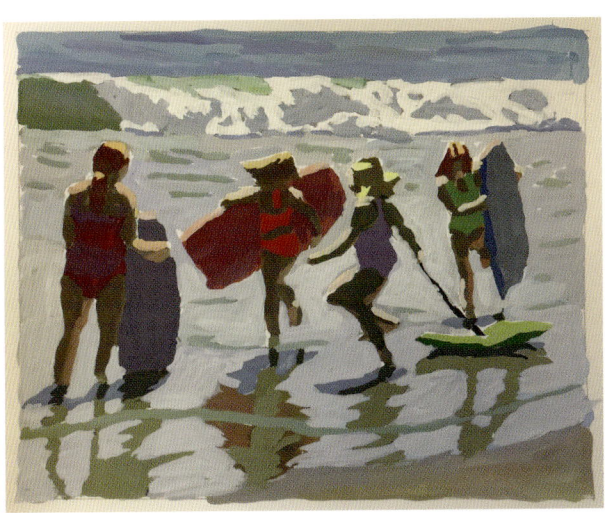

Peggi Kroll Roberts, *Girls with Boogie Boards*, gouache on acid-free paper, 10" × 12" | 25.4 cm × 30.5 cm

The girls' reflections in the backwash describe the ripples and action of the water as well as the light. Reflections always go straight down. Shadows may go diagonally—reflections never. The reflection is darker in the cast shadow. The reflection of the sky, surrounding the girls' reflections, is such a convincing and natural sight that we may not even recognize it as reflection.

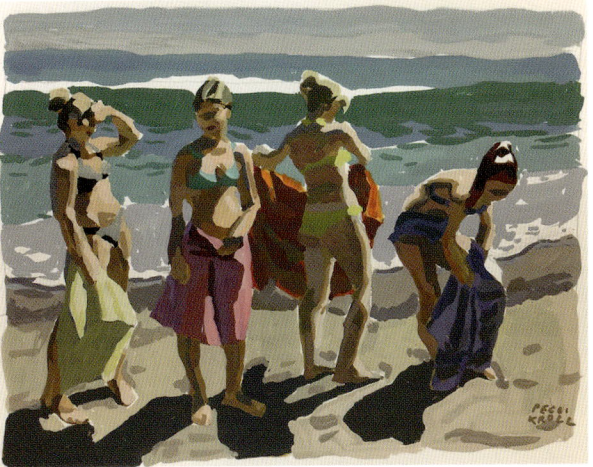

Peggi Kroll Roberts, *Beach Towels*, gouache on acid-free paper, 10" × 12" | 25.4 cm × 30.5 cm

For comparison, girls casting shadows on dry sand.

Reflections go straight down.

Aimee Erickson, *Sunpennies, Oxford Harbor,* oil on muslin panel, 14" × 18" | 35.6 cm × 45.7 cm

Reflections in water clearly have two jobs: describe the surface of the water and have a color relationship to whatever is being reflected. Here, the boats and pilings are backlit, so their shadows block the reflection of the sky that happens everywhere else. With ripples, the top/back side of the ripple is where you see more reflection on the surface, and the front side is where you see less of the surface and more into the water.

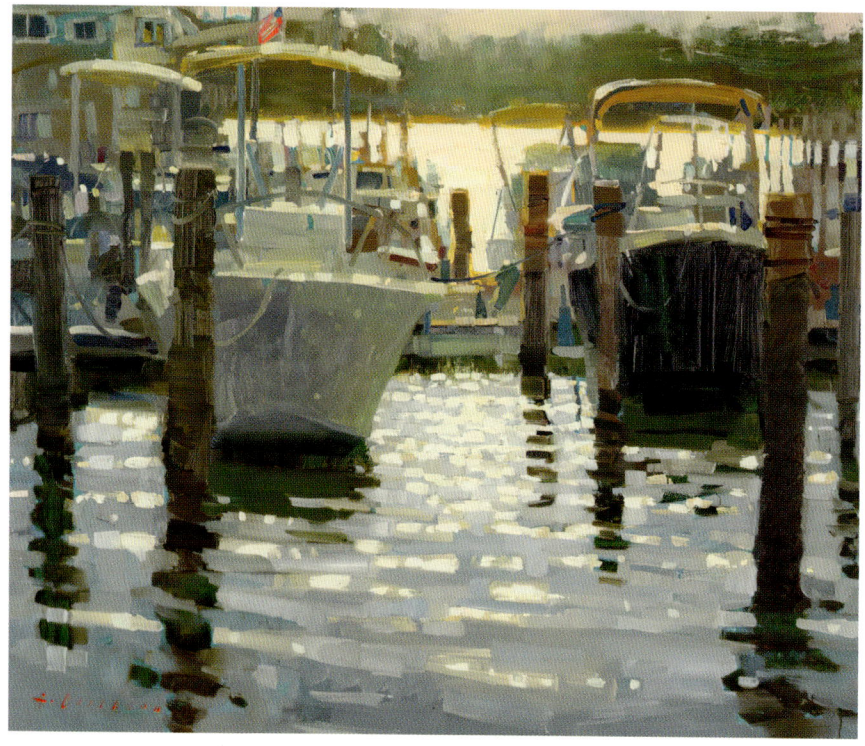

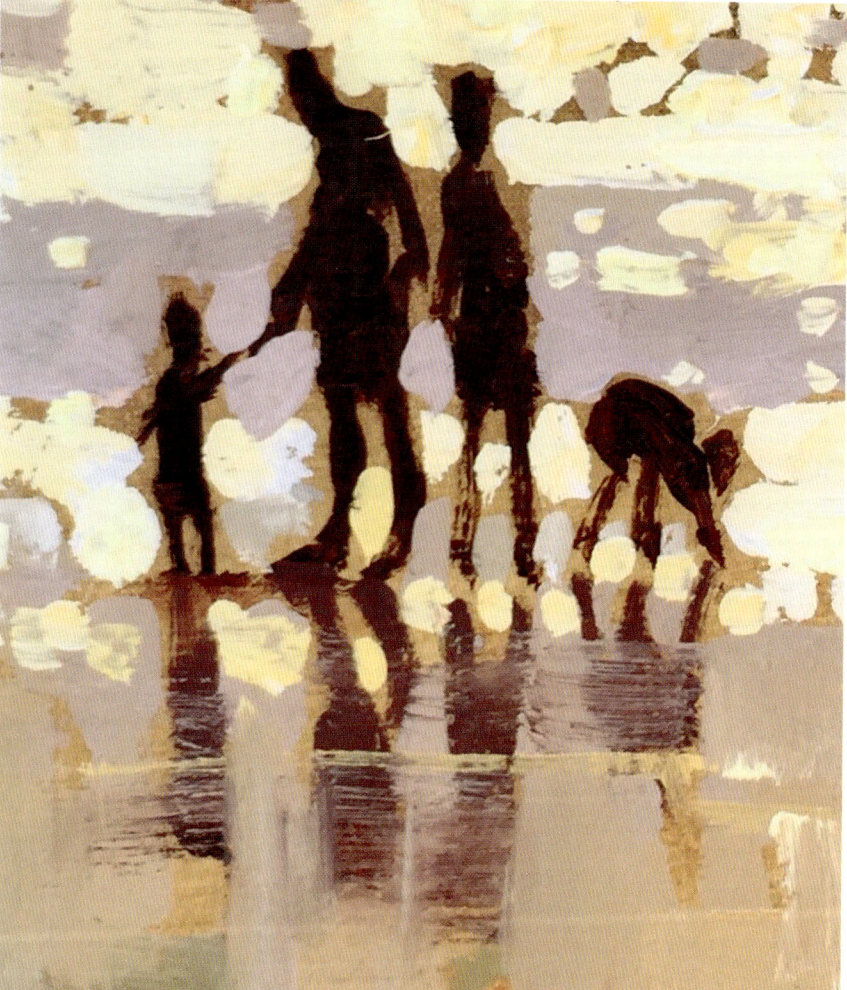

Aimee Erickson, *Sunpennies in the Sea* (detail), oil on muslin panel, 6" × 12" | 15.2 cm × 30.5 cm

Here, the reflections establish a connecting middle color between the dark silhouettes and the lit world of the ocean. In the wet sand, my brushstrokes are vertical for reflections and horizontal for the flatness of the sand.

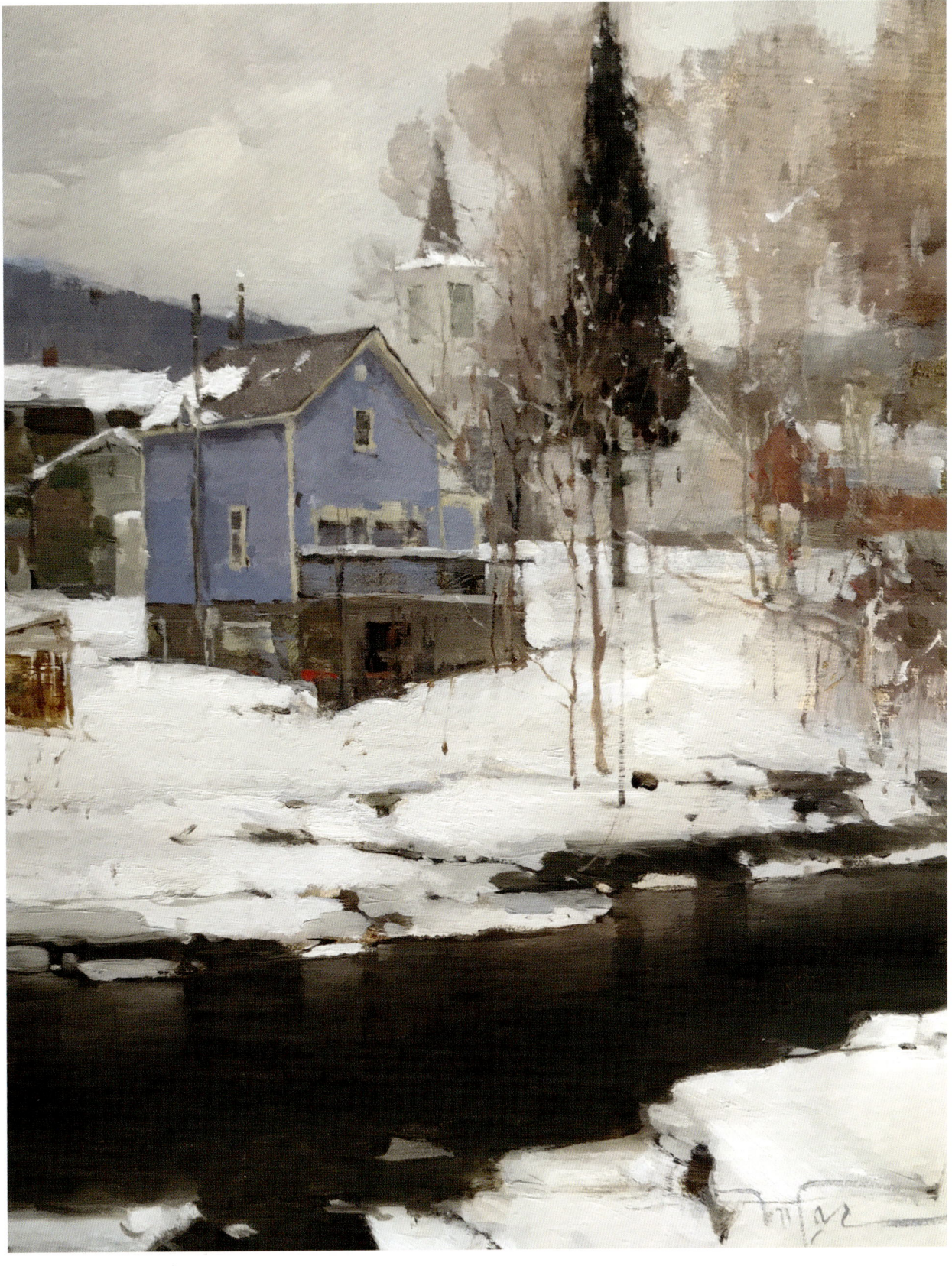

Zufar Bikbov, *Waterville Tale*, oil on linen panel, 14" × 11" | 35.6 cm × 28 cm

Note the snowbanks' subtle reflections in the dark water. Our eyes tend to move toward the light, so these give an upward invitation in the picture.

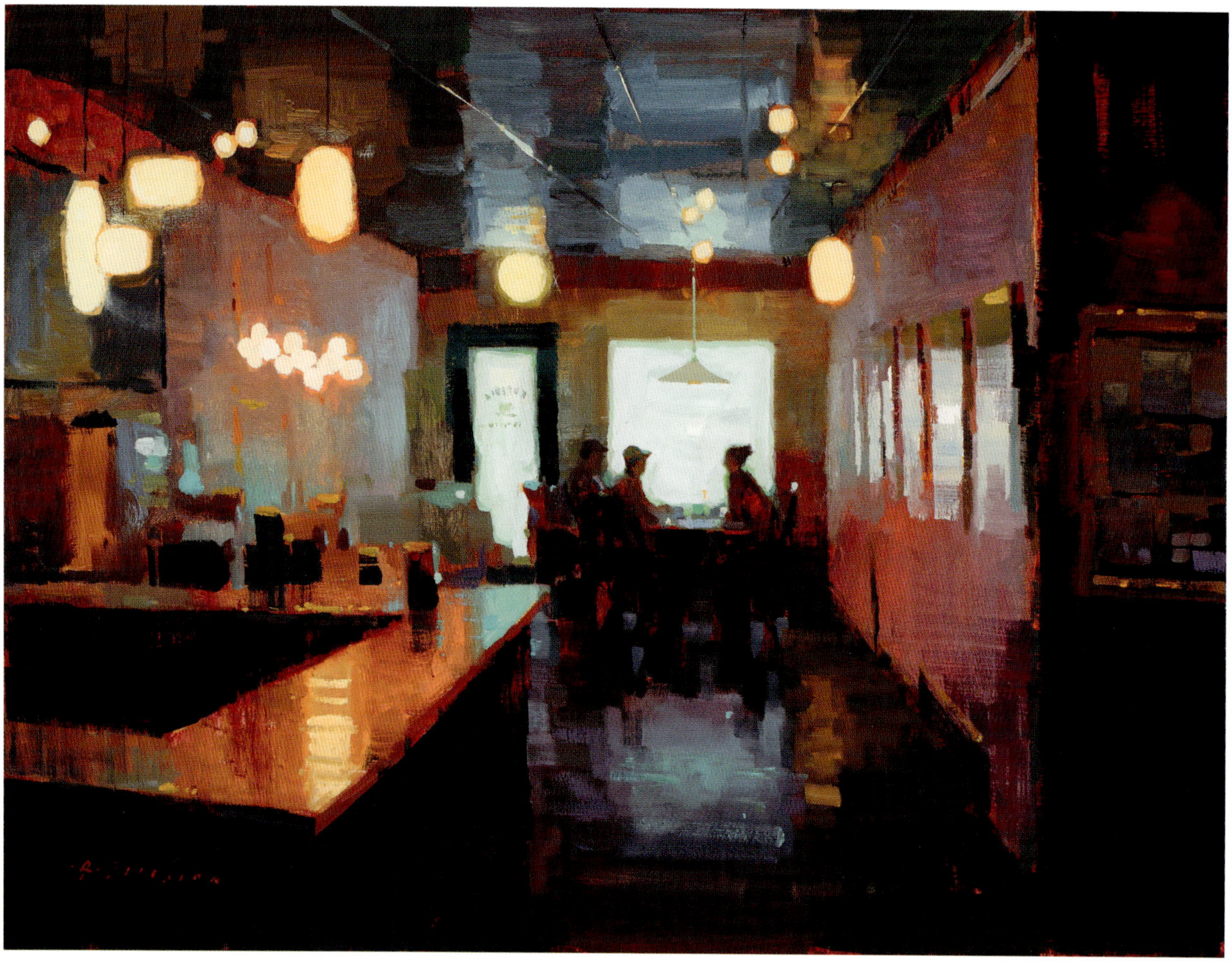

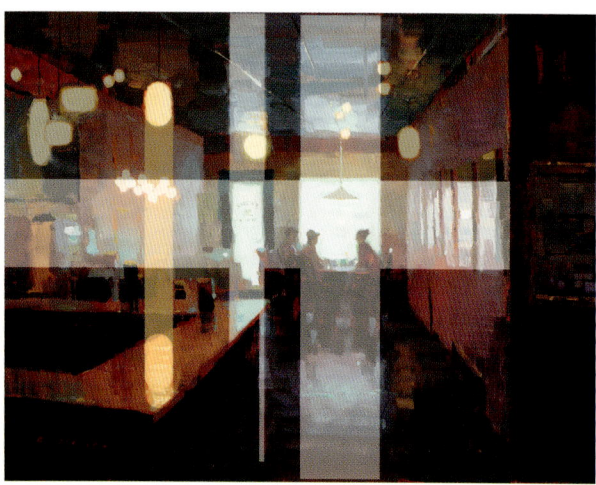

Aimee Erickson, *Interior, a Café*, oil on panel, 23" × 32" | 58.4 cm × 81.3 cm

Analysis of *Interior, a Café* with an overlay showing the pathways of reflections from the major light sources (window, door, and one light fixture).

Reflections' pathways result from the size of the light source and the availability of surfaces to bounce light to your eye. Note the combination of horizontal, vertical, and diagonal elements in this composition. Horizontal and vertical lines indicate either an object that we are facing directly, like the far wall with the window and door, or the shape of a reflection on a receding surface, like the floor—reflections do not conform to perspective. Diagonal lines indicate planes that are receding in space: ceiling, floor, countertop surface, and walls.

REFLECTIVE OBJECTS

A good thing to remember when painting reflective objects, like shiny metal, is that their brightness is deceptive, and reflections are darker than their source. Save room for highlights. Aim low in value when you paint metal.

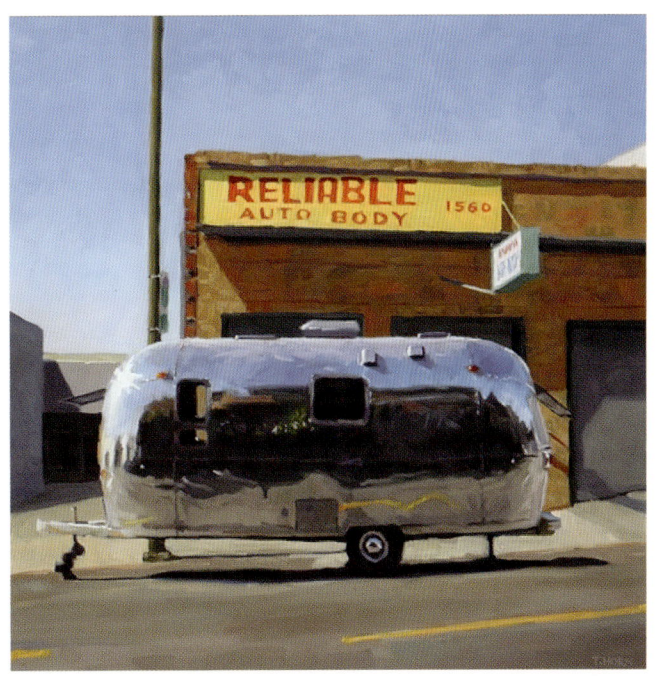

Tim Horn, *Reliable Airstream*, oil on canvas, 24" × 24" | 61 cm × 61 cm

The glorious Airstream shows us the world, reflecting everything around it. Its contours and local color are still apparent.

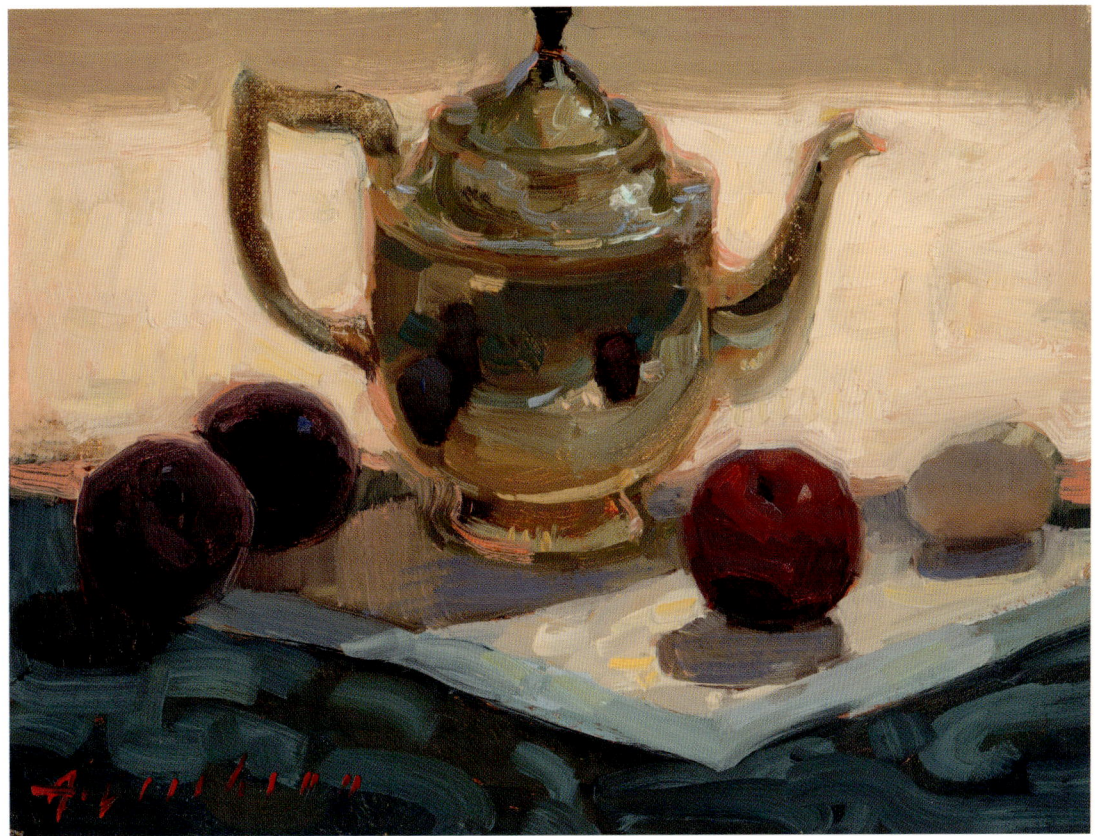

Aimee Erickson, *Still Life with Teapot and Plums*, oil on panel, 9" × 12" | 22.9 cm × 30.5 cm

This teapot is not the cool chrome color of the Airstream but a warmer silver. Sunlight on the tablecloth reflects pink into the underside of the belly of the teapot and also into the egg. Shiny objects have crisper delineations in their reflections than matte objects. Even a little bit of reflection or "bounced light" can go a long way to create conversation in a painting.

HEAVY ATMOSPHERE

FOG, MIST, DUST, AND SMOKE

Heavy atmospheric conditions exaggerate the effects of aerial perspective, with significant color shifts from a sunny day. Look for even more lightening of values from foreground to distance and bigger color shifts depending on the conditions.

On this page are studies from Vermilion Cliffs in northern Arizona, United States of America, all painted with the same palette. The cliffs are named for their color, which is most enhanced when low, golden sunlight amplifies it.

Unpainted corners were blocked by clamps holding these extra-lightweight panels (muslin on Multimedia Artboard) to the box.

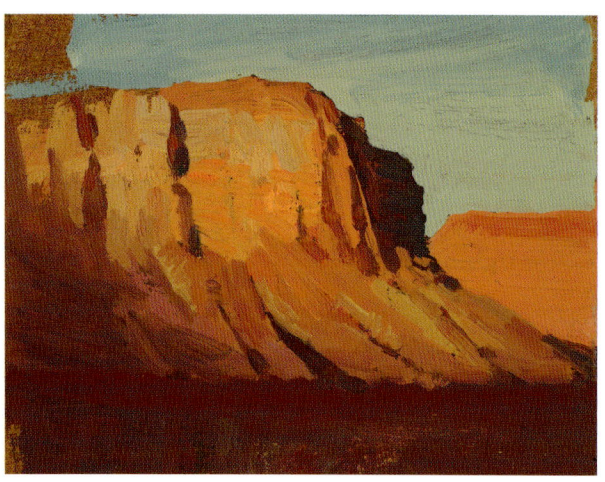

Aimee Erickson, *Study at sundown, Vermilion Cliffs*, oil on muslin panel, 6" × 8" | 15.2 cm × 20.3 cm

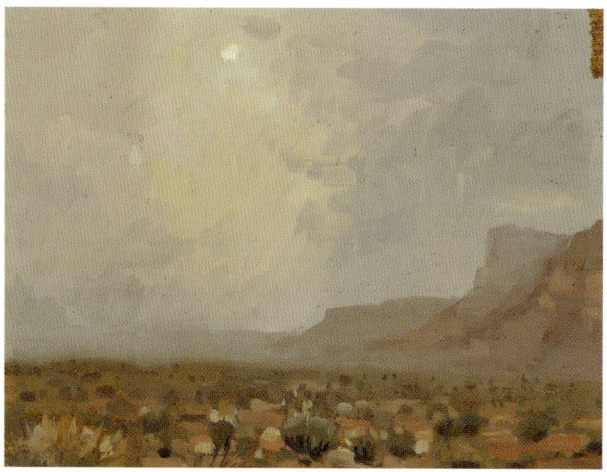

Aimee Erickson, *Study of dust in the air, Vermilion Cliffs*, oil on muslin panel, 6" × 8" | 15.2 cm × 20.3 cm

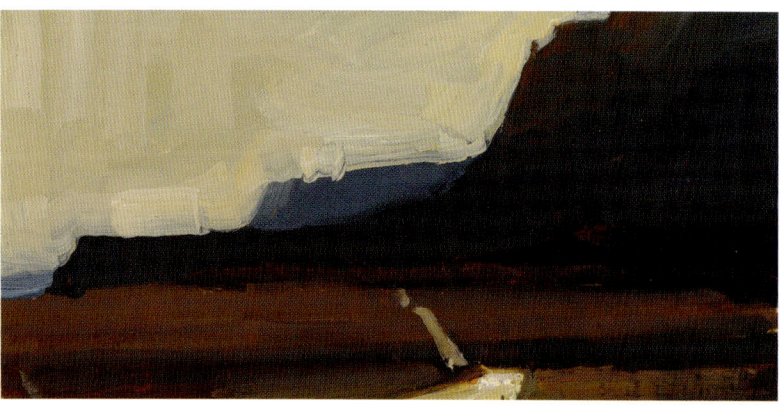

Aimee Erickson, *Dark Earth Study, Vermilion Cliffs*, oil on muslin panel, 4" × 8" | 10.2 cm × 20.3 cm

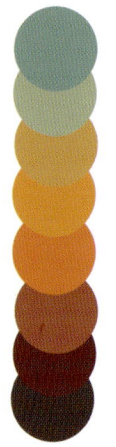
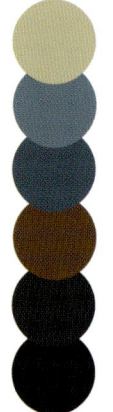
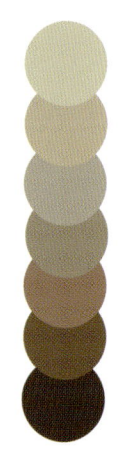

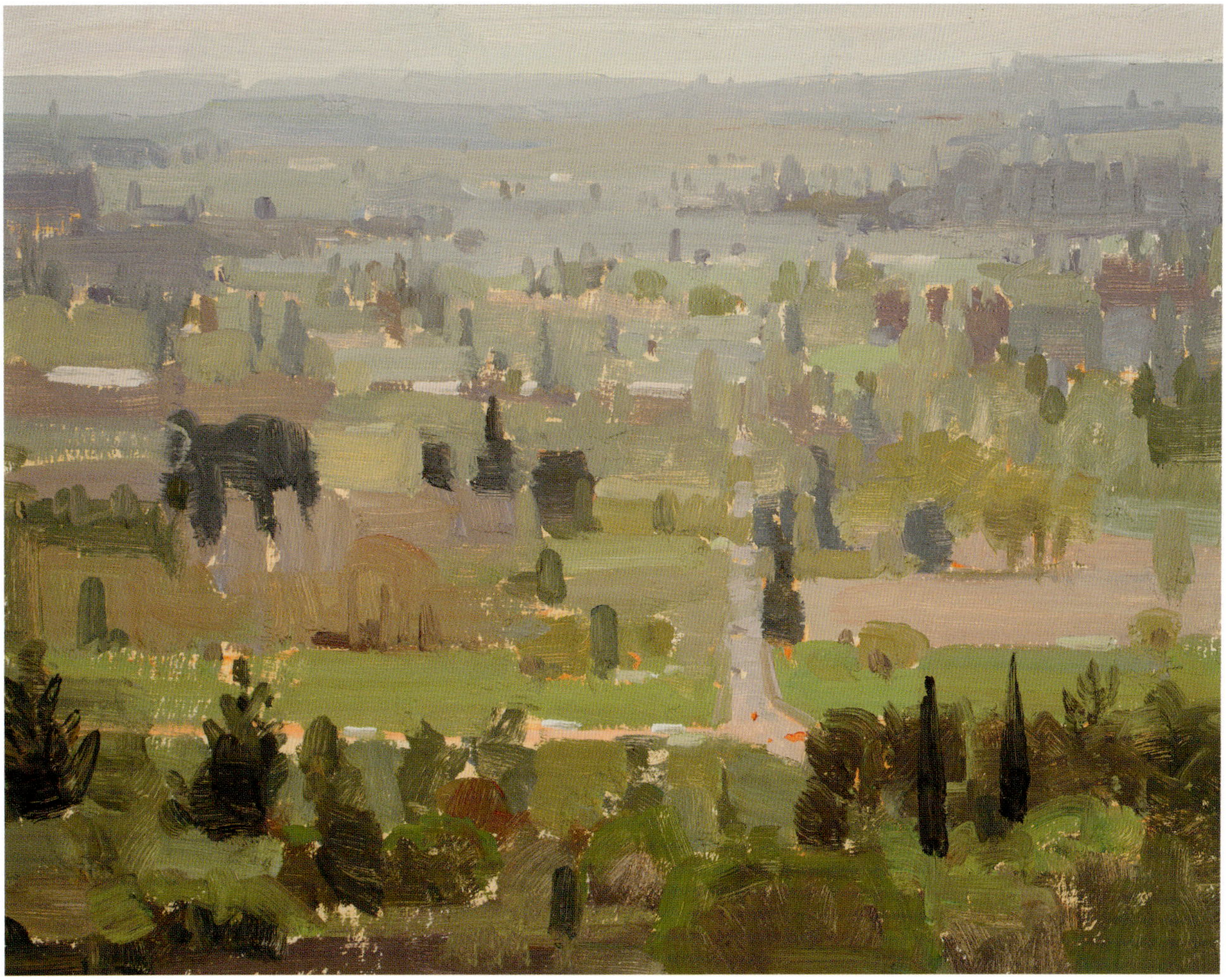

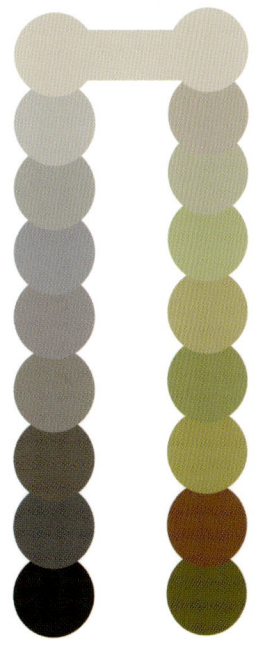

Aimee Erickson, *Hazy Day*, oil on muslin panel, 11" × 14" | 28 cm × 35.6 cm

Here we have high cloud cover and a thin mist in the Oregon air. There's no clear light and shadow, but the ground planes facing the sky—fields and open areas—are better lit than the upright planes—trees and tree-groupings. The two columns of color callouts show a range for each: upright planes on the left and upward-facing planes on the right. At the top of each column is the same color, the sky. Note how all the colors become more similar with distance—in this case, paler and grayer.

DEMONSTRATION:
FOG

KATHLEEN B. HUDSON:
COVE WREATHED IN FOG

A field or shoreline of rocks like this is a fairly complicated subject. You have to put three elements—at the least—in every rock: shadow, turning color, and lit side. In this painting, made on the coast of Maine, United States of America, in the blustery edge of a hurricane, Kathleen B. Hudson manages all the rocks, reflections, and sense of the shoreline's gesture, within a limited color and value range, all while intermittently sheltering from the weather.

DEMONSTRATION NOTES

- Linen panel, 16" × 12" (40.6 cm × 30.5 cm).
- Gear: Hudson uses the Daytripper Easel from Prolific Painter because of its flexibility—it's very lightweight but can handle large works.

- Palette (all Michael Harding paint): Titanium White No. 1, Cadmium Yellow Lemon, Indian Yellow, Cadmium Red Light, Magenta, Transparent Oxide Red, Yellow Ochre, Phthalocyanine Blue Lake (Phthalo Blue), Ultramarine Blue, Cobalt Blue, Raw Umber, Ivory Black, and Neutral Grey.

1. Hudson starts with a graded wash of Ultramarine Blue and Transparent Oxide Red to set the key for the painting, and then blocks in the foggy sky, knowing that's her lightest value.

2. Michael Harding's Raw Umber has a beautiful warm, transparent quality. Hudson used it to design the rocks in the foreground and hold the darkest values before laying in the carefully graded lit colors.

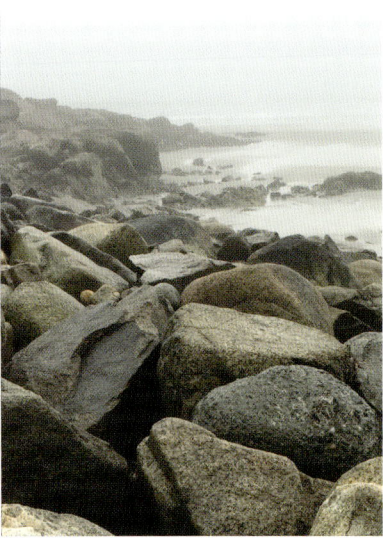

The scene and the weather that day.

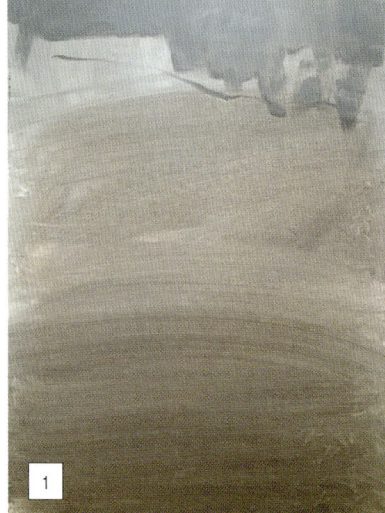

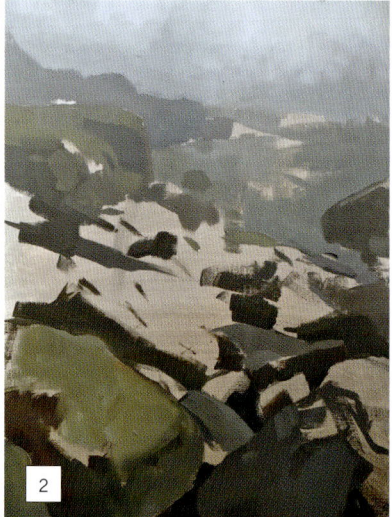

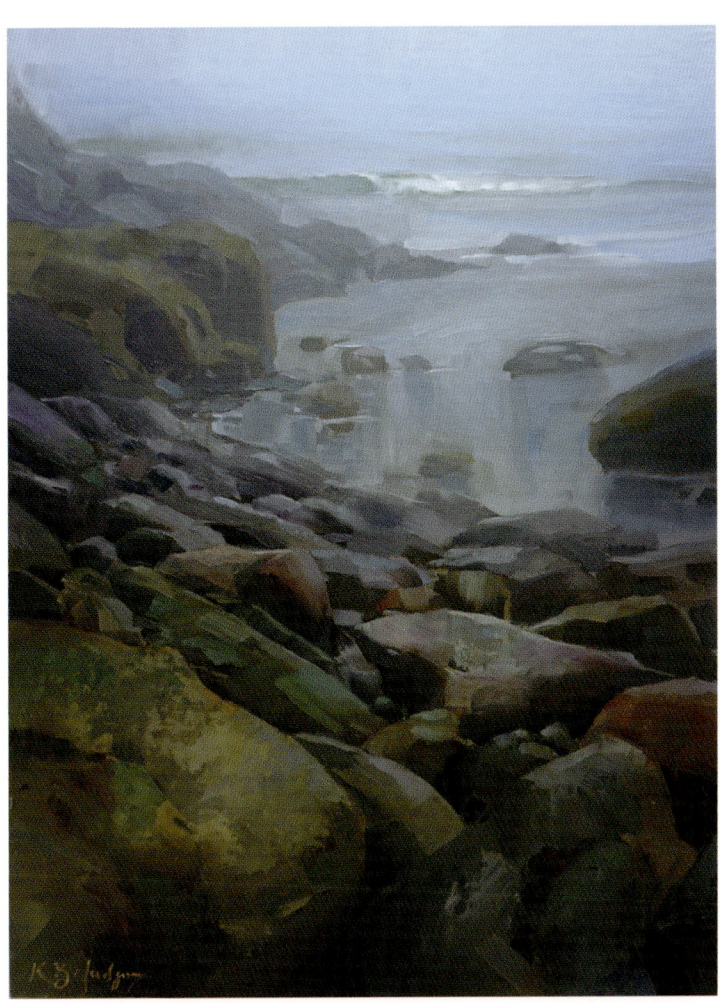

Kathleen B. Hudson, *Cove Wreathed in Fog*, oil on linen panel, 20" × 16" | 50.8 cm × 40.6 cm

"It's the subtle shifts that create a compelling painting."

—KATHLEEN B. HUDSON

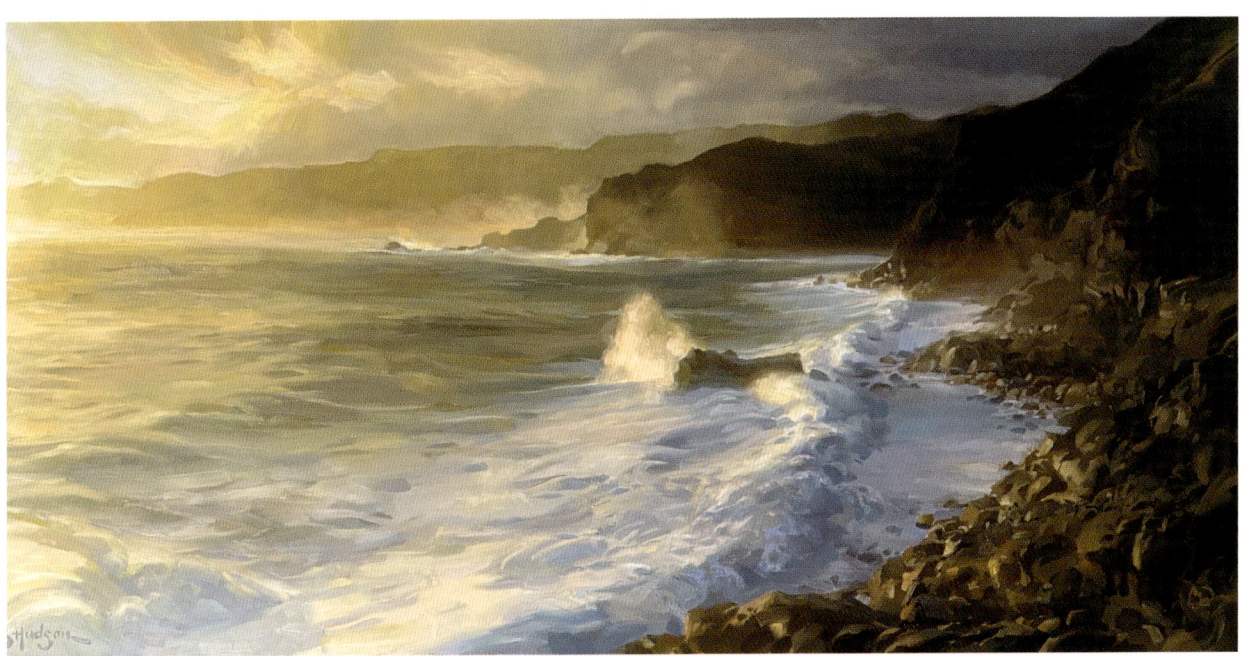

Kathleen B. Hudson, *Light Breaking Through*, oil on linen panel, 12" × 24" | 30.5 cm × 61 cm

Mist in the ocean air holds the glowing light of the setting sun, pushing everything toward gold.

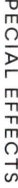

SMOKY SKIES

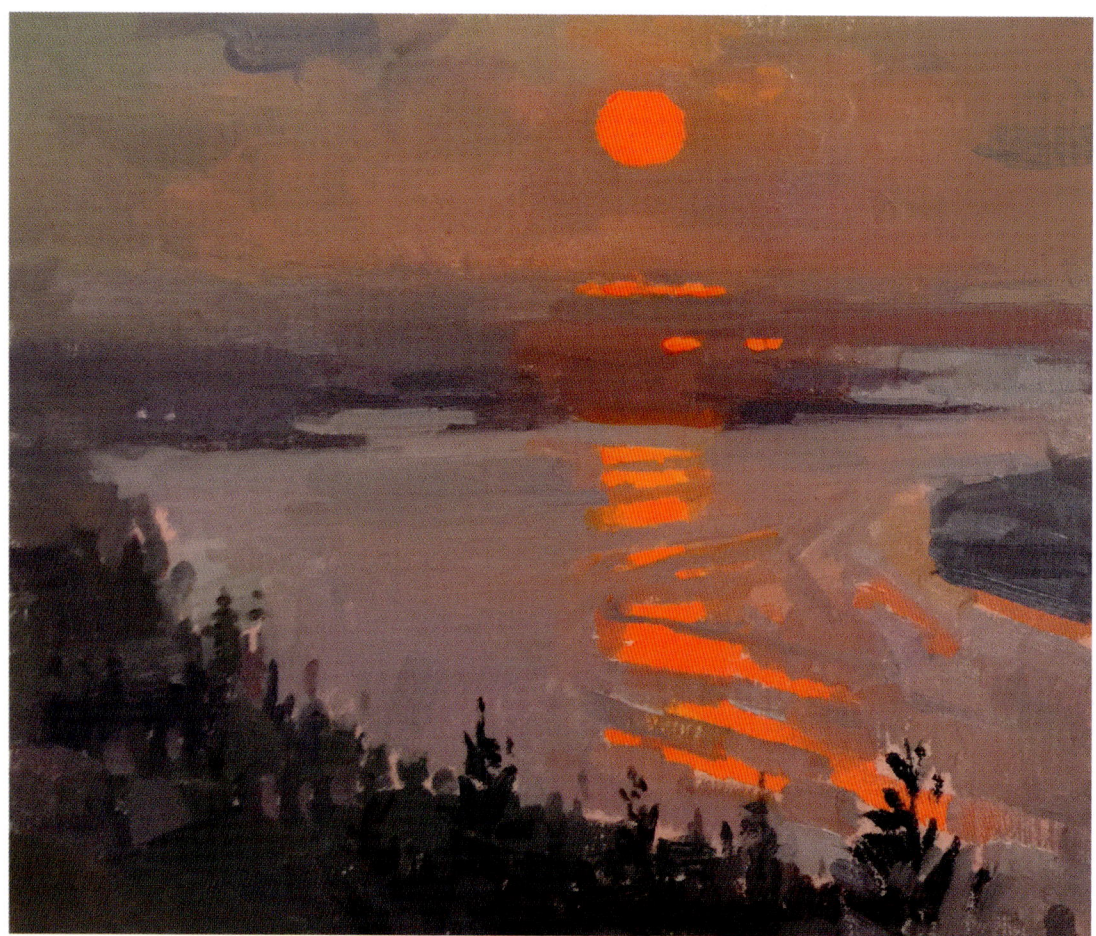

Aimee Erickson, *Smoky Sunset,
Columbia River*, oil on muslin panel,
9" × 12" | 22.9 cm × 30.5 cm

Smoke in the air causes the strange phenomenon of gray skies and a glowing red sun. This poses a challenge because if you paint the sky light gray and the sun red, the sun ends up darker than the sky, which is contrary to what we know about a light source—it *has* to be the lightest thing. In this painting, I made the sun and its reflections on the water as light as I could while keeping the color very intense, and I made the water and sky as dark as I could while still keeping them somewhere in the gray-purple range (or at any rate, less chromatic than the sun).

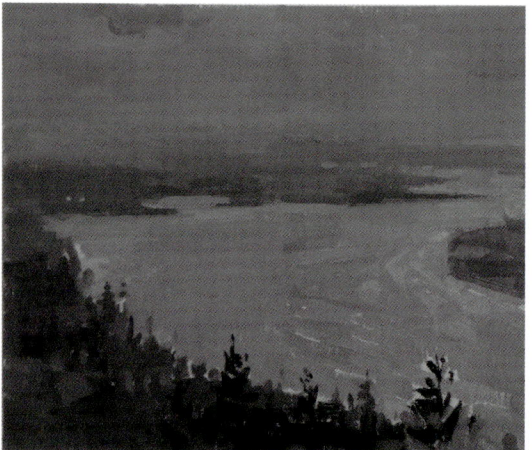

Same image, desaturated. Turns out the sun and the sky are the exact same value. This demonstrates that at the same value, the higher chroma color appears to be *more lit*. Its glow is heightened by the color of the sky surrounding it.

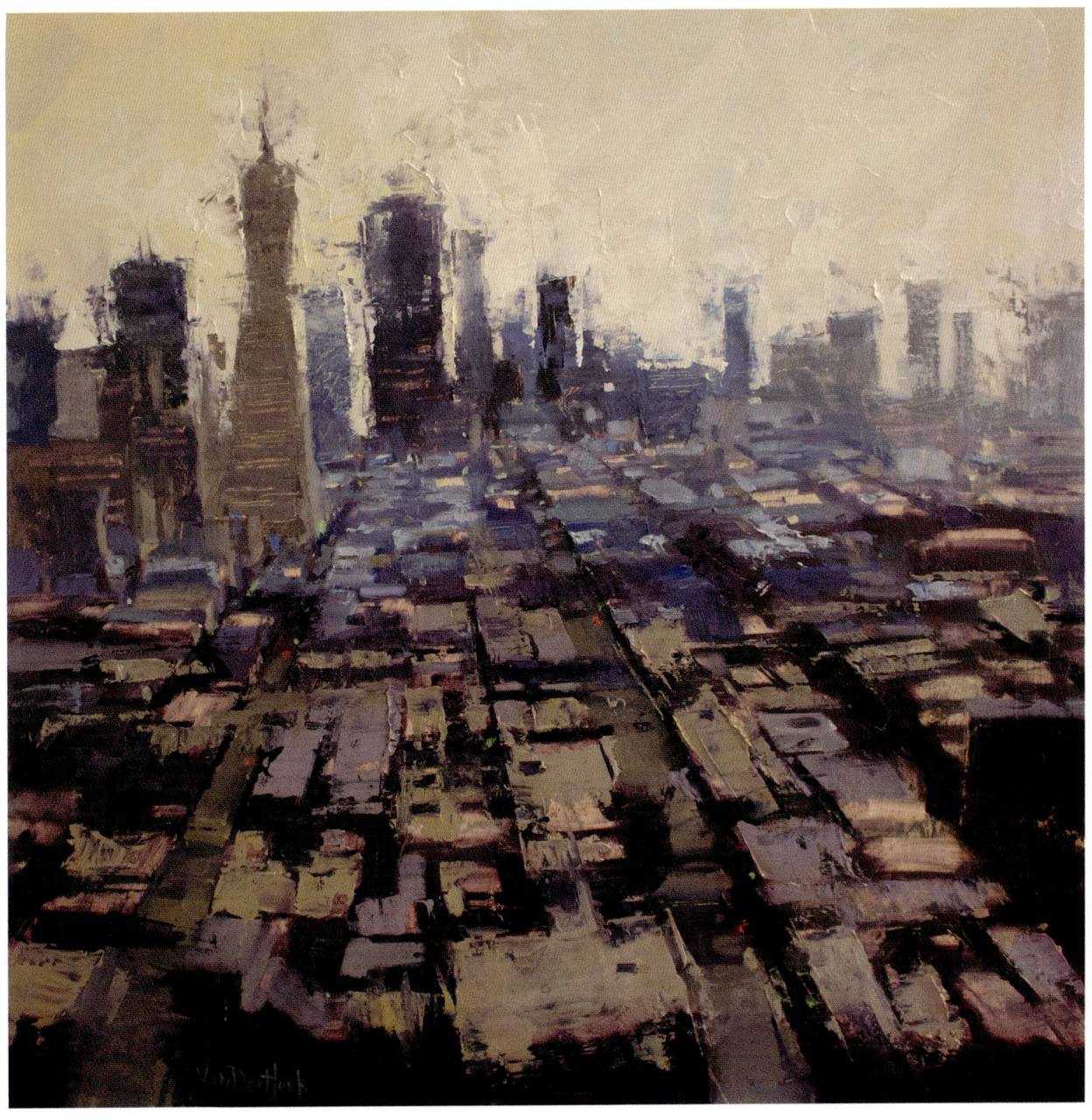

Kim VanDerHoek, *The Maze*, oil on canvas, 24" × 24" | 61 cm × 61 cm

Looking over the city: converging lines and shifting color. The horizon line is not stated, but all the other information makes it clear what our eye level is and which buildings rise past it. Color shifts give a sense of atmosphere settled over the city.

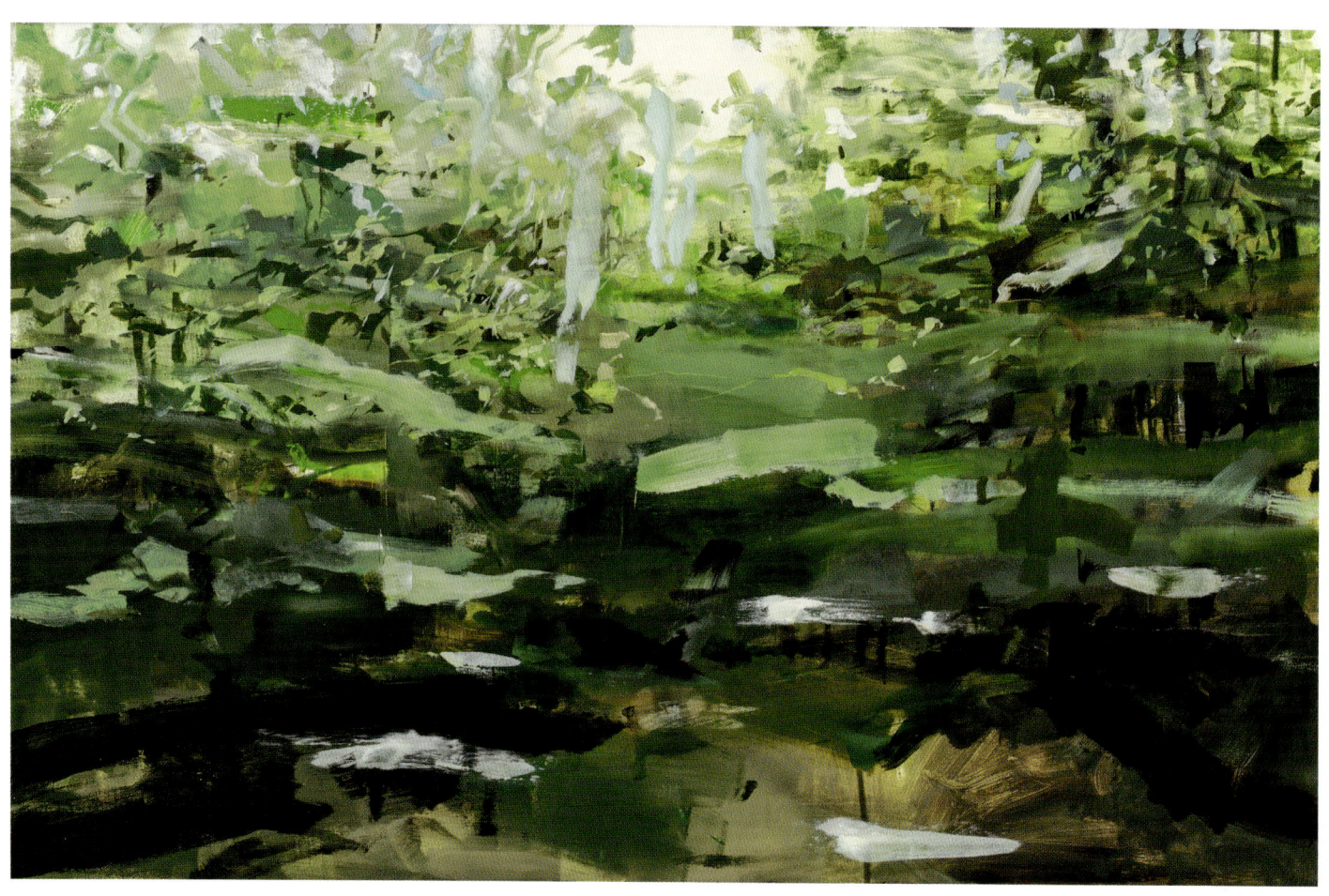

Alex Kanevsky, *New Hampshire Trees*, oil on linen, 36" × 56" | 91.4 cm × 142.2 cm

10

DESIGN AND
THE VISUAL IDEA

The starting point for a painting is a visual idea. The idea is the spark—the "in," the pull, the question that needs an answer—and being visual, it doesn't translate well into words. It wants to be painted.

Having an idea means knowing what you want to make of something. I once heard a legendary painter say, "It's the most valuable thing we have, and we're not in charge of it."

Often, it has to do with wanting to express the *feel* of something, such as the feeling of a hill rising and falling or the feeling of dusk settling over the landscape. Subject matter can be pushy and keep insisting that you get it "right." But human beings are not machines. We *feel* things. We have intention and can make decisions. We can create something original, something artistic, something which takes on its own identity and answers only to itself.

I see stuff all the time: all day, every day. Do I always have an idea for a painting? Not always. But often.

"To put it roughly: Painting is never 'of something.' It is not even 'of something happening to something.' It is when something is next to something else, unrelated, and what happens in between."

—ALEX KANEVSKY

BEYOND REPRESENTATION

A painting can be more evocative than reality. For one thing, it's a painting, and paint has innate beauty. Artistic principles can be applied at every decision point.

We are not photographers: We can choose what goes where. We can emphasize and subordinate elements. Reality is awfully bossy, and there's a strong pull to relay things "as they are." Reality is not fixed. We can tell the truth without being literal.

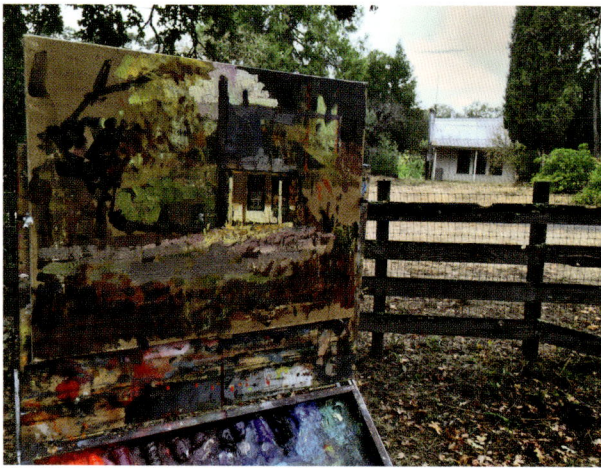

On location in Sonoma, midway through my painting of one of the old farm workers' houses near Glen Ellen.

"Abstract literally means to draw from or separate. In this sense, every artist is abstract . . . a realistic or non-objective approach makes no difference. The result is what counts."

—RICHARD DIEBENKORN

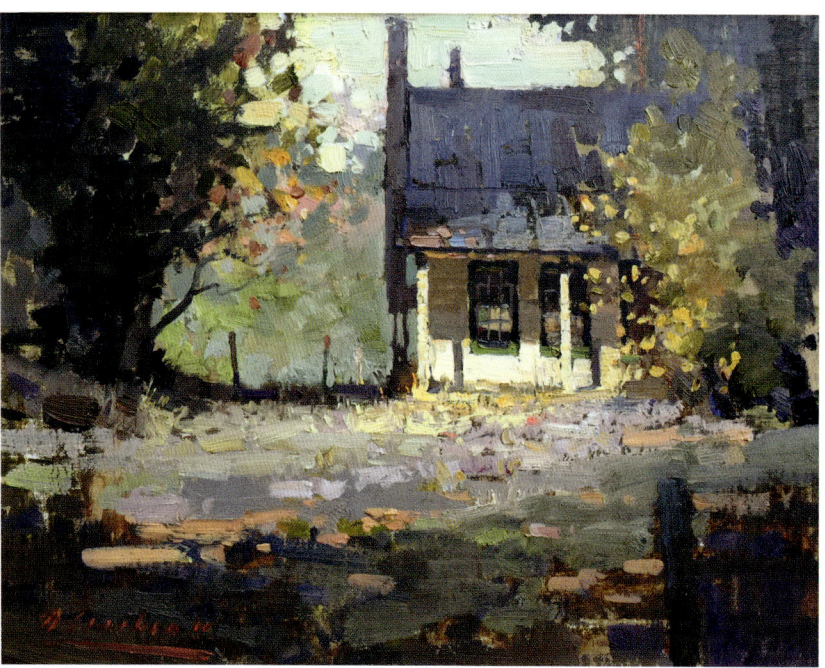

Aimee Erickson, *Sonoma Ranch House*, oil on canvas panel,
11" × 14" | 28 cm × 35.6 cm

TECHNIQUE:
PAINT MANIPULATION

CHARLIE HUNTER:
WINTERBARN

DEMONSTRATION NOTES

- Medium: Cobra Water-Miscible Oils.
- Palette: Vandyke Brown—warm, dark, semitransparent, and very versatile.
- Brushes: Several brushes, including a 1-inch (2.5 cm) flat watercolor brush for square edges, a rigger for twigs, and a smaller flat.
- Tools: A spray bottle, paper towels, a squeegee, cotton swabs, a toothbrush, and various scrapers.

Starting from a series of sketches made on location, Hunter uses a single color to make a painting that is strong in design and has a remarkable variety of paint application. Washes, scrapes, drips, paint pulled off with a squeegee or laid down in an impossible line from the squeegee's edge; water spritzed onto semi-dry paint then blotted with a paper towel to remove the spray pattern; paint spritzed onto the canvas with a toothbrush; the bright canvas in some places untouched; crisp high-contrast edges; edges broken with splatter, with drips, with a brush shoved like a trowel; paint lifted by a paper towel pressed against it—these are all decisions made by a bold and careful mind. The result somehow merges the world of an old sepia-toned photograph with the reality of abstraction.

1. Barn sketches. We can see his thought process in experimenting with various designs—how much space should the barn take up in the frame? What if the utility pole is moved off to the right? Can the cupola be solved as a dark shape or a light one? Note also that the shape of the format is adjusted as he figures out the shape relationships.

continued ▸

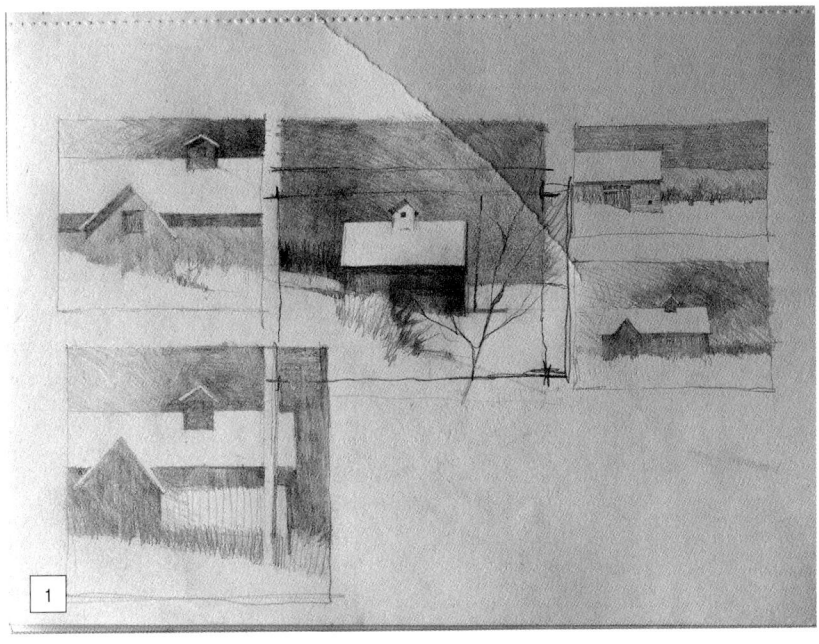

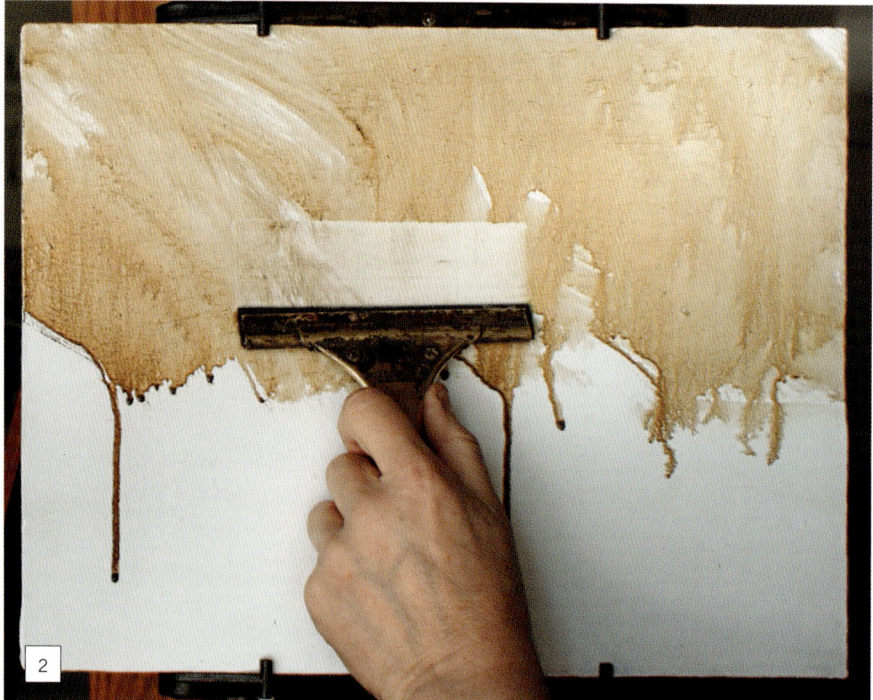

2. A single stroke of the squeegee defines the light shape of the barn's roof. Later, he will use a cotton swab and a smaller brush to remove paint for the cupola.

3. Marking the edge of the roof. We can also see mass tone next to and on top of glaze tone. Hunter uses a soft-haired flat watercolor brush to lay down heavier paint on the side of the barn. A squeegee loaded with paint makes a good straight mark. The paint load and pressure vary. The direction of the stroke indicates the siding.

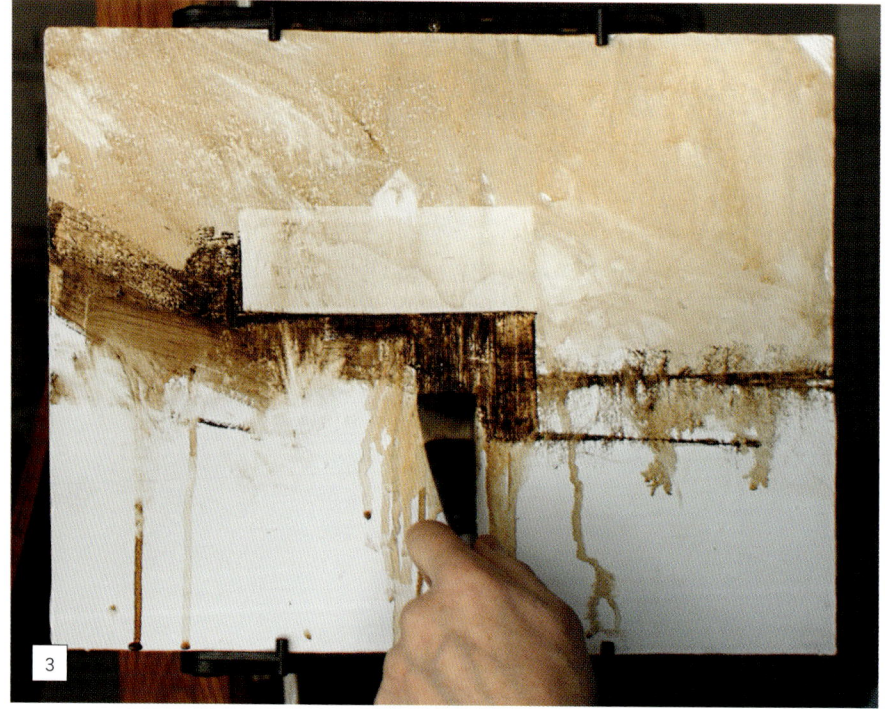

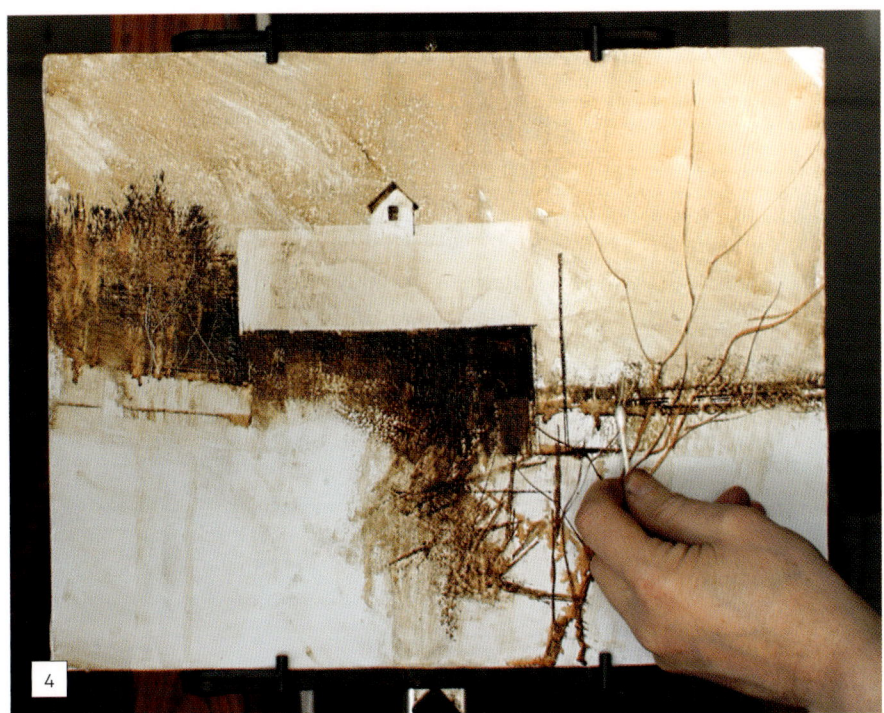

4. A primary concern is the balance between marks. Smooshy wet brushmarks below the barn are the beginning indication of shrubbery. The rigger can make beautiful long fine brushstrokes, which contrast beautifully with the dark mass of the barn. A dampened, finger-sharpened cotton swab pulls out trunks from a mass of trees.

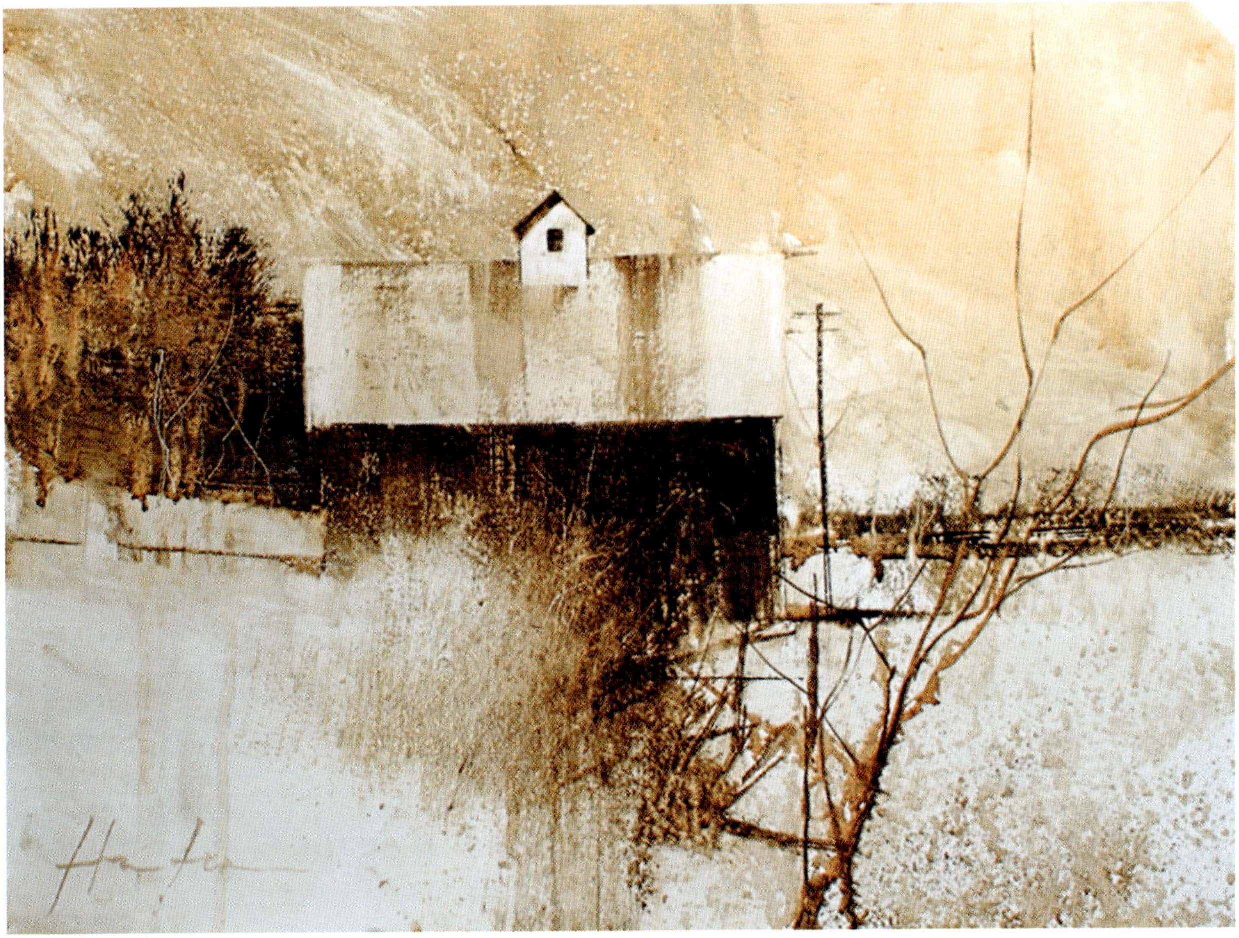

Charlie Hunter, *Winterbarn Demo*, Cobra water-miscible oils on gessoed muslin, mounted on Gator Board, 11" × 14" | 28 cm × 35.6 cm

MULTIPLE SMALL STUDIES

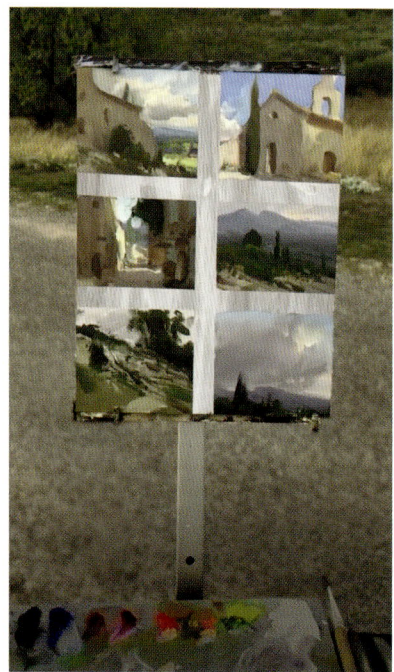

Josh Clare's panel with six studies. He used masking tape to divide the panel and keep clean edges. This is a great solution if you want to do smaller studies and not cope with transporting a bunch of small wet panels. You can use your bigger panels and store them in the usual panel carrier.

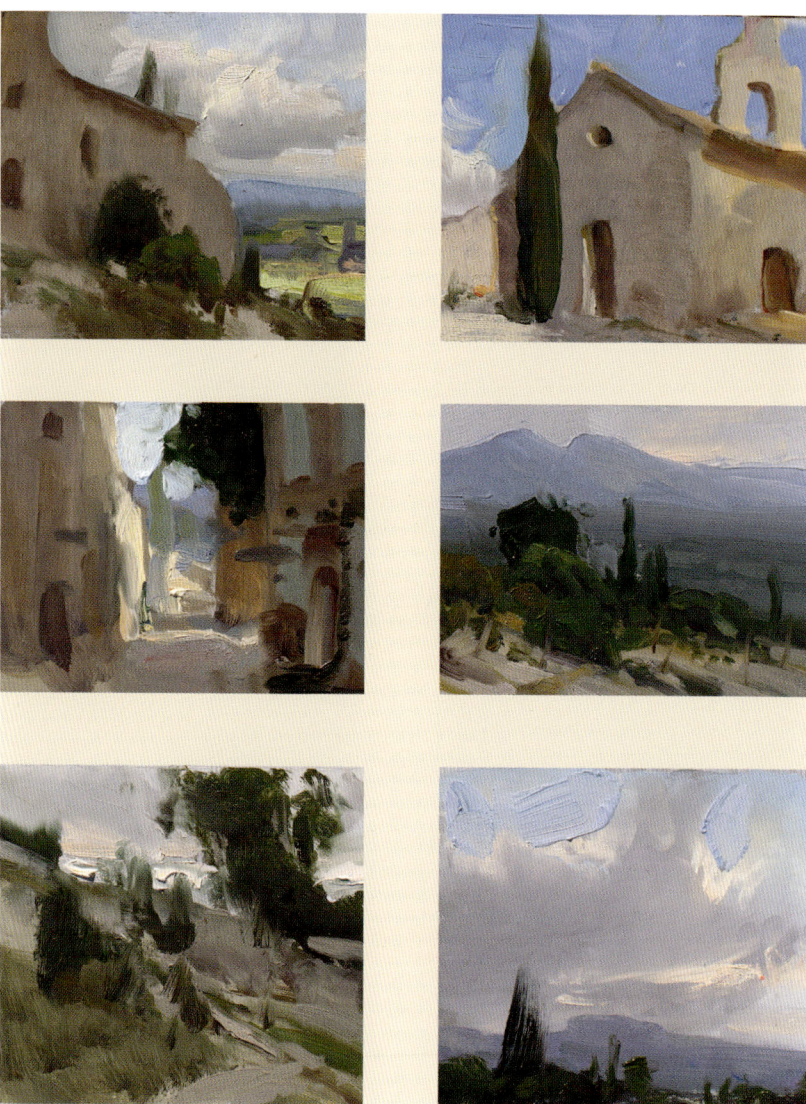

Josh Clare, *six studies from France.*

WORKING TIME AND PACE

Pace is a matter of the artist's intention and what the painting is ready for. Plein air work is often associated with speed, and for good reason, particularly if the aim is to capture the conditions of the day in a single sitting. Some people find it very motivating to work under time pressure. The important thing is to suit yourself and stay in tune with your painting.

STRATEGY:
SERIAL STUDIES OF A SUBJECT

SCOTT GELLATLY AT THE WETLANDS

Painting repeatedly at the same location is an opportunity to study a subject in depth. It's the same place, but the weather's different, the light's different, the temperature's different. Familiarity with a place makes you more sensitive to its character.

DEMONSTRATION NOTES

Location, materials, and working methods remain consistent:

- Location: A wetlands area close to home.
- Medium: Casein.
- Support: Strathmore 400 Series Watercolor Paper Sketchbook.
- Size (taped off): 4½" × 7½" (11.4 cm × 19 cm).
- Brushes: Princeton Aspen and watercolor brushes.
- Palette: Cadmium Yellow Light, Cadmium Orange, Quinacridone Red, Ultramarine Blue, Phthalo Green, and Titanium White.
- Gear: U.GO Plein Air Pochade Box, tripod-mounted.
- Working Time: 30–60 minutes.

. . . and these elements vary:

- Season and time of day.
- Scene selection and color choices.
- Conditions of the day: weather, temperature, and light.

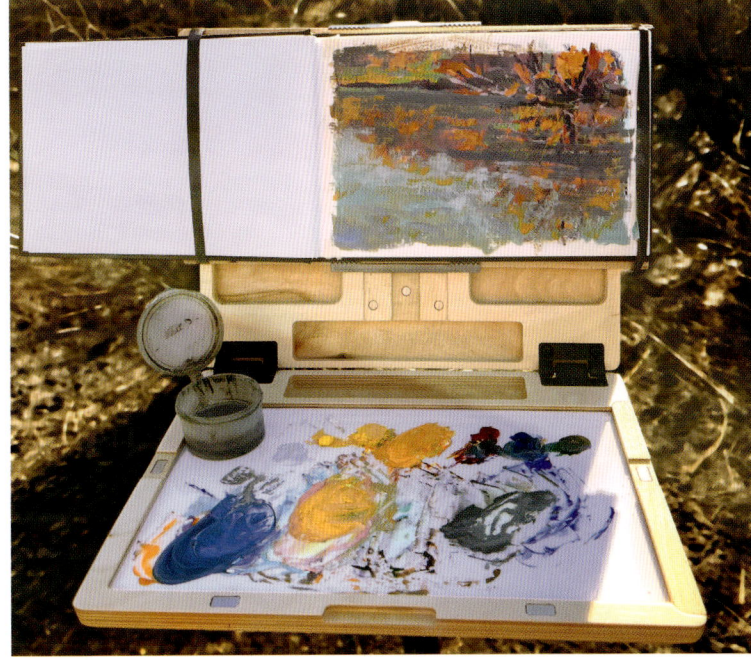

Gellatly's casein setup. He uses a lightweight wooden pochade box with tension hinges. A rubber band keeps the sketchbook pages together.

"In regards to site selection, I have traded searching for the 'grand view' of epic landscapes for the more intimate and familiar."

—SCOTT GELLATLY

continued ▸

These are just a few of the dozens of studies Gellatly has made, filling four sketchbooks over a three-year period. The individual studies become more than standalone sketches: They form a series with its own vocabulary of place, an extended statement about a wetlands and about a painter's vision. They also serve as a springboard for his studio paintings.

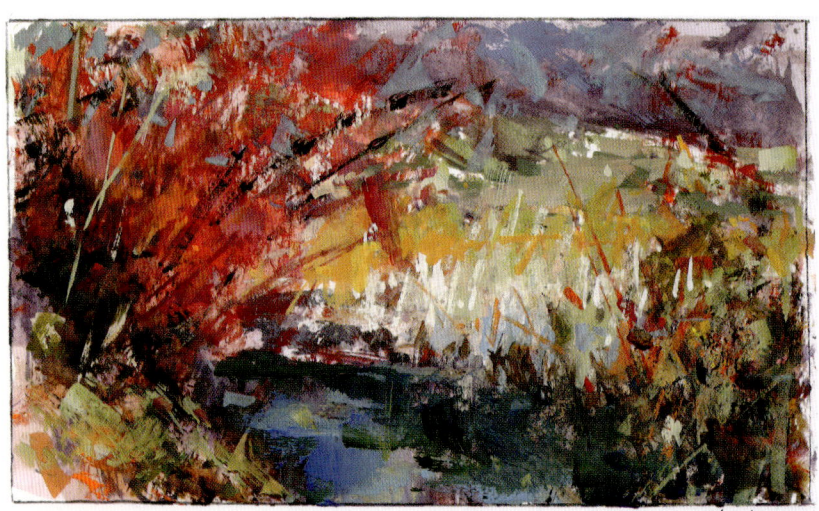

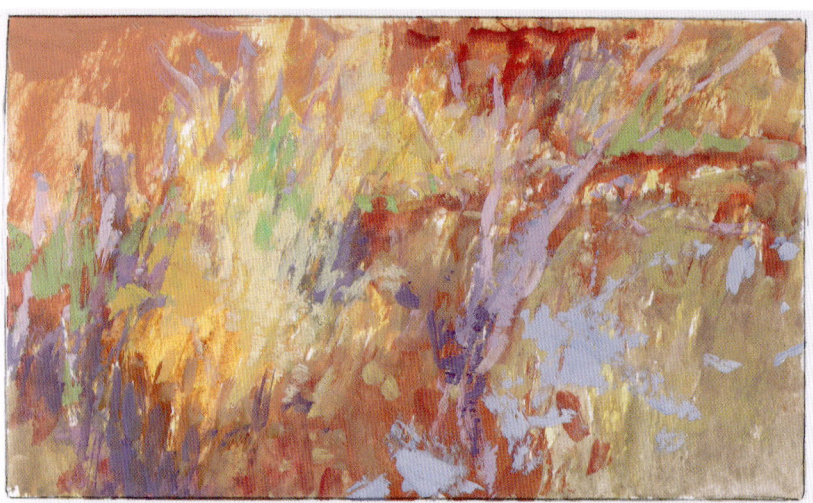

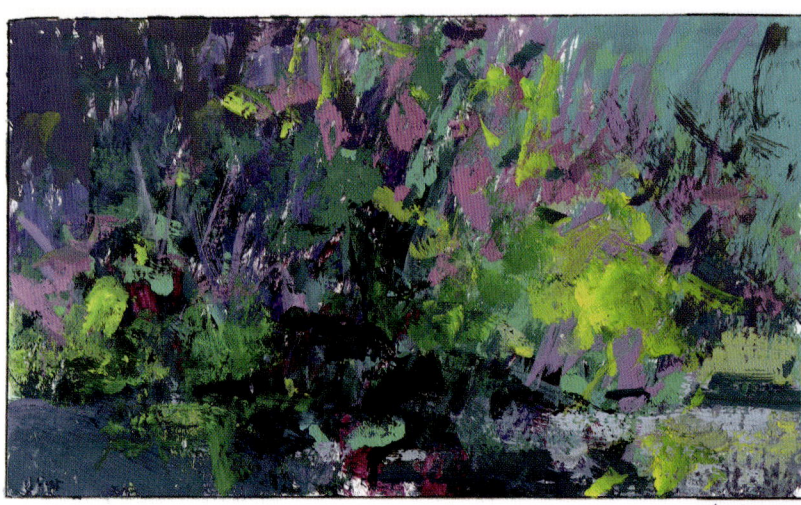

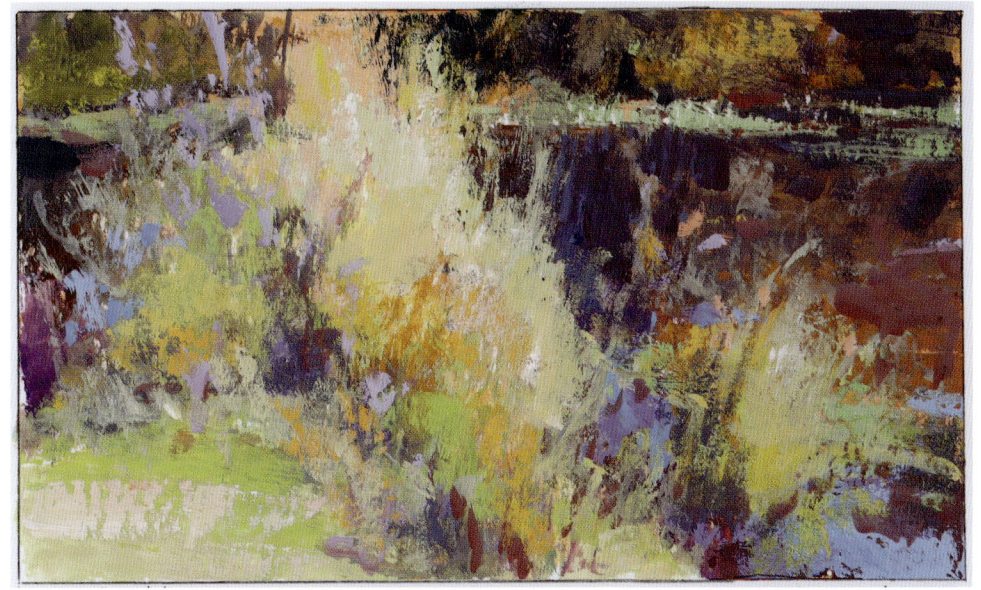

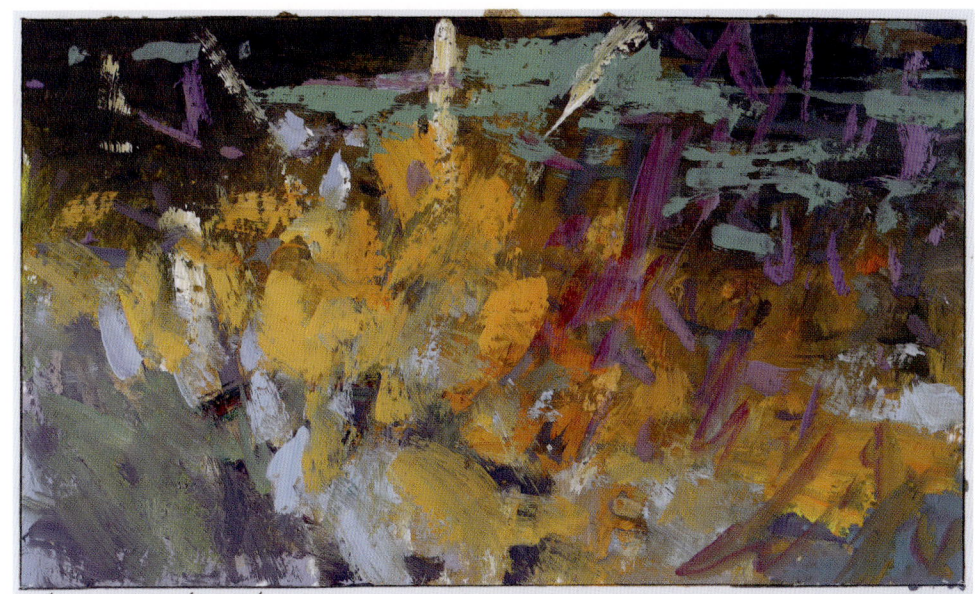

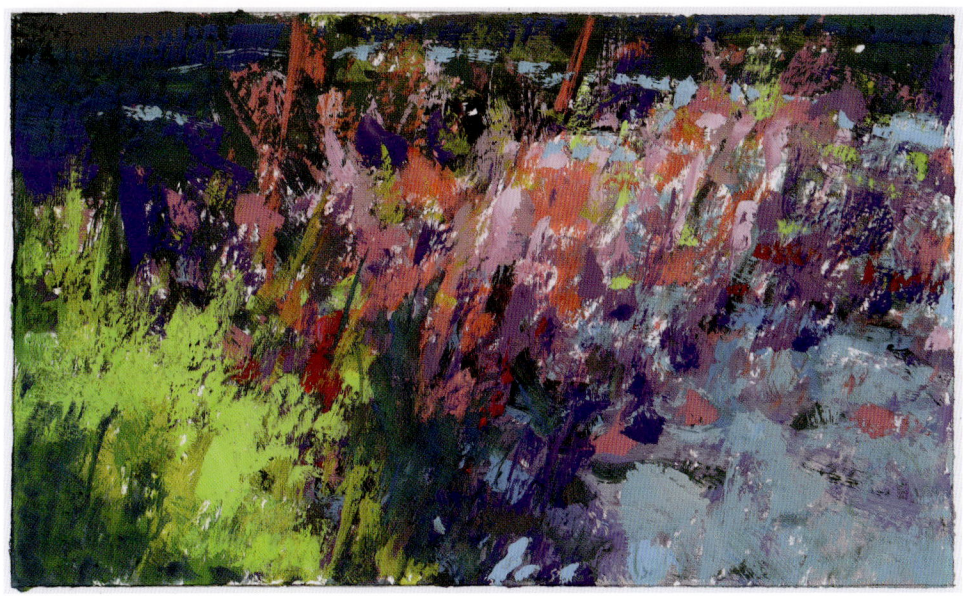

THE CAMERA'S ROLE

Plein air painting is all about being on location and painting, from direct observation, the conditions of the day. It goes without saying that you don't need a camera for that. You need seeing skills to judge intervals and color relationships, and you need the design skills to make effective compositions. But you probably have a camera, and it can help you learn to see differently. Here's one way I use my camera.

Out-of-focus photographs show less detail and more of the gestalt. This helps us perceive the bigger shapes. Colors are generalized or averaged together. Edges are softened. Points of light are rendered by the camera lens as flat disks of color, an effect known as *bokeh*.

In effect, an out-of-focus photograph starts to look something like a painting. It can help us shift our thinking away from detail and into painting mode, where we consider big shapes and color relationships.

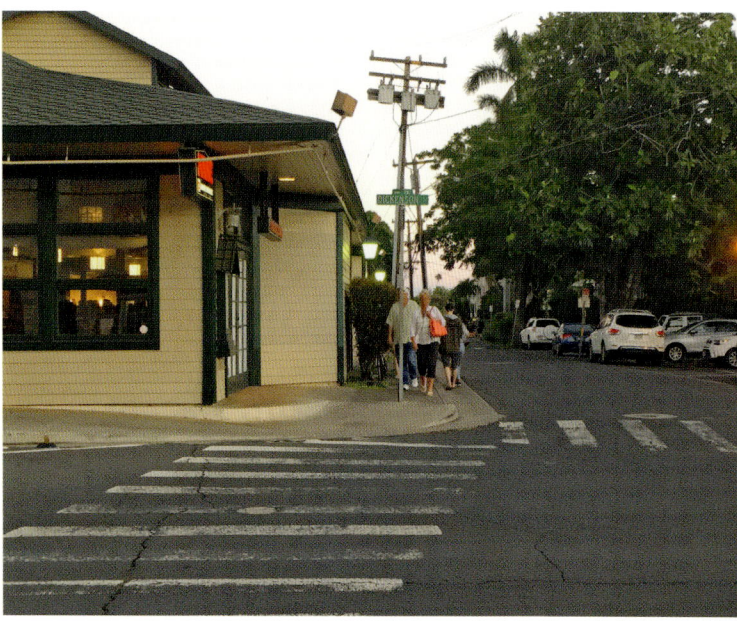

A street corner in Lahaina. This was shot on an iPhone with auto focus and auto exposure.

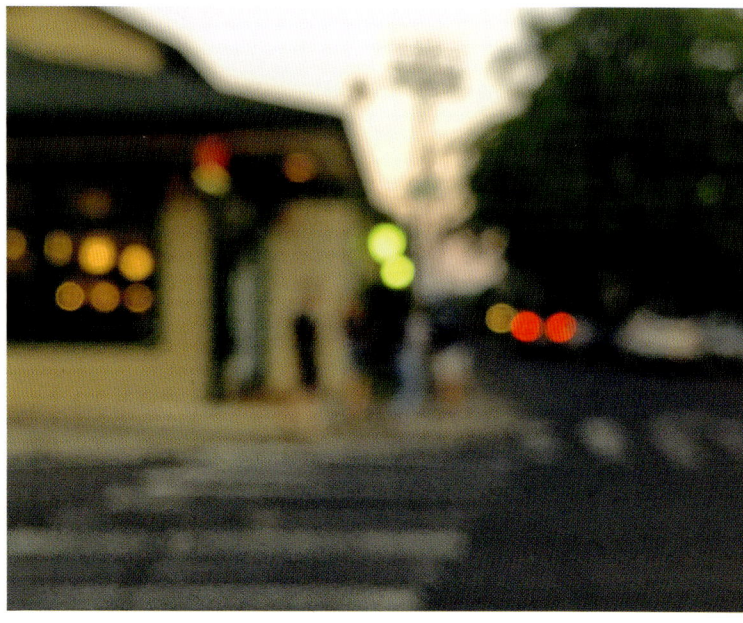

This photo was also shot on an iPhone, using an app with a manual focus adjustment.

IMPROVISATION

To *improvise* is to *make something in the moment with the materials at hand.*

There's no rehearsal—you're prepared, but you don't know precisely what for. You don't know where you're going, but you have intention and momentum.

Consider that on any given day, you can do the painting you can do that day. Your skills and understanding are what they are. In that moment, you are as prepared as you'll ever be *for that moment*. Pause. Gather yourself. See what you can see. There is often a clear and strong feeling of *not knowing* because the process is one of discovery, of being on the edge of the known. If you can stay on that thread and play your way through the painting, you may arrive at something.

A solution that's arrived at is very different from one that is imposed.

There are so many possibilities of depth in the journey of painting, moving out of the shallow end into the deep. It's about the fringes. It's about finding a way in and the territory unexplored. It's about finding solutions in an authentic way. You begin a journey that is your own, with discoveries that are yours.

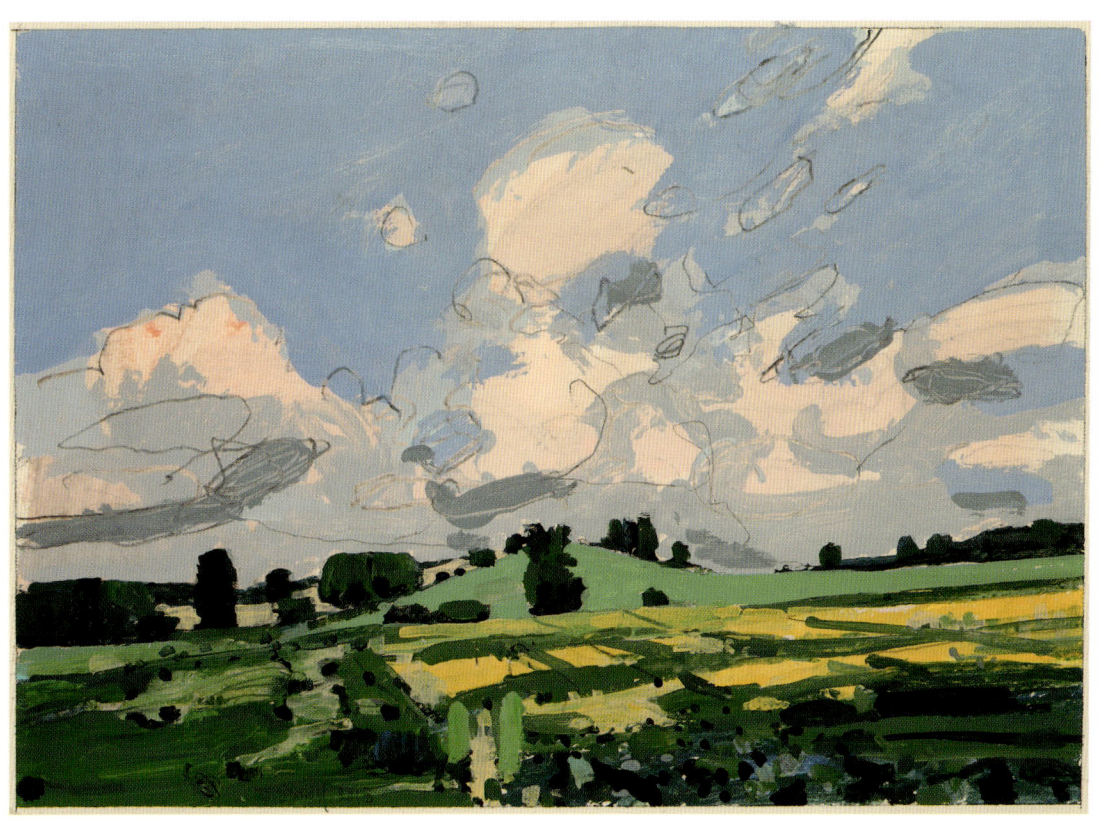

Harry Stooshinoff, *Fallow, Late August,* acrylic on paper, 10" × 14" | 25.4 cm × 35.6 cm

GLOSSARY

Acrylics   Fast-drying water-soluble paints

Bokeh   The way a camera lens renders out-of-focus points of light, commonly as flat discs of color; effects vary depending on the lens shape

Casein   A water-based paint that uses a milk protein as the binder and is insoluble when dry

Chroma   The intensity or saturation of color (The opposite of saturated color is grayed color: for example, fire-engine red and brick red.)

Chromatic arc   Chroma plotted against value for any color plus white (Each pigment's peak chroma is particular to itself.)

Color ladder   A color scale from dark to light, with hue adjustments as desired at every value

Color spot painting   The method of observing a section of color in a scene and aiming to correctly match and put down that color in one attempt

Color study   A small sketch to work out a color question

Contre-jour   Meaning "against the light" or "against daylight" in French, refers to a subject that is lit from behind and is surrounded by a bright field of light

Creative limitation   A theory that limiting available options increases creativity by inviting resourceful thinking

Cutting in   Painting the (usually darker) foreground object first, then painting the (usually lighter) background and using it to refine the shape of the foreground object (Sky holes in trees are often cut in.)

Desirable difficulty   Conditions in a learning environment that apparently create difficulty, but lead to better learning

En plein air   Meaning "in open air" in French, refers to the practice of painting outdoors

Ferrule (fer-uhl)   The crimped metal tube that holds the bristles to the brush handle

Figure-ground   The value relationship of an object to its background, such as a dark figure relationship against a light ground or a lit figure against a dark ground (The figure, or part of it, is "lost" if it is the same value as the background.)

Foamcore   A rigid lightweight layer of open-cell foam sandwiched between layers of paper, used as backing for a support

Gatorfoam   A brand of heavy-duty foamcore

Gesso   A white primer for supports, traditionally oil-based but now commonly acrylic; the Italian word for chalk, a primary ingredient in traditional recipes

Glaze   A semitransparent layer of paint mixed with medium, applied very thinly over a previous layer of dry paint; imparts a unifying effect and can be an intermediate or final step

Gouache (gwäsh)   A highly pigmented opaque watercolor

Ground   The foundation of a painting, usually *gesso*, applied to protect and seal the support and provide a surface of proper absorbency for paint

Impasto   A technique used in painting where the paint is applied thickly, leaving visible brushstrokes, to create depth and texture

Improvisation   Responding in the moment to the materials at hand

Interval   The difference between one *value* and another

Limited value study   A study made with a restricted number of values (usually three to five), to develop a simple and legible value structure for a picture

Local color   The "home" color of an object as we usually think of it–yellow for lemons, green for leaves–as distinguished from that color as affected by light and shadow

Local value   The "home" value (lightness or darkness) of an object as we usually think of it

Masstone   The color and value of a pigment (oil or opaque watermedia) when it is thickly applied; as opposed to *glaze tone*, which is the often very different color and value produced when a pigment is applied thinly, as in a glaze

Medium   1. A type of paint as defined by the solvent or binder, such as watercolor, oil, or acrylic
    2. An additive that affects the flow or consistency of paint

Modulation   Once a clear value separation between light and shadow has been established, modulation is the process of lightening shadow values and darkening lit values, with attention to grazing light (halftones)

Mother color   A single color, often a single pigment, added to every other color in the palette and used to create color harmony

Notan   A compositional study of light-dark balance using black and white only; in its less strict form allows gray

Oils   Oil-based paints that use a drying oil such as linseed oil or walnut oil as the binder; oils have a long open time (i.e., they are slow to dry)

Pochade box   A small wooden paint box that opens to hold a canvas, from the French word *poche*, which means pocket

Raking light   Light coming low and from the side

Rim light   A lighting condition where a subject is backlit against a shadowed background and only the rim of the subject is illuminated

Scumble   1. A very thin layer of semiopaque pigment and medium applied over a dry paint layer; similar to a glaze except for its opacity (and effect)
    2. A scrubbing motion used to apply paint

Support   The base material (or surface) to which media or a coating is applied; usually paper, canvas, or wood

Tinting strength   One color's ability to influence another when mixed together

Transmitted light   Visible light that passes through a semitransparent object

Turps   Short for turpentine and a holdover from the days when gum spirits or rectified turpentine was the only solvent available for oil paint, now commonly used as a blanket term for odorless and nontoxic solvents as well

Value   Lightness or darkness

Value scale   Any number of discrete gray tones ranging from dark to light; traditionally nine values including black, white, and seven grays

Value study   A preliminary study without color, made to work out the value structure; also called a value comp

Viewfinder   A device for framing and isolating a view of the landscape for composing purposes, usually paper or plastic and handheld, but can also be made with your fingers

Watermedia   Any water-soluble paint, such as acrylic, gouache, watercolor, and casein

PLEIN AIR QUICK REFERENCE

FIELD PAINTING STRATEGIES

Stain it, draw it, and throw a bunch of color at it. Stain the canvas with a thin layer of paint (a canvas tone), make whatever marks you need to indicate size and placement of the shapes and relationships, and then go straight to direct laying in of color.

Dark to light. Define the shadow shapes in a single value first, then work your way out of the shadow to the next lighter value, and so on. Keep an eye on the lightest value you'll need and keep everything else darker.

Rubout. Tone the entire canvas and then use a rag or brush or cotton swab to remove paint in the lit areas.

Degree of abstraction. Think of your painting as an abstract study of the subject. A painting is always an abstraction. Acknowledging this and doing it with more intention gives you a stronger position.

Alla prima. Italian for "at the first," this approach lays in one piece of color at a time. The idea is that each stroke, once made, is final. There's no reworking or development.

Make it, break it, and remake it. An intermediate stage of deconstruction can allow the painting to arrive at a more interesting finish.

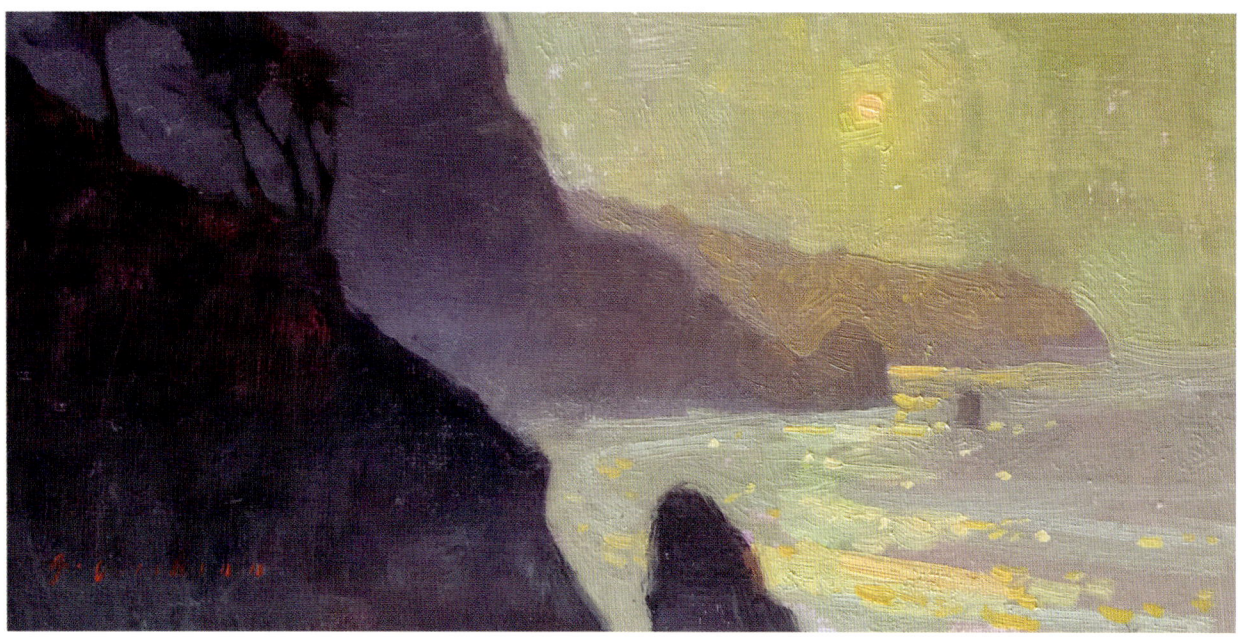

Aimee Erickson, *Oregon Coast Sunrise*, oil on muslin panel, 6" × 12" | 15.2 cm × 30.5 cm

WHAT TO DO IF YOU DON'T HAVE AN IDEA

Try doing less. Limiting some aspect of your scope has the effect of sparking creativity. You can introduce physical limitations, limits to your palette or stylistic approach, or what tools you use.

- Paint with your non-dominant hand.
- Paint with your back to the subject and limit the number of times you can turn to look at it.
- Set a time limit. Try twenty minutes, or less, and reduce the number of decisions you make to fit.
- Work small. On a big canvas, mark off a small box in the corner and do a mini painting.
- Use a single big brush on a small canvas.
- Do the entire painting with a palette knife—or a credit card.
- Work in black and white only.

- Choose a limited palette that has no relation to your subject.
- Limit yourself to four colors only.
- Find something very small to paint—a single well-lit object or a color relationship.
- Make thumbnails and design sketches instead of something more ambitious.
- Paint a familiar subject.
- Make an abstract color study.
- Make vertical brushstrokes only, or horizontal brushstrokes only, or all diagonal brushstrokes.
- Use a toned canvas and keep all your brushstrokes from touching each other; then, make an exception.

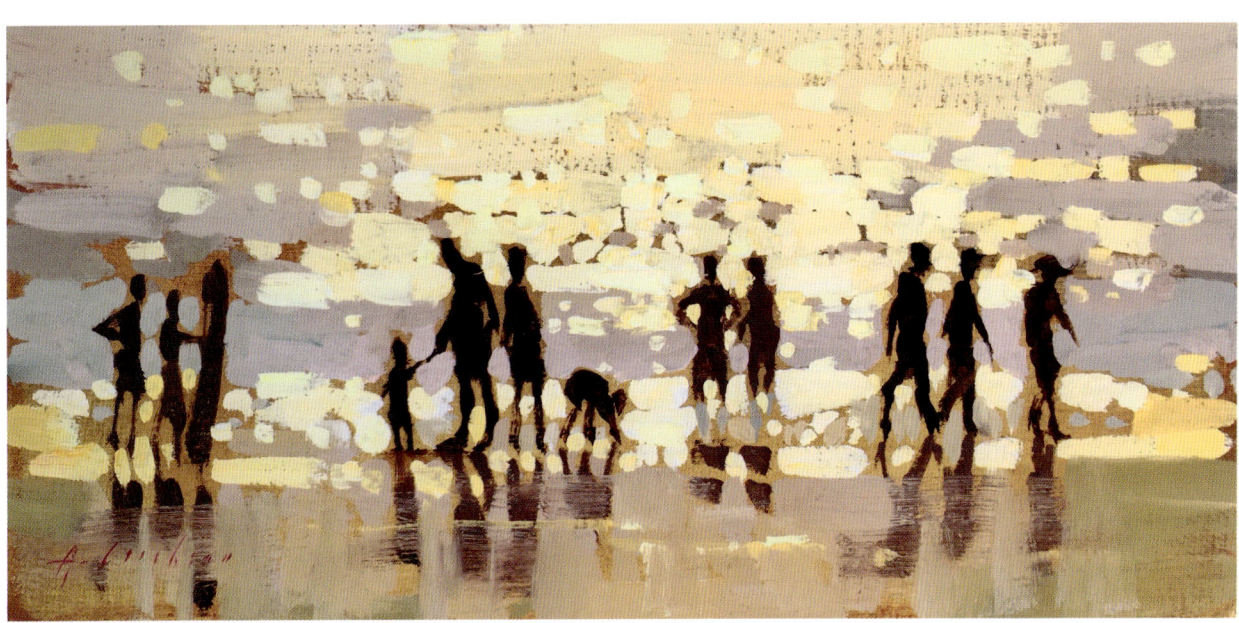

Aimee Erickson, *Sunpennies in the Sea*, oil on muslin panel, 6" × 12" | 15.2 cm × 30.5 cm

SUMMARY OF PERSPECTIVE PRINCIPLES

The general principle is this: *Less* recedes and *more* advances. Of course, there are several ways an element in a painting can be more or less than another. Usually, we employ multiple strategies together to imply distance, and sometimes, one strategy is subordinated to another.

DRAWING SOLUTIONS

Size. This one's easy—a proximate object should be larger in the picture than the same object in the distance. This applies to intervals as well as to things. The tricky part is when nature doesn't cooperate and gives you a small tree in the foreground and a big tree a little ways off. If being true to reality messes up the sense of distance in your picture, change it to make your picture work.

Placement relative to the horizon line. Closer to the horizon line implies farther away. So, in the sky, lower means more distant, and on the ground, higher means more distant. Know where your eye level is in the picture. This is true even in a still life situation, with objects sitting on the tabletop.

Overlapping. This is the placement of objects relative to each other so that one is obscured "behind" the other.

ATMOSPHERIC OR AERIAL PERSPECTIVE: COLOR CHANGES WITH DISTANCE

Value. Dark values advance; light values recede.

Chroma. Stronger color advances; weaker color recedes.

Hue. Hue shifts with distance, but usually it's chroma that changes more. The conditions of the day are the determining factor.

DEVELOPMENT: DETAIL AND PAINT HANDLING

Flatter paint, less developed = distant. More developed, thicker paint = closer.

Distant objects should be simplified and have less detail, less contrast between light and shadow, and less information overall compared to proximate objects.

SCALE INDICATORS

There are some visual cues that instantly communicate scale, with two of the clearest ones being animals (including people) and windows.

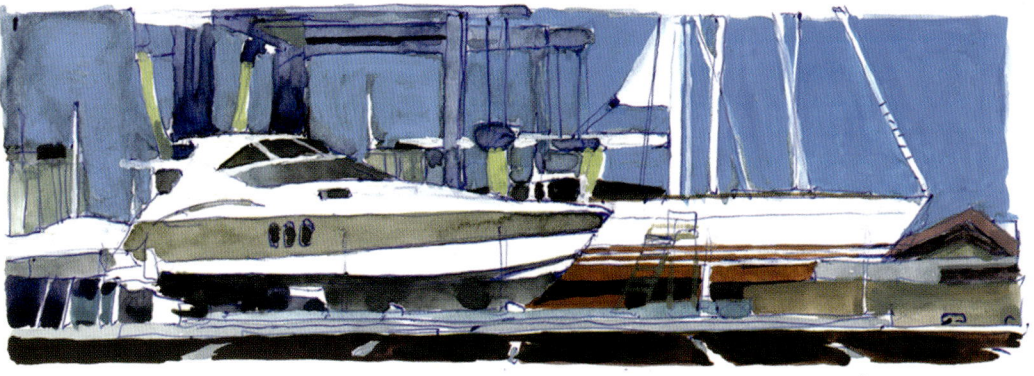

Christian Schellewald, *Marina del Rey*, LAMY ballpoint pen on Holbein watercolor and Holbein gouache on paper, 5" × 8" | 12.7 cm × 20.3 cm

IF YOUR COMPOSITION ISN'T WORKING

- Do I know what the main point of the picture is?
- How many things am I trying to do—are there too many? Can the picture be about one thing?
- Does the rest of the picture support or detract from the idea?
- Can anything be removed?
- Selective focus: As in film, let the subject be sharp and the rest be out of focus/softer, with more detail/development on the main subject. Think about re-creating the effect of looking at one thing and not noticing as much the things in the periphery.

- Is color detracting from the main event? Can I use more color on the subject and intentionally neutralize color in the rest of the picture?
- Spotlight: When the rest of the picture is in shadow, attention will be drawn toward the light.
- Placement: Generally, somewhere central to the picture feels more important.
- Is the subject or area of greatest interest big enough to carry the picture?
- Are there busy areas that can be simplified? Look for "holidays" where a dry brushstroke has left open areas. Are they interesting or distracting?

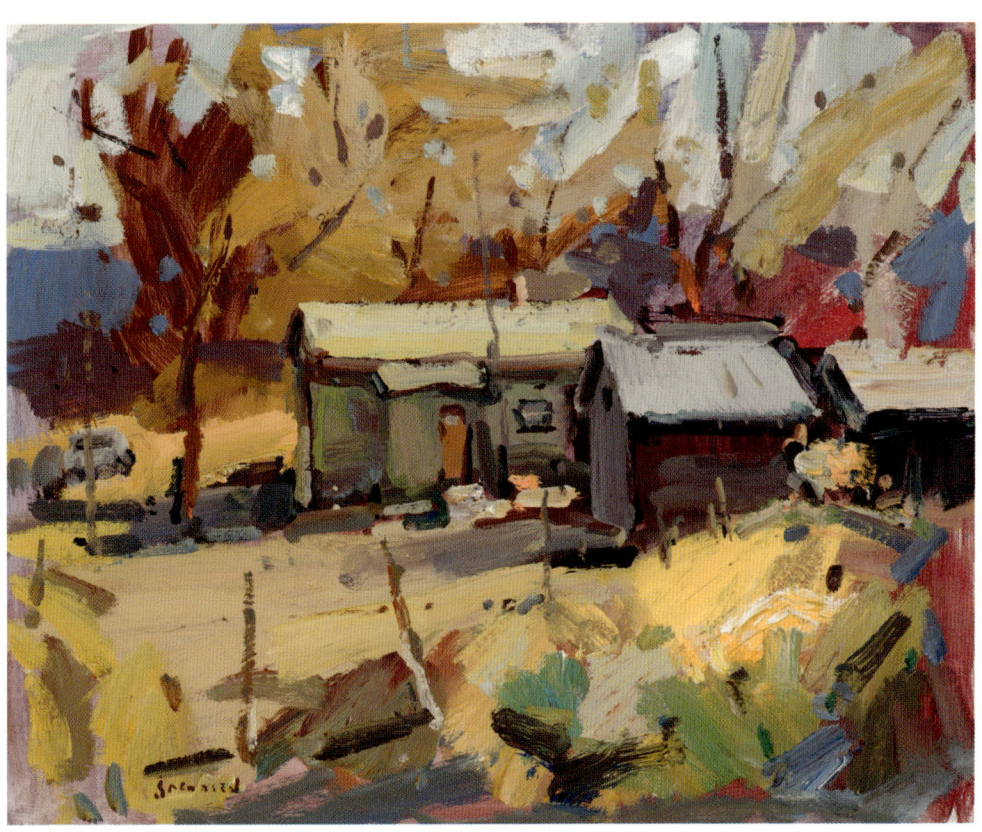

Eric Jacobsen, *The Neighbor's Place*, oil on canvas, 16" × 20" | 40.6 cm × 51 cm

CONTRIBUTING ARTISTS

Mitch Baird
mitchbaird.com

Suzie Baker
suziebaker.com

Tom Balderas
tombalderas.com

Tim Beall
beall-gallery-marine-art.business.site

Zufar Bikbov
zufar.com

Carl Bretzke
carlbretzke.com

Jill Carver
jillcarver.com

Josh Clare
joshclare.com

Marc Dalessio
marcdalessio.com

Kim English
anglinsmith.com/artists/kim-english

Andy Evansen
evansenartstudio.com

Zoey Frank
zoeyfrank.com

Scott Gellatly
scottgellatly.com

Carole Gray-Weihman
gray-weihman.com

A. Hauser

Stephen Hayes
stephenhayes.net

Wyllis Heaton
wyllisheaton.com

Agustina Hein
Instagram: @agustinahein

Mike Hernandez
Instagram: @squatchgouache

Tim Horn
timhornart.com

Kathleen B. Hudson
kathleenbhudson.com

Charlie Hunter
charliehunter.art

Eric Jacobsen
jacobsenfineart.com

Mitchell Johnson
mitchelljohnson.com

Gareth Jones
gejart.com

Alex Kanevsky
somepaintings.net

Peggi Kroll Roberts
peggikrollroberts.com

John P. Lasater IV
lasaterart.com

Patrick Lee
patrickleefineart.com

Leo Mancini-Hresko
Instagram: @leo_mancini_hresko

Callan McDonald

Peter McLaren
petermclarenfineart.com

Michelle Morin
michellemorinart.com

Charles Movalli
wallsgallery.com/project/charles-movalli

Nicholas O'Leary
nicholasoleary.com

Ralph Oberg
ralphoberg.com

Colin Page
colinpagepaintings.com

Ray Roberts
rayrobertsart.com

Jason Sacran
jasonsacran.com

Christian Schellewald
Instagram: @cwschellewald

David Sharpe
sharpegallery.com

L. Sharpe

Harry Stooshinoff
harrystooshinoff.com

Bryan Mark Taylor
bryanmarktaylor.com

Mary Tonkin
Instagram: @mary.tonkin

Michele Usibelli
micheleusibelli.com

Kim VanDerHoek
kimvanderhoek.com

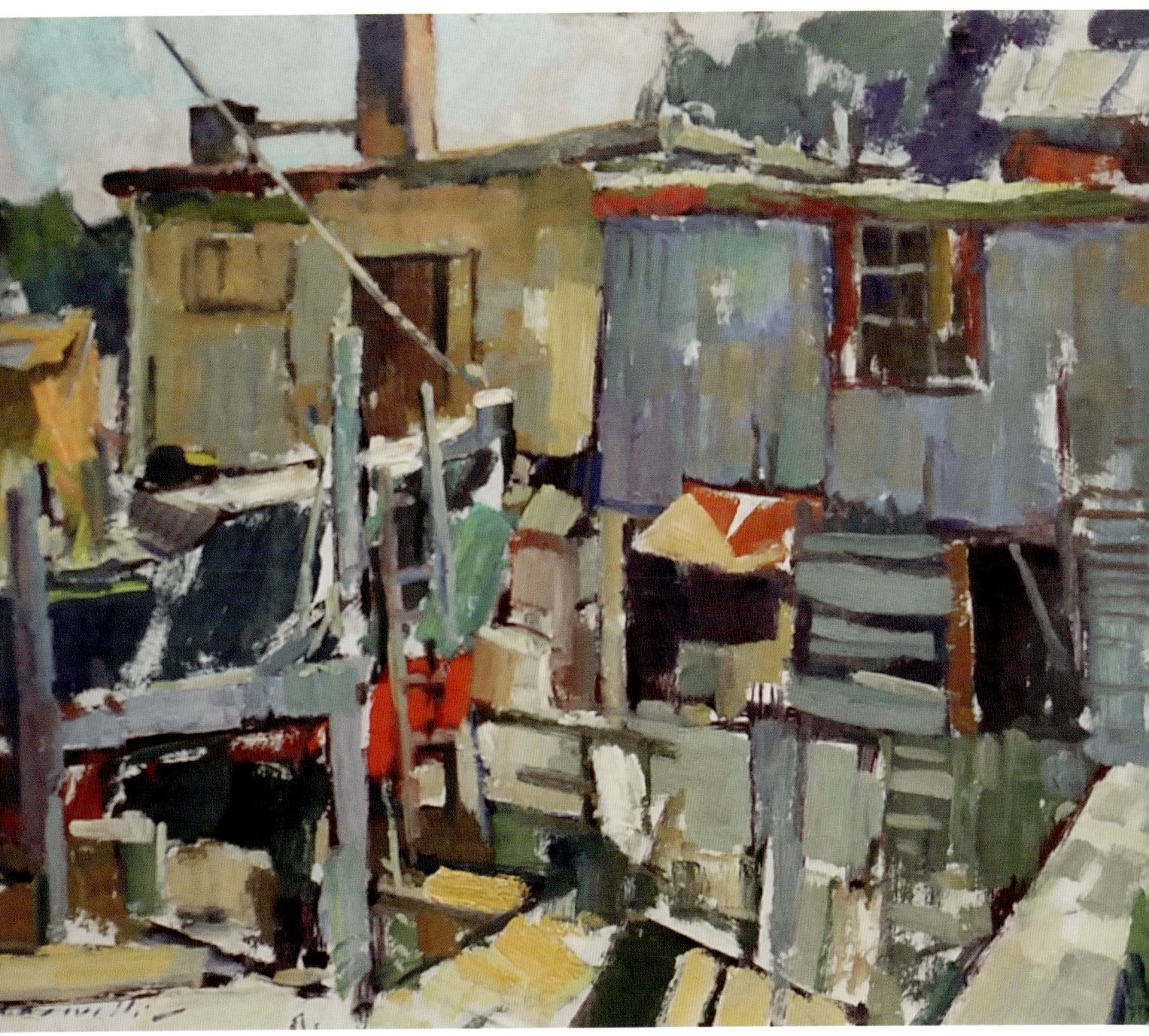

Charles Movalli, *Lobster Shacks*, oil on canvas, 16" × 20" | 40.6 cm × 51 cm

ACKNOWLEDGMENTS

Joy: Thank you for inviting me to write this book. (Everyone: This is Joy, my publisher! She is a seamless professional, and I loved working with her.)

Jed: Thank you for turning down this project and telling Joy to call me.

Sharon: Your artistic sensitivity and gentle love for small things is a continuing delight to me. Thank you for your friendship, for reading my early drafts, and for picking out the most important things.

Scott: For sharing your expertise, for being at least as enthusiastic about color as I am, and for always being up for a paint-out—thank you.

Lindsay, one of the greats: Thank you for being an excellent reader, for your complete confidence, and for showing up every time I needed support.

Jolene: Thank you for all you know about the craft of writing and editing, and for what you know about me.

Eric: Your thoughtfulness on all things paint-related and your generosity in sharing your knowledge have been a gift. Thank you for painting like nobody else, and for being there to talk about Cheez Whiz and improvising and gaining wings.

Mitch A.: As a first-time author, I very much appreciate your support. Thank you for being the voice of experience.

Vivian: Thank you for coming in to help me map the chapters on the studio wall. You are a bright light.

Mom: Thank you for teaching me to love words and books, for signing me up for oil painting lessons when I was six, and for letting me wear that blue knit skirt every day in first grade.

And to all the contributing artists: The second biggest thrill for me in writing this book was to contact artists whose work I love and ask them to let me include their work. The biggest thrill was when every one of you said yes—even those of you I had not yet met. The paintings in this book hold so much knowledge, so many hours of learning in the studio, and so much beauty that it makes my heart sing. I'm grateful for your skill, your artistry, and your generosity.

ABOUT THE AUTHOR

Known for an engaging style and versatility in subject matter, **AIMEE ERICKSON** is an internationally renowned oil painter and instructor who has given lectures and demonstrations at venues nationwide and abroad. A standout at plein air painting competitions, she has won both Best of Show and Artists' Choice at Plein Air Easton, as well as Best of Show at Carmel, Sonoma, Olmsted, Laguna, and Pacific Northwest art festivals. Erickson has been a Portrait Society of America finalist, won Best of Show at an American Women Artists national show, and is a signature member with multiple awards from Oil Painters of America. She has exhibited with international plein air groups in China and Russia, is an inaugural member of Charlie Hunter's En Train Air expedition, and in 1997 painted the official portrait of governor of Oregon Barbara Roberts. Erickson's professional affiliations include Plein Air Painters of America, Oil Painters of America, Laguna Plein Air Painters Association, American Impressionist Society, and the California Art Club, and her work has been featured in *Southwest Art Magazine*, *American Art Collector*, and *Plein Air Magazine*, and on OutdoorPainter.com.

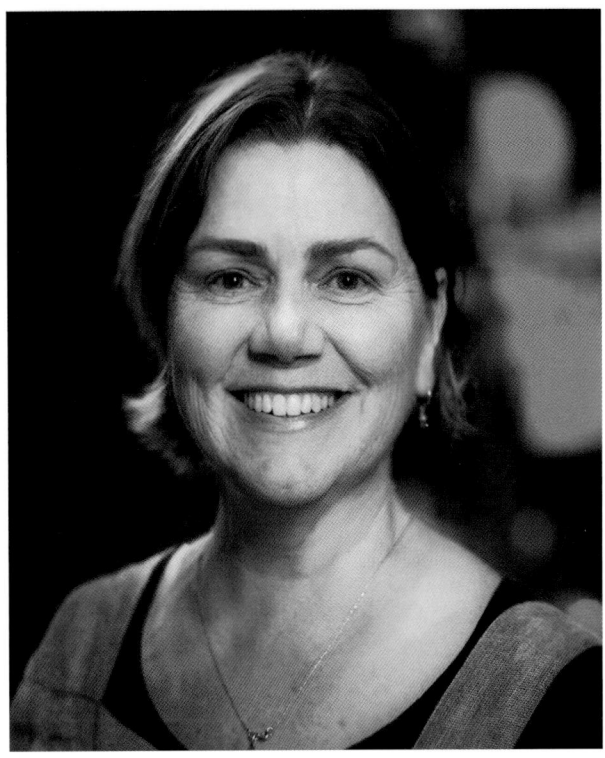

Photo by Jeremy Fenske

Erickson has a BFA in Visual Communication Design with an Illustration emphasis from Brigham Young University. She lives in Portland, Oregon, and carries a sketchbook. To see more of Erickson's work, visit aimeeerickson.com, @1aim on Instagram, and Aimee Erickson Artist on Facebook.

INDEX

A

Abstraction, 164
Acryla gouache, 13
Acrylic gesso, 17
Acrylic paints, 13, 33
Alla prima, 63, 164
Atmospheric (aerial) perspective, 71, 72, 110, 133, 166

B

Backlight(ing), 99–111
Black and white images, 22, 32, 33–34, 35
Bokeh, 160
Bristles (brush), 14
Broad brush, using a, 94
Brushes, 11, 14, 16, 20, 94
Brushstrokes, 14, 15, 63, 131

C

Canvas/canvas panels, 17
Canvas tone, 17, 18
Casein, 13, 33, 157
Cast shadows, 68, 75, 99, 113
Chroma, 43, 46, 48, 72, 104, 166
Clouds, 7, 71, 122, 135
Color(s)
  color chart emphasizing value, 46
  composition and, 23, 25
  exercises, 45–48
  factors related to decisions about, 41
  light(ing) and, 59, 66–67, 133
  painting makeover using more, 120
  palettes, 50–52
  temperature, 44
  value studies and, 54–55
  vocabulary, 42–43
Color chart, 46
Color ladders, 47
Color spot painting, 53
Composition(s), 23, 24–33
  arrangement of shapes in, 25
  with black and white, 32–34
  horizon and, 31
  mark-making, 28
  non-shape-based paintings, 27
  perspective, 29
  on scale from static to dynamic, 24
  on a scale from static to dynamic, 24
  shape-based painting for, 25–26
  thumbnail sketches and, 30, 31
  viewfinder used for, 30
Contre-jour, 99, 102–103

Cutting in, 88, 90–91

D

Dappled light, 78, 82–83, 117
Dark to light, 46, 164
Demonstrations, 60–62, 80–83, 87–89, 129–130, 146–147. *See* also Techniques
Design, 153–155
Development, 71, 111, 166
Dust, 144

E

Easel, 11, 19, 128, 129
Equalization, 27
Exercises, 32, 33–34, 39, 45–48

F

Ferrule (brush), 14
Figure-ground relationship, 116–117
Filtered light, 78, 79
Fog, 144, 146–147
Foreground, 73–75, 90, 110, 111
Front light, 113–123

G

Gatorfoam Board, 17
Gesso, 12, 13, 17, 137
Glare, 131, 137
Glowing light, 134–135
Gouache, 13, 33
Gray(s), 35, 37–38, 43

H

Half-light, 121
Horizon, the, 29, 31, 71, 166
Hue, 43, 48, 72, 166

I

Impasto brushwork, 72, 96, 118–119
Improvisation, 161
Indirect light, 77–97
Interiors, 106, 107–109, 142
Interval, 35

L

Large-scale painting, 80–81
Limited value studies, 37–38
Lines, 23, 28

M

Mark-making, 28
Masonite, 17
Materials and gear, 11–21
Medium, types of, 12–13
Mid-tone canvas, 79
Mist, 145, 147
Moon(light), 59, 66, 126, 134
Motif, 27
Multimedia Artboard, 17
Muslin panel, 17

N

New things, trying, 8
Nocturnes and nighttime painting(s), 125–131
Non-shape paintings, 27
Notan(s), 32–34

O

Oil paint(ing), 12, 17, 19
Opaque watermedia, 13, 19
Overcast light, 77, 84–86
Overlapping, 71, 166

P

Painting(s)
  formal aspects of, 27
  loose start with (demonstrations), 107–109
  makeovers, 92–93, 110–111, 120
  as more than representation, 152
  at the same location, 157–159
  small studies, 156
  strategies, 164
  visual idea for, 151
  where to begin, 63
Palette, 11, 20, 122
Panel size, 11
Paper, 17, 20
Perception, shifting your, 58
Perspective, 29, 71–72, 110–111, 166
Photographs, out-of-focus, 160
Plein air painting
  about, 6–7
  kits, 19–20
Poetic color vocabulary, 42

R

Raking light (side light/crosslight), 68, 72, 92, 101
Reflected light, 95
Reflections, 139–143
Reflective objects, 143
Rim light, 99, 100–101
Rubout, 99, 164

S

Scientific color vocabulary, 43
Shadow(s), 63
  on architecture, 60–62
  color, light, and, 59
  with dappled light, 82, 83
  dropping in shapes of, 64–65
  foreground, 71, 74, 75
  with overcast light, 84
  raking light and, 68
  reflected light and, 95–97
  rim light and, 100
  value contrast and, 72
Shape(s)
  composition and, 23, 25
  in notan, 32
  in value studies, 37
Shape-based painting, 27
Shellac, 12, 17
Side lighting. See Raking light (side light/cross-light)
Single-color palette, 50
Small studies, 156
Smoke, 148
Squeegee, 154
Stain it, draw it, paint it technique, 69–70, 164
Still life, 92–93
Sunlight. See Light(ing)
Support types, 17

T

Techniques, 69–70, 94, 107–109, 118–119
Texture, composition and, 23
Three-value thinking, 79
Thumbnail sketches, 30, 31
Tinting strength, 35
Toned canvas, 17, 18
Transmitted light, 104–105
Transparent watercolor, 13
Triad palettes, 51
Tripod, 19, 20
Twilight, 126
Two-session painting, 87–89

V

Value(s) and value studies, 23, 25, 32, 35–39, 43, 44, 46, 47–48, 54–55, 72, 77, 166
Viewfinder, 30
Visual idea, 151

W

Warm-cool palette, 51
Watercolor(s), 12, 13, 20–21, 33
Water-miscible oils, 12, 36
Windshield wiper method, 30

Z

"The zone," finding the, 8

TITLES IN ROCKPORT'S FOR ARTISTS SERIES

The **For Artists series** expertly guides and instructs artists at all skill levels who want to develop their classical drawing and painting skills and create realistic and representational art.

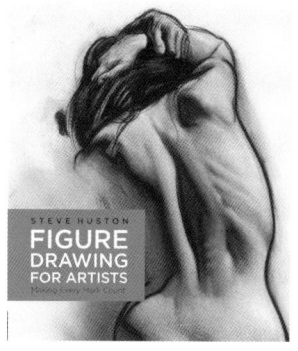

Figure Drawing for Artists
978-1-6315-9065-8

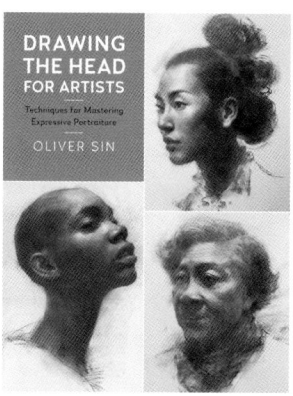

Drawing the Head for Artists
978-1-6315-9692-6

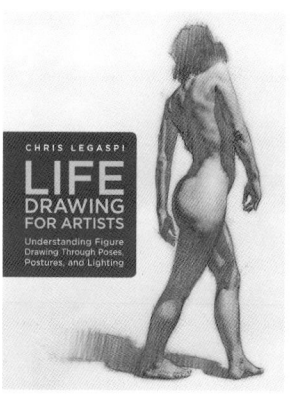

Life Drawing for Artists
978-1-6315-9801-2

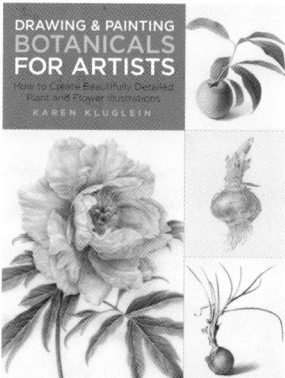

Drawing and Painting Botanicals for Artists
978-1-6315-9857-9

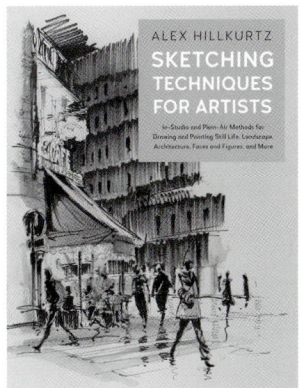

*Sketching Techniques
for Artists*
978-1-6315-9923-1

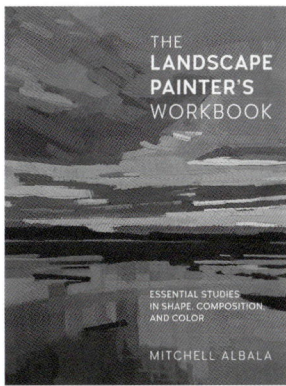

*The Landscape
Painter's Workbook*
978-0-7603-7135-0

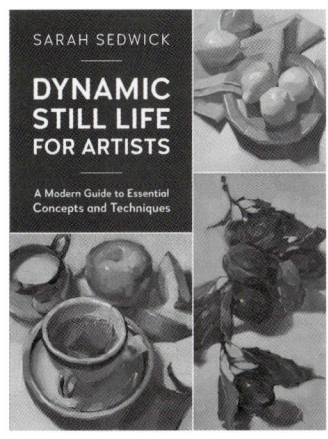

Dynamic Still Life for Artists
978-0-7603-7700-0

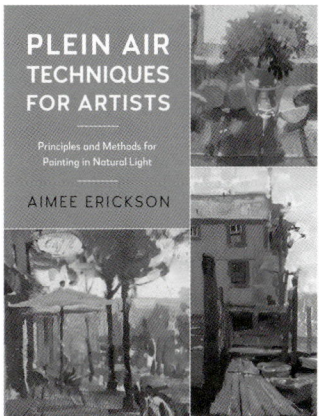

Plein Air Techniques for Artists
978-0-7603-7935-6

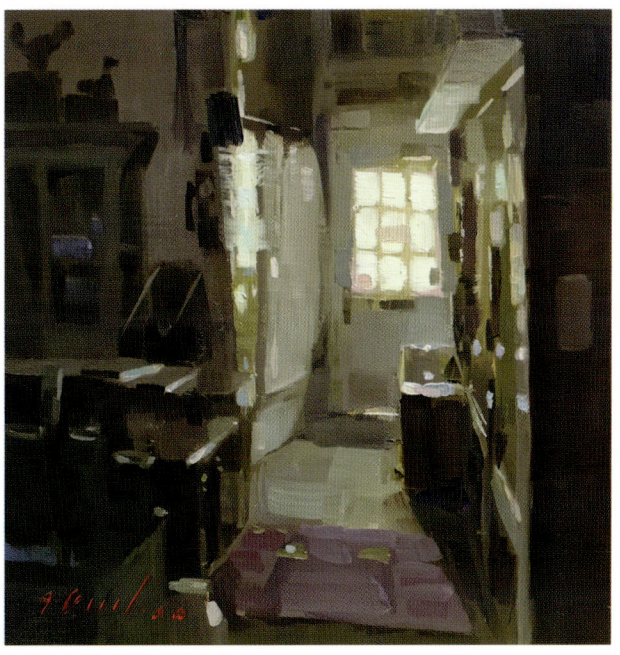

Aimee Erickson, *Decoy*, oil on linen panel,
12" ×12" | 30.5 cm × 30.5 cm

To my teachers, my friends, my students,
and to the grand tradition of plein air painting.

Title page:

Aimee Erickson, *Blue Surfboard*,
watercolor on sketchbook paper,
3" × 4" | 7.6 cm × 10.2 cm

Quarto.com

© 2023 Quarto Publishing Group USA Inc.
Text and images © 2023 Aimee Erickson

First published in 2023 by Rockport Publishers, an imprint of The Quarto Group,
100 Cummings Center, Suite 265-D, Beverly, MA 01915, USA.
T (978) 282-9590 F (978) 283-2742

EEA Representation, WTS Tax d.o.o.,
Žanova ulica 3, 4000 Kranj, Slovenia.
www.wts-tax.si

Rockport Publishers titles are also available at discount for retail, wholesale, promotional, and bulk purchase. For details, contact the Special Sales Manager by email at specialsales@quarto.com or by mail at The Quarto Group, Attn: Special Sales Manager, 100 Cummings Center, Suite 265-D, Beverly, MA 01915, USA.

10 9 8 7 6

ISBN: 978-0-7603-7935-6

Digital edition published in 2023
eISBN: 978-0-7603-7936-3

Library of Congress Cataloging-in-Publication data is available.

Design: Megan Jones Design

Printed in Guangdong, China TT062025